Professional
WCF Programming

Professional
WCF Programming
.NET Development with the Windows®
Communication Foundation

Scott Klein

Wiley Publishing, Inc.

Professional WCF Programming: .NET Development with the Windows® Communication Foundation

Published by
Wiley Publishing, Inc.
10475 Crosspoint Boulevard
Indianapolis, IN 46256
www.wiley.com

Published simultaneously in Canada

ISBN: 978-0-470-08984-2

Manufactured in the United States of America

10 9 8 7 6 5 4 3 2 1

 Library of Congress Cataloging-in-Publication Data:

Klein, Scott, 1966-
  Professional WCF programming: .NET development with the Windows communication foundation /   Scott Klein.
      p. cm.
Includes index.
 ISBN 978-0-470-08984-2 (paper/website)
1. Application software--Development. 2. Microsoft Windows (Computer file) 3. Microsoft .NET. 4. Web services. I.
Title.   QA76.76.A65K6 2007 005.3--dc22
                              2007003318

For general information on our other products and services please contact our Customer Care Department within the United States at (800) 762-2974, outside the United States at (317) 572-3993 or fax (317) 572-4002.

About the Author

Scott Klein is an independent consultant with passions for all things SQL Server, .NET, and XML. He is the author of *Professional SQL Server 2005 XML* by Wrox, writes the bi-weekly feature article for the SQL PASS Community Connector, and has contributed articles to both Wrox (`www.Wrox.com`) and TopXML (`www.TopXML.com`). He frequently speaks at SQL Server and .NET user groups. When he is not sitting in front of a computer or spending time with his family he can usually be found aboard his Yamaha at the local motocross track. He can be reached at `ScottKlein@SqlXml.com`.

Credits

Senior Acquisitions Editor
Jim Minatel

Development Editor
Howard A. Jones

Technical Editor
William G. Ryan

Production Editor
Eric Charbonneau

Copy Editor
Kim Cofer

Editorial Manager
Mary Beth Wakefield

Production Manager
Tim Tate

Vice President and Executive Group Publisher
Richard Swadley

Vice President and Executive Publisher
Joseph B. Wikert

Project Coordinator
Jennifer Theriot

Graphics and Production Specialists
Denny Hager
Jennifer Mayberry
Alicia B. South

Quality Control Technicians
Cynthia Fields
John Greenough

Proofreading and Indexing
Aptara

Anniversary Logo Design
Richard Pacifico

Contents

Contents

Contents

Contents

Contents

Acknowledgments

I don't know if I am just naive or what, but I would have thought that writing a second book would have been easier than writing the first. I quickly learned that no book is easy to write, but to make it go as pain-free as possible you have to surround yourself with the best people possible. Sometimes they find you, and sometimes you have to go find them. Once you have everyone assembled, it is like poetry in motion. Therefore it is only appropriate to thank those individuals who made this project much less painful than it could have been.

First and foremost Clay Andres and Neil Salkind, and everyone at Studio B for that matter, for being who they are and for all that they do. They take care of all of the things I don't want to have to worry about and let me do what I like to do. Man, that is nice.

A huge thanks to the guys at Wrox/Wiley for making this book happen. Jim Minatel, for accepting the book idea and letting me write it and for being patient with me when I was hitting a few walls. That meant a lot Jim. I appreciate it. Howard Jones, my development editor, was a delight to work with. I can't thank Bill Ryan, the technical reviewer, enough for the time and energy he put into this. His comments were priceless.

I learned during the writing of the first book that having that "one person" that you could go to for whatever reason made life so much easier. I had that "one person" during the writing of my first book, but it took me awhile to find that "one person" for this book. But when I found that "one person" for this book, it was like a whole new world opened up. Ralph Squillace, you are the man! Not many people would take the time he did to help me understand a great many things, but he did and I cannot thank him enough. Ralph went far above and beyond my expectations. If his boss is reading this, GIVE RALPH A RAISE!

A large dosage of gratitude also goes out to Clemens Vasters, Brian McNamara, Doug Purdy, Jan Alexander, Michael Green, Laurence Melloul, and Kenny Wolf. A thank you to each of these people for letting me ask questions and providing excellent feedback.

It has been said that you are only as good as those with whom you associate. So enough cannot be said about the love and support of my family, for without them, this book, or anything else I do in life would not be possible. My tremendous wife, Lynelle, who during these times is an anchor for this family, who held the house together for the 8+ months I spent upstairs. And to my children, who were patient with their father knowing that they soon "would get their dad back." I love you all. I swear they weren't that tall when I started this book.

Now, on to book number three...

Introduction

While I was still trying to get the word "Grok" into everyone's mainstream vocabulary (see the introduction in my first book), I happened upon what at the time was called WinFX, later to be renamed .NET Framework 3.0. Shortly thereafter I attended a local MSDN event where they presented some of the new technologies in .NET Framework 3.0, such as Windows Presentation Foundation and Windows Communication Foundation. I could hardly contain myself.

SOA (Service-Oriented Architecture) is an important concept to Microsoft. The problem is that in the past, SOA has had a fairly vague definition, but Microsoft is working hard to clear up the concept. SOA is not simply a set of services. SOA is the policies, frameworks, and practices under which the correct services are provided.

Web services were a great start, but SOA can help deliver the business agility and flexible IT that web services were supposed to deliver. Enter Windows Communication Foundation. Windows Communication Foundation (WCF) is a platform for creating and distributing connected applications. It is a fusion of current distributed system technologies designed and developed from the outset to help solve many of the SOA problems.

Who This Book Is For

This book is for developers who want to learn about Windows Communication Foundation and how it can be a benefit in their environment. Equally, this book is also for those individuals who have spent at least a little time looking at and playing with WCF and would like to dig deeper into the technology—to see what WCF has to offer and how it can enhance current applications.

A good understanding of the .NET Framework and related technologies (such as web services and the WS-* specifications) will be useful when reading this book, but is not required. If you have worked with web services prior to reading this book, then comprehending WCF will certainly be easier; but don't worry too much if you haven't.

What This Book Covers

The focus of this book is in three primary areas. First and foremost is the discussion of Service-Oriented Architecture (SOA) and an introduction to Windows Communication Foundation (WCF). This first section explains what SOA is and how WCF answers many of the SOA needs. The next section jumps into the meat of WCF by first laying down the foundation of WCF and explaining the core makeup of WCF. It then digs deeper by discussing more advanced topics such as security and interoperability. The last section focuses on the management topics of WCF including hosting options and deployment.

How This Book Is Structured

This book is broken out into the following structure:

❏ Part I—Introduction to Windows Communication Foundation

    ❏ Chapter 1—"Windows Communication Foundation Overview." This chapter takes a look at SOA (Service-Oriented Architecture), the need for it, and how Windows Communication Foundation solves those needs.

    ❏ Chapter 2—"Windows Communication Foundation Concepts." This chapter provides an overview of the basic concepts of Windows Communication Foundation and messaging in general.

    ❏ Chapter 3—"Understanding Windows Communication Foundation." This chapter provides a quick walkthrough and explanation of the WCF programming model and service model, and finally walks you through installing WCF.

❏ Part II—Programming Windows Communication Foundation

    ❏ Chapter 4—"Addresses." This chapter discusses WCF addresses and how they are used.

    ❏ Chapter 5—"Understanding and Programming WCF Bindings." This chapter introduces the different WCF bindings, how they are used, and the functionality that each binding provides.

    ❏ Chapter 6—"Understanding and Programming WCF Contracts." This chapter introduces the concept of a WCF contract, the different types of contracts, and how they are used.

    ❏ Chapter 7—"Clients." This chapter discusses WCF from the client side. Specifically it details how clients connect and communicate with WCF services.

    ❏ Chapter 8—"Services." This chapter introduces the concept of behaviors and discusses the different options and behaviors that can be applied to a WCF service.

    ❏ Chapter 9—"Transactions and Reliable Sessions." This chapter discusses the reliable exchange of messages by introducing and discussing the topics of transactions and queues and how to take advantage of these features in WCF.

    ❏ Chapter 10—"Security." This chapter discusses the security aspects of WCF. It shows how to build security into your WCF applications.

    ❏ Chapter 11—"Customizing Windows Communication Foundation." This chapter focuses on the extending and customization of WCF.

    ❏ Chapter 12—"Interoperability and Integration." The focus of this chapter is the integration and interoperability of WCF with existing applications and technology such as MSMQ, WSE, and ASP.NET.

❑   Part III—Deploying Windows Communication Foundation

  ❑   Chapter 13—"Deploying Windows Communication Foundation." This chapter focuses on deployment strategies and issues for your WCF services.

  ❑   Chapter 14—"Managing Windows Communication Foundation." This chapter takes a good look at the available WCF management tools that come with WCF to help debug and configure your WCF services.

  ❑   Chapter 15—"Hosting Windows Communication Foundation Services." This chapter talks about the available options for hosting WCF services.

  ❑   Appendix A—"WCF Template Extensions in Visual Studio." This appendix provides an overview of the Visual Studio templates and add-ins to assist you in building WCF services.

  ❑   Appendix B—"Case Study." This appendix provides a case study that illustrates many of the technologies discussed in the book. Although directly tied into the rest of the contents of the book, you will find Appendix B online rather within these pages, at www.wrox.com. You can find details for accessing it in the section titled "Source Code" toward the end of this introduction.

What You Need To Read This Book

All of the examples in this book require the following:

❑   Visual Studio 2005

❑   .NET Framework 3.0

❑   Visual Studio 2005 Extensions for WCF

Although it is possible to run the products on separate computers, the examples in this book were done with the products running on the same computer.

Conventions

To help you get the most from the text and keep track of what's happening, we've used a number of conventions throughout the book.

> **Boxes like this one hold important, not-to-be forgotten information that is directly relevant to the surrounding text.**

Tips, hints, tricks, and asides to the current discussion are offset and placed in italics like this.

As for styles in the text:

- ❏ We *highlight* new terms and important words when we introduce them.
- ❏ We show keyboard strokes like this: Ctrl+A.
- ❏ We show filenames, URLs, and code within the text like so: `persistence.properties`.
- ❏ We present code in two different ways:

```
In code examples we highlight new and important code with a gray background.
```

```
The gray highlighting is not used for code that's less important in the present
context, or has been shown before.
```

Source Code

As you work through the examples in this book, you may choose either to type in all the code manually or to use the source code files that accompany the book. All of the source code used in this book is available for download at `http://www.wrox.com`. Once at the site, simply locate the book's title (either by using the Search box or by using one of the title lists) and click the Download Code link on the book's detail page to obtain all the source code for the book.

Because many books have similar titles, you may find it easiest to search by ISBN; this book's ISBN is 978-0-470-08984-2.

Once you download the code, just decompress it with your favorite compression tool. Alternatively, you can go to the main Wrox code download page at `http://www.wrox.com/dynamic/books/download.aspx` to see the code available for this book and all other Wrox books.

Errata

We make every effort to ensure that there are no errors in the text or in the code. However, no one is perfect, and mistakes do occur. If you find an error in one of our books, like a spelling mistake or faulty piece of code, we would be very grateful for your feedback. By sending in errata you may save another reader hours of frustration and at the same time you will be helping us provide even higher quality information.

To find the errata page for this book, go to `http://www.wrox.com` and locate the title using the Search box or one of the title lists. Then, on the book details page, click the Book Errata link. On this page you can view all errata that has been submitted for this book and posted by Wrox editors. A complete book list including links to each book's errata is also available at `www.wrox.com/misc-pages/booklist.shtml`.

If you don't spot "your" error on the Book Errata page, go to `www.wrox.com/contact/techsupport.shtml` and complete the form there to send us the error you have found. We'll check the information and, if appropriate, post a message to the book's errata page and fix the problem in subsequent editions of the book.

p2p.wrox.com

For author and peer discussion, join the P2P forums at p2p.wrox.com. The forums are a Web-based system for you to post messages relating to Wrox books and related technologies and interact with other readers and technology users. The forums offer a subscription feature to e-mail you topics of interest of your choosing when new posts are made to the forums. Wrox authors, editors, other industry experts, and your fellow readers are present on these forums.

At http://p2p.wrox.com you will find a number of different forums that will help you not only as you read this book, but also as you develop your own applications. To join the forums, just follow these steps:

1. Go to p2p.wrox.com and click the Register link.

2. Read the terms of use and click Agree.

3. Complete the required information to join as well as any optional information you wish to provide and click Submit.

4. You will receive an e-mail with information describing how to verify your account and complete the joining process.

> *You can read messages in the forums without joining P2P but in order to post your own messages, you must join.*

Once you join, you can post new messages and respond to messages other users post. You can read messages at any time on the Web. If you would like to have new messages from a particular forum e-mailed to you, click the Subscribe to this Forum icon by the forum name in the forum listing.

For more information about how to use the Wrox P2P, be sure to read the P2P FAQs for answers to questions about how the forum software works as well as many common questions specific to P2P and Wrox books. To read the FAQs, click the FAQ link on any P2P page.

Part I

Introduction to Windows Communication Foundation

1

Windows Communication
Foundation Overview

One of the biggest IT topics today has to be the concept of Service-Oriented Architecture (SOA). Service-Oriented Architecture isn't new. You'd think that with the coverage it has received over the past few years that developers and "techy" individuals would understand it better, yet it ranks fairly high on the misunderstood-o-meter because its interpretation, implementation, and use is pretty loose due to the fairly vague definition.

When you want to understand the meaning of something, you usually go to a place that defines it, such as a dictionary. In this case, we turn to the W3C to understand the definition of SOA. The W3C defines Service-Oriented Architecture as "A set of components which can be invoked and whose interface descriptions can be discovered and published" (http://www.w3.org/TR/ws-gloss/). As you sit and ponder this definition, it becomes quite apparent that this definition is fairly broad. It also becomes apparent why the Service-Oriented Architecture picture is somewhat fuzzy, because the definition leaves a lot of room for interpretation.

With this in mind, the purpose of this chapter is twofold. First, to better explain what SOA is and the need for it; and second, to introduce Windows Communication Foundation (WCF) and explain how it answers some of the SOA needs. This chapter covers the following:

❑   The need for SOA

❑   How Windows Communication Foundation addresses the SOA needs

The Need for SOA

To understand Service-Oriented Architecture, take a look at the scenario shown in Figure 1-1.

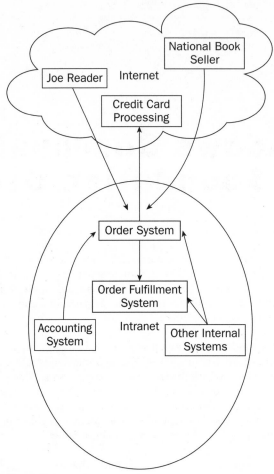

Figure 1-1

The preceding illustration shows the process of a very simplified book publisher order solution. In this example, a book publisher can receive book orders from both a single, individual reader as well as large-quantity book orders from large national book resellers. Orders are received by the Order System application, which collects and processes the orders.

Internally, the Order System application collects and processes the orders, such as validating credit cards and forwarding the order to the Order Fulfillment system. Both the Order System application and the Order Fulfillment application communicate with other internal applications and systems for various reasons.

Over time this publishing company becomes popular because it is hiring great authors and putting out high-quality books, and it becomes apparent that this simple solution is not keeping up with the demand and volume of orders. For example, maybe the current Order System can't keep up with the volume of orders coming in, and thus the Order Fulfillment system is having difficulty handling the amount of orders being handed to it from the Order System.

Service-Oriented Architecture says that the current system can, and should, be flexible enough to allow changes to the existing architecture without disrupting the current architecture and infrastructure currently in place. That is, each piece should be isolated enough that it can be replaced without disturbing the flow and process of the rest of the system. It is the concept of designing the technology processes within a business.

If the developers of the original systems in place were smart, they would have designed the architecture to allow for such a "plug-and-play" type of environment, but at that time their decision was somewhat difficult because of the technologies they had to choose from.

A Look Back

Through the years, developers have had a plethora of technology choices to choose from when it has come to building distributed applications. Lately it has been ASP.NET and WSE (Web Service Enhancements), used to build web services. These allow for the communication of information across different platforms regardless of the client. In addition to these two technologies, the Framework provides .NET Remoting, which provides object communication no matter where the application components reside. Yet even with Remoting you have pros and cons. Many times objects are created remotely, whereas WCF deals with message transmissions natively. .NET Remoting works well in some distributed scenarios yet lacks the ability to be a primary application interface. For example, web services can call Remoting components, but a remote object created outside of your network won't work with Remoting. Prior to that you had COM+ and Microsoft Message Queuing (MSMQ). MSMQ provided a fast and reliable method of application communication through the process of sending and receiving messages.

I remember not many years ago using MSMQ in a fairly large project because the guaranteed delivery of information was critical, yet today I use ASP.NET web services almost religiously because of the many benefits they offer (simplicity, diversity of environments, and so on).

These were, and still are, great technologies that provided great solutions to countless development problems. Yet every time you as a developer had a distributed system problem to solve, you had to ask yourself "which one of these technologies more easily and efficiently solves my problem?" The downside to each one of these is that your method of implementation will vary greatly based on your choice of solution, especially if your solution uses more than one of these technologies.

Given this information, how would you as a developer tackle the responsibility of designing and architecting the book publisher systems given the definition of SOA as described earlier? ASP.NET web services, WSE, and .NET Remoting have been out roughly five years; COM+ and MSMQ have been out a lot longer.

Understanding Service Orientation

Given the book publisher example, this section now looks at it from a Service-Oriented Architecture perspective. Again, SOA says that the current system can, and should, be flexible enough to allow changes to the existing architecture without disrupting the current architecture and infrastructure currently in place.

Building this with service orientation in mind, several changes are made to the architecture, which fulfills the needs of the system without disrupting the process, as shown in Figure 1-2.

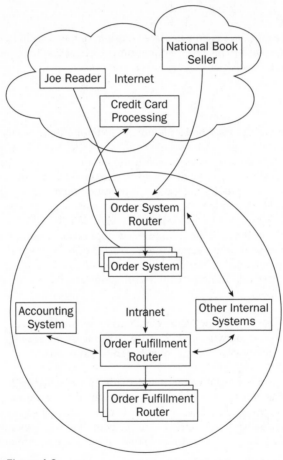

Figure 1-2

To handle the amount of orders coming in, a router was put in front of the Order Process service that then distributes the orders to one of many Order Process services. An Order Fulfillment router was also placed in front of the Order Fulfillment service, which accomplishes the same thing as the Order Process router; that is, it takes the incoming orders from the Order Process service and distributes the orders to one of many Order Fulfillment services.

The other internal systems can still communicate and exchange information with these services without any changes. Externally, Joe Reader and the National Book Seller have no idea that changes were made at the publisher's end — it is all transparent to them. In fact, they might even see a better responding system when placing orders. The key here is that with SOA, major changes can take place behind the scenes completely transparent to the end user and without any interruption of the system.

Software as a service is not a new concept, and in fact if you have been using web services you can start to see where this is going. One could argue that web services was the first step on the road to SOA. Is that statement true? Yes and no. No, in that you can have an SOA solution without using ASP.NET web services. Yes, in that it is a great beginning to something much larger.

It is possible to have a web service that follows no SOA principles and a web service that exhibits wonderful SOA traits. For example, a good web service is almost self-describing, providing useful information. I want to hit a web service that gives me stock quotes, or lets me buy or sell stocks, or tells me how my portfolio is doing. In the case of the book publisher, I want a web service that tells me information about my order. These are web services that exhibit SOA traits.

In contrast, a web service that provides reads as well as writes data to my database shows no SOA. Now, don't get me wrong. Those types of web services have their place and provide great benefits (I have written a few myself). But they don't fit in the SOA realm and don't conform to the SOA principles.

So what are these principles?

Service-Oriented Architecture Principles

Streams of information have been flowing from Microsoft in the forms of articles and white papers regarding its commitment to SOA, and in all of this information one of the big areas constantly stressed are the principles behind service orientation:

❏ Explicit boundaries

❏ Autonomous services

❏ Policy-based compatibility

❏ Shared schemas and contracts

Explicit Boundaries

As you will learn in the next section, SOA is all about messaging — sending messages from point A to point B. These messages must be able to cross explicit and formal boundaries regardless of what is behind those boundaries. This allows developers to keep the flexibility of how services are implemented and deployed. Explicit boundaries mean that a service can be deployed anywhere and be easily and freely accessed by other services, regardless of the environment or development language of the other service.

The thing to keep in mind is that there is a cost associated with crossing boundaries. These costs come in a number of forms, such as communication, performance, and processing overhead costs. Services should be called quickly and efficiently.

Autonomous Services

Services are built and deployed independently of other services. Systems, especially distributed systems, must evolve over time and should be built to handle change easily. This SOA principle states that each service must be managed and versioned differently so as to not affect other services in the process.

In the book publisher example, the Order Process service and Order Fulfillment service are completely independent of each other; each is versioned and managed completely independent of the other. In this way, when one changes it should not affect the other. It has been said that services should be built *not* to fail. In following this concept, if a service is unavailable for whatever reason or should a service depend on another service that is not available, every precaution should be taken to allow for such services to survive, such as redundancy or failover.

Policy-Based Compatibility

When services call each other, it isn't like two friends meeting in the street, exchanging pleasantries, and then talking. Services need to know a little more about each other. Each service may or may not have certain requirements before it will start communicating and handing out information. Each service has its own compatibility level and knows how it will interact with other services. These two friends in fact aren't friends at all. They are complete and total strangers. When these two strangers meet in the street, an interrogation takes place, with each person providing the other with a policy. This policy is an information sheet containing explicit information about the person. Each stranger scours the policy of the other looking for similar interests. If the two services were to talk again, it would be as if they had never met before in their life. The whole interrogation process would start over.

This is how services interact. Services look at each others' policy, looking for similarities so that they can start communicating. If two services can't satisfy each others' policy requirements, all bets are off. These policies exist in the form of machine-readable expressions.

Policies also allow you to move a service from one environment to another without changing the behavior of the service.

Shared Schemas and Contracts

Think "schemas = data" and "contracts = behavior." The contract contains information regarding the structure of the message. Services do not pass classes and types; they pass schemas and contracts. This allows for a loosely coupled system where the service does not care what type of environment the other service is executing on. The information being passed is 100 percent platform independent. As described previously, a service describes it capabilities.

Microsoft's Commitment to SOA

In 2005 Microsoft showed it was serious about SOA by releasing SQL Server 2005 and Visual Studio 2005. VS 2005 introduced several new components that aid in the architecting of service-oriented applications. The first of these tools is the Application Designer. This tool is to help application developers and designers visually build applications that use or make available services.

The second tool is the Logical Datacenter Designer, which provides the ability to create a logical representation of your datacenter. When I first read about this I thought "why would I want this?," but think about it. Nine times out of 10 the environments in which you develop are not the same environments in which your production application will go. Thus, the Logical Datacenter Designer is a tool that allows developers to see important information about the environment in which their application is targeted, providing such information as current software configurations and versions (SQL Server, IIS, and so on).

Not to be left out, SQL Server 2005 hit the street with a ton of new features and enhancements, many of which are SOA-focused such as a new XML data type and the ability to return XML in a Dataset, support for XQuery, and endpoints exposed as web services.

Where is Microsoft going next? Good question. In the next 12 to 18 months, Microsoft will be introducing two new products. This book is the focus of one of them, Windows Communication Foundation. The other is Windows Vista and WinFX. Windows Vista introduces a new XML markup language called XAML (pronounced "zamel"), which uses a declarative syntax for describing user-interface elements. It also includes a brand-new programming interface, further building on the SOA model by unifying all of the messaging models as well as exposing all of the Windows Communication Foundation capabilities.

SOA Wrap-up

Entire books have been written solely for the purpose of describing in great detail SOA and explaining the reasoning behind it. I have tried to sum it up in seven or eight pages. Consider it the *Readers Digest* version, but hopefully in these few pages you have come to understand SOA a little bit and see some of the benefits of it. But for your enjoyment, I will briefly list them here:

❑   Services are platform and location independent. A service does not care where the service is located, and it does not care about the environment of another service to be able to communicate with it.

❑   Services are isolated. A change in one service does not necessitate a change in other services.

❑   Services are protocol, format, and transport neutral. Service communication information is flexible.

❑   Services are scalable. Remember the book publisher example?

❑   Service behavior is not constrained. If you want to move the location of the service, you only need to change the policy, not the service itself.

With that, you can move on to the real reason for this chapter, and realistically, this book. Earlier in this chapter, several other technologies were mentioned when SOA was being introduced and when distributed architecture was being discussed. This begs the question: Wouldn't it be great if all of these were combined into a single SOA solution?

Why Windows Communication Foundation

Windows Communication Foundation (WCF) is a platform, a framework if you will, for creating and distributing connected applications. It is a fusion of current distributed system technologies designed and developed from day one with the goal of achieving SOA nirvana, or coming as close to it as possible.

WCF is a programming model that enables developers to build service solutions that are reliable and secure, and even transacted. It simplifies development of connected applications and offers something to developers that they have not seen in quite a while — a unified, simplified, and manageable distributed system development approach.

Built on top of the 2.0 .NET Framework CLR (Common Language Runtime), the Windows Communication Foundation is a set of classes that allow developers to build service-oriented applications in their favorite .NET environment (VB.NET or C#).

This section begins by taking a detailed look at the architecture of WCF and the components that make WCF what it is.

WCF Architecture

At the heart of WCF is a layered architecture that supports a lot of the distributed application development styles. Figure 1-3 illustrates the layered architecture of Windows Communication Foundation.

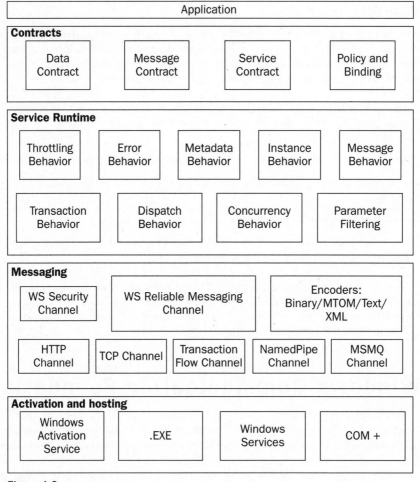

Figure 1-3

This layered architecture, which provides developers a new service-oriented programming model, is discussed in detail in the following sections.

Contracts

WCF contracts are much like a contract that you and I would sign in real life. A contract I may sign could contain information such as the type of work I will perform and what information I might make available to the other party. A WCF contract contains very similar information. It contains information that stipulates what a service does and the type of information it will make available.

Given this information, there are three types of contracts: data, message, and service. More detailed information about contracts is given in Chapter 6, so consider this a primer.

Data

A data contract explicitly stipulates the data that will be exchanged by the service. The service and the client do not need to agree on the types, but they do need to agree on the data contract. This includes parameters and return types.

Message

A message contract provides additional control over that of a data contract, in that it controls the SOAP messages sent and received by the service. In other words, a message contract lets you customize the type formatting of parameters in SOAP messages.

Most of the time a data contract is good enough, but there might be occasions when a little extra control is necessary.

Service

A service contract is what informs the clients and the rest of the outside world what the endpoint has to offer and communicate. Think of it as a single declaration that basically states "here are the data types of my messages, here is where I am located, and here are the protocols that I communicate with."

There is a bit more to it than this, and Chapter 6 covers this in greater detail. But for now, suffice it to say that a service contract is one or more related message interactions.

Policy and Binding

Remember the SOA principles discussed earlier? Remember the one that discusses policies? Here is where they come into play. Policy and binding contracts specify important information such as security, protocol, and other information, and these policies are interrogated looking for the things that need to be satisfied before the two services start communicating.

Service Runtime

The Service Runtime layer is the layer that specifies and manages the behaviors of the service that occur during service operation, or service runtime (thus "service runtime behaviors"). Service behaviors control service type behaviors. They have no control over endpoint or message behaviors. Likewise, endpoint and message behaviors have no control over service behaviors.

The following lists the various behaviors managed by the Service Runtime layer:

❑ **Throttling Behavior:** The Throttling behavior determines the number of processed messages.

❑ **Error Behavior:** The Error behavior specifies what action will be taken if an error occurs during service runtime.

❑ **Metadata Behavior:** The Metadata behavior controls whether or not metadata is exposed to the outside world.

❑ **Instance Behavior:** The Instance behavior drives how many instances of the service will be available to process messages.

❑ **Message Inspection:** Message Inspection gives the service the ability to inspect all or parts of a message.

❑ **Transaction Behavior:** The Transaction behavior enables transacted operations. That is, if a process fails during the service runtime it has the ability to rollback the transaction.

❑ **Dispatch Behavior:** When a message is processed by the WCF infrastructure, the Dispatch Behavior service determines how the message is to be handled and processed.

❑ **Concurrency Behavior:** The Concurrency behavior determines how each service, or instance of the service, handles threading. This behavior helps control how many threads can access a given instance of a service.

❑ **Parameter Filtering:** When a message is acted upon by the service, certain actions can be taken based on what is in the message headers. Parameter Filtering filters the message headers and executes preset actions based on the filter of the message headers.

Messaging

The Messaging layer defines what formats and data exchange patterns can be used during service communication. Client applications can be developed to access this layer and control messaging details and work directly with messages and channels.

The following lists the channels and components that the Messaging layer is composed of:

❑ **WS Security Channel:** The WS Security channel implements the WS-Security specification, which enables message security.

❑ **WS Reliable Messaging Channel:** Guaranteed message delivery is provided by the WS Reliable Messaging channel.

❑ **Encoders:** Encoders let you pick from a number of encodings for the message.

❑ **HTTP Channel:** The HTTP channel tells the service that message delivery will take place via the HTTP protocol.

❑ **TCP Channel:** The TCP channel tells the service that message delivery will take place via the TCP protocol.

❑ **Transaction Flow Channel:** The Transaction Flow channel governs transacted message patterns.

❑ **NamedPipe Channel:** The NamedPipe channel enables inter-process communication.

❑ **MSMQ Channel:** If your service needs to interoperate with MSMQ, this is the channel that enables that.

Activation and Hosting

The Activation and Hosting layer provides different options in which a service can be started as well as hosted. Services can be hosted within the context of another application, or they can be self-hosted. This layer provides those options.

The following list details the hosting and activation options provided by this layer:

❑ **Windows Activation Service:** The Windows Activation Service enables WCF applications to be automatically started when running on a computer that is running the Windows Activation Service.

❑ **.EXE:** WCF allows services to be run as executables (.EXE files).

❑ **Windows Services:** WCF allows services to be run as a Windows service.

❑ **COM+:** WCF allows services to be run as a COM+ application.

The Makeup of WCF

Now that you have an idea of the architecture behind Windows Communication Foundation, a few pages need to be spent covering those things that make WCF what it is. That is, why all the hype surrounding WCF and what makes it so unique?

If you have been paying attention during this chapter, you can more than likely pick out a small handful of things that really make WCF stand out. On the surface, you might make the incorrect assumption that WCF is just a bunch of "add-ons" to the already existing framework. Not so. As you dig into WCF you will really start to see that a lot of thought and time went into developing what you see in front of you. To help you out, this section lists a number of the great focus points that WCF has to offer. Think of it as the personality of WCF:

❑ Programming model

❑ Scalability

❑ Interoperability

❑ Enhanced communication

❑ Enterprise enabled

Programming Model

The great thing about WCF is that there is no "right way" to get from point A to point B. If fact, WCF lets users start at point A and go to point B any way they see fit. This is because the programming model in WCF lets developers control how and when they want to code things and yet gives them the ability to do that with a minimum amount of code.

As you have seen from the architecture, there are only a small handful of major components that a developer will need to work with to build high-class services. However, WCF also lets developers drill down to lower-level components if they desire to get more granular with their options. WCF makes this very simple. The WCF programming model lets a developer take whichever approach he or she desires. There is no single "right" way.

The programming model also combines many of the earlier technologies, such as the ones mentioned earlier in the chapter (MSMQ, COM+, WSE, and so on), into a single model.

Scalability

WCF services scale, and they scale in all directions. Not just up or out, but in all directions. They scale out via routing mechanisms and farms. Remember the book publisher example? The Order Process service was scaled out by providing an Order Process router, which routed orders to multiple Order Process services.

Services scale up by not being tied to a single OS or processor. Services scale up by the pure ability to deploy them on bigger and better servers and taking advantage of the new processor technologies that are starting to appear.

Services scale in by way of cross-process transports, meaning on-machine and cross-machine messaging and Object-RPC.

Services scale down by interfacing and communicating with devices such as printers, scanners, faxes, and so on.

Interoperability

How sweet is it to be able to build high-class services using a single programming model and at the same time take advantage of earlier technologies (see "Programming Model"), irrespective of the OS, environment, or platform? WCF services operate independent of all of these.

WCF services also take advantage of the WS architecture utilizing the already established standards as far as communication and protocols are concerned.

Enhanced Communication

Services aren't picky as far as transports, formats, or much else. You as a developer can choose from a handful of transports, different message formats, and surplus of message patterns.

Along these same lines, WCF is like the country of Switzerland (nice segue, heh?), in that services are neutral as far as transports and protocols are concerned. A service can use TCP, HTTP, Named Pipes, or any other protocol to communicate. The same goes for transports. In fact, if you want to build and use your own, feel free to do so.

The reason it is this way is because, as you hopefully have figured out by now, communication is completely separate from the service. They are completely independent from one another.

Enterprise Enabled

A lot of times there is a give-and-take relationship when dealing with web services, interoperability, and other important features geared toward enterprises. As a developer you have to weigh performance versus security, or reliability. At what cost does adding transactional capabilities add to your solution? Up until now, having the best of all worlds was a mere pipe dream.

Well, now it is time to wake up and smell the technology because WCF provides the ability to have security and reliability without sacrificing performance. And you can throw transactions into the mix as well.

A lot of this comes from the standards of the web service architecture, allowing you to build enterprise-class applications.

Now that you know what makes WCF tick, the chapter wraps up by discussing some of the great things you can do with WCF.

WCF Features

A lot of the topics just discussed can almost be included here, because things such as communication, scalability, and the enterprise are very much considered features as well. Yet they were put in their own section because those are things that define the great characteristics of WCF. As you read this section, keep those topics in mind also, because they are indeed features of WCF.

This section, however, discusses a few of those topics that make WCF feature rich. You know, those topics that make you say "whoa, that is cool." Though this list is by no means complete, it hopefully lists the top few. This chapter has already discussed communication and the programming model (all of which are discussed in greater detail in later chapters), so what are those features?

Transactions

A transaction is a unit of work. A transaction ensures that everything within that transaction either succeeds as a whole or fails as whole. For example, if a transaction contains three items of work to perform, and during the execution of that transaction one of those items fails, then all three fail. The transaction succeeds only if all three statements of work succeed, unless a Checkpoint is issued. You commonly see this in database operations.

WCF incorporates this same transactional processing into its communication. You as a developer can now group communications into transactions. On the enterprise level, this feature lets you execute transactional work across different platforms. Transactions are discussed in Chapter 9.

Hosting

WCF hosting allows services to be hosted in a handful of different environments, such as Windows NT Services, Windows Forms, and console applications, and well as IIS (Internet Information Services) and Windows Activation Services (WAS).

Hosting a service in IIS has added benefits in that the service can take full advantage of many of the native IIS features. For example, IIS can control the starting and stopping of the service automatically. Hosting is discussed in Chapter 15.

Security

What good would Windows Communication Foundation be without security? Trust me on this, WCF certainly isn't lacking in this department. Everything from messages to clients and servers get authenticated, and WCF has a feature that ensures messages aren't messed with during transit. WCF includes message integrity and message confidentiality.

WCF also enables you to integrate your application into an existing security infrastructure, including those that extend beyond the standard Windows-only environments by using secure SOAP messages. Security is discussed in Chapter 10.

Queuing

If you are at all familiar with MSMQ (Microsoft Message Queuing), this topic will sound familiar. WCF provides queuing, allowing messages to be safely stored, providing a consistent state of communication. Queuing collects and stores sent messages from a sending application and forwards them on to the receiving application. This provides a safe and reliable message delivery mechanism.

WCF enables queuing by providing support for the MSMQ transport. Queuing is discussed in Chapter 9.

Of course there are other features. Each of us can put together our own list of nice features, so hopefully you will add your favorite features to this list.

Summary

Windows Communication Foundation is Microsoft's next step in building service-oriented applications. This chapter began by building a nice foundation, delving a little bit into Service-Oriented Architecture. This foundation is important because it helps you understand the rest of the chapter, the importance of Widows Communication Foundation, and what it can do for you.

The discussion of SOA talked about what SOA is and some of the principles that SOA exhibits. An example was given, the book publisher, which showed how using SOA a system can be upgraded and improved without disrupting other components, keeping the entire process intact.

From there the chapter moved on to introducing Windows Communication Foundation (WCF) and discussed its architecture, benefits, and capabilities. This section took a look at the layered architecture of WCF and explained what each layer provides and their purpose. The makeup of WCF was then discussed to better understand what makes WCF tick. Lastly, the chapter covered some of the great features of WCF.

The next chapter discusses the basic Windows Communication Foundation concepts needed to proceed through the rest of the book.

Windows Communication Foundation Concepts

Chapter 1 gave a background of SOA (Service-Oriented Architecture) and built upon that foundation by introducing the topic of this book, Windows Communication Foundation. With that introduction out of the way, this chapter focuses on the main concepts of WCF.

Chapter 1 also spent a few pages discussing the architecture of WCF, which helped build a nice foundation for understanding how WCF is laid out and intricately put together, and how all those layers work together. For example, one of the layers discussed was the Messaging layer, which defines what formats and data exchange patterns can be used when communicating with services. The Service Runtime layer was also discussed, which specifies the behaviors of the service or endpoint.

This chapter goes into a bit more depth in discussing those components, so before diving into the nitty-gritty of WCF and starting to work with it, it would be helpful to understand the components and definitions that make up the basic and fundamental pieces of WCF and some of the basic concepts that make up WCF. In other words, in order to "walk-the-walk" of WCF, you need to "talk-the-talk" of WCF. To understand WCF, it helps to understand messages and services, their behaviors, and other related aspects. By the time you finish this chapter, you will be able to explain what a message is, what a service is and how it works, and how they are related to endpoints.

Therefore, this chapter defines and discusses the following topics:

❑   Messages

❑   Channels

❑   Services

❑   Behaviors

Messages

In its simplest terms, a message is a packet of data containing several pieces of important information being routed from a source to a destination. Applications written using the Windows Communication Foundation communicate through messages that are sent from a source to a destination.

All messages are SOAP messages, formatted in XML as SOAP envelopes. The W3C defines a message as "The basic unit of communication between SOAP nodes." In the case of WCF, these SOAP nodes are services and endpoints, sending these SOAP messages from one location to another to exchange information.

This section discusses the structure of a message, the different types of messaging programs, and the different patterns a message can use to exchange information.

Message Structure

As stated previously, Windows Communication Foundation uses messages to pass data, or exchange information, from one point to another. These messages are little more than a packet of data and must conform to a specific format in order for the exchange of information to take place. Figure 2-1 shows the basic structure of a SOAP message.

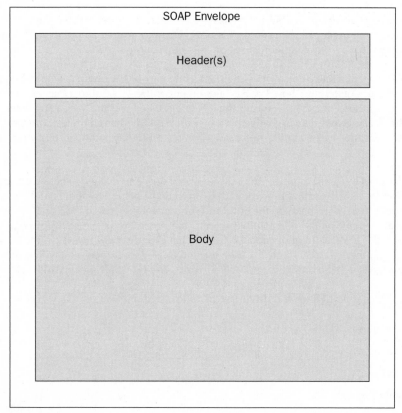

Figure 2-1

As you can see by the figure, there are basically three general components that make up a SOAP message:

❑ The SOAP envelope

❑ The SOAP header

❑ The SOAP body

The following sections discuss each of the components in more detail.

SOAP Envelope

The outermost component of a SOAP message is the SOAP envelope. The SOAP envelope, although extremely important, is nothing more than a container for the two most important pieces of a SOAP message, the SOAP header and the SOAP body.

A SOAP envelope contains several pieces of key information in the form of *elements*. They include the following:

❑ The name of the envelope

❑ A namespace name

❑ An optional <header> element

❑ A required <body> element

*The namespace name must be "*http://www.w3.org/2003/05/soap-envelope*".*

The following code snippet shows the basic code necessary to create a SOAP message:

```
<env:Envelope xmlns:s="http://www.w3.org/2003/05/soap-envelope"
  xmlns:a="http://schemas.xmlsoap.org/ws/2004/08/addressing">
  ...
</env:Envelope>
```

You'll notice in the code fragment that it contains the name of the envelope and a namespace name. The envelope name is given by the following:

```
env:Envelope
```

The rest of the code fragment contains the namespace name. It was mentioned earlier that a SOAP envelope also contains an optional <header> element and a required <body> element. Although those do not appear in the previous code fragment, they are added next.

SOAP Header

The SOAP header is a collection of zero or more header blocks. It is possible for a SOAP message to contain no headers, so the SOAP header collection can contain zero or more SOAP headers. If a header is included, it must be the first child element of the envelope element.

The SOAP header contains important information regarding things that may not be directly related to the message, and is a good place to put optional information regarding the message.

The following code sample illustrates the basic format for including a message header:

```
<env:Envelope xmlns:s="http://www.w3.org/2003/05/soap-envelope"
  xmlns:a="http://schemas.xmlsoap.org/ws/2004/08/addressing">
  <env:Header>
  </env:Header>
</env:Envelope>
```

The header element needs to contain a header name and the namespace of "http://www.w3.org/2003/05/soap-envelope" if it has not already been specified with the envelope element.

SOAP Body

The SOAP body is a collection of data items to be used at a specific target (SOAP receiver). Like the SOAP header, a message can contain zero or more bodies.

A SOAP body, which is simply a child element of the envelope, contains all the necessary information for communication with the SOAP receiver.

The following code sample illustrates the basic format for including a message body:

```
<env:Envelope xmlns:s="http://www.w3.org/2003/05/soap-envelope"
  xmlns:a="http://schemas.xmlsoap.org/ws/2004/08/addressing">
  <env:Header>
  </env:Header>
  <env:Body>
  </env:Body>
</env:Envelope>
```

Given all of this information, a SOAP message might look like that shown in Figure 2-2. According to this figure, the SOAP message contains a SOAP header and a SOAP body.

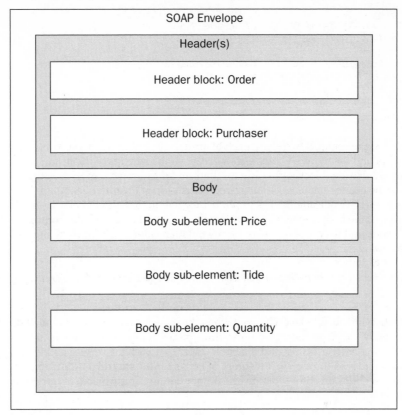

Figure 2-2

The XML representation for this SOAP message might look like the following:

```
<env:Envelope xmlns:s="http://www.w3.org/2003/05/soap-envelope"
  xmlns:a="http://schemas.xmlsoap.org/ws/2004/08/addressing">
  <env:Header>
    <o:order xmlns:o="http://www.wrox.com/order" env:mustUnderstand="true">
      <o:orderreference>591aef96-0c0d-4534-a1d2-4253b910b0b6</o:orderreference>
      <o:orderdate>05/15/2006</o:orderdate>
    </o:orderreference>
    <p:purchaser xmlns:o="http://www.wrox.com/purchaser" env:mustUnderstand="true">
      <p:name>John Spano</p:name>
      <p:creditcardnum>1234-5678-9012-3456</p:creditcardnum>
    </p:orderreference>
  </env:Header>
  <env:Body>
    <c:price xmlns:c="http://www.wrox.com/bookcost">
      <c:cost>
        <c:retailcost>$49.99</c:retailcost>
        <c:salecost>$39.99</c:salecost>
      </c:cost>
```

```
      </c:price>
      <q:quantity xmlns:q="http://www.wrox.com/quantity">
        <q:orderquantity>1</q:orderquantity>
      </q:quantity>
      <t:title xmlns:t="http://www.wrox.com/title">
        <t:booktitle>WCF for Dummies</t:booktitle>
      </t:title>
    </env:Body>
  </env:Envelope>
```

This SOAP message contains two elements that are specific to the envelope. Those are the optional header element and the required body element. Any child elements of the header element are called "header blocks." Header blocks provide a mechanism for grouping logical data together. In the preceding example, the header element contains two header blocks: the order header block and the purchaser header block. These two header blocks provide information that, though not required, can be useful in the processing of the body element of the message. For example, the header contains the name of who ordered the book and the order reference number. Both header blocks must be processed by the receiving service.

> *What information goes in the header and what information goes in the body are entirely up to you and are determined at design time.*

Any information intended to be exchanged when the message reaches the intended destination goes in the message body. In the preceding example, three pieces of information are included in the message body: the title, the order quantity, and the book price. The receiving service (SOAP receiver) might use this information to look through its inventory of books for the specific title and, based on the order quantity, decrement its inventory total by the order quantity. These pieces of information are expected to be understood by the receiving service.

Now, depending on how both the client and service were coded, the client might or might not expect a response, and the service might or might not send a response. If the client does not expect a response and the service does not send a response, the whole operation is complete. However, if you are like me and like order confirmations when you order something, it is completely valid to have the client expect a response and the service to send a response. If this is the case, the response message sent by the service might look something like the following:

```
<env:Envelope xmlns:s="http://www.w3.org/2003/05/soap-envelope">
  <env:Header>
    <o:order xmlns:o="http://www.ogcs.com" env:mustUnderstand="true">
      <o:orderreference>591aef96-0c0d-4534-a1d2-4253b910b0b6</o:orderreference>
      <o:orderdate>05/15/2006</o:orderdate>
    </o:orderreference>
    <p:purchaser xmlns:o="http://www.ogcs.com" env:mustUnderstand="true">
      <p:name>John Spano</p:name>
      <p:creditcardnum>1234-5678-9012-3456</p:creditcardnum>
    </p:orderreference>
  </env:Header>
  <env:Body>
    <ShippingInfo xmlns=="http://www.ogcs.com"/>
      <OrderStatus>Success></OrderStatus>
```

```
      <ShipDate>5/16/2006</ShipDate>
      <ArrivalDate>5/22/2006</ArrivalDate>
    </ShippingInfo>
  </env:Body>
</env:Envelope>
```

When the client receives the response, it knows that the order was placed successfully, when the order will ship, and a tentative date of when it will arrive.

Obviously a lot more information would be needed to place a book order, and this example is simply used to illustrate how messages are structured. With this information deeply embedded in your head, it is time to move on to the different types of programs that can exchange messages.

Messaging Programs

In WCF, different types of applications can send and receive messages. They are the following:

❑   Clients

❑   Services

❑   Intermediaries

What is important to understand is that each of these programs is very unique in several ways. You as a programmer will program the clients and services, but not the intermediaries, and as such, you need to understand that the client and services have very distinct roles. How so? Think of what a client does versus what the service provides. A service will never initiate communication. It will answer a request, but it will never start the flow of communication. That is the role of the client, to "open the flow of communication," per se, and send the initial message. Because they have separate roles, they will be developed somewhat differently, and understanding this from the outset will help smooth the development process. The following section discusses each of the messaging programs.

Clients

After all that this chapter has covered so far, you should have a pretty good idea of what a client is (especially after reading the preceding paragraph), but just in case, it's discussed again here. A client is the piece in the whole WCF picture that initiates communication via the sending of a message. The client sends a message to a service and waits for a response. The service, which is discussed in detail in the next section, receives and processes the message and sends a response.

Figure 2-3 illustrates the sending of a message from a client to a service.

Figure 2-3

In this example, the client has initiated communication by sending a message to the service. Also, in the example no message reply was sent back to the client from the service. However, the client can also receive messages, which means that the service can send a response back to the client as part of the communication. The important thing to remember is that it is the client that drives the communication.

Services

With everything you have learned so far, can you define what a service is and what it does? A service is a program that receives messages and performs predefined actions based on the contents of the message. Services simply respond to incoming messages. The receiving of a message triggers code to be executed, performing an action (or behavior).

These actions, or behaviors, could be a number of things ranging from reading or writing to/from a database, performing some file I/O operations, or even performing more messaging operations such as responding to the client or even sending a message to another service (see the section titled "Service Chains," immediately following this section).

In Figure 2-3, you see a service receiving a message from a single client. In reality, however, services typically serve more than one client. Figure 2-4 illustrates a single service communicating with multiple clients. Both clients send a message to the service and the service can respond to the client.

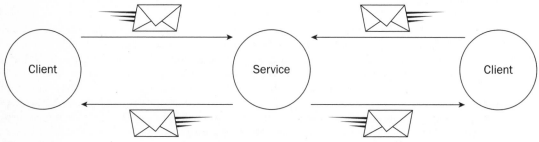

Figure 2-4

One of the important things to remember about services serving multiple clients is that the service is completely able to hold each session's state and keep it totally isolated from other session. Two clients can call the same endpoint of the same service at the same time, and the service will be able to maintain session state for each client so that the operations of one client do not step on the operations of the other client.

Service Chains

Service chains simply mean that a service can act like a client and send messages to other services in response to an incoming message. Remember that a service cannot initiate communication. Instead, it reacts to the incoming message and sends a message to another service. When the service sends a message in response to an incoming message, it is acting as a client.

Figure 2-5 illustrates a service chain in action. The client initiates the communication by sending a message to a service, the first service in the chain. The service processes the incoming message and, based on the predefined behaviors, sends another message to the second service in the chain. In this scenario, the first service in the chain behaves both like a client and a service.

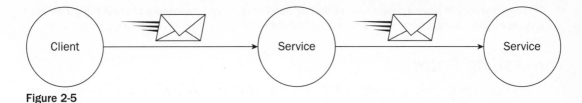

Figure 2-5

Putting this in perspective, the chaining of services has great appeal and tremendous possibilities. Consider for a moment the book publisher example from the first chapter. One of the services put in place was the Order Fulfillment system. Part of the responsibility of this service could be to check shipping options for the incoming order. To do this, the Order Fulfillment system could send a message to several shipping companies requesting shipping amounts.

The flow of communication for this process would be something like this:

- ❏ Client places book order
- ❏ Order received by Order service, which sends a message to the Order Fulfillment service
- ❏ Order Fulfillment service sends message to Shipping service requesting shipping pricing information
- ❏ Shipping service responds with shipping pricing information

In this scenario, you have a service chain of three services communicating with each other, all for the simple process of ordering a book.

Intermediaries

To finish the topic of messaging programs it will be helpful to understand one last concept, and that is the concept of intermediaries. An intermediary is not a service in a chain of services. In fact, the client and the service have no idea that the intermediary even exists. The intermediary does, nonetheless, sit in between the client and service.

An intermediary is not required nor does it perform any action against the message; for example, it does not consume the message. The intermediary might take a peek inside the message but the body of the message is only intended for the destination service. The intermediary might interrogate the message for a variety of reasons, but it does not perform any action in response to the message, such as modifying values or encrypting the message.

The purpose of the intermediary can be one of many things. In the book publisher example that was modified to include a Shipping service, an intermediary can be a gateway between the two companies in which the message passes as it travels between the publisher and the shipping company. The intermediary can also be a firewall that more than likely both companies have in place.

In either case, neither the client nor the service knows of the existence of the intermediary and, in reality, neither of them cares about its existence. However, the intermediary performs an important role nonetheless: It can prevent unwanted messages from getting in and it can take various other actions on messages, such as routing messages or acting as a gateway. An intermediary can also monitor message activity.

By now you should have a good grasp of both the architecture of a message and the different types of messaging programs. It is now time to discuss the different types of messaging patterns.

Messaging Patterns

If you have been keeping up on WSDL (Web Service Description Language) at all and if you have done some reading on Microsoft or the W3C web sites, you should be familiar with the concept of messaging patterns.

Messaging patterns basically describe how programs exchange messages. When a program sends a message, it must conform to one of several patterns in order for it to successfully communicate with the destination program. Likewise, the destination program must conform to the same basic patterns.

There are three basic messaging patterns that programs can use to exchange messages. Those patterns include the following:

- ❑ Simplex
- ❑ Duplex
- ❑ Request-Reply

The next sections discuss these messaging patterns individually.

Simplex

The Simplex message pattern is simply a one-way communication from Program A to Program B. No response is generated by Program B, thus causing the one-way communication. Figure 2-6 illustrates a Simplex message pattern.

Figure 2-6

In this scenario, the client initiates communication and sends a message to the service. The service consumes the message and performs some action or behavior but does not communicate back to the client. The client in the Simplex message pattern suffers from short-term memory loss. When the client sends the message, it has no idea it sent a message because it is not expecting a response.

Duplex

If the client wants a response it uses the Duplex messaging pattern. This pattern allows for both programs to communicate openly and allows information exchanges in both directions. Figure 2-7 illustrates the Duplex message pattern.

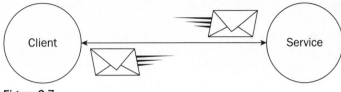

Figure 2-7

A fax machine would be an example of Duplex messaging communication. When you send a fax through the phone line, the sending machine and receiving machine make a connection and start communicating back and forth, sending information to each such as baud rate and receive status. This sending fax machine sends the scanned document to the receiving fax machine, while the receiving fax machine sends back received status information.

The concept with this messaging pattern is that neither the sending program nor the receiving program waits for a response from the other program.

Request-Reply

Unlike the Duplex messaging pattern, the Request-Reply messaging pattern doesn't allow bi-directional communication to happen freely. In this pattern, the client sends a response and then waits for reply. The service doesn't communicate anything until it receives a message. Figure 2-8 illustrates the Request-Reply message pattern.

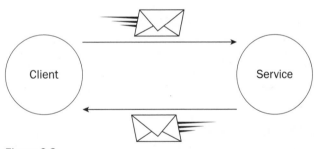

Figure 2-8

When you surf the web, you are witnessing the Request-Reply messaging pattern in action. When you browse to http://www.wrox.com, your browser sends information to that URL requesting information from that web site. That web site then sends back the information your browser requested.

You also see this type of messaging pattern in the form of distributed objects. WCF services have the ability to communicate using this message pattern as well as the Duplex message pattern. This information is discussed in more detail in Chapter 8 when services are discussed.

Channels

OK, enough about messages. By now you should have a good understanding of what messages are, the different types of programs that exchange messages, and how messages are communicated and exchanged. From here, the topic of channels needs to be discussed because channels play a pivotal role in the delivery of messages.

The topic of channels is being discussed for two reasons. First, it is through this medium that messages are exchanged. A message cannot be sent without first establishing a channel through which to send the message. Second, it is through these mediums that a WCF program has access to some of the great features of Windows Communication Foundation.

A channel, as mentioned, is the medium through which messages are exchanged. The channel is created by the client specifying the address of the service and the type of channel to create. Once this information is established, the channel is created and opened.

Figure 2-9 illustrates the steps taken when creating a channel and sending a message.

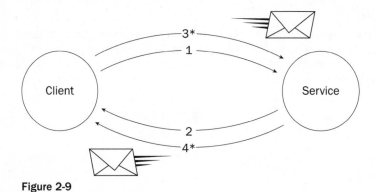

Figure 2-9

The steps are defined in order as follows:

- ❑ The client establishes a channel to the service
- ❑ The service accepts the client's request to open a channel
- ❑ The client sends the message request via the channel
- ❑ The service sends a reply to the client via the channel

Keep in mind that in order for this process to work, the service must already be listening for requests. For example, the service might be listening on `http://OrderServer/AcceptOrder` for incoming requests. This is the address the client will use to establish a channel and send subsequent messages.

Also, it is the responsibility of the client to close and dispose of the channel once it is done using the channel.

Channel Stacks

This chapter needs to spend a page or two on the topic of channel stacks because it is through channel stacks that interoperability with other platforms comes into the picture. If you remember back to Chapter 1 where the discussion revolved round service-orientation and Service-Oriented Architecture, one of the big bonuses of SOA was interoperability. On top of that, it is through channel stacks that additional features needed by the message are provided, such as binding and security.

So, what are channel stacks? Think of a channel as a pipe or tube. When a message is sent from the sender to the receiver, the message is sent through the channel "pipe." Now imagine gluing a number of these pipes together, with each pipe or tube performing a specific function needed by the message. You now have a channel stack.

The following is a list of some of the functionality available that can be utilized to create and string together a channel stack:

❑   Security

❑   Interoperability

❑   Message Patterns

❑   Transports

Security

Two basic levels of security are available: transport security and message security. Transport security can be provided by several protocols including as HTTPS. SOAP message security offers quite a list of functionality, including authentication, message integrity and confidentiality, and auditing.

You can take advantage of several message security features that already exist such as Windows authentication (Windows NTLM and Kerberos) and X.509. Keep in mind that one of the key features of WCF is that it is extensible, meaning that you can write custom extensions to add additional security features such as custom credentials, tokens, and authorization. Pretty nifty.

Interoperability

These first two chapters have talked quite a bit about the importance of interoperability, especially the first chapter, and the role it plays in Windows Communication Foundation. A lot of the first chapter talked about the need to be able to communicate with other platforms for a pure service-oriented and distributed architecture.

By combining different components you can build a channel that communicates and operates with the other platforms seamlessly. Keep in mind those platforms you want to interoperate with. You have several to choose from and most, if not all, have been talked about already. Those include MSMQ interoperability, .NET interoperability, and WS-* interoperability.

MSMQ interoperability allows your WCF application to communicate with your MSMQ installation. .NET interoperability lets you communicate with .NET platforms on both ends of the communication channel, and WS-* interoperability allows you to take advantage of those platforms using the WS-* protocols, such as SOAP, MTOM, WSDL, WS-Security, ReliableMessaging, and WS-Policy, as well as others. Interoperability rocks. Interoperability is discussed in Chapter 12.

If you have been doing any work with WSE 3.0, you will be glad to hear that WCF interoperates extremely well with WSE 3.0, which Chapter 12 discusses. Any existing WSE 3.0 services can, and do, work with WCF with very little work on your part.

Message Patterns

Message patterns were discussed earlier in this chapter, and how you build your message pattern channel depends on what message patterns are available to you. Remember that the three message patterns are Simplex, Duplex, and Request-Reply. When interoperability comes into play you need to keep in mind the types of message patterns of other platforms. You may design for one message pattern but the platform you want to interoperate with may not support that message pattern. For example, MSMQ doesn't communicate in a request-reply fashion.

Transports

Windows Communication Foundation supports four different transports: HTTP, TCP, MSMQ, and Named Pipes. These transports are the medium in which communication takes place in a channel. Some of these transports have built-in security, and others do not. For example, HTTP has HTTPS.

The HTTP transport is useful when connection state does not need to be maintained, such as a web-browser client communicating with a web server. Because the HTTP protocol is not connection-based, no connection state is maintained once the response is sent. However, the HTTP protocol is very useful in interoperability with legacy systems.

TCP is useful when connection-based communication is important. In this scenario, a communication session between participants is created prior to the exchange of data. If all communicating participants are using WCF, bindings using this protocol or the Named Pipes protocol perform better. The TCP transport in WCF is specifically designed for the scenario where both participants are using WCF.

Named Pipes is useful for single machine processing between processes. It can be used for single (one-way) or duplex communication between processes on a single computer. This transport should be used when communication from another machine is to be prevented and communication between WCF applications on the same machine is required.

The MSMQ transport can be used when the reliable delivery of messages is required.

As you select your transport, keep in mind the target environment and the platforms you might encounter, especially if your channel crosses boundaries (a domain boundary, geographic boundary, and so on). The transport you select can have a performance and communication cost associated with it.

From here the next concept to discuss is that of services.

Services

Of all the things that I get excited about, services rank really high. When I was writing my first book, *Professional SQL Server 2005 XML*, one of my favorite chapters to write was the one on SOAP support and endpoints in SQL Server 2005. Why? Because it dealt with SOAP, WSDL, and endpoints. It is possible now to create multiple endpoints within SQL Server 2005 and communicate with those endpoints regardless of the client. As long as my client application can talk SOAP, I can communicate with those endpoints.

Windows Communication Foundation is not that much different. WCF is made up of services and endpoints that communicate with clients, regardless of the platform. However, as you have learned, WCF builds on this to offer interoperability with other platforms and allows for the extension of WCF in many areas.

A Windows Communication Foundation service is comprised of a service description and a collection of endpoints, as illustrated in Figure 2-10.

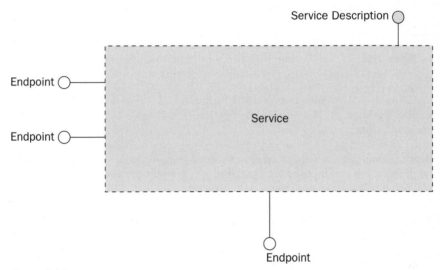

Figure 2-10

The service description is basically what broadcasts how the service can be accessed and what functionality the service provides. There are a small handful of standards in which to communicate and broadcast the service information, the most common being the WSDL (Web Service Description Language). However, you also can use an XSD Schema, a WS-Policy, and WS-MEX (WS-Metadata Exchange).

If your message contains any complex data structures, the XSD Schema can be used to help describe these. WS-Policy is the format in which a service's policy is defined.

Neither this chapter, nor this book, really, get into any great depth of WSDL or schemas. Whole books are dedicated to those topics, and to cover them here would be outside the scope of this book. However, they are defined and briefly discussed here as a mechanism for understanding how services operate and communicate.

OK, time to dig a little deeper and understand what a service looks like "under the hood." Figure 2-11 shows what a service looks like once the hood is lifted, allowing us to take a look inside.

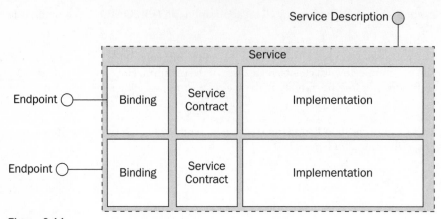

Figure 2-11

From the outside, a service contains a service description and one or more endpoints. However, when you look under the hood you'll notice that there are also bindings, service contracts, and code for the service implementation.

In the preceding example, each endpoint has an associated binding, service contract, and implementation. Though this is a very simplistic example, it is very possible for a service to contain multiple endpoints, multiple bindings, and multiple service contracts.

Each endpoint has a unique address that distinguishes it from the other endpoints on the same service. To this end, the binding for each service must also be unique. However, service contracts can be shared among the endpoints.

There is one last piece of information regarding services, and that is to explain what happens when a service is executed. As the service receives a message, service execution takes place, at which time a CLR runtime instance is created of the service description and implementation code. As messages come in, the first thing that happens is that an instance of the ServiceDescription class is created.

The WCF runtime controls several aspects of the service including message formatting, and the sending and receiving of messages. The runtime also oversees handing the message over to the correct operation for processing and execution.

On top of all of this is the ServiceHost. The ServiceHost is responsible for providing a host for the endpoints as well as making available the service behaviors.

At any given point a service can be in one of six states:

❑ Created

❑ Opening

❑ Opened

❑ Closing

❑   Closed

❑   Faulted

Most of these states should be self-explanatory, such as opened and closed.

Endpoints have been mentioned quite a bit in this chapter, yet they haven't really been discussed. It is time to do that. Once endpoints are discussed, bindings, contracts, and addresses will quickly follow.

Endpoint

Think of a service as a collection of one or more endpoints. A service must have at least one endpoint, otherwise, what would there be to connect to? An endpoint is the component of the service that communicates with the client and provides the service operations.

As stated in the previous section, each endpoint has its very own address, which makes it distinguishable from the other endpoints on the service.

You can sort of get an idea of the inner workings of an endpoint by revisiting Figure 2-11. Each endpoint has a unique address. For example, the top endpoint might have an address of `http://OrderSrver/Order` with a transport binding of HTTP and no security binding. The service contract implements the service interface, defining the actions the endpoint will take.

In the previous section you took a look under the hood of a service to inspect its inner workings and saw the relationship between the endpoints and their associated addresses, bindings, and contracts. The following sections discuss those in a bit more detail. There are also complete chapters dedicated to each topic as well.

Addresses

You should have a pretty good idea by now that all endpoints are addressed by their address. However, don't make the mistake of thinking that all services are hosted within IIS or that they all have an "http://..." address. Not correct.

Several things determine the format of an address, such as the transport used and whether or not IIS is hosting the service. It is entirely possible to host a service using TCP or MSMQ. For example, if you were using the service using TCP, the prefix would be net.tcp and the address would look something like this:

```
net.tcp://localhost/BookOrder
```

Addresses are discussed in much more detail in Chapter 4.

Bindings

Bindings are what define how an endpoint communicates with the outside world. Each endpoint must have a binding. The binding, which is simply a set of properties, defines things like the transport pattern, the security pattern, and the message pattern. At the very least, a binding should specify the transport.

Windows Communication Foundation comes with nine predefined bindings. These bindings are then selected based on the features you need. The following table shows the different binding types and their features (default values are in parentheses).

Binding	Interoperability	Security	Sessions	Message Pattern
BasicHttpBinding	Basic Profile 1.1	(none), Transport, Message	None, (None)	n/a
WSHttpBinding	WS	Transport, (Message), Mixed	(None), Transport, Reliable	n/a
WSDualHttpBinding	WS	(Message)	Reliable	Yes
WSFederationHttpBinding	WS	(Message)	(None), Reliable	No
NetTcpBinding	.NET	(Transport), Message	Reliable, (Transport)	Yes
NetNamedPipeBinding	.NET	(Transport)	None, (Transport)	Yes
NetMsmqBinding	.NET	Message, (Transport), Both	(None)	No
NetPeerTcpBinding	Peer	(Transport)	(None)	Yes
MsmgIntegrationBinding	MSMQ	(Transport)	(None)	n/a

For you hard-core programmers, WCF allows you to create your own custom bindings. Is that cool, or what?

Contracts

Contracts define certain aspects of the service such as the format and structure of the message, and equally important, the behavior of the service. Service contracts are well-formed XML documents, typically found in the format of WSDL or XSD.

Windows Communication Foundation supports the following three types of contracts:

- ❑ Service contracts
- ❑ Message contracts
- ❑ Data contracts

Service Contracts

Service contracts define the operations that a service will perform when executed. They tell the outside world a lot about the service such as message data types, operation locations, the protocols the client will need in order to communicate with the service, and the operations the service provides.

In the book publisher example, a service might exist that has a PlaceOrder operation, which accepts order information (name, title, payment type, and so on) and returns success or failure (and if success, an order number). In this scenario the service contract could inform the clients that the service contract contains a PlaceOrder operation and the address of this operation and the type of protocols needed to communicate with this service. As well, the information could include the data types needed for this message.

Message Contracts

Message contracts allow the control of SOAP messages that are produced and consumed by WCF. Basically it boils down to being able to customize the format of contract parameters and the placing of elements within a SOAP message, or in other words, having control of the structure as well as the contents of a SOAP message. If you have this need, then this is for you.

It is highly recommended that if you don't need this level of control, you should consider using data contracts.

Data Contracts

Data contracts specifically define the data that is being exchanged between a client and service. The data contract is an agreement, meaning that the client and the service *must* agree on the data contract in order for the exchange of data to take place. Note that they don't have to agree on the data types, just the contract.

This is made available due to the fact that all data is serialized to XML and deserialized from XML during the processing of the message. This means that a number of different types can be serialized with no extra preparation. These types include .NET primitive types such as System.Boolean and System.Single, as well as special types (System.DateTime, for example).

Serialization is provided via a new serialization engine in WCF, called the DataContractSerializer. This engine provides the translation between .NET Framework objects and XML, and vice versa. Serialization occurs at runtime when the message is created and ready to send. WCF selects the serializer based on service contract encoding. The DataContractSerializer is used by default but you can also use the XmlSerializer (currently used in ASMX) by annotating the service contract with an attribute, such as the following:

```
[ServiceContract, XmlSerializerFormat]
public interface IWCFService
{
   //add Operation Contracts...
}
```

Contracts are covered in greater detail in Chapter 6.

Behaviors

This chapter has mentioned service behaviors on many occasions, so it closes out by discussing the different types of service runtime behaviors. A behavior controls the runtime characteristics of a service or endpoint. Behaviors are grouped according to their scope, in that they control aspects relevant to the object to which they are applied. For example, service behaviors affect aspects related to the service, and endpoint behaviors affect only properties related to the endpoint. Likewise, endpoints get to share many of the common behaviors, but some behaviors only apply to individual endpoints and cannot be shared (such as security information), yet throttling behavior is applied to, and affects, the service-level aspects.

There is a small list of behaviors that a service can use during execution. They include the following:

❑ **Throttling:** Determines the number of threads, instances, and messages that can be processed by a service concurrently.

❑ **Security:** Determines the security characteristics.

❑ **Instancing:** Determines the number of instances of the service implementation class to be created.

    ❑ **PerCall:** A new InstanceContext is created for each client request.

    ❑ **PerSession:** A new InstanceContext is created per client session and maintained throughout the lifetime of the session.

    ❑ **Single:** A single InstanceContext is used for all client requests during the lifetime of the application.

❑ **Error handling:** Lets you determine how errors will be handled when encountered and if they should be returned to the calling application.

❑ **Concurrency:** Controls the number of threads that are active within an InstanceContext at any given time.

    ❑ **Multiple:** Each instance of the service can have multiple threads that are concurrently processing messages.

    ❑ **Single:** Each InstanceContext can have only one thread that is processing messages at a time.

    ❑ **Reentrant:** Each instance of the service can only process messages one at a time but can accept re-entrant operation calls.

❑ **Transactions:** Determines if the service can accept and execute a transaction from the client. Transactions are controlled by the client, meaning that the client will tell the service if it can accept and execute a transaction and also controls the lifetime of the transaction.

Summary

This chapter covered a lot of information in a few pages, but luckily there are entire chapters dedicated to most of the main topics in this chapter, such as services (Chapter 8), binding (Chapter 5), contracts (Chapter 6), and addresses (Chapter 4). Clients are discussed in Chapter 7 as well.

This chapter was designed to provide you with the fundamental basics of the major components that make up Windows Communication Foundation. Equally important was the discussion on messaging. You can't use the WCF without using messaging. The beginning of this chapter spent quite a bit of time on messaging and related topics, such as different messaging programs and messaging patterns, because data is exchanged via this mechanism, and it is critical that this be understood so you will know how they work and how they are exchanged.

The rest of the chapter was spent discussing the fundamental components of WCF such as services, channels, endpoints, addresses, and binding. Although most of these are discussed in more detail later, it was important that the foundation be laid here so that you will have a good grasp of each topic when you get to that particular chapter.

The section on services took a dissected look at the makeup of a service, including endpoints, and what makes them tick. The different types of bindings were discussed as well as the different behaviors that a service can implement.

This section of the book wraps up by discussing the Windows Communication Foundation programming model in Chapter 3.

3

Understanding Windows Communication Foundation

On the surface, Windows Communication Foundation seems a bit daunting. If you understand WSDL (Web Service Description Language) and web services, grasping the concept of WCF may be less of a task, but if you are not familiar with WSDL/web services, understanding Windows Communication Foundation might seem a bit overwhelming based on what you have read so far, given its multiple layers and many components. A look underneath the hood would expose an API consisting of hundreds of classes.

The beauty of WCF, however, comes from the simplicity of its programming and service models. Although the underlying foundation of WCF is quite large, WCF is built on the .NET Framework and it therefore takes advantage of programming languages and a platform that you already know. Even better, to write WCF services you only need to know how to use a fraction of those many classes.

The best way to learn how to build Windows Communication Foundation services is to jump in with both feet and actually build one. This chapter does just that. After digging into the WCF programming model and service model, the last part of this chapter allows you to begin slinging code and building a WCF service.

This chapter covers the following topics:

- ❑ WCF programming model
- ❑ Installing WCF
- ❑ Building a WCF service

WCF Programming Model

In all my reading on this great technology, I read over and over about the "WCF Programming Model," yet nowhere does it explain, or define, what it *is*. They say what it can *do*, but not what it *is*. This chapter answers that question and explains the many benefits it provides to you as a developer.

This section discusses several aspects that will help answer that question, and it does so by discussing some very important aspects that apply to, and belong to, Windows Communication Foundation.

SO or OO

Chapter 1 spent a few pages digging into the why's and what's regarding service-orientation. Over the past few years Microsoft has provided a lot of support for service-oriented programming by adding exceptional capabilities to the .NET Framework via the System.Web.Services class. Microsoft's dedication to service-orientation was further proven by adding additional support via the Web Service Enhancements.

The support for service-oriented programming was provided with the SOA principles discussed in Chapter 1 in mind. The goal for developing SOA applications is to be able to provide a solution that follows those principles.

With that being said, where does object-oriented programming fit in? I'm going to go out on a limb here and state that if you are reading this book, you have been writing object-oriented code and applications for a while. Object-oriented software development has been around a long time and continues to be a strong component in the .NET Framework.

When developing WCF services, which do you use? Do you use a service-oriented approach or an object-oriented approach to developing a WCF solution? The answer is, both. Simply put, object-oriented programming is used to develop applications, and service-oriented programming is used to connect those applications. The trick is to understand the distinction between the two and understand when and how they are used and the benefits they provide.

Think "object-orientation = tightly coupled, and service-orientation = loosely coupled." Object-oriented applications are two or more class libraries that are dependent on each other and share a common type system. These class libraries communicate with each other via distributed object calls, with each object class communicating with the other classes' exposed interface.

Service-oriented applications are programs that know nothing about each other, thus are loosely coupled. Each application communicates with other applications via messages, and what makes this approach ideal is that these messages can be sent from one application to another regardless of the platform of each service.

When developing WCF services, the trick is to understand how to link OO and SO together. The terms *classes* and *interfaces* are extremely familiar to the object-oriented developer, and they are still used when developing WCF services. This is the OO part of the equation. The SO part of the equation comes in when you apply the WCF attributes to define the entities.

For example, the following class defines an object-oriented interface:

```
public interface coolservice
{
  decimal CalculateShipping(string state, int shiptype)
  {
    //do something
  }
  decimal CalculateTax(string state, decimal bookcost)
  {
    //do something
  }
}
```

The first step is to define the interface using your favorite .NET programming language, in this case, C#. Now comes the SO part, which is to add the necessary attributes used to designate this interface as a WCF contract. The preceding code now looks like this:

```
[ServiceContract]
public interface coolservice
{
  [OperationContract]
  decimal CalculateShipping(string state, int shiptype)
  {
    //do something
  }
  [OperationContract]
  decimal CalculateTax(string state, decimal bookcost)
  {
    //do something
  }
}
```

Though this example is fairly simple (don't worry, it will get more detailed throughout the book), this shows the fusion of object-oriented programming and service-oriented programming. You get to use a language that you already know while taking advantage of the great benefits of service-orientation.

Don't worry about understanding the [ServiceContract] and [OperationContract] attributes just yet. All of this, and much more, is explained in due time.

Service Model

If you have done any sort of web service development, this model will look somewhat familiar. When you create a web service you are indeed creating a *service*. A web service contains an XML document that is used to describe everything there is to know about the service. This document is the Web Service Description Language (WSDL) for the service and contains three parts or sections:

❑ Service

❑ Binding

❑ portType

The first part, the *service* part, contains information as to where the service is. The second part, the *binding* section, contains information as to how this service will communicate, such as what protocols the service will use, and so on. The third part, the *portType* section, explains what the service will do.

Coincidently, the Windows Communication Foundation service model is very similar to the web service model. Using the service model, you specify where the service is (that is, URI), how it communicates, and what the service can do. Hmmm, just like the WSDL. The only difference is the naming of the parts. In WCF, they are not called *service*, *binding*, and *portType*. In WCF, they are called *address*, *binding*, and *contract*.

Simply put, a service is an application or piece of software that communicates with other services or applications. That service has one or more *endpoints*. Each of those endpoints contains an address, binding, and contract.

This service model is provided by the System.ServiceModel namespace and, as mentioned earlier, contains too many classes to count. Luckily you don't need to know all of them. The following section discusses a few of the important classes of the System.ServiceModel namespace.

System.ServiceModel

In Windows Communication Foundation, the System.ServiceModel namespace is used to model and develop the service application and how it communicates. This namespace provides a large number of classes that allow developers to be flexible with respect to how their service will be developed. From the outset, a developer can model the service to communicate a certain way, for instance, using the service model. Some time later, the requirements may change and the need to modify how the service communicates may necessitate changes and modifications. The service model provided via the System.ServiceModel namespace provides this flexibility. It is a full-featured service-oriented infrastructure.

The following table lists some of the more commonly used classes used to model and build your service.

Class	Description
BasicHTTPBinding	The binding that service endpoints can use to communicate with clients and web services (ASMX).
NetMsmqBinding	The binding that service endpoints can use to communicate with MSMQ clients and other services.
NetNamedPipeBinding	The secure binding that service endpoints can use to communicate with clients/services on the same machine.
NetTCPBinding	The secure binding that service endpoints can use to communicate with clients/services across machines.
WSHTTPBinding	The binding that service endpoints can use to communicate with clients/services using distributed transactions and secure and reliable sessions.
EndpointAddress	The means by which a unique address is provided and accessible to clients for communication with the endpoint.

Class	Description
EndpointAddressBuilding	The mechanism in which to create new endpoint addresses with specific property values.
ChannelFactory	The mechanism in which different types of channels are created and managed, and made available to clients to send messages to endpoints.
Identity	The means by which an identity is specified, enabling authentication between endpoints when messages are exchanged.
MessageHeader	Represents the contents of a SOAP message header.
ServiceHost	The mechanism by which a host is provided for services.
ReliableSession	Provides access to the properties of a reliable session binding element. This is only available when using one of the predefined bindings.

Obviously there are many more classes, and you may have your own "commonly used" list. For example, there are all the security classes such as BasicHTTPSecurity, which is used to configure security settings for the BasicHTTPBinding. This list, however, is to provide you with a base foundation of the classes you might choose to have in your "WCF Utility Belt."

System.ServiceModel.Channels

The System.ServiceModel.Channels namespace provides a means by which developers determine how their service will communicate. The System.ServiceModel namespace, discussed previously, provides the developer a way to define and model the service from the communication aspect.

The following table lists some of the more commonly used classes used to define the communication of your service.

Class	Description
AddressHeader	A header that contains address information used to identify and communicate with an endpoint
AddressHeaderCollection	A collection of address headers
Binding	A collection of binding elements, each binding defining how an endpoint will communicate with the outside world
BindingContext	Provides address and binding information needed to build channel factories and channel listeners
BindingElement	Represents a binding element, which is used to build bindings
CustomBinding	Used to define and build a custom binding from a set of binding elements

Table continued on following page

Class	Description
Message	A unit of communication between endpoints
MessageHeader	The content of a message SOAP header
MessageHeaders	A collection of message headers

Obviously if you were to look at the list of classes in the System.ServiceModel.Channels namespace you would see close to 10 times the number of classes than those listed here. The point of this list is to provide a base for you to start with and build from, and to point out those classes that might be most beneficial to you as you begin modeling your service.

For example, the following code snippet illustrates a number of the classes listed in both the System.ServiceModel and System.ServiceModel.Channels namespaces:

```
class TestWCFApp
{
  static void Main()
  {
    Uri baseAddress = new Uri(ConfigurationManager.AppSettings["address"]);

    AddressHeader ah =
AddressHeader.CreateAddressHeader("service1","http://localhost:8080/service");

    EndpointAddress ea = new EndpointAddress(new
Uri("http://localhost:8081/testservice/service"), ah);

    ServiceEndpoint se = new
ServiceEndpoint(ContractDescription.GetContract(typeof(BookOrderService)), new
WSHttpBinding), ea);

    ServiceHost sh new ServiceHost(typeof(BookOrderService), baseAddress);

    sh.Description.Endpoints.Add(se);

    sh.Open();

    sh.close();
  }
}
```

In this small example, the AddressHeader class is used to define an address header for the endpoint. The endpoint is then defined using the address header. A service endpoint is then defined, followed by the defining of a service host, which is used to provide a host for the service being created. The endpoint description is then set, and finally the service host is opened, which creates listeners and starts listening for messages.

System.Transactions

Transactions provide a way to gather a set of operations and package them into a single unit of execution. A transaction event must have the following properties:

❑   Transactions must be atomic, meaning that all operations in the transaction must complete successfully and be committed. If any one of the operations fails, all the operations get rolled back to their previous state.

❑   Transactions must be consistent, in that the operations in the transaction correctly change the state of the system.

❑   Transactions must be isolated, meaning that one operation within the transaction cannot see the results of another operation within the transaction.

❑   Transactions must be durable, meaning that anything committed to a managed resource must survive a failure. Surviving the failure means that no damage has been done to the resource if the operation fails (such as changing data in a database).

New to version 2 of the .NET Framework is the System.Transactions namespace. This namespace provides the ability to create and participate in a transaction with one or more parties. You can also write your own transactional application and resource manager.

This namespace also comes with two new built-in transaction managers: the Lightweight Transaction Manager (LM) and OleTx Transaction Manager.

Windows Communication Foundation provides the ability to pass transactions from the client to a service, and the great thing is that WCF inherits the .NET transaction capabilities discussed earlier so no additional components are needed to enable transactions in WCF.

Transactions are covered in more detail in Chapter 9.

SvcUtil.exe

This little handy-dandy utility will nearly become your best friend. In fact, it should be one of your favorite utilities in your WCF Utility Belt. This tool does two things:

❑   Creates service model code from your metadata documents

❑   Creates metadata documents from your service code

How cool is that?

The tool is in the \Program Files\Microsoft SDKs\Windows\v1.0\Bin directory and is a command-line tool, meaning you'll need to open a command window and execute the executable followed by several parameters. This section lists the parameters and the available options that can be used with the SvcUtil utility. You can find the same information by typing the following at the command line:

```
Svcutil.exe /?
```

The general syntax for the utility is as follows:

```
SvcUtil [options] [metadatapath* | assemblypath* | metadataUrl*]
```

The following list explains the parameters that can be used with the SvcUtil utility:

❑ metadatadocumentpath — Path to the metadata document that contains the contract information to import into .wsdl, .xsd, .wspolicy, or .wsmex code.

❑ assemblyinfopath — Path to the assembly file that contains the service contracts that will be exported to metadata.

❑ url — URL to a service endpoint that contains metadata available for download via the WS-Metadata Exchange or HTTP-Get.

The following tables list and explain the options available to the SvcUtil utility, broken out by option type.

Common Usages

Parameter	Short Form	Description
/directory:<directory>	/d:<directory>	Directory in which to create the files. If a directory is not specified, the current directory is used as the default.
/target:<output type>	/t:	Specifies the output to be generated by this tool. Available values are code, metadata, and XmlSerializer.
/config:<file1>[, <file2>]		Instructs the SvcUtil utility to generate a configuration file. If a single name is provided, that is the name of the configuration file. If two filenames are supplied, the first file is an input configuration file whose contents are combined with the generated configuration file and written into the second file.
/noConfig		Does not generate a configuration file.

Code Generation

Parameter	Short Form	Description
/out:<file>	/o:<file>	Filename for the generated code. If a filename is not specified, the name of the file is taken from the WSDL filename, service name, or the target-Namespace of the schema document.
/mergeConfig		Merges the generated config file into an existing file instead of overwriting the existing configuration file.

Parameter	Short Form	Description
/language:<language>	/l:<language>	Specifies the programming language to use when generating code. Must be either a language name or a fully qualified name of a class that implements the System.CodeDom.Compiler.CodeDomCompiler namespace. Language name values include CS, VB, VJS, C#. Default is C#.
/namespace: <string, string>	/n:<string, string>	Specifies a mapping from WSDK or schema target namespace to CLR namespace. Specifying ' * ' for the target namespace will map all target-Namespaces without an explicit mapping to that CLR namespace.
/messageContract	/mc	Generates Message Contract types.
/enableDataBinding	/edb	Implements the INotifyPropertyChanged interfaces on all Data Contract types to enable data binding.
/serializer:Auto	/ser:Auto	Automatically selects the serializer that uses the Data Contract serializer. The XmlSerializer is used if the Data Contract serializer fails.
/serializer: DataContractSerializer	/ser:Data ContractSerializer	Generates data types that use the Data Contract serializer for serialization and deserialization.
/serializer:XmlSerializer	/ser:XmlSerializer	Generates data types that use the XmlSerializer for serialization and deserialization.
/importXmlTypes		Configures the Data Contract serializer to import non-Data Contract types as IXmlSerializable types.

Metadata Export

Parameter	Short Form	Description
/serviceName: <serviceConfig		Specifies the configuration name of a service to be exported. An executable and an associated configuration file must be passed as input if this option is used.
/reference:<file path>	/r	Adds the specified assembly to the set of assemblies used for resolving type references. This option helps locate extension assemblies that are not in the GAC, especially if you are using a service that uses third-party extensions.
/dataContractOnly	/dconly	Instructs the SvcUtil utility to operate on Data Contract types only. Service Contracts will not be processed.

Serialization / Message

Parameter	Short Form	Description
/typedMessage	/tm	Generates code that uses Typed Messages.
/useXmlSerializer	/uxs	Generates code that uses the XmlSerializer.
/importXmlType	/ixt	Imports non-DataContract types as IXmlSerializable.
/enableDataBinding	/edb	Implements INotifyPropertyChanged interface on all XmlFormatter types to enable data binding.

Advanced

Parameter	Short Form	Description
/async	/a	Generates asynchronous method signatures. The default is to generate synchronous methods.
/internal	/i	Generates classes marked internal. The default is to only generate public classes.
/reference:<file path>	/r:<file path>	References the specified assembly.
/noStdLib		Does not reference the standard library mscorlib.dll.
/CollectionType:<type>	/ct:<type>	Fully qualified or assembly qualified name of the type to use as referenced collection type.
/excludeType:<type>	/et:<type>	Fully qualified or assembly qualified name to exclude from referenced types.
/serializable	/s	Generates classes marked Serializable.

Miscellaneous

Parameter	Short Form	Description
/svcutilConfig:<configfile>		Custom configuration file to use in place of the application configuration file. This can be used to change the metadata configuration without changing the tool's configuration file.
/validate	/v	Validates services. A configuration file defining a service is loaded when an exe for the configuration file is passed as input to the tool.
/noLogo		Suppresses the copyright and banner messages.
/help	/?	Displays the command syntax and tool options.

You will notice that several options do not have a short form. This is by design, and when using those options the full parameter needs to be used.

A number of these parameters and options are put to good use throughout the book, and more explanation is given when they are used.

WCF Programming Methods

Windows Communication Foundation supports a number of different methods, or approaches, of programming, each with its pros and cons. The great thing about WCF is that there is always more than one way to accomplish something. For example, you can specify an endpoint in code or in a configuration file.

You also do not need to stick to a specific method or approach, and in fact the best approach is to combine the methods to get the most flexibility out of your service.

This section discusses the three common methods of developing WCF services:

❑   Declarative

❑   Explicit

❑   Configuration

Declarative

Declarative programming is accomplished via attributes. These attributes are used to define the contracts and specify the behavior of the service. They are used to specify additional parameters that change the details of the contracts and service behavior.

For example, the following code shows the beginnings of a simple service contract:

```
[ServiceContract]
public interface coolservice
{
  [OperationContract]
  decimal CalculateShipping(string state, int shiptype)
  {
    //do something
  }
  [OperationContract]
  decimal CalculateTax(string state, decimal bookcost)
  {
    //do something
  }
}
```

For declarative programming, the attributes are added as shown in the following modified code:

```
[ServiceContract(Session=true)]
public interface coolservice
{
  [OperationContract(IsOneWay=true)]
  decimal CalculateShipping(string state, int shiptype)
```

```
    {
      //do something
    }
    [OperationContract(IsOneWay=true)]
    decimal CalculateTax(string state, decimal bookcost)
    {
      //do something
    }
  }
```

There is a whole list of available attributes, which are discussed in further detail later on in this book.

Explicit

Explicit programming lets you work directly with all of the many classes and interfaces provided by the WCF object model. Working directly with the object model gives you as a developer much more flexibility and control over your code, and is much more extensive than that of attributes (declarative programming) or using configuration files. This is because you as a developer can use your object-oriented programming knowledge in a language you are already familiar with to take advantage of the rich WCF object model.

The following code, used earlier in this chapter, illustrates a simple example of how to create and start a service using the object model:

```
class TestWCFApp
{
  static void Main()
  {
    Uri baseAddress = new Uri(ConfigurationManager.AppSettings["address"]);

    AddressHeader ah =
AddressHeader.CreateAddressHeader("service1","http://localhost:8080/service");

    EndpointAddress ea = new EndpointAddress(new
Uri("http://localhost:8081/testservice/service"), ah);

    ServiceEndpoint se = new
ServiceEndpoint(ContractDescription.GetContract(typeof(BookOrderService)), new
WSHttpBinding), ea);

    ServiceHost sh new ServiceHost(typeof(BookOrderService), baseAddress);

    sh.Description.Endpoints.Add(se);

    sh.Open();

    sh.close();
  }
}
```

Though this example is fairly simple, it does illustrate the use of the object model. The depth of the object model is discussed throughout the chapters of this book to give you a better understanding of its many capabilities.

Configuration

Just like declarative programming, there are many things that you can specify regarding the behavior of a service via the configuration file of the service. The nice thing about using "configuration-based" programming is that any changes do not necessitate a recompile of the service.

The following example uses a configuration file to define a service endpoint with an address, binding, and contract:

```xml
<?xml version="1.0" encoding="UTF-8" ?>
<configuration>
<system.serviceModel>
  <services>
    <service type="MyTestService">
      <endpoint address="http://localhost:8080/MyTestService/"
         bindingConfiguration="usingDefaults"
         binding="MyTestBinding"
         contract="MyTestService">
      </endpoint>
    </service>
  </services>
</system.serviceModel>
</configuration>
```

Which One Wins?

As mentioned earlier, you don't need to pick a method and stick with it throughout your service development. The best approach is normally a combination of all three methods. However, as a note of caution, it is important to know the "pecking order" when all three are used together. It is possible to accomplish the same task using multiple methods. So it is entirely possible to use the object model to tell the service to do one thing, then apply some attributes to tell it to do something completely different. In this case, which one takes precedence?

Windows Communication Foundation does indeed have an execution order. First, attributes are applied. Second, settings from the configuration file are applied. Settings in the configuration file will override those of the attributes if there is a conflict. Lastly, code is executed. Again, any settings or definitions will override those in the configuration file if a conflict is found.

Having said that, it might take some time to figure out the best way to use which method, depending on your service and scenario.

WCF Programming Levels

The Windows Communication Foundation programming model offers the developer several options as to the level of control when dealing with data types, parameters, return values, and the overall development of WCF services.

Typed

With typed services, parameters and return types can be simple or complex data types. From a developer standpoint, this level will be more familiar to developers and most likely the level of choice for many. This is because at this level the development is similar to object-oriented programming. At this level, service operations are very similar to functions, in that parameters and return values are used.

At this level, the developer does not need to deal with messages directly. In fact, serialization and deserialization of the parameters and return values happens automatically, but you also have the ability to use message contracts if you need a bit more control of the parameters and return values.

Untyped

The untyped level is similar to the typed level in many ways, but with a few differences. Like typed services, untyped services are like functions, such that operations have parameters and return types. The difference with untyped services is that the parameters and return types are messages, not data types.

Another difference between the two types is that at this level the developer can access the messages directly, providing more control over the sending and receiving of messages. You don't have this level of control at the typed level, so this level would come in handy if you need more granularity over messages.

Through code you can create messages, interrogate messages, and make decisions based on the contents of the message.

Messaging

You would program at this level for two reasons. First, you are a control freak. Second, you are not a control freak but you need to have access to more than what the first two levels provide. For example, if you need to create your own routers, you must program at this level because the other two levels do not support these operations.

At this level the developer has more control over every aspect of the service, including working with messages and channels, as well as other details of communication.

The Development Process

Lastly is the decision as to how to approach the development of your service. As you should have gathered by now, there is no one "right way" to develop a WCF service. There is always more than one way to accomplish a task. The same goes for deciding your approach for developing your service. Do you start with code, or start with the contract? There are pros and cons to each approach.

If you want to code first, this means that you will start by coding the implementation of your service. Once you have the implementation in place, your contracts are based on this code, and using the SvcUtil utility described earlier you can generate metadata describing your service. A "con" to this approach is that you need to be cognizant about your types. Not all types can be converted to XSD Schema, so you might have problems transitioning between XSD and WSDL.

Starting with contracts first means that you begin with the metadata and generate your code from there. The benefit of this approach is that you have a big help in creating the code.

And the Answer Is . . .

So, I'm going to ask the same question I asked on the second page of this chapter. What is the WCF programming model? Do you have an answer yet? Let me give you my answer.

The Windows Communication Foundation programming model is a combination of existing technologies (.NET Framework) with new and improved technologies, methods, and programming approaches. WCF is specifically designed to provide a manageable approach to building distributed applications while supporting extensive interoperability and support for SOA.

The goal of WCF is to simplify distributed application development via a whole new service-oriented programming model. This model helps developers that are already familiar with existing technologies such as ASP.NET, Web Services, and .NET remoting to be able to dive right in and feel comfortable with the new WCF technology.

Installing WCF

It is time to put all of this great new knowledge to work. Although reading about this amazing, new technology is fun, now the real fun begins. But first, you need to install the necessary components to work with WCF.

Windows Communication Foundation is part of the .NET Framework 3.0. Initially, WCF was part of the WinFX Runtime Components, but on June 9th of 2006 it was officially announced that WinFX would be renamed to the .NET Framework 3.0. The change was in name only and does not affect the technology or functionality found in WinFX.

The .NET Framework 3.0 will ship as part of Windows Vista and is available as a separate download for Windows XP and Windows Server 2003 (which is what you need to do here).

To develop WCF services, you need a few things. The supported operating systems were just mentioned, but you will also need a development environment and the .NET Framework 3.0. This section assumes that you already have the appropriate development environment (Visual Studio .NET 2005 is the preferred and recommended environment and the environment this book uses for all the examples), but it walks you through installing the .NET Framework 3.0.

To install the latest build of .NET Framework 3.0, go to the following URL:

`http://msdn.microsoft.com/windowsvista/downloads/products/getthebeta/default.aspx`

Under the section "Downloads for Running .NET Framework 3.0 Applications," click the link "download and install the .NET Framework 3.0 Runtime Components." This will download a file called `dotnetfx3setup.exe`.

Next, go to the following URL:

`http://www.microsoft.com/downloads/details.aspx?FamilyID=9221A6AA-AC1C-4604-A326-B8CF2B12B6EB&displaylang=en`

Click the download button to download a file called Setup.exe. Once you have downloaded the files, you should have the two files shown in Figure 3-1.

Figure 3-1

The first thing to install is the .NET Framework 3.0. Double-click the file dotnetfx3setup.exe. The screen shown in Figure 3-2 will appear. Click "I have read and ACCEPT the terms of the License Agreement" and then click the Install button.

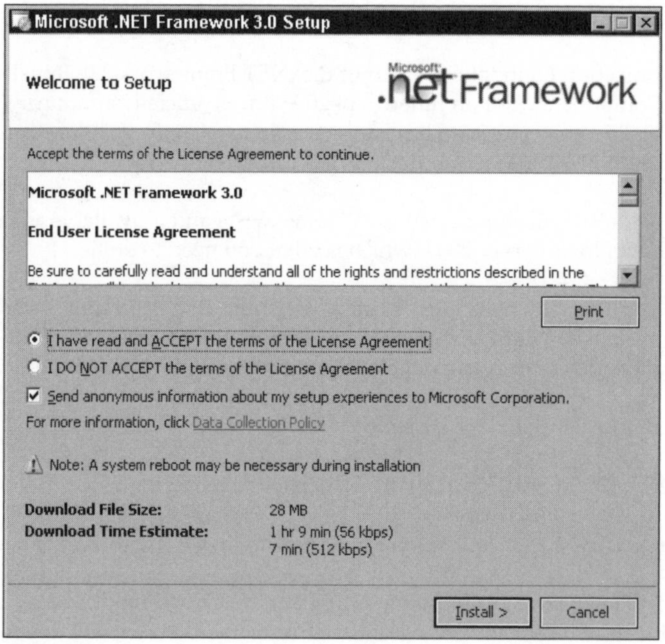

Figure 3-2

You'll notice in Figure 3-1 that the size of the `dotnetfx3setup.exe` file is not that large. Two and a half megabytes for the .NET Framework seems kind of small. Well, that is because when you click Next on the screen in Figure 3-2, you get the screen in Figure 3-3, which downloads the .NET Framework 3.0 from Microsoft.

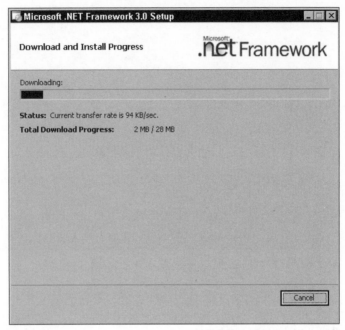

Figure 3-3

Depending on your connection, it could be quick or it could take a while. I am somewhere in the middle. My transfer rate ranged between 90 KB/sec and 180 KB/sec.

Once downloaded, it will automatically start installing the Framework, as shown in Figure 3-4.

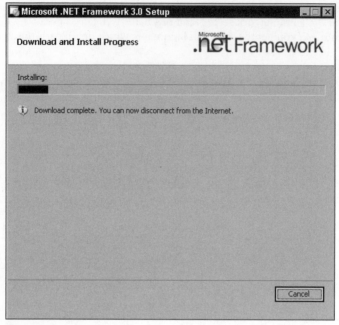

Figure 3-4

Once the install is finished, click the Exit button, and you are all done. With the .NET Framework 3.0, Visual Studio .NET 2005, and the appropriate operating system, you are ready to develop your first Windows Communication Foundation service.

The second file you downloaded is not necessary to create Windows Communication Foundation services, but it does install the Windows Software Development Kit (SDK), which contains documentation and samples for WCF. Like the previous install, the `setup.exe` is not a full install. It will install the SDK by downloading from the Microsoft web site the files it needs. This install, depending on your Internet connection, might take a while because it is quite a large install, but very worthwhile.

Because the SDK is out of the scope of this book, the install of the SDK is not covered; however, I do recommend running the install.

Creating Your First WCF Service

OK, are you ready? Great.

I am going to throw out a disclaimer before you begin this example. There are two ways that you can create a service. The first is manually. The second is to use the templates and extensions that are available when you install the Development Tools for .NET Framework 3.0.

This example uses the former, rather than the latter. Why? Because by building the service manually you will get a better understanding of the components and procedures necessary to build a WCF service. When using the built-in templates, all the necessary components and references are added to the project for you, and it is easy to miss something important that the template added for you. However, if you really must know how to use the templates, Appendix A walks you through using the available WCF templates and add-ins. But I think you can wait, trust me.

This example walks you through creating a very simple WCF service that is hosted in IIS. This service is going to be built manually, starting from the ground up.

So, with that said, time to begin. The first step is to open up Internet Information Services and expand the Default Web Site node, shown in Figure 3-5.

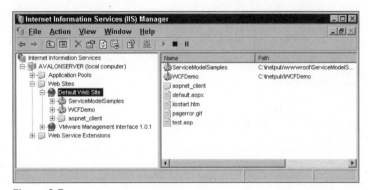

Figure 3-5

Right-click the Default Web Site and select New ➪ Virtual Directory from the context menu. This will start the Virtual Directory Creation Wizard. The first page of this wizard is the Welcome Screen. Simply click the Next button on this step of the wizard.

The second page of the wizard is shown in Figure 3-6. This step in the wizard asks you to specify an alias for the virtual directory you are creating. For this example, type in WCFDemoService, then click the Next button.

The next step in the wizard is the Web Site Content Directory page, shown in Figure 3-8. This page allows you to specify where the files for your web site, or in this case the WCF service, will be stored. At this point you don't have one, so click the Browse button.

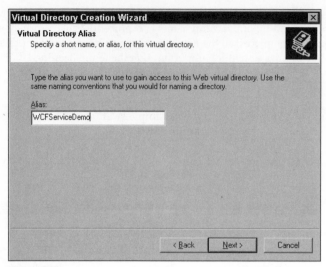

Figure 3-6

Clicking the Browse button brings up the Browse For Folder dialog, shown in Figure 3-7, which lets you browse to your destination directory. In this example you will create a new directory, and this dialog allows for that. Navigate to the Inetpub/wwwroot directory and click the wwwroot node to highlight it, then select the Make New Folder button. This will create a new folder and let you rename it. Name the new folder WCFServiceDemo (as shown in Figure 3-7) and click the OK button.

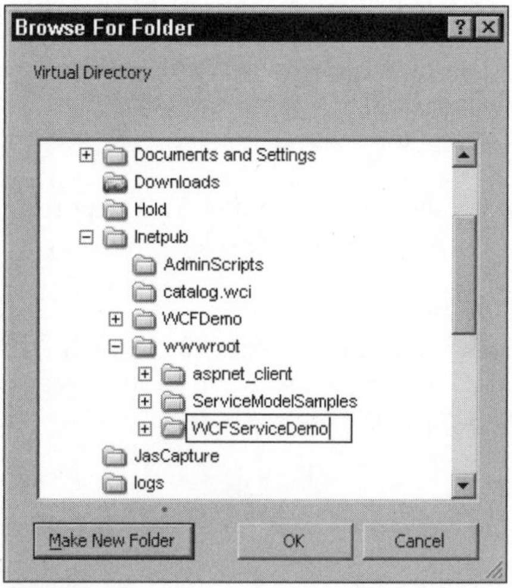

Figure 3-7

Clicking OK on the Browse For Folder dialog will bring you back to the Web Site Content Directory page in the Virtual Directory Creation Wizard. This page should now look like Figure 3-8. Click the Next button to close this dialog.

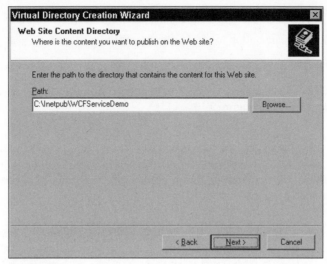

Figure 3-8

The next step in the wizard is the Virtual Directory Access Permissions page. You don't need to make any changes to this page in the wizard, so go ahead and click Next. This brings you to the Finish page. Woohoo, you're almost done! Click Finish to create the virtual directory.

There are a few things you need to configure on this virtual directory to let you access it and make it completely functional, so right-click the WCFDemoService virtual directory and select Properties from the context menu. This will bring up the WCFServiceDemo Properties shown in Figure 3-9.

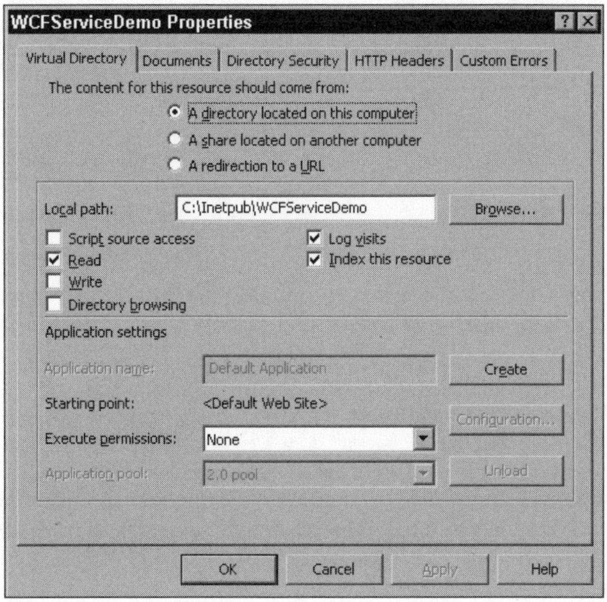

Figure 3-9

On this Properties page you need to do two things:

❑ First, click the Create button in the Application Settings section

❑ Second, set the Execute Permissions to Scripts only

Once you have made these changes, click the Apply button. Your WCFServiceDemo Properties dialog should now look like the one in Figure 3-10.

As a side note, quite a few months ago I installed the examples that come with the SDK. In order to run those examples you first need to run a batch file that does a few things to IIS, one of which creates a new Application Pool called 2.0 pool. It is not necessary for you to do this. If your Application Pool says DefaultAppPool, that is good enough for this example, so there is no need to panic if your app pool setting looks different than the one in Figure 3-10.

Figure 3-10

Your work in IIS is now done. Go ahead and click OK on the WCFServiceDemo Properties dialog. You should now see a virtual directory called WCFServiceDemo in your IIS Manager, such as the one in Figure 3-11.

It is now time to get to the good stuff, the WCF piece.

Fire up Visual Studio .NET 2005 and from the File menu, select New ➪ Web Site. This will bring up the New Web Site dialog shown Figure 3-12. In the New Web Site dialog, under the Visual Studio Installed Templates section, you will see a number of Web Site templates. If you have installed the .NET Framework 3.0 development tools, you will see a template called WCF Service. I know you are tempted to select that one, but stay with me.

Figure 3-11

Select the ASP.NET Web Service template and set the location to File System. For simplicity, this example uses a directory called WCFDemoService in the root of the C drive, but you can place it anywhere you'd like. Set the Language to C# (sorry, VB'ers) and click OK. Visual Studio will now create a new ASP.NET web service project with all the associated components.

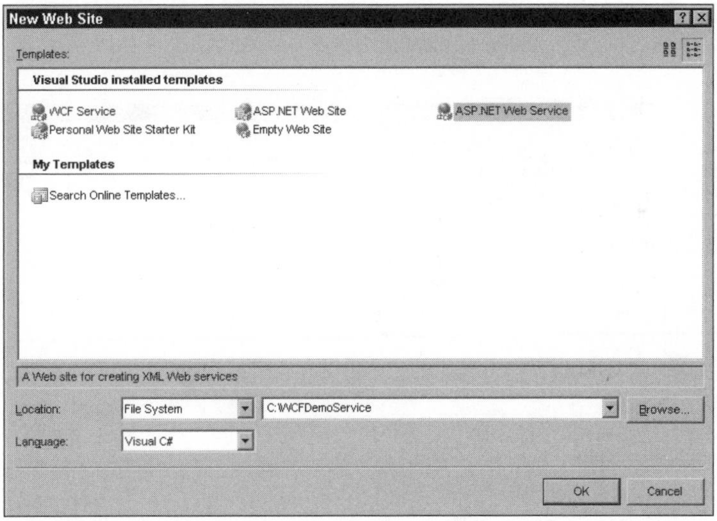

Figure 3-12

The first step is to take a look in the Solution Explorer for your new project. Figure 3-13 shows what your Solution Explorer should look like. You will notice that because this is an ASP.NET web service project Visual Studio has provided the `Service.asmx` page and all the other necessary components.

Because this will soon become a WCF service, you can actually get rid of the `.asmx` file. So, right click the `Service.asmx` file and select Delete from the context menu. Everything else can remain the same, and as you'll find out later on in the book, the rest of the solution is very similar to what the actual WCF service template would create.

Figure 3-13

Now that you have deleted the `.asmx` file, you need to add a couple of files that are important to a WCF service. If you have built any ASP.NET web services, you will be familiar with one of the items you need to add. Go ahead and right-click the WCFDemoService project and select Add New Item. This will bring up the Add New Item dialog. Select the Web Configuration File from the Visual Studio Installed Templates section, make sure it is named `Web.config`, which should be done by default, and select Add.

The next item you need to add is not listed in the Add New Item dialog, but go ahead and bring up the Add New Item dialog again and this time select Text File from the available templates. However, make sure it is named `Service.svc` as shown in Figure 3-14. Select Add.

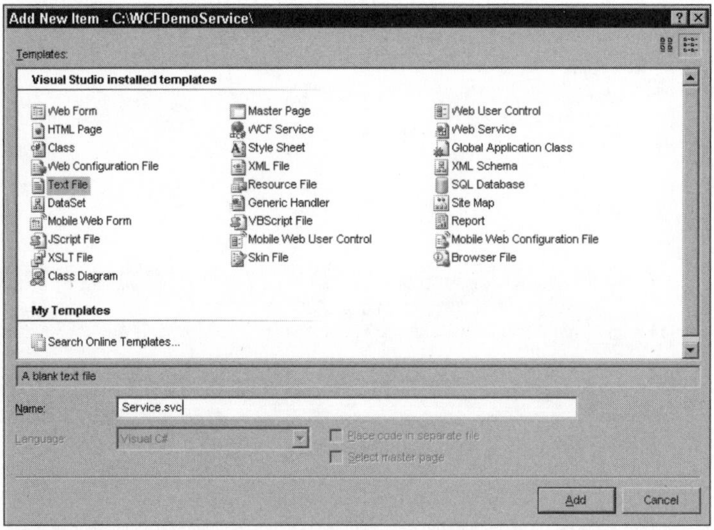

Figure 3-14

Your Solution Explorer should now look like Figure 3-15. You should see a `Web.config` file and a file called `Service.svc`, as well as the other service components.

Figure 3-15

The next step is probably the most vital step in this whole process, and that is to add a reference to the System.ServiceModel library. Right-click the WCFDemoService project again and select Add Reference. If you are using a CTP or RC1 you will probably need to browse to this file. If not it will be listed on the .NET tab. Because this example is using RC1, select the Browse tab and browse to the `Windows\ Microsoft.NET\Framework\v3.0\Windows Communication Foundation` directory, shown in Figure 3-16.

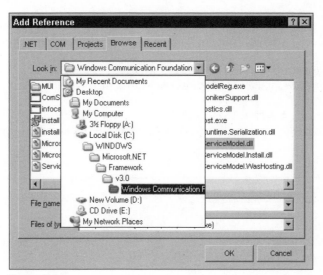

Figure 3-16

In that directory is a file called `System.ServiceModel.dll` as shown in Figure 3-17. Select this file and click OK.

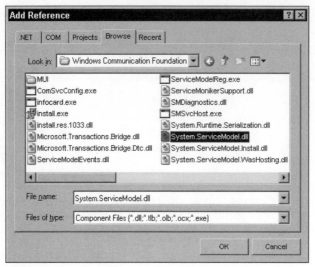

Figure 3-17

The `System.ServiceModel.dll` is the heart and soul of WCF. As explained earlier in this chapter, it provides all the necessary functionality of Windows Communication Foundation.

Time to write some code. If you have not worked with WCF before, some of this will be unfamiliar territory for you. Don't worry, at the end of this example all of this is explained so you aren't left hanging.

The first step is to write the service code. In Solution Explorer, double-click the `Service.cs` file underneath the App_Code folder and modify the contents of the file, replacing the code that is there with the following code:

```
using System;
using System.ServiceModel;
using System.Runtime.Serialization;

[ServiceContract]
public interface IMyWCFService
{
    [OperationContract]
    string Operation1(string myvalue);
}

public class MyWCFService : IMyWCFService
{
    public string Operation1(string myvalue)
    {
        return "Hello: " + myvalue;
    }
}
```

Save the `Service.cs` file and open up the `Service.svc` file and add the following to it:

```
<% @ServiceHost Language=C# Debug="true" Service="MyWCFService"
CodeBehind="~/App_Code/Service.cs" %>
```

The last step is to modify the Web.config file. Open up the Web.config and replace the contents of that file with the following:

```
<?xml version="1.0"?>
<configuration xmlns="http://schemas.microsoft.com/.NetConfiguration/v2.0">
<system.serviceModel>
  <services>
    <service name="MyWCFService" behaviorConfiguration="returnFaults">
      <endpoint contract="IMyWCFService" binding="wsHttpBinding"
                address="http://localhost/WCFServiceDemo/service.svc"/>
    </service>
   </services>
   <behaviors>
     <serviceBehaviors>
       <behavior name="returnFaults">
         <serviceMetadata httpGetEnabled="true"/>
       </behavior>
     </serviceBehaviors>
   </behaviors>
</system.serviceModel>
   <system.web>
     <compilation debug="true"/>
   </system.web>
</configuration>
```

That is all there is to it. Save all the files, and from the Build menu, select Build Project. The next step is to publish your newly created WCF service to the virtual directory you created earlier. To do this, right-click the WCFDemoService project and select Publish Web Site from the context menu, as shown in Figure 3-18.

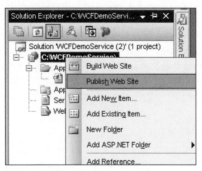

Figure 3-18

Selecting this menu will open the Publish Web Site dialog, shown in Figure 3-20. The Target Location will be pre-populated with a fairly lengthy path to a location that won't do you any good for this example because your target location is IIS, not a directory. Don't fret, however, because this is easily remedied. Simply click the ellipsis button to the right of the Target Location, which will display a second Publish Web Site dialog, this one shown in Figure 3-19.

If it is not already selected, select the Local IIS icon on the left of the form. This will display the available virtual directories in the Default Web Site. Select the virtual directory you created earlier, WCFServiceDemo, and click Open.

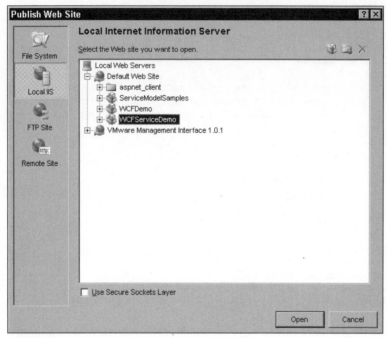

Figure 3-19

After you click the Open button on the Publish Web Site dialog shown in Figure 3-19, you will be taken back to the first Publish Web Site dialog, which now will contain the appropriate target location information, as shown in Figure 3-20. No other changes need to be made on this form, so click the OK button.

When you click the OK button, Visual Studio will copy, or publish, all of the service contents to the virtual directory you selected. Once the publish is finished, the Visual Studio status bar will display a message stating "Publish Succeeded."

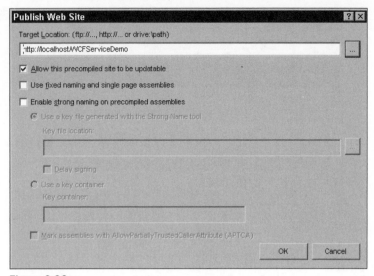

Figure 3-20

The next step is to test your web service. This is easily accomplished by opening up Internet Explorer and typing in the following address URL:

```
http://localhost/WCFServiceDemo/Service.svc
```

Figure 3-21 shows the results that are returned when you access the service. The page returned contains a few pieces of information that will be helpful when creating your client. This information is very similar to the information returned when accessing a .NET web service asmx file.

This page also contains helpful information about how to use the SvcUtil utility to generate the necessary files and include them in your client project to be able to access this service. As well, it contains a couple of code snippets, one in C# and the other in VB (Figure 3-21 was resized to only include the C# portion) to help you start putting together your client application. Very helpful.

This information is helpful if you plan on using the SvcUtil utility to generate the proxy code to include in your client project. However, the other option is to add a reference to the WCF service from within your client application. In fact, that is how this example will do it. However, as a note of recommendation, I would not totally abandon the SvcUtil utility. It is very helpful and useful. I may even use it in a couple of examples during the course of this book.

So, while you have this page open, highlight the link displayed on the top of the page, except for the svcutil.exe, and copy it to the clipboard. You will need this in a few more steps.

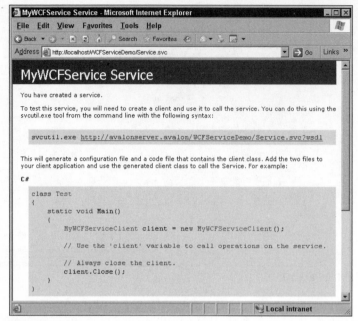

Figure 3-21

Now that you have successfully tested your service, it is time to put that service to use. Fire up another instance of Visual Studio, and this time create a standard C# Windows application. For the sake of this example, name the project WCFDemoClient.

Just like the service, the client also needs to "talk" WCF, and in order to do that a reference needs to be added to the System.ServiceModel.dll. So, just like you did for the service, add a reference to the System.ServiceModel.dll.

The second step is to add a reference to the WCF service. This step is a lot like adding a reference to a standard ASP.NET web service, except that instead of selecting a Web Reference, you select a Service Reference. To do this, right-click the References node of the WCFDemoClient project in Solution Explorer (you may need to click the "show all files" button in the Solution Explorer to see the References node), and from the context menu, select Add Service Reference, as shown in Figure 3-22.

Selecting the Add Service Reference menu displays the Add Service Reference form shown in Figure 3-23. There are two ways you can add the reference to this form. Remember the link you copied to the clipboard a few steps earlier? Paste that into the Service URI field. That is the first way. The second way is to click the Browse button, which will display the Add Web Reference dialog.

Once you have entered the Service URI, enter a Service Reference Name. This is the name that your client application will use to reference the WCF service. Enter WCFServiceDemo into the Reference Name box and click OK.

Taking a look at your client application in Solution Explorer, you should now have a reference to the System.ServiceModel library and to the WCF service you created earlier. Figure 3-24 shows what your Solution Explorer should look like.

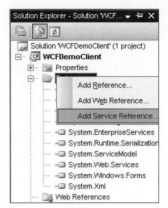

Figure 3-22

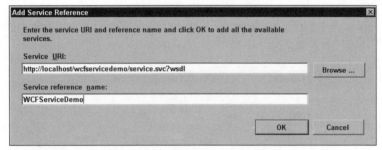

Figure 3-23

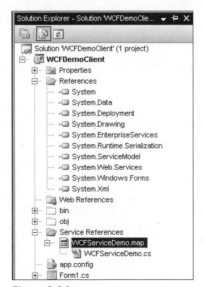

Figure 3-24

The last step is to modify the form and add code to it. Double-click Form1 to open the form in design mode and place a button and a text box on the form. The location does not matter. Name the text box txtResult and set the Text property of the button to "Click Me."

Once you have the button and text box on the form, double-click the button to display the code for the form. In the Click event for the button, add the following code (the highlighted code is what you need to add). If you really want to personalize this example, replace my name with your own name.

```
private void button1_Click(object sender, EventArgs e)
{
WCFServiceDemo.MyWCFServiceClient client = new WCFServiceDemo.MyWCFServiceClient();
txtResult.Text = client.Operation1("Scott");
}
```

Believe it or not, you're done! You are ready to test your web service via your client application. From the Build menu, select Build Project. Press the F5 key to run your client application. When the application runs and the form displays, click the button.

When the button is pressed, the text box will display "Hello: Scott" (or your own name if you put your own name in the code), as shown in Figure 3-25.

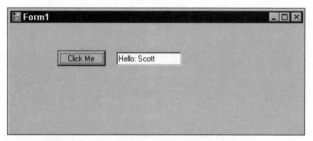

Figure 3-25

Congratulations! You have successfully created your first Windows Communication Foundation service.

Now, before this chapter ends, you probably want an explanation as to how everything worked like I promised at the beginning of this example. I will certainly do that, but I am going to do it at the 30,000 foot view, a brief overview, because many of the things I will mention are discussed in much greater detail in following chapters.

If you have any experience with ASP.NET web services, then what you just went through should have some familiarity to you. What will be new to you is WCF service piece and how that works, but if you take a good look at the `Service.svc` file you will notice that the contents look very similar to an ASP.NET web service `.asmx` file. That is no coincidence. The `Web.config` file and how it is used should look familiar as well. The contents may be a bit strange but that will all become second hand to you in the remaining chapters as well. The following section takes a brief look at each piece.

Service Code

In an ASP.NET web service, methods that you want to expose to the public are annotated by the WebMethod annotation, for example:

```
<WebMethod()> _
Public Function HelloWorld() As String
  Return "HelloWorld"
End Function
```

In Windows Communication Foundation, you expose those methods to the public by defining "Service Contracts." This is accomplished by annotating an interface (or class) and method with attributes. In the example in this chapter, you annotated the IMyWCFService with the [ServiceContract] annotation. This basically announces to the public "This is a WCF service!" You then annotated the Operation1 method with the [OperationContract] annotation, which states that this method will be made available to the public. These annotations, and contracts in general, are covered in detail in Chapter 6.

```
[ServiceContract]
public interface IMyWCFService
{
    [OperationContract]
    string Operation1(string myvalue);
}

public class MyWCFService : IMyWCFService
{
    public string Operation1(string myvalue)
    {
        return "Hello: " + myvalue;
    }
}
```

Service.svc

The `Service.svc` file is used much like the `.asmx` file in an ASP.NET web service. In a way it is like a stub for IIS, but this file contains the all the information necessary to operate a WCF service successfully. This file contains things like the language (C# or VB), the name of the service, and where the code for the service resides.

It is possible to put your service code in this file. Not recommended, only because it is not good practice.

Web.config

In Chapter 1 you learned about the principles of SOA, and one of those was policy-based compatibility. The example was given of two people meeting on the street and striking up a conversation. The `Web.config` has a lot to do with this. The `Web.config` contains information that is used to communicate with the client, such as its address, the binding it is using, and the contract information. This information is specified for the endpoint, as shown in the following code:

```
<services>
  <service name="MyWCFService" behaviorConfiguration="returnFaults">
    <endpoint contract="IMyWCFService" binding="wsHttpBinding"
              address="http://localhost/WCFServiceDemo/service.svc"/>
  </service>
</services>
```

Addresses are discussed in Chapter 4, bindings are discussed in Chapter 5, and contracts are discussed in Chapter 6. You will have a really good understanding of each of these, as well as endpoints, when you are done with those, and a couple more chapters.

Summary

The purpose of this chapter was twofold. First, to introduce you to the Windows Communication Foundation programming model and explain the components and architecture that make up the programming model. Topics such as service-oriented programming versus object-oriented programming and how they apply to WCF were discussed to give you an understanding of how they differ yet how they work together to build a nice framework in which to model your service.

Other topics such as service model, specifically the System.ServiceModel namespace, were discussed to introduce you to some of the classes that you will need to know and will probably use to architect your WCF services. Topics such as programming approaches and levels were also discussed to show you the many different ways a service can be approached and built.

Second, the end of the chapter walked you through the building of a WCF service from the ground up. This piece is important because it will be the model on which the rest of the book builds.

Chapter 4, as well as the rest of the chapters, builds on this chapter to delve deeper into the individual aspects of WCF. Next, Chapter 4 discusses addresses in detail.

Part II

Programming Windows Communication Foundation

4

Addresses

Chapter 2 spent quite a bit of time explaining the makeup of endpoints, and one of the main concepts discussed was that of addresses and how they apply to endpoints and the important role they play in communication. As you learned, every endpoint must have an address so that other programs can communicate with it. An address basically declares "here I am" to the outside world.

This chapter builds on the brief introduction in Chapter 2 and delves deep into addresses by discussing the different types and formats of addresses, and then the rest of the chapter shows you how to program addresses.

This chapter discusses the following:

- ❏ Address types
- ❏ Address formats
- ❏ Programming addresses

WCF Addresses

Chapter 2 discussed the three components that make up an endpoint. Those three are the address, binding, and contract. Not being one to start an argument, but if I had to make a choice as to which of those was the most important component of the endpoint, I would have to say it is the address, only because without the address, you wouldn't be able to find the endpoint to begin with. Without the address, the endpoint is basically useless.

Now, you could argue the same for the binding and contract. Without either of those, the endpoint would be rendered useless as well, and I would agree with that. But you have to first find the endpoint, and that is what the address does. It specifies where the service endpoint is. You have to be able to find it and get to it to be able to use it, and this is what the address does.

Every endpoint must have an address to which the endpoint is associated. This allows client applications to find and identify the endpoints of a service.

Taking a detailed look at an endpoint address, you would discover it contains the following:

❑ The transport protocol, or scheme, such as `http:`

❑ The name of the machine running the service, such as `//localhost` or `//www.wrox.com`

❑ The path to the specific service endpoint, such as `/MyWCFService`

For example, an address might look like the following:

```
http://mymachine:8080/myservice
```

Or:

```
http://mymachine/myservice
```

It should be noted that there can be an optional fourth part, the port, over which the service is being accessed. In the preceding example, the port is specified after the machine name.

In this example all three items are specified. The transport protocol is specified as highlighted here:

```
http://mymachine:8080/myservice
```

The name of the machine running the service is specified as highlighted here:

```
http://mymachine:8080/myservice
```

The path to the specified service endpoint is specified as highlighted here:

```
http://mymachine:8080/myservice
```

To understand addresses, you also need to know the different types of addresses, which are discussed next.

Address Types

Windows Communication Foundation lets you use several types of addresses to associate with each endpoint, and it is through these addresses that the client communicates with the endpoint.

Endpoint Address

Just like the preceding example address, an endpoint address specifies the address of a specific service endpoint. The client can access the service via the endpoint address such as the following:

```
http://mymachine:8080/myservice/
```

Once the client has accessed the service via the endpoint address, the client can talk to the service, and all communication to and from the service goes through this endpoint at this address.

Base Address

Base addresses provide a way to specify a single, primary address for a given service and assign relative addresses to each individual endpoint. For example, suppose you have a service with three exposed endpoints. You can assign a given service the following primary, or base, address:

```
http://mymachine:8080/myservice/
```

With the base address assigned to the service, you can then assign the three endpoints the following relative addresses:

```
http://mymachine:8080/myservice/service1
http://mymachine:8080/myservice/service2
http://mymachine:8080/myservice/service3
```

The base address is associated to the service, allowing you to assign relative addresses to the individual endpoints.

MEX Address

MEX addresses allow a client to gather information about a particular service. MEX, meaning metadata exchange, is an HTTP endpoint address used to obtain service information. For example, the following address is an MEX address:

```
http://mymachine:8080/myservice/mex
```

MEX addresses provide the client a way to obtain information about the service. This information is provided through the service metadata, which describes the service.

Now that you have an understanding of the different types of addresses, this next section covers the format of addresses.

Address Formats

Endpoint addresses are formatted based on the selected transport used in communication. As shown in the first example of the chapter, the transport, or scheme, is the part of the address that specifies and determines the transport that will be used. The key here is that it is you, the developer, who can choose the address and how it is deployed. However, it is important to remember that no matter the format, the client must be able to get to the address to get to and consume the service.

There are a few things to keep in mind as you develop a service:

❑   The environment in which the service will be hosted. The environment may enforce or require that addresses be formatted a certain way, or in other words, a specific transport might need to be used.

❑   Where the address will be specified. You have the option of storing it in a configuration file or you can hard-code it into the application. (Good programming practice dictates that you avoid the latter approach.)

This section of the chapter discusses the different types of address formats to give you an idea of the flexibility and different options you have at your fingertips when developing and deploying services.

What you will notice is that the format of most of these addresses is nearly identical. For example, most of the address formats contain the following parts:

❑ **Scheme:** The scheme that specifies the protocol.

❑ **DomainName:** A fully qualified domain name. Typically during development this portion of the address would contain *localhost* or a specific machine name.

❑ **Port:** If you plan on running the service on a specific port, it is specified in this option. If left out, it defaults to port 80.

❑ **Path:** The specific path to the service. Multiple paths can be specified by separating each path with a forward slash (/).

What makes them unique in and of themselves is their scheme, which identifies the protocol, and how they are used. The sections that follow point out the differences and uses of each address format.

HTTP Address

Probably one of the most common address formats for a service is that of an HTTP address. The format of an HTTP address is shown as follows:

```
http://domainname|machinename [:port]/path
```

The HTTP address format contains four parts. The following is an example of an HTTP address using all the parts:

```
http://www.sqlxml.com:8080/myservice
```

An address with multiple paths would look like the following:

```
http://www.sqlxml.com:8080/myservice/bookorder/
```

As a note of caution, it is recommended that you run your service on a port other than 80 so that there are no conflicts with IIS on that port.

HTTPS Address

HTTP addresses can be secured by using SSL (Secure Socket Layer), which are then specified as HTTPS. Other than the scheme, HTTPS address formats are no different than normal HTTP addresses. The following example shows an HTTPS address:

```
https://www.sqlxml.com:8080/myservice
```

When using HTTPS, you are required to obtain a certificate from a valid certificate authority such as Verisign or Thawte.

TCP Address

The format of a TCP address is as follows:

```
net.tcp://www.sqlxml.com:8080/myservice
```

MSMQ Address

The MSMQ address format differs from the others a bit. The format of this address is as follows:

```
net.msmq://hostname / [private] / queue-name
```

For example, the following address follows the MSMQ address format:

```
net.msmq://localhost/msmqshare/bookorder
```

In this address format, the following parts are identified:

❑   **Scheme:** The scheme that specifies the MSMQ protocol.

❑   **HostName:** A fully qualified domain name of the machine running MSMQ or localhost if MSMQ is installed on the local machine.

❑   **[private]:** This is optional, but when used it contains the address of a target queue that is a private queue. This value is not specified when accessing a public queue.

❑   **Queue-name:** The name of the MSMQ queue.

MSMQ provides both public and private queues to work with. An example of a private queue would be a queue on a local machine. A public queue would be a queue found on your network, such as one accessed via Active Directory.

Named Pipe Address

The Named Pipe address is formatted as follows:

```
net.pipe://localhost/myservice
```

There are two things to notice about this address format:

❑   There is no port number. This is because ports don't matter in Named Pipe addresses. They really don't benefit the address or add any value at all.

❑   Communication using named pipes cannot be "cross-machine," meaning between two separate machines.

IIS Address

Last are IIS addresses. These addresses, like the MSMQ address, have a slightly different address format. This is because an IIS address requires a virtual directory name as well as a service (.svc) filename. The format for the IIS address is as follows:

```
http://domainname|machinename [:port]/virtualdirectoryname [.svc filename]
```

The following list explains the parts of an IIS address:

❑   **Scheme:** The scheme that specifies the HTTP protocol.

❑   **DomainName:** A fully qualified domain name. Typically during development this portion of the address would contain *localhost* or a specific machine name.

❑ **Port:** If you plan on running the service on a specific port, it is specified in this option. If left out, it defaults to port 80.

❑ **Virtual Directory Name:** The name of the virtual directory where the service is residing.

❑ **Service filename:** The name of the service (.svc) file.

The following is an example of an IIS address:

```
http://www.sqlxml.com/myservice/coolservice.svc
```

In an IIS address, the service (.svc) file is what defines the service, that is, how the service is hosted and referenced. You can find more information about hosting a service in IIS in Appendix A.

Alright then, with address types and formatting understood, it is time to delve into the good stuff, programming Windows Communication Foundation addresses.

Programming WCF Addresses

Programming Windows Communication Foundation addresses provides additional flexibility when working with endpoints and services because you can also programmatically define and manipulate base addresses.

As a note, it typically is not common practice to create endpoints and endpoint addresses via code because the addresses and bindings you use during the development process will more than likely be different than the addresses and bindings used in production. It is general practice to define endpoints and addresses in the configuration.

So why, then, is the rest of this chapter discussing how to program addresses? One of the great benefits of WCF is its flexibility, and there might just be a time when programming an address is necessary.

The rest of this chapter covers the following:

❑ The EndPointAddress class, which provides a way for you the developer to create a unique network address accessible by clients, allowing them to communicate with your service.

❑ Programming endpoint addresses. The examples in this chapter are of the conceptual kind, meaning, for now, there won't be a need to fire up Visual Studio just yet. All of the information you learn in this chapter will come in handy in Chapter 5 when the addresses are combined with bindings to create a service.

EndpointAddress Class

As stated just a bit ago, the EndpointAddress class provides the mechanism for uniquely identifying service endpoints. In its simplest form, an address is a URI (Uniform Resource Identifier) but can also contain an identity and a collection of headers.

The optional identity property allows for the authentication of an endpoint by other endpoints so that messages can be exchanged between endpoints.

The header collection, although optional, provides additional addressing information. An endpoint is specified by its URI address, but there are occasions when endpoints might share the same URI, or multiple instances of the service have an endpoint that share the same address. It is in these cases where a header collection comes in handy by providing additional address information on top of the information already specified by the endpoint. This information would include issues such as how to handle incoming messages and what endpoint should process the message.

For example, the following is a simple example of the EndpointAddress used to create a new instance of the class, specifying a URI string of an address:

```
EndpointAddress ea = new _ EndpointAddress("http://localhost:8080/
testservice/service");
```

The following sections describe the Identity and Headers properties of the EndpointAddress class.

Identity Property

The Identity property sets the identity for the associated endpoint used to authenticate it. As stated earlier, this property is optional, but when included it specifies the identity of the service that is being accessed and called by the client. This value is used by the client to verify the validity of the service.

When the client begins the communication process with a service endpoint, the service endpoint then authenticates itself with the client. At this point an identity comparison takes place. The client compares the value of the endpoint identity with the value that was returned to the client via the authentication process. If everything matches, communication flow continues between client and endpoint because the client at this point knows that it is communicating with the appropriate and correct endpoint. This prevents what is commonly known as "phishing," preventing a client from being redirected to the wrong endpoint.

There are six types of identities, and they are detailed in the following table.

Identity Type	Description
DNS (Domain Name Service)	Checks the specified credentials in the DNS name
Certificate	Returns an X.509 certificate value that is compared on the client
Certificate Reference	The same as the Certificate option except that this option allows you to specify the name and store location from which to obtain the certificate
RSA	Returns an RSA key value to compare on the client
UPN (User Principle Name)	Returns the UPN under which the service is running
SPN (Service Principle Name)	Returns the SPN associated with the service's account

Normally there is no need to specify an endpoint identity because the client credential type determines the identity type exposed. However, you can change the default service identity by using the `<identity>` element in the configuration file or by setting it programmatically in code.

The following example sets the identity for a specific endpoint in code:

```
ServiceEndpoint sep = MyServiceHost.AddServiceEndPoint(typeof(IMyWCFService), new
WSHttpBinding(), String.Empy);
EndpointAddress ea = new _ EndpointAddress(new
Uri("http://localhost:8080/testservice/service"),
EndpointEdentity.CreateDnsIdentity("BookOrder.com"));;
sep.Address = ea
```

In the configuration file it would like the following:

```
<?xml version="1.0" encoding="UTF-8" ?>
<configuration>
<system.serviceModel>
  <services>
    <service type="MyWCFService">
      <endpoint address="http://localhost:8080/MyTestService/service"
         bindingConfiguration="usingDefaults"
         binding="MyWCFBinding"
         contract="MyWCFService">
      </endpoint>
      <identity>
       <dns value="BookOrder.com"/>
      </identity>
     </service>
  </services>
</system.serviceModel>
</configuration>
```

Headers Collection

As explained earlier, the headers collection is the method in which additional information can be provided to the endpoint addresses. The first step is to create new address headers and add them to an array:

```
AddressHeader ah1 = AddressHeader.CreateAddressHeader("service1",
"http://localhost:8080/testservice /service", 1);
AddressHeader ah2 = AddressHeader.CreateAddressHeader("service2",
"http://localhost:8080/testservice /service", 2);
```

Once the address headers are created, the next step is to add the address headers into an array:

```
AddressHeader[] addressHeaders = new AddressHeader[2] {ah1, ah2};
```

With the address collection created and populated, the collection can then be added to an instance of the EndpointAddress class. Using the previous EndpointAddress example, the code can be modified as follows:

```
EndpointAddress ea = new _ EndpointAddress("http://localhost:8080/testservice/
service"), addressHeaders);
```

There are a few other properties and methods of the EndpointAddress class, but the ones already discussed are the most vital and they provide the basic functionality needed to program addresses. Speaking of which, the next section discusses exactly that.

Programming Addresses

Having the flexibility to work with addresses is one of the key aspects of WCF. You as a developer now have at your fingertips the ability to work with endpoint addresses, base addresses, and endpoints directly through your code. This chapter finishes up by discussing how to program WCF addresses.

Base Address

The previous chapter talked a lot about the System.ServiceModel namespace. One of the major classes of that namespace is the ServiceHost class. This class provides a host in which a service is configured, exposed, and made available to client applications when the service is not being hosted in IIS.

Through the ServiceHost class, a base address can be specified via one of the class's overloaded constructors, specified as a URI. The following example illustrates the creation of a base address using the ServiceHost class:

```
Uri ba = new Uri("http://localhost:8080/testservice");
ServiceHost sh = new ServiceHost(typeof(Service), ba));
```

In this example, the service is exposing a single base address, but a service can expose more than one base address. In the real world, a service will normally have more than one endpoint, and those endpoints might use different protocols and transports. Luckily for you, the constructor on the ServiceHost class can accept more than one base address, as shown here:

```
Uri[] bas = new Uri[] {new Uri("http://localhost:8080/testservice"),
    new Uri("net.tcp://localhost:8090/testservice")};
```

Keep in mind that only one base address per transport can be specified. Once the base addresses have been defined, they can be added using the ServiceHost class as shown here:

```
ServiceHost sh = new ServiceHost(typeof(Service), bas));
```

Now the host can be opened and used:

```
sh.Open();
```

It is good practice to wrap this code within a try/catch statement to catch any errors.

Endpoint Address

With base addresses defined, you can now define endpoint addresses which can be either an absolute address or relative to the base address.

You can define the endpoint address in one of following ways:

❑   Via a configuration file
❑   Via code

Using the configuration file is discussed first.

Of the two, the configuration file method is preferable because it provides much more flexibility after the application is deployed. On the other hand, coding gives developers stricter control over service and client components, and configuration settings can be overridden if necessary.

Specifying in a Configuration File

As mentioned, the preferred method of specifying endpoints and addresses is via a configuration file. This is accomplished by adding the `address` attribute to the `endpoint` element.

The following example illustrates how to specify an endpoint and address via a configuration file for the `MyTestService` service:

```xml
<?xml version="1.0" encoding="UTF-8" ?>
<configuration>
<system.serviceModel>
  <services>
    <service type="MyTestService">
      <endpoint address="http://localhost:8080/MyTestService/"
          bindingConfiguration="usingDefaults"
          binding="MyTestBinding"
          contract="MyTestService">
      </endpoint>
    </service>
  </services>
</system.serviceModel>
</configuration>
```

In this example, the endpoint for the `MyTestService` service is specified in the configuration file. In the configuration, the address is specified via an attribute on the endpoint element. You can also see the binding and contract information as well, which are discussed in the next couple of chapters.

The configuration in the preceding example defines a single endpoint, but you are not confined to a single endpoint, so you can specify multiple endpoints in a configuration file. The following configuration file defines two endpoints and their addresses:

```xml
<?xml version="1.0" encoding="UTF-8" ?>
<configuration>
<system.serviceModel>
  <services>
    <service type="MyTestService">
      <endpoint address="http://localhost:8080/MyTestService1/"
          bindingConfiguration="usingDefaults"
          binding="MyTestBinding"
          contract="MyTestService">
      </endpoint>
      <endpoint address="http://localhost:8080/MyTestService2/"
          bindingConfiguration="usingDefaults"
          binding="MyTestBinding"
          contract="MyTestService">
      </endpoint>
    </service>
  </services>
</system.serviceModel>
</configuration>
```

Specifying the address in the configuration file is the preferred method, but you can also specify it in code, which is discussed next. Typically, defining endpoints in code is not convenient because the bindings and/or addresses of a service being deployed are different than those used in development.

Specifying in Code

Endpoint addresses can be specified in your code, and as you saw earlier, you have several options when doing so. Earlier in the chapter, a few examples were given in which different constructors are available to instantiate the EndpointAddress class.

You also have several options of specifying the endpoint address, depending on whether you are using a relative or base address.

The following example illustrates how you would specify a full endpoint address:

```
ServiceHost sh = new ServiceHost(typeof(), new WsHttpBinding(),String.Empty);
```

The following shows how a base endpoint address is specified:

```
ServiceHost sh = new ServiceHost(typeof(), String.Empty);
```

The following shows how a relative address is specified:

```
Sh.AddEndPoint(typeof(), new WsHttpBinding(),String.Empty);
```

In all of these examples, once the endpoint address is specified, the host can be opened by simply calling the Open method of the ServiceHost:

```
sh.Open();
```

Lastly, the following section discusses how to use relative addresses.

Relative Address

Earlier in the chapter you learned the difference between absolute and relative addresses. As a recap, relative addresses are addresses that contain a base address. You can use relative addresses in code as well as configuration files.

The following configuration file example illustrates how to specify a relative address:

```
<?xml version="1.0" encoding="UTF-8" ?>
<configuration>
<system.serviceModel>
  <services>
    <service type="MyTestService">
      <endpoint address="TestEndpoint"
          bindingConfiguration="usingDefaults"
          binding="MyTestBinding"
          contract="MyTestService">
      </endpoint>
    </service>
```

```
      </services>
   </system.serviceModel>
   </configuration>
```

Equally important is the fact that the address attribute in your configuration file can be left blank. This signifies that the endpoint address and the base address of the service are the same. The following configuration file example shows a blank endpoint address attribute:

```
<?xml version="1.0" encoding="UTF-8" ?>
<configuration>
<system.serviceModel>
   <services>
      <service type="MyTestService">
         <endpoint address=""
            bindingConfiguration="usingDefaults"
            binding="MyTestBinding"
            contract="MyTestService">
         </endpoint>
      </service>
   </services>
</system.serviceModel>
</configuration>
```

As you can see, you have several options when programming endpoint addresses. These options let you be flexible in your approach in developing your WCF service endpoints.

Summary

Well, there you have it. Short and sweet, yet to the point. The purpose of this chapter was to show you how to work with addresses. The chapter began by discussing the different types of addresses and address formats. The chapter then provided examples on how to program these addresses and the flexibility that Windows Communication Foundation provides in programming endpoint addresses.

Chapter 5 takes a detailed look at bindings, and you will be able to build some examples using the information you learned in this chapter as well as what you learn in Chapter 5.

5

Understanding and
Programming WCF Bindings

The preceding chapter discussed addresses and how they are used in specifying the location of a service. As mentioned previously, an address is one of the three main components that make up an endpoint. This chapter discusses the second component of those three, bindings.

Like addresses, bindings are one of the three critical components of an endpoint. Bindings specify how the endpoint will communicate; specifically, they dictate how a client needs to connect to an endpoint. Each service endpoint in WCF requires that a binding be well-specified, meaning that a binding must specify all the necessary information for a client to properly connect to and communicate with an endpoint, such as the transport, protocol, and encodings.

This chapter discusses bindings and all the information associated with bindings such as their properties and how to apply a binding to an endpoint. This chapter covers the following:

- ❑ An understanding of WCF bindings
- ❑ The WCF predefined bindings
- ❑ Binding properties
- ❑ Programming bindings

Understanding WCF Bindings

Bindings are the mechanism by which communication details are specified to make connecting to a service's WCF endpoint possible. WCF bindings can vary in levels of complexity. These levels can be anywhere on the spectrum of very simple to extremely complex. When defining a binding, the information you specify will typically fall into one of several categories:

❑ **Protocol:** Defines information to be used in the binding such as security, transaction capability, or reliable messaging capability. This information is provided by the protocol stack.

❑ **Transport:** Defines the base protocol to be used in communication.

❑ **Encoding:** Defines the encoding to be used by messages during communication.

Using bindings is a two-step process, as follows:

1. Select the binding from the predefined list of WCF bindings that you will use for a particular endpoint. When selecting a predefined binding you have the option of keeping or changing the binding's properties to meet your needs. For example, you can configure security and reliable messaging behavior options through optional parameters of the constructor or by adding the appropriate behavior elements to the configuration file. If you find that a predefined binding does not meet your needs, you have the option of creating a custom binding.

2. Create an endpoint that utilizes the binding that you have selected or created. This entails defining the endpoint, either in code or configuration, and specifying the corresponding binding and address. If the endpoint is being created in code, the endpoint must be added to a ServiceHost instance that is hosting the service.

The great thing about WCF is that it comes with a number of predefined bindings that should meet most of your development criteria and contain the information listed earlier. Chapter 1 listed the predefined bindings that come with Windows Communication Foundation. The following section re-lists those again and discusses the properties and characteristics of each.

Predefined Bindings

The following table lists the predefined bindings that are shipped with Windows Communication Foundation. The values listed in parentheses are the default values for that specific binding feature.

Binding	Interoperability	Security	Sessions	Transactions
BasicHttpBinding	Basic Profile 1.1	(none), Transport, Message	None, (None)	(None)
WSHttpBinding	WS	Transport, (Message), Mixed	(None), Transport, Reliable	(none), Yes
WSDualHttpBinding	WS	(Message)	Reliable	(none), Yes
WSFederationHttpBinding	WS	(Message)	(None), Reliable	(none), Yes
NetTcpBinding	.NET	(Transport), Message	Reliable, (Transport)	(none), Yes
NetNamedPipeBinding	.NET	(Transport)	None, (Transport)	(none), Yes

Binding	Interoperability	Security	Sessions	Transactions
NetMsmqBinding	.NET	Message, (Transport), Both	(None)	(none), Yes
NetPeerTcpBinding	Peer	(Transport)	(None)	None
MsmgIntegrationBinding	MSMQ	(Transport)	(None)	(none), Yes

In the preceding table, the features are defined as follows:

❑ **Interoperability:** Defines the protocol or technology that the binding will use to guarantee the exchange and use of information.

❑ **Security:** Dictates how the channel will be secured.

❑ **Sessions:** Specifies session contract support.

❑ **Transactions:** Specifies the enabling of transactions.

From a security standpoint, several options are available when securing the channel. You can choose not to secure the SOAP message, which means that the client will not be authenticated when initializing communication. This would only be recommended if the data is guaranteed not to be of a sensitive nature. You also have the option of securing at the transport layer or message layer. Transport-level security hands the security responsibility off to the transport layer, and message-level security gives the security responsibility to the message layer. If the binding supports mixed security (transport and message), both layers share and divide up the responsibility. The message layer takes care of any claims within the message, and the transport layer takes care of the message integrity and confidentiality.

BasicHttpBinding

This binding is probably the most comprehensive binding when talking in terms of interoperability. If you have written ASPX web services in the past, then you have used BasicHttpBinding in your web service even if you weren't aware that you were doing so. BasicHttpBinding uses HTTP as the transport protocol and Text/XML as the default message encoding. It represents bindings that a service can use to communicate with ASMX-based clients and web services.

Though simple to use, employment of the BasicHttpBinding presents some issues that developers need to be aware of. These issues are as follows:

❑ Security is disabled by default. To add security to this binding you can use the BasicHttpSecurityMode enumeration and set the value to anything other than None.

❑ This binding does not provide WS-* functionality and is fairly weak on the interoperability. It does not provide SOAP security or any transaction support.

BasicHttpBinding Properties

The following table shows a list of attributes, and their descriptions, that are available to be used with the BasicHttpBinding binding.

Attribute	Description
allowCookies	Boolean value, default of False, which specifies whether or not the client accepts cookies and to propagate them of any future requests.
bypassProxyOnLocal	Boolean value, default of False, which specifies whether or not to bypass the proxy server for local Internet resources.
closeTimeout	A time interval value, which must be greater than zero, that specifies the amount of time for a close operation to complete. The default value is 1 minute (00:01:00).
hostnameComparisonMode	Specifies the HTTP hostname comparison node used to parse URIs. Acceptable values are Exact, StrongWildCard, and Weak-WildCard. The default value is StrongWildCard.
maxBufferPoolSize	Specifies the maximum buffer size for a buffer pool, which stores messages processed by the binding. This is an integer value with a default of 512*1024, or 524388.
maxBufferSize	Specifies the maximum buffer size for a buffer, which stores messages processed by the binding. This is an integer value with a default of 65536.
maxReceivedMessageSize	Specifies the maximum size of a message, including headers. The number is specified in bytes with a default value of 65536. If a message is larger than the value specified, the sender receives a SOAP fault message and the receiver drops the message and creates an event in the trace log.
messageEncoding	Defines the type of encoding used to encode the message. Acceptable values are Text (text encoding) and Mtom (Message Transmission Organization Mechanism 1.0 encoder). Default is Text.
Name	A unique string value that contains the configuration name of the binding.
openTimeout	A time interval value that specifies the amount of time a message has to complete. Value should be greater than zero. Default is 1 minute (00:01:00).
proxyAddress	Used in conjunction with the useDefaultWebProxy attribute. This attribute is a URI that specifies the address of the HTTP proxy. If the useDefaultWebProxy attribute is set to True, this value must be null.
receiveTimeout	A time interval value that specifies the amount of time a receive operation has to complete. Value should be greater than zero. Default is 1 minute (00:01:00).
sendTimeout	A time interval value that specifies the amount of time a send operation has to complete. Value should be greater than zero. Default is 1 minute (00:01:00).

Attribute	Description
textEncoding	Specifies the character encoding set. Acceptable values are UnicodeFffeTextEncoding, Utf16TextEncoding, and Utf8TextEncoding. Default is Utf8TextEncoding. This value is used for emitting binding messages.
transferMode	A valid TransferMode value that specifies whether messages are buffered or streamed during a response or request.
useDefaultWebProxy	Boolean value, default of True, which specifies whether the auto-configured HTTP proxy should be used if one exists.

The following example illustrates some of the properties being configured in a configuration file:

```
<system.serviceModel>
  <bindings>
    <basicHttpBinding>
      <binding name = "basichttpbind"
        closeTimeout = "00:00:30"
        openTimeout = "00:00:30"
        sendTimeout = "00:00:30"
        receiveTimeout = "00:00:30">
      </binding>
    </basicHttpBinding>
  </bindings>
</system.ServiceModel>
```

The same can be done through code, as illustrated in the following code snippet:

```
Uri ba = new Uri("http://localhost:8080/WroxService");
BasicHttpBinding binding = new BasicHttpBinding();
binding.CloseTimeout = 30000;
binding.OpenTimeout = 30000;
binding.SendTimeout = 30000;
binding.ReceiveTimeout = 30000;
ServiceHost host = new ServiceHost(serviceType, baseAddresses);
sh.AddServiceEndpoint("", binding, ba);
```

Notes of Interest

Windows Communication Foundation relies quite heavily on buffers. Creating and destroying buffers every time they are used is very expensive. Garbage collection for buffers is also very expensive. The solution is to employ buffer pools, which take a buffer from the pool, use it as needed, and then return it to the pool when the task is completed. This method still requires garbage collection cleanup but the overhead of creating and destroying buffers is eliminated.

The hostnameComparisonMode attribute is of the type HostnameComprisonMode enumeration of the System.ServiceModel namespace. The HostnameComparisonMode enumeration has the following members:

❑   `StrongWildCard` ignores the hostname when performing URI matching. This means that a service is reachable via any valid hostname.

❑   `Exact` requires that an exact match must be found with the URI specified. No equivalence matching between short hostnames and fully qualified domain names is performed.

❑   `WeakWildCard` performs matches by ignoring the hostname if no strong match was found.

WSHttpBinding

The WSHttpBinding offers a lot more functionality in the area of interoperability. Unlike BasicHttpBinding, WSHttpBinding supports WS-* functionality and distributed transactions with reliable and secure sessions using SOAP security. It uses the HTTP and HTTPS transport for communication as well. This option is the best for those developers looking for this level of WS-* interoperability.

WSHttpBinding Properties

The following table shows a list of attributes, and their descriptions, that are available to be used with the WSHttpBinding.

Attribute	Description
allowCookies	Boolean value, default of False, which specifies whether or not the client accepts cookies and to propagate them of any future requests.
bypassProxyOnLocal	Boolean value, default of False, which specifies whether or not to bypass the proxy server for local Internet resources.
closeTimeout	A time interval value, which must be greater than zero, that specifies the amount of time for a close operation to complete. The default value is 1 minute (00:01:00).
hostnameComparisonMode	Specifies the HTTP hostname comparison node used to parse URIs. Acceptable values are Exact, StrongWildCard, and Weak-WildCard. The default value is StrongWildCard.
maxBufferPoolSize	Specifies the maximum buffer size for a buffer pool, which stores messages processed by the binding. This is an integer value with a default of 512*1024, or 524388.
maxReceivedMessageSize	Specifies the maximum size of a message, including headers. The number is specified in bytes with a default value of 65536. If a message is larger than the value specified, the sender receives a SOAP fault message and the receiver drops the message and creates an event in the trace log.
messageEncoding	Defines the type of encoding used to encode the message. Acceptable values are Text (text encoding) and Mtom (Message Transmission Organization Mechanism 1.0 encoder). Default is Text.
Name	A unique string value that contains the configuration name of the binding.

Attribute	Description
openTimeout	A time interval value that specifies the amount of time a message has to complete. Value should be greater than zero. Default is 1 minute (00:01:00).
proxyAddress	Used in conjunction with the useDefaultWebProxy attribute. This attribute is a URI that specifies the address of the HTTP proxy. If the useDefaultWebProxy attribute is set to True, this value must be null.
receiveTimeout	A time interval value that specifies the amount of time a receive operation has to complete. Value should be greater than zero. Default is 1 minute (00:01:00).
sendTimeout	A time interval value that specifies the amount of time a send operation has to complete. Value should be greater than zero. Default is 1 minute (00:01:00).
textEncoding	Specifies the character encoding set. Acceptable values are UnicodeFffeTextEncoding, Utf16TextEncoding, and Utf8TextEncoding. Default is Utf8TextEncoding. This value is used for emitting binding messages.
transactionFlow	Boolean value, default of False, which specifies whether the binding supports flowing WS-Transactions.
useDefaultWebProxy	Boolean value, default of True, which specifies whether the auto-configured HTTP proxy should be used if one exists.

The following example illustrates some of the properties being configured in a configuration file:

```
<system.serviceModel>
  <bindings>
    <wsHttpBinding>
      <binding name = "wshttpbind"
        allowcookies = "true"
        textencoding = "utf-8"
        closeTimeout = "00:00:30"
        receiveTimeout = "00:00:30">
      </binding>
    </wsHttpBinding>
  </bindings>
</system.ServiceModel>
```

The same can be done through code, as illustrated here:

```
WSHttpBinding wsb = new WSHttpBinding();
wsb.AllowCookies = true;
wsb.TextEncoding = UTF-8;
wsb.ReceiveTimeout = 30000;
wsb.CloseTimeout= 30000;
```

WSDualHttpBinding

The WSDualHttpBinding is almost a mirror image of the WSHttpBinding except for one aspect, which is that WSDualHttpBinding supports duplex services. A duplex service is a service that uses duplex message patterns. These patterns provide the ability for a service to communicate back to the client via a callback.

The WSDualHTTPBinding also supports communication via SOAP intermediaries. Intermediaries are discussed in Chapter 2. They are not a part of WCF but certainly can have a hand in dealing with WCF services and messages in areas such as routing and load balancing. This binding allows the communication through intermediaries.

With WSDualHttpBinding, reliable sessions are enabled by default. Not so with WSHttpBinding. In WSHttpBinding, reliable sessions are disabled by default and must be enabled if you want to use them.

WSDualHttpBinding Properties

The following table is a list of attributes, and their descriptions, that are available to be used with the WSDualHttpBinding.

Attribute	Description
bypassProxyOnLocal	Boolean value, default of False, which specifies whether or not to bypass the proxy server for local Internet resources.
clientBaseAddress	A URI that specifies the base address that the client listens to for response messages from the service. The default is null.
closeTimeout	A time interval value, which must be greater than zero, that specifies the amount of time for a close operation to complete. The default value is 1 minute (00:01:00).
hostnameComparisonMode	Specifies the HTTP hostname comparison node used to parse URIs. Acceptable values are Exact, StrongWildCard, and Weak-WildCard. The default value is StrongWildCard.
maxBufferPoolSize	Specifies the maximum buffer size for a buffer pool, which stores messages processed by the binding. This is an integer value with a default of 512*1024, or 524388.
maxReceivedMessageSize	Specifies the maximum size of a message, including headers. The number is specified in bytes with a default value of 65536. If a message is larger than the value specified, the sender receives a SOAP fault message and the receiver drops the message and creates an event in the trace log.
messageEncoding	Defines the type of encoding used to encode the message. Acceptable values are Text (text encoding) and Mtom (Message Transmission Organization Mechanism 1.0 encoder). Default is Text.
Name	A unique string value that contains the configuration name of the binding.

Attribute	Description
openTimeout	A time interval value that specifies the amount of time a message has to complete. Value should be greater than zero. Default is 1 minute (00:01:00).
proxyAddress	Used in conjunction with the useDefaultWebProxy attribute. This attribute is a URI that specifies the address of the HTTP proxy. If the useDefaultWebProxy attribute is set to True, this value must be null.
receiveTimeout	A time interval value that specifies the amount of time a receive operation has to complete. Value should be greater than zero. Default is 1 minute (00:01:00).
sendTimeout	A time interval value that specifies the amount of time a send operation has to complete. Value should be greater than zero. Default is 1 minute (00:01:00).
textEncoding	Specifies the character encoding set. Acceptable values are UnicodeFffeTextEncoding, Utf16TextEncoding, and Utf8TextEncoding. Default is Utf8TextEncoding. This value is used for emitting binding messages.
transactionFlow	Boolean value, default of False, which specifies whether the binding supports flowing WS-Transactions.
useDefaultWebProxy	Boolean value, default of True, which specifies whether the auto-configured HTTP proxy should be used if one exists.

The following example illustrates some of the properties being configured in a configuration file:

```
<system.serviceModel>
  <bindings>
    <wsDualHttpBinding>
      <binding name = "wsDualhttpbind"
        clientbaseaddress = "http://localhost:8080/client"
        transactionflow = "false"
        closeTimeout = "00:00:30"
        receiveTimeout = "00:00:30">
      </binding>
    </wsDualHttpBinding>
  </bindings>
</system.ServiceModel>
```

The same can be done through code, as illustrated here:

```
WSDualHttpBinding wsdb = new WSDualHttpBinding();
wsdb.ClientBaseAddress = "http://localhost:8080/client";
wsdb.TransactionFlow = false;
wsdb.ReceiveTimeout = 30000;
wsdb.CloseTimeout = 30000;
```

Notes of Interest

The clientBaseAddress attribute, if specified, is a combination of the base address plus a per-channel GUID and is used for listening by the client to see if any responses are coming from the service. If this attribute is not specified, the client base address is created in a transport-specific manner.

WSFederationHttpBinding

To understand this binding, you need to understand Federations and Realms. A Realm is a single unit of security administration or trust, such as a domain. A Federation is a collection of Realms that have an established trust. This level of trust can differ, but at the least it would include authentication.

A few years ago, Microsoft got together with IBM, BEA, RSA Security, and VeriSign and held meeting designed to define a mechanism that allows different security realms to federate by allowing and brokering trust of identities, attributes, and authentication between web services.

The result of this meeting is the WS-Federation specification and protocol, which is designed to be a building block used in conjunction with other web service technology to provide and support a wide variety of security models.

The WSFederationHttpBinding, therefore, is a binding that offers security and interoperability that supports the WS-Federation protocol. The goal of this binding is to provide a support mechanism for those organizations within a federation to easily and efficiently authenticate users.

WSFederationHttpBinding Properties

The following table is a list of attributes, and their descriptions, that are available to be used with the WSFederationHttpBinding.

Attribute	Description
bypassProxyOnLocal	Boolean value, default of False, which specifies whether or not to bypass the proxy server for local Internet resources.
closeTimeout	A time interval value, which must be greater than zero, that specifies the amount of time for a close operation to complete. The default value is 1 minute (00:01:00).
hostnameComparisonMode	Specifies the HTTP hostname comparison node used to parse URIs. Acceptable values are Exact, StrongWildCard, and WeakWildCard. The default value is StrongWildCard.
maxBufferPoolSize	Specifies the maximum buffer size for a buffer pool, which stores messages processed by the binding. This is an integer value with a default of 512*1024, or 524388.
maxReceivedMessageSize	Specifies the maximum size of a message, including headers. The number is specified in bytes with a default value of 65536. If a message is larger than the value specified, the sender receives a SOAP fault message and the receiver drops the message and creates an event in the trace log.

Attribute	Description
messageEncoding	Defines the type of encoding used to encode the message. Acceptable values are Text (text encoding) and Mtom (Message Transmission Organization Mechanism 1.0 encoder). Default is Text.
Name	A unique string value that contains the configuration name of the binding.
openTimeout	A time interval value that specifies the amount of time a message has to complete. Value should be greater than zero. Default is 1 minute (00:01:00).
privacyNoticeAt	A string value that specifies the URI where the privacy notice is located.
privacyNoticeVersion	An integer value that specifies the version of the current privacy notice.
proxyAddress	Used in conjunction with the useDefaultWebProxy attribute. This attribute is a URI that specifies the address of the HTTP proxy. If the useDefaultWebProxy attribute is set to True, this value must be null.
receiveTimeout	A time interval value that specifies the amount of time a receive operation has to complete. Value should be greater than zero. Default is 1 minute (00:01:00).
sendTimeout	A time interval value that specifies the amount of time a send operation has to complete. Value should be greater than zero. Default is 1 minute (00:01:00).
textEncoding	Specifies the character encoding set. Acceptable values are UnicodeFffeTextEncoding, Utf16TextEncoding, and Utf8TextEncoding. Default is Utf8TextEncoding. This value is used for emitting binding messages.
transactionFlow	Boolean value, default of False, which specifies whether the binding supports flowing WS-Transactions.
useDefaultWebProxy	Boolean value, default of True, which specifies whether the auto-configured HTTP proxy should be used if one exists.

The following example illustrates some of the properties being configured in a configuration file:

```
<system.serviceModel>
  <bindings>
    <wsFederationHttpBinding>
      <binding name = "wsfedhttpbind"
        privacynoticeat = "http://localhost:8080/privacynotice"
        privacyversion = "1"
        messageencoding = "utf8textencoding"
        receiveTimeout = "00:00:30">
      </binding>
```

```
        </wsFederationHttpBinding>
      </bindings>
    </system.ServiceModel>
```

The same can be done through code, as illustrated here:

```
WSFederationHttpBinding wsfb = new WSFederationHttpBinding();
wsfb.PrivacyNoticeAt = "http://localhost:8080/privacynotice";
wsfb.PrivacyNoticeVersion = 1;
wsfb.MessageEncoding = UTF8TextEncoding;
wsfb.ReceiveTimeout = 30000;
```

NetTcpBinding

The NetTcpBinding provides a secure and reliable binding environment for .NET-to-.NET cross-machine communication. It uses the TCP protocol and provides full support for SOAP security, transactions, and reliability.

At runtime the NetTcpBinding creates a communication stack using the WS-ReliableMessaging protocol for reliability, Windows Security for message security and authentication, and TCP for message delivery.

The WS-ReliableMessaging protocol is an interoperable protocol used by both sender and receiver to ensure safe and reliable delivery of messages between the sender and receiver. The guaranteed delivery is specified as a delivery assurance, and it is the responsibility of the sender and receiver to fulfill the delivery assurance, or generate an error.

NetTcpBinding Properties

The following table is a list of attributes, and their descriptions, that are available to be used with the NetTcpBinding.

Attribute	Description
closeTimeout	A time interval value, which must be greater than zero, that specifies the amount of time for a close operation to complete. The default value is 1 minute (00:01:00).
hostnameComparisonMode	Specifies the HTTP hostname comparison node used to parse URIs. Acceptable values are Exact, StrongWildCard, and WeakWildCard. The default value is StrongWildCard.
listenBackLog	Specifies the maximum number of channels waiting to be accepted on the listener. This value is a positive integer with a default of 10.
maxBufferPoolSize	Specifies the maximum buffer size for a buffer pool, which stores messages processed by the binding. This is an integer value with a default of 512*1024, or 524388.
maxBufferSize	Specifies the maximum buffer size for a buffer that stores messages processed by the binding. This is an integer value with a default of 65536.

Attribute	Description
maxConnections	A positive integer that specifies the maximum number of inbound and outbound connections that the service will create/accept. The default value is 10. Connections that exceed the specified value are queued until a space below the specified value becomes available.
maxReceivedMessageSize	Specifies the maximum size of a message, including headers. The number is specified in bytes with a default value of 65536. If a message is larger than the value specified, the sender receives a SOAP fault message and the receiver drops the message and creates an event in the trace log.
Name	A unique string value that contains the configuration name of the binding.
openTimeout	A time interval value that specifies the amount of time a message has to complete. Value should be greater than zero. Default is 1 minute (00:01:00).
portSharingEnabled	A Boolean value with a default of False, applied only to services, which specifies whether TCP port sharing is enabled for a connection. If false, each binding uses its own specific port.
receiveTimeout	A time interval value that specifies the amount of time a receive operation has to complete. Value should be greater than zero. Default is 1 minute (00:01:00).
sendTimeout	A time interval value that specifies the amount of time a send operation has to complete. Value should be greater than zero. Default is 1 minute (00:01:00).
transactionFlow	Boolean value, default of False, which specifies whether the binding supports flowing WS-Transactions.
transactionProtocol	Specifies the transaction protocol to be used with this binding. Available values are OleTransaction and WS-AtomicTransaction. The default is OleTransaction.
transferMode	A valid TransferMode value that specifies whether messages are buffered or streamed during a response or request.

The following example illustrates some of the properties being configured in a configuration file:

```
<system.serviceModel>
  <bindings>
    <netTCPBinding>
      <binding name = "nettcpbind"
        portsharingenabled = "true"
        listenbacklog = "10"
        closeTimeout = "00:00:30"
        transactionflow = "true">
      </binding>
```

```
        </netTCPBinding>
    </bindings>
</system.ServiceModel>
```

The same can be done through code, as illustrated here:

```
NetTcpBinding nettcp = new NetTcpBinding();
nettcp.PortSharingEnabled = true;
nettcp.ListenBacklog = 10;
nettcp.CloseTimeout = 30000;
nettcp.TransactionFlow = true;
```

Notes of Interest

The maxConnections attribute handles both inbound and outbound connections. If the total number of connections, both inbound and outbound, exceeds the number of specified connections, the connection is queued until the number of connections falls below the specified limit.

The transactionProtocol attribute is of the type TransactionProtocol and is used to specify the transaction protocol when flowing transactions.

The transferMode attribute is of the TransferMode enumeration and specifies whether messages are streamed or buffered on a request or response. The TransferMode enumeration is comprised of the following:

- ❏ Buffered signifies that the request and response messages are buffered.
- ❏ Streamed signifies that the request and response messages are streamed.
- ❏ StreamedRequest signifies that the request message is streamed and the response message is buffered.
- ❏ StreamedResponse signifies that the request message is buffered and the response message is streamed.

NetNamedPipeBinding

The NetNamedPipeBinding provides a secure and reliable binding environment for cross-process (same machine) communication. It uses the NamedPipe protocol and provides full support for SOAP security, transactions, and reliability.

NetNamedPipeBinding Properties

The following table is a list of attributes, and their descriptions, that are available to be used with the NetNamedPipeBinding.

Attribute	Description
closeTimeout	A time interval value, which must be greater than zero, that specifies the amount of time for a close operation to complete. The default value is 1 minute (00:01:00).
hostnameComparisonMode	Specifies the HTTP hostname comparison node used to parse URIs. Acceptable values are Exact, StrongWildCard, and Weak-WildCard. The default value is StrongWildCard.
maxBufferPoolSize	Specifies the maximum buffer size for a buffer pool, which stores messages processed by the binding. This is an integer value with a default of 512*1024, or 524388.
maxBufferSize	Specifies the maximum buffer size for a buffer that stores messages processed by the binding. This is an integer value with a default of 65536.
maxConnections	A positive integer that specifies the maximum number of inbound and outbound connections that the service will create/accept. The default value is 10. Connections that exceed the specified value are queued until a space below the specified value becomes available.
maxReceivedMessageSize	Specifies the maximum size of a message, including headers. The number is specified in bytes with a default value of 65536. If a message is larger than the value specified, the sender receives a SOAP fault message and the receiver drops the message and creates an event in the trace log.
Name	A unique string value that contains the configuration name of the binding.
openTimeout	A time interval value that specifies the amount of time a message has to complete. Value should be greater than zero. Default is 1 minute (00:01:00).
receiveTimeout	A time interval value that specifies the amount of time a receive operation has to complete. Value should be greater than zero. Default is 1 minute (00:01:00).
sendTimeout	A time interval value that specifies the amount of time a send operation has to complete. Value should be greater than zero. Default is 1 minute (00:01:00).
transactionFlow	Boolean value, default of False, which specifies whether the binding supports flowing WS-Transactions.
transactionProtocol	Specifies the transaction protocol to be used with this binding. Available values are OleTransaction and WS-AtomicTransaction. The default is OleTransaction.
transferMode	A valid TransferMode value that specifies whether messages are buffered or streamed during a response or request.

The following example illustrates some of the properties being configured in a configuration file:

```
<system.serviceModel>
  <bindings>
    <netNamedPipeBinding>
      <binding name = "netnamedpipebind"
        maxconnections = "50"
        openTimeout = "00:00:30">
      </binding>
    </netNamedPipeBinding>
  </bindings>
</system.ServiceModel>
```

The same can be done through code, as illustrated here:

```
NetNamedPipeBinding nnpb = new NetNamedPipeBinding();
nnpb.MaxConnections = 90;
nnpb.OpenTimeout = 30000;
```

NetMsmqBinding

The NetMsmqBinding provides a secure and reliable queued communication for cross-machine environments. Queuing is provided by using the MSMQ (Microsoft Message Queuing) as a transport, which enables support for disconnected operations, failure isolation, and load leveling. Each of these three is described in detail next.

A disconnected operation means that the client and the service do not have to be online at the same time. The client can initiate the transaction and disconnect. The service can accept the assignment and begin working on it while the client is disconnected.

Load leveling is the process of managing incoming messages so that the receiving service is not completely overwhelmed by the number of incoming messages.

Failure isolation means that messages can fail without affecting the processing of other messages. If a message is received by a service and the receiving service fails, the client can continue to send messages, which will be received by the message queue. When the failed receiving application is up and running again, it will start pulling messages off of the queue. This process guarantees message reliability and system stability.

NetMsmqBinding Properties

The following table is a list of attributes, and their descriptions, that are available to be used with the NetMsmqBinding.

Attribute	Description
closeTimeout	A time interval value, which must be greater than zero, that specifies the amount of time for a close operation to complete. The default value is 1 minute (00:01:00).
customDeadLetterQueue	A string value that contains a URI that specifies the location of expired messages or messages that have failed delivery.

Attribute	Description
deadLetterQueue	A string value that contains a URI that specifies the location of the dead letter queue.
Durable	A Boolean value that specifies whether a message is durable or unstable in the queue.
exactlyOnce	A Boolean value that specifies whether each message processed by this binding is only delivered a single time.
maxBufferPoolSize	Specifies the maximum buffer size for a buffer pool, which stores messages processed by the binding. This is an integer value with a default of 512*1024, or 524388.
maxImmediateRetries	An integer value that specifies the maximum number of retry attempts per message that is ready from the application queue. These retries are immediate. The default is 5.
maxReceivedMessageSize	Specifies the maximum size of a message, including headers. The number is specified in bytes with a default value of 65536. If a message is larger than the value specified, the sender receives a SOAP fault message and the receiver drops the message and creates an event in the trace log.
maxRetryCycles	An integer value that specifies the maximum number of retry cycles used by the poison message feature. A message becomes poisoned when it fails all delivery attempts. The default is 3.
Name	A unique string value that contains the configuration name of the binding.
openTimeout	A time interval value that specifies the amount of time a message has to complete. Value should be greater than zero. Default is 1 minute (00:01:00).
poisonMessageHandling	Allows the service to enable or disable poison message handling. Valid values are Disabled and EnabledIfSupported. The default is EnabledIfSupported.
queueTransferProtocol	A valid QueueTransferProtocol value that specifies the queued communication channel transport that this binding will use.
recieveTimeout	A time interval value that specifies the amount of time a receive operation has to complete. Value should be greater than zero. Default is 1 minute (00:01:00).
rejectAfterLastRetry	A Boolean value that specifies the action to be taken for a failed message delivery after the maximum number of retries. True signifies a negative acknowledgment is sent to the sender and the message is dropped. False signifies that the message is sent to the poison queue. The default is False.

Table continued on following page

Attribute	Description
retryCycleDelay	A time interval value that specifies the minimum time delay between retry cycles for failed message delivery. Value should be greater than zero. Default is 10 minutes (00:10:00).
sendTimeout	A time interval value that specifies the amount of time a send operation has to complete. Value should be greater than zero. Default is 1 minute (00:01:00).
timeToLive	A time interval value that specifies the amount of time a message is valid before it expires and is sent to the dead letter queue. Default is 1 day (1.00:00:00).
usingActiveDirectory	A Boolean value that specifies whether the queue addresses should be converted using AD (Active Directory).
useMsmqTracing	A Boolean value that specifies whether messages processed by this binding should be traced. The default value is False.
useSourceJournal	A Boolean value that specifies whether copies of process messages should be stored in the source journal. The default is False.

The following example illustrates some of the properties being configured in a configuration file:

```
<system.serviceModel>
  <bindings>
    <netMsmqBinding>
      <binding name = "netmsmqbind"
        exactlyonce = "true"
        durable = "true"
        usemsmqtracing = "false"
        openTimeout = "00:00:30">
      </binding>
    </netMsmqBinding>
  </bindings>
</system.ServiceModel>
```

The same can be done through code, as illustrated here:

```
NetMsmqBinding nmqb = new NetMsmqBinding();
nmqb.ExactlyOnce = true;
nmqb.Durable = true;
nmqb.UseMsmqTracing = false;
nmqb.OpenTimeout = 30000;
```

Notes of Interest

The dead letter queue is a queue on the queue manager of the sending application. This queue is for expired messages that have failed to be delivered. The URI that is specified by the customDeadLetterQueue property must use the net.msmq scheme.

A durable message survives a queue manager crash, whereas an unstable or volatile message does not survive. Why would you send a volatile message? Your application might require a lower latency and an occasional lost message is not a big deal. As a note, if the exactlyOnce attribute is set to True, this attribute must be True as well.

When using SOAP Reliable Messaging Protocol, MSMQ does not support Active Directory addressing. Therefore, the QueueTransferProtocol attribute must not be set to a value of Srmp or SrmpSecure when the useActiveDirectory attribute is set to True.

A poison message is a message that has reached, or exceeded, the maximum number of delivery attempts to the awaiting application. This could happen because an application fails to successfully process a message due to errors that occur during the processing of the message. MSMQ 3.0 does not support message poisoning, so any WCF applications deployed using this binding should take this into consideration. This attribute can be disabled and enabled based on the underlying platform support as well, meaning that an application can choose to disable poison handling if the application will contain its own poison-message mechanism. You could disable poison-message handling via the configuration file, and then when the environment is upgraded to MSMQ 4.0 (which supports poison-messaging), the configuration can simply be modified to enable to poison-messaging.

The timeToLive attribute helps to ensure that time-sensitive messages are delivered in a quick timeframe and do not expire before they are processed by the receiving application. Any message that is not consumed within the time interval specified by this attribute expires and is sent to the dead letter queue.

When using the useActiveDirectory attribute, keep in mind that MSMQ queue addresses can be in several formats, including path names and direct format names. With a path name, MSMQ can resolve the computer using Active Directory. Not so with direct format names, which in this case MSMQ will use DNS, NetBIOS, or IP to resolve the computer name. WCF will convert the URI of a message queue to a direct format name, and when this property is set to True, this allows an application to dictate that the queued transport should resolve the computer name via AD.

A source journal provides queued applications the ability to keep a copy of any outgoing messages via the outgoing queue. Basically it works like this:

❑   The sending application sends a message to the receiver.

❑   The receiver sends a message back to the sender acknowledging that the message was received by the receiver.

❑   When the acknowledgment is received by the sender, a copy of the original message is stored in the sender's journal queue.

❑   The useSourceJournal attribute enables this functionality, but it is disabled by default. Set this attribute to True to enable this functionality.

NetPeerTcpBinding

The NetPeerTcpBinding provides a secure binding for peer-to-peer environments and network applications. It uses the TCP protocol and provides full support for SOAP security, transactions, and reliability.

NetPeerTcpBinding Properties

The following table is a list of attributes, and their descriptions, that are available to be used with the NetPeerTcpBinding.

Attribute	Description
closeTimeout	A time interval value, which must be greater than zero, that specifies the amount of time for a close operation to complete. The default value is 1 minute (00:01:00).
listenIPAddress	A string value that specifies the IP address on which the peer node will listen for TCP messages. The default is NULL.
maxBufferPoolSize	Specifies the maximum buffer size for a buffer pool, which stores messages processed by the binding. This is an integer value with a default of 512*1024, or 524388.
maxReceivedMessageSize	Specifies the maximum size of a message, including headers. The number is specified in bytes with a default value of 65536. If a message is larger than the value specified, the sender receives a SOAP fault message and the receiver drops the message and creates an event in the trace log.
Name	A unique string value that contains the configuration name of the binding.
openTimeout	A time interval value that specifies the amount of time a message has to complete. Value should be greater than zero. Default is 1 minute (00:01:00).
port	An integer value that specifies the network port on which this binding will process peer TCP messages. The default value is 0.
recieveTimeout	A time interval value that specifies the amount of time a receive operation has to complete. Value should be greater than zero. Default is 1 minute (00:01:00).
sendTimeout	A time interval value that specifies the amount of time a send operation has to complete. Value should be greater than zero. Default is 1 minute (00:01:00).

The following example illustrates some of the properties being configured in a configuration file:

```
<system.serviceModel>
  <bindings>
    <netpeertcpBinding>
      <binding name = "netpeertcpbind"
        listenipaddress = "192.168.10.150"
        port = "80"
        openTimeout = "00:00:30"
        closeTimeout = "00:00:30">
      </binding>
```

```
        </netpeertcpBinding>
      </bindings>
</system.ServiceModel>
```

The same can be done through code, as illustrated here:

```
NetPeerTcpBinding nptcpb = new NetPeerTcpBinding();
nptcpb.ListenIPAddress = "192.168.10.150";
nptcpb.Port = 80;
nptcpb.OpenTimeout = 30000;
nptcpb.CloseTimeout = 30000;
```

MsmqIntegrationBinding

The MsmqIntegrationBinding differs from the NetMsmqBinding in that the MsmqIntegrationBinding provides direct integration between Windows Communication Foundation and MSMQ. With NetMsmqBinding, MSMQ is the transport and communicates with other WCF applications, whereas with MsmqIntegrationBinding your WCF application communicates directly with an MSMQ deployment.

The benefit here is that your MSMQ installation will not need to be modified to be able to communicate with your WCF application. Plug-n-play, baby.

MsmqIntegrationBinding Properties

The following table is a list of attributes, and their descriptions, that are available to be used with the MsmqIntegrationBinding.

Attribute	Description
closeTimeout	A time interval value, which must be greater than zero, that specifies the amount of time for a close operation to complete. The default value is 1 minute (00:01:00).
customDeadLetterQueue	A string value that contains a URI that specifies the location of expired messages or messages that have failed delivery.
deadLetterQueue	A string value that contains a URI that specifies the location of the dead letter queue.
Durable	A Boolean value that specifies whether a message is durable or unstable in the queue.
exactlyOnce	A Boolean value that specifies whether each message processed by this binding is only delivered a single time.
maxImmediateRetries	An integer value that specifies the maximum number of retry attempts per message that is ready from the application queue. These retries are immediate. The default is 5.

Table continued on following page

Attribute	Description
maxReceivedMessageSize	Specifies the maximum size of a message, including headers. The number is specified in bytes with a default value of 65536. If a message is larger than the value specified, the sender receives a SOAP fault message and the receiver drops the message and creates an event in the trace log.
maxRetryCycles	An integer value that specifies the maximum number of retry cycles used by the poison message feature. A message becomes poisoned when it fails all delivery attempts. The default is 3.
Name	A unique string value that contains the configuration name of the binding.
openTimeout	A time interval value that specifies the amount of time a message has to complete. Value should be greater than zero. Default is 1 minute (00:01:00).
poisonMessageHandling	Allows the service to enable or disable poison message handling. Valid values are Disabled and EnabledIfSupported. The default is EnabledIfSupported.
recieveTimeout	A time interval value that specifies the amount of time a receive operation has to complete. Value should be greater than zero. Default is 1 minute (00:01:00).
rejectAfterLastRetry	A Boolean value that specifies the action to be taken for a failed message delivery after the maximum number of retries. True signifies a negative acknowledgment is sent to the sender and the message is dropped. False signifies that the message is sent to the poison queue. The default is False.
retryCycleDelay	A time interval value that specifies the minimum time delay between retry cycles for failed message delivery. Value should be greater than zero. Default is 10 minutes (00:10:00).
sendTimeout	A time interval value that specifies the amount of time a send operation has to complete. Value should be greater than zero. Default is 1 minute (00:01:00).
serializationFormat	The format used for message body serialization. Attribute is of type MsmqMessageSerializationFormat.
timeToLive	A time interval value that specifies the amount of time a message is valid before it expires and is sent to the dead letter queue. Default is 1 day (1.00:00:00).
useMsmqTracing	A Boolean value that specifies whether messages processed by this binding should be traced. The default value is False.
useSourceJournal	A Boolean value that specifies whether copies of process messages should be stored in the source journal. The default is False.

The following example illustrates some of the properties being configured in a configuration file:

```
<system.serviceModel>
  <bindings>
    <msmqintegrateBinding>
      <binding name = "msmqintegratebind"
        durable = "true"
        retrycycledelay = "00:00:10"
        usesourcejournal = "false"
      </binding>
    </msmqintegrateBinding>
  </bindings>
</system.ServiceModel>
```

The same can be done through code, as illustrated here:

```
MsmqIntegrationBinding mib = new MsmqIntegrationBinding();
mib.Durable = true;
mib.RetryCycleDelay = 10000;
mib.UseSourceJournal = false;
```

Programming WCF Bindings

The following example uses what you learned in this chapter regarding bindings as well as the information you learned in Chapter 4 regarding addresses.

Chapter 4 stated that the preferred method of defining endpoints and addresses is via configuration files instead of straight through code. There are several reasons for this:

❑ First, it is likely that any addresses and bindings you use during the development process will change or be different than those of the production environment.

❑ Second, if either environment changes, a code change and recompilation are necessary. Using configuration files eliminates these issues.

This section illustrates using both code and configuration. Using code is illustrated first to provide a foundation as to how addresses and bindings work. That is followed up by a section on how to use configuration files.

Using Code

To use code, implement the following steps:

1. Create a directory in the root of your C drive called Wrox, as shown in Figure 5-1.

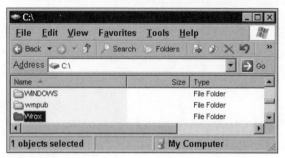

Figure 5-1

2. Inside that directory, create a text file named WCFServiceTest.txt.

3. Open the new text file and type a simple, one-line text string such as shown in Figure 5-2.

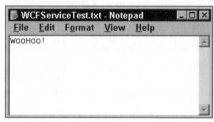

Figure 5-2

4. Save the text file.

OK, now you are ready for the good stuff:

1. Open up Visual Studio 2005 and create a new C# Class Library Project, as shown in Figure 5-3. Give this project a name of WCFService and let it create the project directory. For simplicity, set the Location of the project to the root of the C drive (C:\).

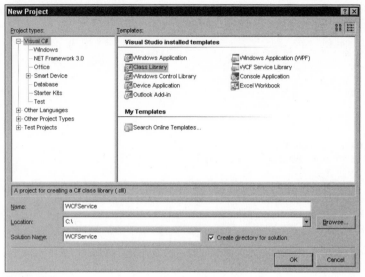

Figure 5-3

2. Rename the `Class1.cs` file to `ServiceClass.cs`. This is simply to have things named properly.

3. Add a reference to the System.ServiceModel namespace. Right-click the References node in Project Explorer and select Add Reference. The Add Reference dialog will come up. If you have done the examples in previous chapters, you can simply select the Recent tab on this dialog and select the component from there. Otherwise, select the Browse tab and browse to the `Windows\Microsoft.NET\Framework\v3.0\Windows Communication Foundation` directory and select System.ServiceModel.dll.

Your Solution Explorer should now look like what you see in Figure 5-4.

Figure 5-4

4. You are now ready to add code. Double-click the `ServiceClass.cs` file to open it in code view. Replace the existing code with the following code:

```csharp
using System;
using System.ServiceModel;
using System.Collections.Generic;
using System.IO;

namespace WCFService
{
    [ServiceContract]
    public interface IServiceClass
    {
        [OperationContract]
        string GetText();

        [OperationContract]
        int MultiplyNumbers(int firstvalue, int secondvalue);
    }

    public class ServiceClass : IServiceClass
    {
        string IServiceClass.GetText()
        {
            StreamReader sw = new StreamReader(@"c:\wrox\WCFServiceTest.txt");
            return sw.ReadLine();
        }

        int IServiceClass.MultiplyNumbers(int firstvalue, int secondvalue)
        {
            return firstvalue * secondvalue;
        }

    }
}
```

In this example, one service contract and two operation contracts are defined. An interface is defined called the IServiceClass interface in which the `[ServiceContract]` attribute is applied, specifying that this is a WCF service and provides available operations. Two `[OperationContract]` attributes are applied to the methods on the interface that define the exact operations of this service.

This service does two very simple operations. The first operation is the `GetText()` method, which reads the text file you created earlier and returns that to the calling client. The second operation is a simple multiplication operation, which takes two numbers as parameters and multiplies them together and returns the results as an integer.

For example, the following code is identical to the preceding code except that an extra method is defined, the AddNumbers method. However, this method will not be exposed by the endpoint because no operation contract has been defined in the interface of the service.

```csharp
namespace WCFService
{
    [ServiceContract]
```

```
public interface IServiceClass
{
    [OperationContract]
    string GetText();

    [OperationContract]
    int MultiplyNumbers(int firstvalue, int secondvalue);
}

public class ServiceClass : IServiceClass
{
    string IServiceClass.GetText()
    {
        StreamReader sw = new StreamReader(@"c:\wrox\WCFServiceTest.txt");
        return sw.ReadLine();
        //return "Hello World";
    }

    int IServiceClass.MultiplyNumbers(int firstvalue, int secondvalue)
    {
        return firstvalue * secondvalue;
    }

    int AddNumbers(int firstvalue, int secondvalue)
    {
        return firstvalue + secondvalue;
    }

}
}
```

1. On the toolbar, select the project to compile in Release mode, and then from the Build menu, select Build Solution. Your WCF service is now built and compiled. Now you need something to host that service in. In Chapter 3 you hosted the WCF service in IIS, but this example uses a standard Windows application to host the service.

2. Open another instance of Visual Studio and this time create a C# Windows application with the name of WCFServiceHost, and like the WCFService, let it create the project directory, again setting the location to the root of the C drive. The project will be created with a default form, Form1. Double-click Form1 in the Solution Explorer; this will display Form1 in design mode. On Form1, drag and drop a label from the Toolbox onto Form1.

3. Because this is hosting the WCF service, this project also needs a reference to System.ServiceModel, so go ahead and add that reference as well. However, you also need to add a reference to the WCF service itself because this project is the one that is hosting the service. Add another reference again, but this time select the Browse tab in the Add Reference dialog. Browse to the location where the WCF is located. This would be in the bin\Release folder of the WCFService project. Figure 5-5 shows where the file is located if you created your host project in the root of your C: drive.

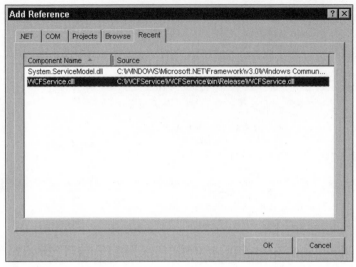

Figure 5-5

Once you have added the appropriate references, your Solution Explorer should look like Figure 5-6.

Figure 5-6

4. With the references added, you are now ready to start adding code. The last two chapters talked about addresses and bindings, and so this example is going to use both of those to make available the service you just created. So, right-click Form1 and select View Code from the context menu. Replace the existing code with the following code:

```csharp
using System;
using System.Collections.Generic;
using System.ComponentModel;
using System.Data;
using System.Drawing;
using System.Text;
using System.Windows.Forms;
using System.ServiceModel;
using System.ServiceModel.Description;
using WCFService;

namespace WCFServiceHost
{
    public partial class Form1 : Form
    {
        ServiceHost sh = null;

        public Form1()
        {
            InitializeComponent();
        }

        private void Form1_Load(object sender, EventArgs e)
        {

            Uri tcpa = new Uri("net.tcp://localhost:8000/TcpBinding");

            sh = new ServiceHost(typeof(ServiceClass), tcpa);

            NetTcpBinding tcpb = new NetTcpBinding();

            ServiceMetadataBehavior mBehave = new ServiceMetadataBehavior();
            sh.Description.Behaviors.Add(mBehave);

            sh.AddServiceEndpoint(typeof(IMetadataExchange),
                MetadataExchangeBindings.CreateMexTcpBinding(), "mex");

            sh.AddServiceEndpoint(typeof(IServiceClass), tcpb, tcpa);

            sh.Open();

            label1.Text = "Service Running";
        }

        private void Form1_FormClosing(object sender, FormClosingEventArgs e)
        {
            sh.Close();
        }
    }
}
```

5. From the Build menu, select Build Solution. Once it compiles, press the F5 key to run the project. When the project runs, the form will display and inform you that the service is running, as illustrated in Figure 5-7.

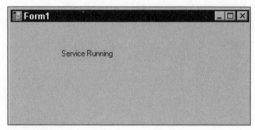

Figure 5-7

So far, you have created the service and are hosting it in a standard C# Windows application. Take a quick look at hosting code. Based on what you learned in Chapter 4, the first line defines a TCP address scheme, defining the transport the service will use to communicate. This example also defines the specific port over which to communicate, which is port 8000.

A ServiceHost is created using the address that was just identified. The very next line defines the binding that this service endpoint will use to communicate. This example uses the NetTcpBinding, which you learned about earlier in this chapter.

The next couple of statements define the behavior of the service and publish the metadata for the service. Service behaviors are provided via the Descriptions class of the System.ServiceModel namespace. When a behavior has been added to the ServiceHost.Descriptions.Behaviors property, this allows the ability to publish the metadata at the mex endpoint, but it does *not* publish the metadata. It only provides the ability.

To publish the metadata you must take the next step, which is to add an endpoint to the service whose contract is "IMetadataExchange." That is what the following line in the host code does. The first two lines define the metadata behavior for the service and the second two lines add the endpoint:

```
ServiceMetadataBehavior mBehave = new ServiceMetadataBehavior();
sh.Description.Behaviors.Add(mBehave);

sh.AddServiceEndpoint(typeof(IMetadataExchange),
MetadataExchangeBindings.CreateMexTcpBinding(), "mex");
```

The remaining two lines of code define the endpoint that the client will use to communicate with the service, and the last line opens the service host.

With the host application running, open a command window and type in the following:

```
Netstat -a -n | more
```

Browse through the open connections, and you should see the port listed in which your service is running. In Figure 5-8, you will see that port 8000, the port you specified in your host application code for the defined TCP address, is indeed open and listening.

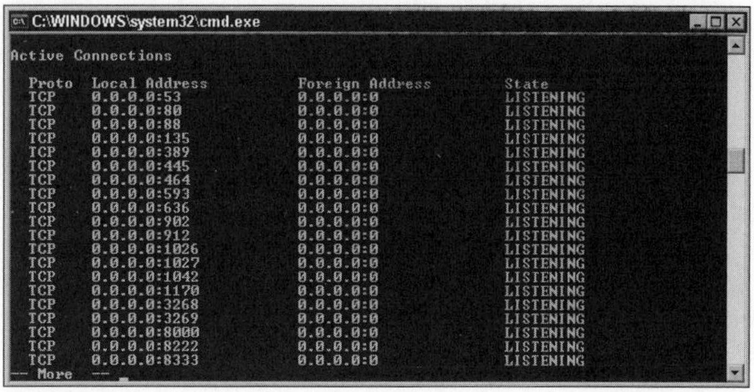

Figure 5-8

The last step is to create the client that will use this service, so open a third instance of Visual Studio and create another C# Windows application. Name this one WCFClientApp and let it create the directory for the solution, again setting the location to the root of the C drive.

As with the other two projects, add a reference to System.ServiceModel. This project will also have a Form1, and so open that form in design mode and drop two text boxes and two buttons on the form. Set the text for button1 to "Go - Get Text" and set the text property of button2 to "Go – Multiply."

The next piece of information you need is vital to the success of the client application, and if you have done any sort of .aspx web service programming, you know that what is needed is to consume the web service, and to do that you need a reference to the web service.

You can get that information simply by knowing what address the service endpoint is using, and you know that because you specified it in the host code when you defined the TCP address, shown in the following code:

```
Uri tcpa = new Uri("net.tcp://localhost:8000/TcpBinding");
```

In Solution Explorer, right-click the References node and select Add Service Reference from the context menu. This will display the Add Service Reference dialog. In the Service URI text box, enter in the net.tcp address from the preceding line of code, and give it a reference name of TCP, as shown in Figure 5-9.

117

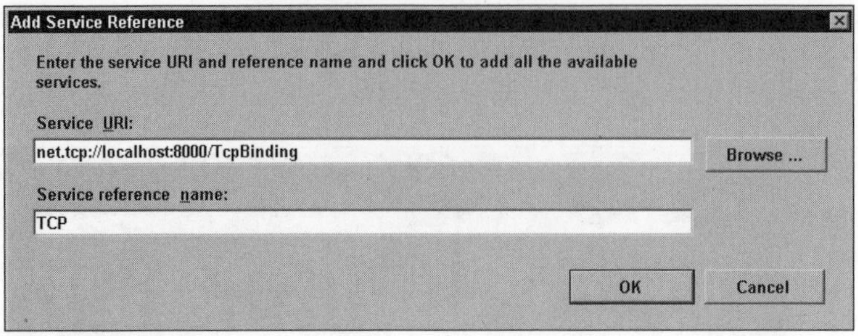

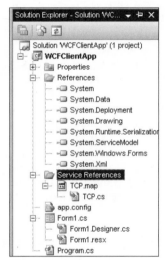

Figure 5-9

Once the reference to the service has been added, take a good look at your project in Solution Explorer. Besides the addition of the service reference, you will also notice that an `app.config` file was added, as shown in Figure 5-10.

Figure 5-10

Open the `app.config` file and take a look at its contents. Figure 5-11 shows you what the contents should look like. Pay close attention to the information it contains. The configuration file contains two critical sections: the binding information and the endpoint information.

The `<bindings>` element contains all the necessary binding and transport information for the client and service to effectively communicate. You read a lot in this chapter about the available parameters for the bindings. Notice that because no parameter values were specified when the bindings were defined in code, WCF automatically added them to the configuration file with the appropriate default values for each.

The next section, the `<client>` element, contains the endpoint configuration information to make a successful connection to the endpoints. This section contains an `<endpoint>` element, which defines the address, binding, and contract information of the endpoint so that the client can successfully communicate with that endpoint.

```xml
<?xml version="1.0" encoding="utf-8" ?>
<configuration>
    <system.serviceModel>
        <bindings>
            <netTcpBinding>
                <binding name="NetTcpBinding_IServiceClass" closeTimeout="00:01:00"
                    openTimeout="00:01:00" receiveTimeout="00:10:00" sendTimeout="00:01:00"
                    transactionFlow="false" transferMode="Buffered" transactionProtocol="OleTransactions"
                    hostNameComparisonMode="StrongWildcard" listenBacklog="10"
                    maxBufferPoolSize="524288" maxBufferSize="65536" maxConnections="10"
                    maxReceivedMessageSize="65536">
                    <readerQuotas maxDepth="32" maxStringContentLength="8192" maxArrayLength="16384"
                        maxBytesPerRead="4096" maxNameTableCharCount="16384" />
                    <reliableSession ordered="true" inactivityTimeout="00:10:00"
                        enabled="false" />
                    <security mode="Transport">
                        <transport clientCredentialType="Windows" protectionLevel="EncryptAndSign" />
                        <message clientCredentialType="Windows" />
                    </security>
                </binding>
            </netTcpBinding>
        </bindings>
        <client>
            <endpoint address="net.tcp://localhost:8000/TcpBinding" binding="netTcpBinding"
                bindingConfiguration="NetTcpBinding_IServiceClass" contract="WCFClientApp.TCP.IServiceClass"
                name="NetTcpBinding_IServiceClass">
                <identity>
                    <userPrincipalName value="Scott@Avalon" />
                </identity>
            </endpoint>
        </client>
    </system.serviceModel>
</configuration>
```

Figure 5-11

The final step is to add the code to the form. Right-click Form1 and select View Code from the context menu. Replace the default code in the form with the following code:

```csharp
using System;
using System.Collections.Generic;
using System.ComponentModel;
using System.Data;
using System.Drawing;
using System.Text;
using System.Windows.Forms;

namespace WCFClientApp
{
    public partial class Form1 : Form
    {
        public Form1()
        {
            InitializeComponent();
        }

        private void button1_Click(object sender, EventArgs e)
        {
            TCP.ServiceClassClient client = new
                WCFClientApp.TCP.ServiceClassClient("NetTcpBinding_IServiceClass");
```

```
            textBox1.Text = client.GetText();
        }

        private void button2_Click(object sender, EventArgs e)
        {
            TCP.ServiceClassClient client2 = new
                WCFClientApp.TCP.ServiceClassClient("NetTcpBinding_IServiceClass");
            textBox2.Text = client2.MultiplyNumbers(5, 5).ToString();
        }
    }
}
```

Before you run the app, take a quick look at the code. When the `Click()` event for button1 is fired, two things happen:

1. First, a channel is opened to the service using the appropriate binding.

2. Second, the `GetText()` method of the WCF service is called and returns the results to the text box. If you remember from earlier, the `GetText()` method opens and reads a text file. The content of the text file is displayed in the first text box.

The `Click()` event for button2 executes similar code. First, just like button 1, a channel is opened to the service with the appropriate binding, then the `MultiplyNumbers()` method of the WCF service is called passing two numbers as parameters. The WCF service multiplies those together and returns the results, which are then displayed in the second text box.

Press the F5 key to run the client app. When the app runs, it will display Form1. Click both buttons to retrieve the text from the text file and to multiply numbers. The results of both of these are shown in Figure 5-12.

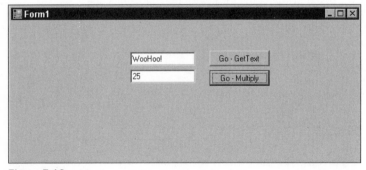

Figure 5-12

You can see by clicking the buttons that you get the desired results. At this point, look at some more advanced functionality by adding another address and binding. Close down the client application and close down the host application.

Go back to the WCFServiceHost project and modify the form load code as follows (new code is high-lighted):

```
Uri bpa = new Uri("net.pipe://localhost/NetNamedPipeBinding");
Uri tcpa = new Uri("net.tcp://localhost:8000/TcpBinding");

sh = new ServiceHost(typeof(ServiceClass), bpa, tcpa);

NetNamedPipeBinding pb = new NetNamedPipeBinding();
NetTcpBinding tcpb = new NetTcpBinding();

ServiceMetadataBehavior mBehave = new ServiceMetadataBehavior();
sh.Description.Behaviors.Add(mBehave);

sh.AddServiceEndpoint(typeof(IMetadataExchange),
    MetadataExchangeBindings.CreateMexTcpBinding(), "mex");

sh.AddServiceEndpoint(typeof(IMetadataExchange),
    MetadataExchangeBindings.CreateMexNamedPipeBinding(), "mex");

sh.AddServiceEndpoint(typeof(IServiceClass), pb, bpa);
sh.AddServiceEndpoint(typeof(IServiceClass), tcpb, tcpa);

sh.Open();

label1.Text = "Service Running";
```

The added lines define an address, binding, behavior, and endpoint for the NamedPipe protocol. The address uses the NamedPipe address format of net.pipe://, which is then passed on to the ServiceHost.

From the Build menu, select Build Solution. Once it compiles, press the F5 key to run the project. With the host app running again, go back to the client app and open the Solution Explorer. A reference to the new endpoint needs to be added so right-click the References node and select Add Service Reference. The address for this reference can be retrieved from the preceding code, which is the following:

```
net.pipe://localhost/NetNamedPipeBinding
```

For the service reference name, enter the name of NamedPipe. The Add Service Reference information should look like Figure 5-13. Once you have filled out everything, click OK.

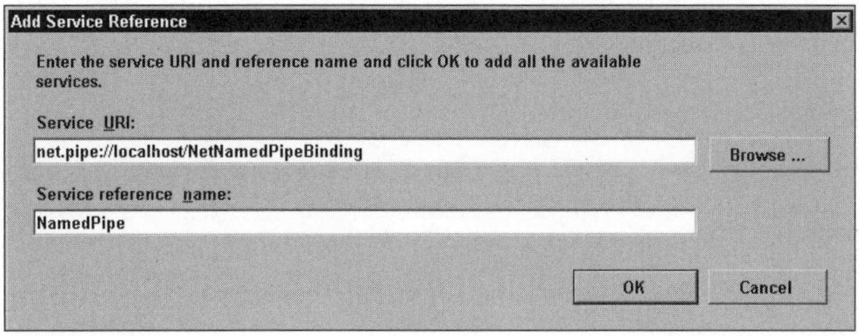

Figure 5-13

The Service References node in your Solution Explorer should now have two references in it, one for the NamedPipe endpoint reference and another for the TCP endpoint reference, as shown in Figure 5-14.

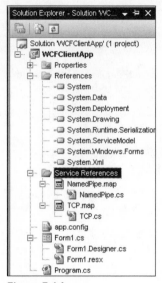

Figure 5-14

The next step is to modify the form design a little bit to accommodate these changes. Open Form1 in design mode and add three radio buttons to the left of the text boxes. Set the Text property of RadioButton1 to TCP, the Text property of RadioButton2 to NamedPipe, and RadioButton3 to Http.

Next, modify the code as follows:

```
using System;
using System.Collections.Generic;
using System.ComponentModel;
using System.Data;
using System.Drawing;
using System.Text;
using System.Windows.Forms;
using System.ServiceModel;

namespace WCFClientApp
{
  public partial class Form1 : Form
  {
      private int _Selection;

      public Form1()
      {
          InitializeComponent();
      }

      private void button1_Click(object sender, EventArgs e)
```

```
        {
          switch (_Selection)
          {
            case 0:
              TCP.ServiceClassClient client = new
                WCFClientApp.TCP.ServiceClassClient("NetTcpBinding_IServiceClass");
              textBox1.Text = client.GetText();
              break;

            case 1:
              NamedPipe.ServiceClassClient client1 = new
WCFClientApp.NamedPipe.ServiceClassClient("NetNamedPipeBinding_IServiceClass");
              textBox1.Text = client1.GetText();
              break;

            case 2:
              break;
          }
        }

      private void button2_Click(object sender, EventArgs e)
      {
        switch (_Selection)
        {
          case 0:
            TCP.ServiceClassClient client = new
              WCFClientApp.TCP.ServiceClassClient("NetTcpBinding_IServiceClass");
            textBox2.Text = client.MultiplyNumbers(5, 5).ToString();
            break;

          case 1:
            NamedPipe.ServiceClassClient client1 = new
WCFClientApp.NamedPipe.ServiceClassClient("NetNamedPipeBinding_IServiceClass");
            textBox2.Text = client1.MultiplyNumbers(5, 5).ToString();
            break;

          case 2:
          break;
        }
      }

      private void radioButton1_CheckedChanged(object sender, EventArgs e)
      {
          _Selection = 0;
          textbox1.Text = "";
          textbox2.Text = "";
      }

      private void radioButton2_CheckedChanged(object sender, EventArgs e)
      {
          _Selection = 1;
          textbox1.Text = "";
          textbox2.Text = "";
      }
```

```
            private void radioButton3_CheckedChanged(object sender, EventArgs e)
            {
                _Selection = 2;
            }
        }
    }
```

The changes made to the form allow you to be able to select the protocol that the client and service will communicate with. Run the client application and select the desired protocol and button to display the result. Figure 5-15 shows an example of the results using the NamedPipe protocol.

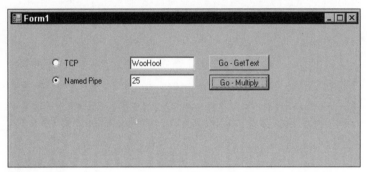

Figure 5-15

Your homework assignment for this chapter is two things: First, to modify the host code to host and run the service using the Http protocol with the appropriate endpoint, and second, to wire up the third radio button to utilize the new Http endpoint.

So far the examples have shown how to define addresses and bindings via code. The other (and pre-ferred method) is to use configuration.

Using Configuration Files

This section takes a quick look at using configuration files to set the address, binding, and contract instead of in your code, and to do this you will modify the previous example. Luckily, there isn't much to change, and the only changes you need to make are to the host application code.

The first step is to add a configuration file to the host application. Right-click the solution and select Add ⇨ New Item from the context menu. From the Add New Item dialog, select Application Configuration File from the list of installed templates. The Name should default to app.config but if it does not, name it app.config and click Add.

The app.config file will be added to your project and will open with some default configuration infor-mation. Delete the contents of the app.config file and replace them with the following:

```
<?xml version="1.0" encoding="utf-8" ?>
<configuration>
  <system.serviceModel>
```

```
<services>
  <service name ="WCFService.ServiceClass">
    <endpoint contract ="WCFService.IServiceClass"
              name="NetTcpBinding_IServiceClass"
              binding ="netTcpBinding"
              address ="net.tcp://localhost:8000/TcpBinding"/>
    <endpoint contract ="WCFService.IServiceClass"
              name="netNamedPipeBinding_IServiceClass"
              binding ="netNamedPipeBinding"
              address ="net.pipe://localhost/NetNamedPipeBinding"/>
  </service>
</services>
<bindings>
  <netTcpBinding>
    <binding name ="NetTcpBinding_IServiceClass"/>
  </netTcpBinding>
  <netNamedPipeBinding>
    <binding name ="netNamedPipeBinding_IServiceClass"/>
  </netNamedPipeBinding>
</bindings>
<behaviors>
  <serviceBehaviors>

  </serviceBehaviors>
</behaviors>
  </system.serviceModel>
</configuration>
```

The next step is to modify the form load code. Modify the form load code in the host application as follows:

```
private void Form1_Load(object sender, EventArgs e)
{

    sh = new ServiceHost(typeof(WCFService.ServiceClass));
    sh.Open();

    label1.Text = "Service Running";
}
```

To test it, select Build WCFServiceHost from the Build menu. Once it is finished compiling and building, press the F5 key to run the host application. Form1 will appear, letting you know that the service is running. Now go over to the client application and run it. When the form comes up, select the protocol you want to test and click the buttons to call the service endpoints.

Take a look at the changes that were made. In the first example, the endpoints were defined in code. The addresses and bindings were also defined in code and applied to those endpoints. Thus, no configuration file was needed.

In the second example, much less code was needed and all the address, binding, and endpoint defining was done within the configuration file. The only code needed in the host application was to create the ServiceHost and specify the Service information.

The configuration file in the host application follows the same format as the configuration file in the client application. There is a `<bindings>` section where the bindings are defined and a `<service>` section in which the endpoints (addresses and bindings) are defined.

When defining endpoints in a configuration file the service name should be in the format of NAMESPACE.CLASSNAME, and the endpoint contract name should be in the format of NAMESPACE.INTERFACECLASS. In the preceding example, the service namespace is WCFService with a class name of ServiceClass, and the interface is named IServiceClass. Therefore the service and endpoints are defined in the configuration file as the following:

```
<service name ="WCFService.ServiceClass">
  <endpoint contract ="WCFService.IServiceClass"
     name="NetTcpBinding_IServiceClass"
     binding ="netTcpBinding"
     address ="net.tcp://localhost:8000/TcpBinding"/>
  <endpoint contract ="WCFService.IServiceClass"
     name="netNamedPipeBinding_IServiceClass"
     binding ="netNamedPipeBinding"
     address ="net.pipe://localhost/NetNamedPipeBinding"/>
</service>
```

Having gone through this now, you can see how beneficial it is to use the configuration file approach over the inline code approach. Now, the second part of your homework is to define a third endpoint using the Http protocol using the configuration file approach.

Summary

The purpose of this chapter was to give you an in-depth look at bindings and their properties as well as to show you how to use bindings to communicate with service endpoints. This chapter began by defining the concept of a binding and then spent quite a few pages discussing the built-in, preexisting bindings and their attributes. These bindings should be able to cover most application requirements.

The last part of this chapter provided several examples to illustrate how to implement bindings and the options you have available to take advantage of the predefined bindings.

Custom bindings are discussed later in this book.

Chapter 6 focuses on some of the information you used in this chapter, contracts.

6

Understanding and Programming WCF Contracts

This chapter discusses the last letter in the Windows Communication Foundation alphabet. Chapter 4 discussed the first letter in the WCF alphabet, letter "A," covering the topic of addresses. Chapter 5 covered the second letter, "B," discussing the topic of WCF bindings. This chapter discusses the final letter, "C," and talks about the very important topic of contracts.

The "ABCs" of Windows Communication Foundation help you easily understand the concepts and components that make up a WCF service. Contracts are vital to WCF services and so this chapter discusses WCF contracts and provides some examples of how to define and program them.

All of the examples you have seen and worked on up until now have used and implemented contacts. One of the big things to consider when writing a book is how to lay things out and talk about topics in a way and order that makes sense. This applies to WCF just as easily because as you have seen when building a service, you can start with almost any aspect of it. Chapter 4 just as easily could have discussed contracts and waited until this chapter to discuss addresses. Regardless of the order, hopefully you have started to get an idea of what these contracts do, but if you haven't this chapter will help you better understand the different types of contracts.

With that, this chapter discusses the following:

❑   The types of WCF contracts

❑   How to define the different types of contracts

❑   Examples of WCF contracts

WCF Contracts

Contracts in Windows Communication Foundation provide the interoperability they need to communicate with the client. It is through contracts that clients and services agree as to the types of operations and structures they will use during the period that they are communicating back and forth. Without contracts, no work would be accomplished because no agreement would happen.

Three basic contracts are used to define a Windows Communication Foundation service:

❑ **Service Contract:** Defines the methods of a service, that is, what operations are available on the endpoint to the client.

❑ **Data Contract:** Defines the data types used by the available service methods.

❑ **Message Contract:** Provides the ability to control the message headers during the creation of a message.

Just like nearly everything else in WCF, contracts are defined using concepts you are already familiar with. Everything you have seen so far when dealing with WCF has used object-oriented architecture, and contracts are not any different.

Contracts are defined using tried-and-true classes and interfaces. In the last chapter you learned that bindings are defined by annotating defined classes and interfaces. Contracts are defined the exact same way, by annotating classes and interfaces.

Contracts and Their Relationship with the CLR

The types of contracts easily translate between internally existing .NET types and the externally shared XML representation. The following lists the relationship of the contracts and their .NET Framework CLR (Common Language Runtime) equivalent:

❑ **Service Contracts:** CLR and WSDL (Web Service Description Language).

❑ **Data Contracts:** CLR and XSD (XML Schema Definition).

❑ **Message Contracts:** CLR and SOAP (Simple Object Access Protocol).

This chapter discusses each of these contract types in detail in the following sections and follows that up by providing examples to show how everything works.

Service Contracts

As explained, a service contract defines the operations, or methods, that are available on the service endpoint and is exposed to the outside world. It also defines the basic message exchange patterns, such as whether the message behaves in a request/reply, one-way, or duplex behavior.

A service contract exposes specific information to the client, which enables the client to understand what the service has to offer. This information includes the following:

- ❏ The data types in the message

- ❏ The locations of the operations

- ❏ The protocol information and serialization format to ensure the proper and successful communication

- ❏ Operation grouping

- ❏ Message exchange pattern (MEPs)

A service contract is defined by simply applying the [ServiceContract] annotation to an interface or class. The following example shows how to define an interface as a service contract:

```
[ServiceContract]
public interface IBookOrder
{
  //do some stuff
}
```

Service operations are specified by applying the [OperationContract] annotation on the methods of an interface, as illustrated in this example:

```
[OperationContract]
bool PlaceOrder(string orderdate, string bookisbn);

[OperationContract]
bool CheckOrder(int ordernumber);
```

Put these two together to make a complete service contract, as shown here:

```
[ServiceContract]
public interface IBookOrder
{
  [OperationContract]
  bool PlaceOrder(string orderdate, string bookisbn);

  [OperationContract]
  bool CheckOrder(int ordernumber);
}
```

Once the interface for the service is defined, the defined interface can then be implemented. The following example implements the IBookOrder interface defined in the preceding code:

```
public class BookOrder : IBookOrder
{
  Public bool PlaceOrder(string orderdate, string bookisbn)
  {
    //do something
  }
  public bool CheckOrder(int ordernumber)
  {
    //do something
  }
}
```

As you learned in Chapter 3, you can combine these two steps into a single implementation, as follows:

```
[ServiceContract]
public class BookOrder : IBookOrder
{
  [OperationContract]
  Public bool PlaceOrder(string orderdate, string bookisbn)
  {
    //do something
  }
  [OperationContract]
  public bool CheckOrder(int ordernumber)
  {
    //do something
  }
}
```

For a review on why you would want to do one way over the other, go back and read the section in Chapter 3 called "WCF Programming Methods."

Up until now you have been using these attributes the way they are illustrated in the preceding example. What is meant by this is that attributes (such as [ServiceContract]) are applied without parameters. However, both the [ServiceContract] and the [OperationAttribute] attributes have many parameters that can be used to specify special details pertaining to each attribute. Functions would be of little value if parameters could not be employed; the same holds true for attributes. These next sections explain the parameters that can be used with these two attributes.

[ServiceContract] Attribute

The [ServiceContract] attribute identifies an interface or class as a service contract. This attribute explicitly defines the interface as a CLR interface and enables it to carry out WCF contract operations, with each [ServiceContract] attribute being mapped to an equivalent WDL portType declaration.

The following list contains the parameters available for use with the [ServiceContract] attribute. More than one parameter can be applied to the attribute, and these parameters can be used in any order:

- CallbackContract
- ConfigurationName
- Name
- Namespace
- ProtectionLevel
- SessionMode

The following sections discuss these parameters in detail.

CallbackContract

The CallbackContract parameter gets or sets the type of callback contract when the contract is communicating in duplex mode. This parameter contains a Type value that specifies the callback contract. The Type value should contain a `CallbackContract = typeof(ClientContract)` that represents the required opposite contract in a two-way (duplex) message exchange operation, or in other words, the client callback contract.

It is possible to have callback contracts on one-way operations as well. In this scenario, the callback contract represents outgoing calls from the service that can be received by the client.

Specifying this parameter informs the client that it needs to listen for inbound method calls coming from the service. These inbound method calls operate independently of other client activity.

The following example shows the CallbackContract attribute in use:

```
[ServiceContract(CallbackContract = typeof(IClientContract))]
public interface IBookOrder
{
    ...
}
```

In this example, the service specifies a callback contract, IClientContract. The default value for this parameter is a null reference.

ConfigurationName

The ConfigurationName parameter gets or sets the name used to locate the service element in a configuration file. This value is a string data type. If not specified, the default is the name of the service implementation class.

The following example uses the ConfigurationName parameter to specify the service element in the service configuration file:

```
[ServiceContract(ConfigurationName = "service")]
public interface IBookOrder
{
    ...
}
```

The application configuration file for the preceding example would look like the following:

```
<configuration>
  <system.servicemodel>
    <services>
      <service name = "BookOrder">
      </service>
    </services>
  </system.servicemodel>
</configuration>
```

Name

The Name parameter gets or sets the name for the `<portType>` element in WSDL (Web Service Description Language). The default value for this parameter is the name of the service class or interface to which this parameter is applied.

As a refresher, the `<portType>` element in WSDL contains all the necessary information for a service, such as the operations it can perform and the messages that are involved.

The Name parameter for the `[ServiceContract]` attribute sets the name of this element. The following example sets the Name parameter:

```
[ServiceContract(Name="IBookOrder")]
public interface IBookOrder
{
    ...
}
```

Namespace

The Namespace parameter gets or sets the namespace for the `<portType>` element in WSDL (Web Service Description Language). The default value for this parameter is "http://tempuri.org".

The Namespace parameter for the `[ServiceContract]` attribute sets the namespace of this element. The following example sets the Namespace parameter:

```
[ServiceContract(Namespace="http://www.WonderBooks.com")]
public interface IBookOrder
{
    ...
}
```

ProtectionLevel

The ProtectionLevel parameter specifies the protection-level binding requirement. This includes encryption, digital signature, or both, for each endpoint that exposes the contract.

The value of this parameter comes from the System.Net.SecurityLevel.ProtectionLevel enumeration. The following enumeration values are available:

❑ **EncryptAndSign** — Encrypt and sign data to ensure the confidentiality and integrity of transmitted data.

❑ **None** — Authentication only.

❑ **Sign** — Sign data to help ensure the integrity of the transmitted data, but do not encrypt.

The following example sets the protection level of the service contract to that of None, meaning that only simple authentication is required:

```
[ServiceContract(ProtectionLevel = System.Net.Security.ProtectionLevel.None)]
public interface IBookOrder
{
    ...
}
```

This property has a hierarchical structure, in that the topmost value establishes the default for all lower-level scopes ([OperationContract] attribute) unless a specific value is specified for the lower-level scopes. It is important to note that the value specified on this property is the default value for all operation messages.

If the associated binding supports security and no protection level is specified on the contract, the protection level defaults to EncryptAndSign for the entire contract. If the binding does not support security, the protection level defaults to None.

SessionMode

The SessionMode attribute specifies the type of support for reliable sessions that a contract requires or supports.

The value of this parameter comes from the SessionMode enumeration. The following enumeration values are available:

❑ **Allowed:** Specifies that the contract supports reliable sessions if the incoming connection supports them.

❑ **NotAllowed:** Specifies that the contract never supports reliable sessions.

❑ **Required:** Specifies that the contract requires a reliable session at all times.

The following example sets the session mode of the service contract to Required, signifying that a service contract must always use reliable sessions:

```
[ServiceContract(SessionMode = SessionMode.Required)]
public interface IBookOrder
{
    ...
}
```

Reliable sessions are implemented via the WS-Reliable Messaging protocol (discussed in Chapter 5). WCF reliable messaging is implemented to provide reliable end-to-end message transfer between two SOAP endpoints, regardless of the number of intermediaries between the two endpoints. You should consider using reliable sessions in the following scenarios:

❑ You want sessions over HTTP.

❑ You have intermittent connectivity between the endpoints.

❑ Proxy intermediaries or transport bridges exist.

❑ SOAP intermediaries exist between endpoints.

Service Types

In Windows Communication Foundation there are three types of services, ranging from simple to somewhat complex. The three types of services are as follows:

❑ Typed

❑ Untyped

❑ Typed message

Typed

A typed service is the simplest of services, and is very similar to the methods in a class, in that both the parameters and method return values can be both simple or complex data types. A typed service can also return a value or return a modified parameter value. The following example illustrates a typed service in which typed operations are used:

```
[ServiceContract(SessionMode = SessionMode.Required)]
public interface IBookOrder
{
  [OperationContract]
  void PlaceOrder(string title, decimal cost);
}
```

This next example shows the use of the ref parameter to return a modified parameter value:

```
[ServiceContract(SessionMode = SessionMode.Required)]
public interface IBookOrder
{
  [OperationContract]
  void PlaceOrder(string title, decimal cost, ref ordernumber);
}
```

Data contracts provide the ability to extend this functionality and accept complex data types as parameters or returned results.

This is very similar to traditional object-oriented programming methodology, so this should not seem unfamiliar.

Typed Message

A typed message service accepts and returns message information via custom classes that are defined by message contracts. You learn about message contracts later in this chapter, but for now suffice it to say that this type of service type allows you to handle incoming requests and corresponding responses as messages, providing more structure to the data.

With a typed message service the operation accepts a custom message parameter in the form of a message class, and the responsibility of deciphering the message falls upon the service operation.

The following example shows a service contract along with a defined typed message that is used as a parameter in a typed service operation:

```
[ServiceContract]
public interface IBookOrder
{
  [OperationContract]
  void PlaceOrder(Contract MyContract);
}

[MessageContract]
public class MyContract
{
  [MessageHeader]
  string Title;
  [MessageBodyMember]
  decimal cost;

}
```

Untyped

Untyped services let you do your work at message level, so this is the most complex of the service types. At this level the service operation accepts and returns *message objects* so it is recommended that you use this type of service only when you need this level of control, that is, working directly with the message. The following example shows an operation contract passing a message object as an untyped service operation:

```
[ServiceContract(SessionMode = SessionMode.Required)]
public interface IBookOrder
{
  [OperationContract]
  void PlaceOrder(message IncomingMessage);
}
```

[OperationContract] Attribute

The [OperationContract] attribute includes the method as part of the service contract and identifies the method as a service operation. A method marked as an operation contract is exposed to the public. Methods not marked with this attribute are not exposed externally. [OperationContract] attributes are also mapped to an equivalent WSDL operation definition.

The following list contains the parameters available for use with the [OperationContract] attribute. More than one parameter can be applied to the attribute, and these parameters can be used in any order:

❑   Action

❑   AsyncPattern

❑   IsInitiating

❑   IsOneWay

❑   IsTerminating

❑   Name

❑   ProtectionLevel

❑   ReplyAction

The following sections discuss these parameters in detail.

Action

The Action parameter gets or sets the WS-Addressing of the request message. It defines the action that identifies the current operation.

The following example illustrates using the Action parameter:

```
[OperationContract(Action = true)]
void PlaceBookOrder(string isbn, int quantity);
```

Windows Communication Foundation uses this property to determine which method to send the incoming message to. This makes it necessary for each contract operation to contain a unique action. WCF uses this action to transmit an incoming message to the appropriate method, therefore messages used within a contract operation must have unique actions. This parameter does have a default action, and that is a combination of the contract namespace, the interface or class name, and the operation name. Specifically specifying an action replaces and overrides this default.

You can also specify that an operation handles all incoming messages by specifying an asterisk (*) for this parameter. This comes with a few caveats, though. To enable this type of functionality, the operation needs to do one of the following:

❑   The operation method can only accept a message object and return a message object.

❑   The operation method can only accept a message object and return nothing.

❑   The operation method can be void and accept an IChannel object.

This parameter interacts very closely with the IsInitiating parameter. For more information on this interaction, see the following "IsInitiating" section.

AsyncPattern

The AsyncPattern parameter specifies that an operation is an asynchronous operation. Service operations can be either synchronous or asynchronous. Asynchronous operations are implemented using a BeginXXX and EndXXX method pair within the service contract. It is the AsyncPattern property that tells the runtime that a Begin method has a corresponding and matching End method. Windows Communication Foundation routes incoming messages to the Begin method, and the results of the End method are sent to the outbound message. The AsyncPattern parameter must also be set to true.

The following example illustrates using the AsyncPattern parameter:

```
[OperationContract(AsyncPattern = true)]
IAsyncResult BeginCheckBookOrderStatus(string OrderNumber, AsyncCallback callback,
object state);
void EndCheckBookOrderStatus(IAsyncResult ar);
```

You should notice that the Begin method contains two additional parameters: the `AsyncCallback` and `state` object. To use the AsyncPattern parameter correctly, the Begin operation returns an IAsyncResult object, and the End operation accepts that IAsyncResult result as a parameter and returns the appropriate service operation result.

IsInitiating

The IsInitiating parameter specifies whether or not an operation implemented by the associated method can initiate a session on the server. Session instancing is the ability to have separate instances of a class be maintained for each client channel. This property controls whether an operation is allowed to be the first operation called when a session is created. The default for this parameter is true, meaning that the specified operation can be the first called on a channel. In this scenario, all following calls to this method have no effect (meaning, no other sessions are created). If this parameter is set to false, the client is forced to call other methods prior to calling this method.

This comes in handy when you are trying to set an "order of operation," meaning that you need a specific method to be called first because the other methods called depend on something returned from the first method.

For example, the following contains three methods, or service operations. The first operation creates the session and must be the first method called. The final operation, Logout, closes the session:

```
[ServiceContract]
public interface IBuyStock
{
    [OperationContract(IsInitiating = true, IsTerminating = false)]
    void Login(user);
    [OperationContract(IsInitiating = false, IsTerminating = false)]
    void BuyStock(string stocksymbol, int quantity);
    [OperationContract(IsInitiating = false, IsTerminating = true)]
    void Logout(user);
}
```

Once the initiating method has been called, subsequent calls can be made to that method with no effect to its initiating properties.

If any method other than the initiating method is called first, the following error is returned:

```
The operation 'operationname' cannot be the first operation to be called because
IsInitiating is false.
```

The initiating method must be called first, then other operations can be called.

As mentioned earlier, there is some important interaction between this parameter and the `Action` parameter. A service contract can only have one operation where the `Action` property is set to "*". When the `IsInitiating` property is set to False, those service contracts that implement a service class can have more than one service operation with the `Action` property set to "*". However, the opposite is true when the `IsInitiating` property is set to True. In those cases, only a single service method can have an `Action` property set to "*".

IsOneWay

As you have probably gathered by now, service communication can be either one-way or bi-directional. Service communication by default is bi-directional. Bi-directional service communication means that a service operation can receive incoming messages and send a reply.

The IsOneWay parameter specifies whether a service operation returns a reply message. The default value for this parameter is false, meaning that the method does not return a reply message.

The following example illustrates a one-way communication:

```
[ServiceContract]
public interface IBuyStock
{
  [OperationContract(IsOneWay = true)]
  void Login(user);
  [OperationContract(IsOneWay = false)]
  void BuyStock(string stocksymbol, int quantity);
}
```

In a one-way communication, the client initiates the communication and continues code execution and does not wait for a response from the service. In a two-way communication, it waits for a response from the service before continuing code execution.

The downside to using one-way communication is that the caller has no way of knowing whether or not the service processed the message successfully.

Any methods that return a value where the IsOneWay property is set to false will return an exception.

IsTerminating

The IsTerminating property specifies whether a called service operation is to terminate the communication session. The following example, taken from the earlier IsInitiating example, shows the last call, Logout(), has the IsTerminating property set to true:

```
[ServiceContract]
public interface IBuyStock
{
  [OperationContract(IsInitiating = true, IsTerminating = false)]
  void Login(user);
  [OperationContract(IsInitiating = false, IsTerminating = false)]
  void BuyStock(string stocksymbol, int quantity);
  [OperationContract(IsInitiating = false, IsTerminating = true)]
  void Logout(user);
}
```

When the IsTerminating property is set to true, the session is closed after the reply message is sent (if a reply message needs to be sent). On the client side, an IsTerminating value of true tells WCF to close the channel only after the reply arrives at the client.

Name

The Name property is used to get or set the name of the operation. This property overrides the `<operation>` element in WSDL and if this property is left blank, the default name is taken from the method.

In the following example, the Name property sets the name to UserLogin:

```
[ServiceContract]
public interface IBuyStock
{
   [OperationContract(Name = "UserLogin")]
   void Login(user);
}
```

Had the Name property not been specified, the default would have been Login.

ProtectionLevel

The ProtectionLevel parameter specifies the encryption level of the message of an operation. This includes encryption, digital signature, or both, for each endpoint that exposes the contract.

The value of this parameter comes from the System.Net.SecurityLevel.ProtectionLevel enumeration. The following enumeration values are available:

❑ **EncryptAndSign:** Encrypt and sign data to ensure the confidentiality and integrity of transmitted data.

❑ **None:** Authentication only.

❑ **Sign:** Sign data to help ensure the integrity of the transmitted data, but do not encrypt.

The following example sets the protection level of the service contract to that of None, meaning that only simple authentication is required. However, a protection level on the Login and BuyStock operations is supplied, setting the protection level to EncryptAndSign. In this scenario, both the Login and BuyStock operations carry the EncryptAndSign protection level, and any other methods inherit the service-level protection level of None.

```
[ServiceContract(ProtectionLevel = System.Net.Security.ProtectionLevel.None)]
public interface IBuyStock
{
   [OperationContract(ProtectionLevel =
System.Net.Security.ProtectionLevel.EncryptAndSign)]
   void Login(user);
   [OperationContract(ProtectionLevel = System.Net.Security.ProtectionLevel.
EncryptAndSign)]
   void BuyStock(string stocksymbol, int quantity);
   . . .
}
```

This property has a hierarchical structure, in that the topmost value establishes the default for all lower-level scopes (`[OperationContract]` attribute) unless a specific value is specified for the lower-level scopes.

ReplyAction

This property specifies a reply action for an incoming message. The value for this parameter is a URL, which can be a full URI or simple operation name. If this parameter is left off, the default value will contain the name of the contract plus the name of the reply action. It is also possible to specify an asterisk (*), which tells Windows Communication Foundation not to add a reply action to the message.

The following example shows a ReplyAction specifying a full URI response operation:

```
[ServiceContract]
public interface IBuyStock
{
    [OperationContract(ReplyAction = "http://tempuri.org/IBuyStock/StockBought")]
}
```

Data Contracts

Simply, a data contract describes the data that is to be exchanged. In Chapter 1 you learned that one of the principles of Service-Oriented Architecture is policy-based compatibility. That section gave an example of a couple of strangers meeting on the street and wanting to start up a discussion. However, before these two strangers can start talking, they each need to agree on the "data" that they will be passing back and forth. This is a data contract. It is a formal agreement between the two parties that contains information regarding the data that they will be exchanging.

The important thing to remember is that the two parties don't have to share the same data types to be able to start talking; they only need to share the same data contracts. The data contract specifically defines what each parameter and return type will be serialized/deserialized to and from (Binary and XML) in order be exchanged from one party to the other.

It is important to understand how serialization and deserialization apply to Windows Communication Foundation. Serialization is the act of taking structured data and converting it into a format that can be communicated or sent over a wire; for example, reading data from a database and converting it to a series of bytes to be sent over your network. Deserialization is the opposite. It takes the data coming in over the wire and converts it back to structured data. This chapter doesn't go into serialization, but a complete chapter has been dedicated to that topic. Therefore, serialization in Windows Communication Foundation is covered in detail in Appendix B.

It is time to dig into data contracts.

[DataContract] Attribute

Data contracts are defined declaratively just like service contracts and operation contracts. To define a data contract, you simply decorate a class or enumeration with the [DataContract] attribute. For example:

```
[DataContract]
public class BuyStock
{
    ...
}
```

I should back up and say that there is one difference between defining a service contract and a data contract. With service contracts, you can annotate a class or interface. Not so with data contracts. Data contracts can be defined by annotating a class, enumeration, or even a structure, but not an interface.

The preceding example defines a data contract. Once you have the data contract defined, you can define the members of a data contract. These members are the fields or properties of your class. Taking the previous example, the following example defines some data members for within the data contract:

```
[DataContract]
public class BuyStock
{
    [DataMember] public string symbol;
    [DataMember] public int quantity;
    [DataMember] public decimal price;
}
```

Once the data contract and its members are defined, you can choose to include that information in a service contract as follows:

```
[ServiceContract]
public interface IBuyStock
{
    [OperationContract]
    Void BuySomeStock(BuyStock stock);
}
```

Each data contract must have a unique name, but as a default these values are pulled from the class. It is important to also note that each member of the contract must be explicitly defined using the [DataMember] attribute. This helps to ensure that the developer meant to expose the data.

Like the [ServiceContract] attribute, the [DataContract] attribute has a number of parameters that are used to specify details about the contract. Those attributes are discussed next.

Name

The Name property is used to get or set the name of the data contract. This property is used as the name of the type in the XML schema. If this property is left blank, the default name is taken from the class in which the attribute is applied.

In the following example, the Name property sets the name to StockPurchase:

```
[DataContract(Name="StockPurchase")]
public class BuyStock
{
    ...
}
```

Usually the default name is sufficient, but there are a couple of reasons why changing the name would be beneficial:

❏ To allow the creation of XML element names that are considered invalid as type names. For example, "%Name" is an invalid type name but is a valid value for this property.

❏ There might be a mismatch between the data and the associated contract. For example, the data contract is expecting, or requires, the element name to be "CompanyName," but the typed name is actually "Name." In this case the contract would fail because of the discrepancy. However, using the Name property solves this problem by letting you define or provide a name for the contract, so in this example you would set the property to a value of "CompanyName."

Namespace

The Namespace parameter, a URI, specifies the namespace for the data contract. The default value for this parameter comes from the CLR namespace. The following example specifies a namespace to identify the data contract:

```
[DataContract(Namespace="http://www.WonderBooks.com")]
public class BookOrder
{
    ...
}
```

[DataMember] Attribute

The [DataMember] attribute is applied to all members of the data contract type to identify it as a data member. Specifying this attribute identifies that member as member whose data will be serialized by the DataContractSerializer.

Just like the [DataContract] attribute, the [DataMember] attribute has a number of parameters to help specify details of the data member.

EmitDefaultValue

The EmitDefaultValue property specifies whether or not to serialize the default value for a field or property being serialized. Types have a concept of default values within the .NET Framework. As such, WCF can take advantage of this by omitting a data member from the serialized data because it has a default value and the data member is set to the default value.

The default value for this property is true, so to take advantage of this functionality the property value must be set to false. In fact, setting the property value to true is not recommended and should only be used to decrease the size of the message or for interoperability reasons.

The following sets the EmitDefaultValue property to false on several data members:

```
[DataContract]
public class BookOrder
{
    [DataMember]
    public string BookTitle = null;

    [DataMember]
```

```
    public int OrderQuantity = 0;

    [DataMember(EmitDefaultValue=false)]
    public string Address2 = null;

    [DataMember(EmitDefaultValue=false)]
    public string Country = null;

}
```

In this example, the BookTitle and OrderQuantity values will be written because the EmitDefaultValue property is defaulting to true, yet the Address2 and Country data members will not be written because the EmitDefaultValue for those data members have specifically been set to false.

IsRequired

The IsRequired parameter is used to inform the serialization engine that a data member must be present. A value of true indicates that a member must be present. If false, a member is not required.

The following example tells the serialization engine that the symbol member of the data contract is not required:

```
[DataContract]
public class BuyStock
{
    [DataMember(IsRequired="false"]
    public string symbol;
}
```

Name

The Name property is used to get or set the name of the data member. This property overrides the default name of the data member. If this property is not specified, the default name is taken from the method that the attribute is applied to.

In the following example, the Name property sets the name to UserLogin:

```
[DataContract]
public class BuyStock
{
    [DataMember(Name="Symb"]
    public string symbol;
}
```

Had the Name property not been specified, the default would have been Symbol.

Order

The Order parameter is used to specify the order in which the data members are serialized and deserialized. In other words, the order determines how the data is to be sent or received (and as such, where it will be physically located) in the XML.

143

The following example illustrates how to specify the processing order of the data members:

```
[DataContract]
public class BuyStock
{
    [DataMember(Order=0)] public string symbol;
    [DataMember(Order=1)] public int quantity;
    [DataMember(Order=2)] public decimal price;
}
```

As a note, there are a few rules when determining order:

❑ If a data contract type is part of an inheritance hierarchy, data members of its base types are always ordered first.

❑ The current type's data members that do not have the Order property set are next in order, in ascending order.

❑ Any members that have the Order property set follow next. The order of these are determined by the Order property first, then alphabetically if more than one of a certain order exists.

[KnownType] Attribute

When data is transmitted between a sender and receiver, a type needs to be found at runtime for the data arriving at the receiver. The type is looked for by searching all of the available known types. These known types are specified via the [KnownType] attribute. The [KnownType] attribute provides the ability to specify the types that should be used for deserialization, and it lets you specify these types in advance.

The [KnownType] attribute is specified in addition to the [DataContract] attribute as shown in the following example:

```
[DataContract]
[KnownType]
public class BuyStock
{
    . . .
}
```

There are two properties, or parameters, that can be specified with this attribute: MethodName and Type. Both are discussed next.

MethodName

The MethodName property specifies the name of the method that contains a list of types recognized during serialization. The referenced method must be a static method, must accept no parameters, and return an array of Type objects.

In the following example, the MethodName parameter is used to specify a method:

```
[DataContract]
[KnownType(TypeOf(NumberTypes))]
```

```
public class BuyStock
{
  ...
}

[DataContract]
public class NumberTypes : BuyStock
{
  Public NumberTypes(double StockPrice)
  ...
}
```

Type

The Type property returns the type recognized by the DataContractSerializer during the serialization or deserialization process. The DataContractSerializer serializes and deserializes an instance of a type into either an XML stream or document via the data contract.

Message Contracts

Message contracts provide the ultimate control over the formatting of the SOAP messages. In most cases you will not need to employ this level because data contracts provide most of the control you will need. However, should the need arise for this level of customization, message contracts are available.

Probably the biggest reason you would need to obtain this level of control is interoperability. A message contract provides the level of interoperability you would need when you need to communicate with clients or other systems that may use a particular WSDL or schema, or cases when there is some question or concern regarding the SOAP message structure, such as controlling security issues.

What message contracts allow you to do is to have more control over the way contract parameters are formatted in SOAP messages, such as whether or not information goes in the message body or message headers. You should keep in mind that WCF does this automatically, but if you want to override this, you need to use message contracts.

Message contracts are defined just like all the other attributes you have learned about so far in this chapter. This section discusses the [MessageContract], [MessageHeader], and [MessageBodyMember] attributes along with their associated parameters.

[MessageContract] Attribute

Message contracts are defined by applying the [MessageContract] attribute. You then specify specifics for each message using the [MessageBodyMember] and [MessageHeader] attributes. The following example illustrates these three attributes by defining a simple message contract:

```
[MessageContract]
public class BuyStock
{
  [MessageHeader]
  Public string Title;
  [MessageBodyMember]
  Public decimal Cost;
}
```

The [MessageContract] attribute defines a strongly typed class that is associated with a SOAP message. This in turn creates a typed message, which then enables the passing of messages between services (service operations). It also provides the ability to use custom messages as parameters within these same services (and service operations).

The following sections discuss the available parameters that can be used with the [MessageContract] attribute.

HasProtectionLevel

The HasProtectionLevel parameter specifies the message protection level. A message can be encrypted, signed, or both. The available values for this property are true and false. If the value is set to true, the message must be either encrypted, signed, or both. A value of false means that no protection level is needed. The default value is false.

The following example indicates that the message has a protection level:

```
[MessageContract(HasProtectionLevel=true)]
public class BookOrder
{
    ...
}
```

IsWrapped

A message can be formatted in several ways. One of those ways is the document/wrapper form. In this XML document form, the outer XML element is called the wrapper element.

The IsWrapped parameter is a Boolean value that specifies that the message is in the document/wrapper form and that the XML document contains a wrapper element:

```
[MessageContract(IsWrapped = True)]
public class BookOrder
{
    ...
}
```

PretectionLevel

The ProtectionLevel property specifies the protection level of the message. The message can be encrypted, signed, or both.

The value of this parameter comes from the System.Net.SecurityLevel.ProtectionLevel enumeration. The following enumeration values are available:

- ❑ **EncryptAndSign:** Encrypt and sign data to ensure the confidentiality and integrity of transmitted data.
- ❑ **None:** Authentication only.
- ❑ **Sign:** Sign data to help ensure the integrity of the transmitted data, but do not encrypt.

The following example sets the protection level of the service contract to that of None, meaning that only simple authentication is required:

```
[MessageContract(ProtectionLevel = System.Net.Security.ProtectionLevel.None)]
public interface IBookOrder
{
    ...
}
```

WrapperName

The WrapperName parameter works in conjunction with the IsWrapped parameter, in that if the IsWrapped parameter is True, this parameter specifies the name of the outer XML element. The following example illustrates how to use the WrapperName parameter:

```
[MessageContract(IsWrapped=true, WrapperName="Order")]
public class BookOrder
{
    ...
}
```

WrapperNamespace

The WrapperNamespace parameter also works in tangent with the IsWrapped parameter. This parameter allows you to set the namespace of the wrapper element. The following example uses the WrapperNamespace of the XML element on the associated message contract:

```
[MessageContract(IsWrapped=true, WrapperNamespace="http://www.WonderBooks.com",
WrapperName="Order")]
public class BookOrder
{
    ...
}
```

[MessageHeader] Attribute

The [MessageHeader] attribute maps a SOAP message header to fields and properties of a type marked with the [MessageHeader] attribute. The fields or properties can be a simple or composite type that can be serialized:

```
[MessageContract]
public class BuyBook
{
    [MessageHeader]
    Public string Title;
}
```

The following sections list the available parameters used with the [MessageHeader] attribute. As a note, Windows Communication Foundation does not process any of the following attribute properties on incoming messages except for the MustUnderstand property. You can, however, read and write these attributes.

Actor

As messages are sent from sender to receiver, WCF provides a mechanism to specify that a specific message is targeted to a specific endpoint. The Actor parameter provides this functionality in that it allows you to specify the node in which the message header is targeted:

```
[MessageContract]
public class BuyBook
{
   [MessageHeader(Actor="http://http://www.WonderBooks.com/WCF2")]
   Public string Title;
}
```

The version of SOAP being used determines the attribute mapping. In SOAP 1.1, the attribute is mapped to the actor header, whereas in SOAP 1.2 this is mapped to the role header attribute.

MustUnderstand

The MustUnderstand parameter is used in conjunction with the Actor parameter. The MustUnderstand parameter is a true/false parameter. If this parameter is set to True, the URI specified in the Actor parameter must understand the associated incoming header in order to appropriately process the header.

The following example shows the Actor and MustUnderstand parameters in use:

```
[MessageContract]
public class BuyBook
{
   [MessageHeader(Actor="http://http://www.WonderBooks.com/WCF2"
MustUnderstand="true")]
   Public string Title;
}
```

It should be noted that a fault will be generated if the MustUnderstand property is set to true and the receiving application does not understand the header. WCF does not process any message header attributes on incoming messages other than the MustUnderstand attribute.

Name

The Name parameter specifies the name of the message contract element. The value specified must be a valid XML element name:

```
[MessageContract]
public class BuyBook
{
   [MessageHeader(Name="Title")]
}
```

Namespace

The Namespace parameter specifies the namespace of the message contract element:

```
[MessageContract]
public class BuyBook
{
   [MessageHeader(Namespace="http://www.WonderBooks.com/WCF2/Title")]
}
```

Relay

The Relay parameter tells the endpoint that it is processing the message to pass, or relay, the message to the next endpoint specified in the Actor parameter once the current endpoint is finished processing the message:

```
[MessageContract]
public class BuyBook
{
   [MessageHeader(Actor="http://http://www.WonderBooks.com/WCF2" Relay="true")]
   Public string Title;
   [MessageHeader(Actor="http://http://www.WonderBooks.com/WCF3" Relay="false")]
   Public string Title;
}
```

[MessageBodyMember] Attribute

The [MessageBodyMember] attribute identifies the members who are to be serialized as a SOAP body element:

```
[MessageContract]
public class BookOrder
{

   [MessageHeader]
   public string ISBN

   [MessageBodyMember]
   public int Quantity
```

This code snippet defines a message contract, as well a message header and a message body member. The value of ISBN will be a data member as a SOAP message header, and the value of Quantity will be serialized into the SOAP body.

Name

The Name property of the [MessageBodyMember] attribute defines the name of the element for this member:

```
[MessageContract]
public class BookOrder
{

   [MessageHeader]
   public string ISBN

   [MessageBodyMember(Name="BookOrderQuantity"]
   public int Quantity
```

This property must follow XML standards and be a valid XML element. For example, in this code snippet, the Name parameter is applied to the `[MessageBodyMember]` attribute with a value of BookOrderQuantity, which will be the name of the SOAP message XML element.

Order

The Order property of the `[MessageBodyMember]` attribute specifies the ordinal position in which each message body member will be serialized into the SOAP message body:

```
[MessageContract]
public class BookOrder
{

  [MessageHeader]
  public string ISBN

  [MessageBodyMember(Order=1)]
  public int Quantity

  [MessageBodyMember(Order=2)]
  public string FirstName

  [MessageBodyMember(Order=3)]
  public string LastName
```

In this example, the Order attribute is applied to all the `[MessageBodyMember]` attributes in the message contract, thus the XML SOAP message will contain the XML elements in the specified order. If no Order parameter is specified, the elements are ordered alphabetically.

[MessageProperty] Attribute

Last, but not least, is the `[MessageProperty]` attribute. The attribute specifies those members who will not be serialized into the SOAP message, but contains data that is included with a custom message:

```
[MessageContract]
public class BookOrder
{

  [MessageHeader]
  public string ISBN

  [MessageProperty]
  public string FirstName
  {
    get { return firstname; }
    set { firstname = value; }
  }
```

This attribute allows you to attach data to a custom message and pass it through the WCF system without it being serialized.

Name

Like all the other Name properties, this Name property lets you give a name to the MessageProperty:

```
[MessageContract]
public class BookOrder
{

  [MessageHeader]
  public string ISBN

  [MessageProperty(Name="BuyerFirstName"]
  public string FirstName
  {
    get { return firstname; }
    set { firstname = value; }
  }
```

Programming WCF Contracts

OK, enough of the detail stuff and time to get to the good part. Dust off your mouse and fire up Visual Studio.

The examples you have done up until this chapter, specifically in Chapters 3 and 5, used contracts in their service definition. The example in Chapter 5 defined a service contract along with several operation contracts. The examples in this chapter, while still utilizing service and operation contracts, focus on the other contract types you learned about in this chapter, specifically, data and message contracts.

This next section walks you through two examples. The first example is building and consuming a data contract. The second example does the same using a message contract.

Data Contract

Open up your WCFService project. Before you write any code, a new reference needs to be added to the project. In Solution Explorer, right-click Add Reference. When the Add Reference dialog opens, verify that the .NET tab is selected and scroll down until you see the System.Runtime.Serialization namespace. This namespace is necessary to work with data contracts. Why? As explained earlier in the chapter, when the client and service communicate, they do not need to share the same types; they only need to share the same data contracts. These data contracts define what will be serialized and deserialized in order for the two to communicate. The System.Runtime.Serialization namespace, new to the .NET 3.0 Framework, performs these functions.

So, add the reference, and then modify your service code to look like the following:

```
using System;
using System.ServiceModel;
using System.Collections.Generic;
using System.Runtime.Serialization;
```

```
using System.IO;

namespace WCFService
{
    [ServiceContract]
    public interface IServiceClass
    {
        [OperationContract]
        ExplicitNumbers Add(ExplicitNumbers en1, ExplicitNumbers en2);
        [OperationContract]
        ExplicitNumbers Subtract(ExplicitNumbers en1, ExplicitNumbers en2);
    }

    [DataContract]
    public class ExplicitNumbers
    {
        [DataMember]
        public double Explicit1;

        [DataMember]
        public double Explicit2;

        public ExplicitNumbers(double explicit1, double explicit2)
        {
            this.Explicit1 = explicit1;
            this.Explicit2 = explicit2;
        }
    }

    public class ServiceClass : IServiceClass
    {

        public ExplicitNumbers Add(ExplicitNumbers en1, ExplicitNumbers en2)
        {
            return new ExplicitNumbers(en1.Explicit1 + en2.Explicit1, en1.Explicit2
+ en2.Explicit2);
        }

        public ExplicitNumbers Subtract(ExplicitNumbers en1, ExplicitNumbers en2)
        {
            return new ExplicitNumbers(en1.Explicit1 - en2.Explicit1, en1.Explicit2
- en2.Explicit2);
        }
    }
}
```

A lot of this should look familiar, and some of it should look new. The [ServiceContract] and [OperationContract] pieces should look familiar because all of the examples have used them, and if you remember, those attributes define the service and its operations.

What should look new to you is the [DataContract] and [DataMember] attributes. These two attributes are part of the System.Runtime.Serialization namespace. In fact, if you try and add those attributes prior to adding the namespace, those attributes will not show up as attribute options.

Once the service and operations are defined, the very next statements define the data contract, that is, what data will be turned into XML (serialized). In this example, two data members are defined, Explicit1 and Explicit2, both with a data type of double. Both the [DataContract] and [DataMember] attributes are applied to the definition of the ExplicitNumbers class telling the service what will be available to communicate.

After you have made the code changes to the service, compile and build the service. The next step is to modify the host to accommodate the service. Realistically, no code changes need to be made to the host, but this example modifies the host configuration file.

In the WCFServiceHost application, modify the app.config to look like the following:

```xml
<?xml version="1.0" encoding="utf-8" ?>
<configuration>
  <system.serviceModel>
    <services>
      <service name ="WCFService.ServiceClass"
behaviorConfiguration="metadataSupport">
        <host>
          <baseAddresses>
            <add baseAddress="http://localhost:8080/WCFService"/>
            <add baseAddress="net.pipe://localhost/WCFService"/>
            <add baseAddress="net.tcp://localhost:8000/WCFService"/>
          </baseAddresses>
        </host>
        <endpoint address="" binding="wsHttpBinding"
contract="WCFService.IServiceClass"/>
        <endpoint address="tcpmex"
                  binding="mexTcpBinding"
                  contract="IMetadataExchange"/>
        <endpoint address="namedpipemex"
                  binding="mexNamedPipeBinding"
                  contract="IMetadataExchange"/>
      </service>
    </services>
    <behaviors>
      <serviceBehaviors>
        <behavior name="metadataSupport">
          <serviceMetadata httpGetEnabled="false" httpGetUrl=""/>
        </behavior>
      </serviceBehaviors>
    </behaviors>
  </system.serviceModel>
</configuration>
```

The changes were made to the host config to dig a little deeper into service addressing. Realistically, you probably didn't need to make any changes to the config, but the purpose of these examples is to build upon each example to increase your knowledge and understanding of how WCF works.

Thus, this example does addressing more correctly. How? All of the examples up until this point have used absolute addresses and have contained no base addresses. Not that that is necessarily bad, but using absolute addresses and no base addresses is fairly fragile. The more flexible way to accomplish addressing is to specify a base address so that you can use relative ones. This makes the service available at the base address. In the programmatic version, meaning, when using code to define the addresses and endpoints, you don't usually have to think about the base address. However, you do when using a configuration file. A base address must be provided in order for automatic metadata publication to work, unless an absolute address is supplied in your endpoints or for the httpGetUrl property.

You should have a better understanding of addresses, both base and relative, by now, so the next step is to move on to the client. Open the WCFClientApp project. If you haven't made any changes to it, specifically the service references, right-click each reference and delete them. This example re-adds them using the new addressing.

Once you have service references deleted, add back the two references. Add the TCP reference back, as shown in Figure 6-1. Remember that to add the service references you will need to run the host application.

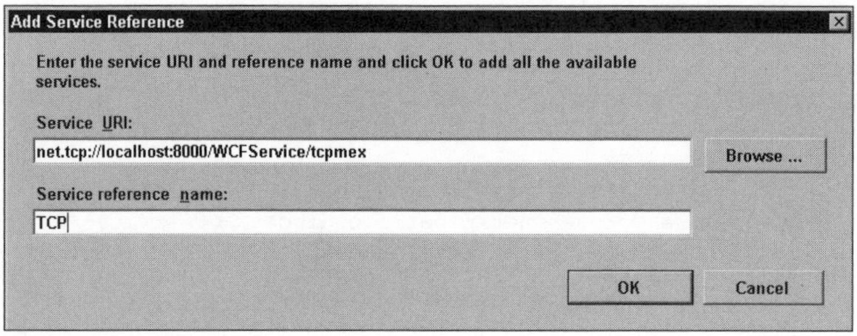

Add Service Reference

Enter the service URI and reference name and click OK to add all the available services.

Service URI:

net.tcp://localhost:8000/WCFService/tcpmex   Browse ...

Service reference name:

TCP

OK   Cancel

Figure 6-1

Notice the difference in the Service URI in the preceding figure versus the Service URI you have used previously. The difference is that you are referencing the service via a combination of the TCP base address (net.pipe://localhost/WCFService) and the endpoint relative address (tcpmex).

Specify the service reference name of TCP (same name you have used previously).

Now add the service reference to the Named Pipe transport, as shown in Figure 6-2.

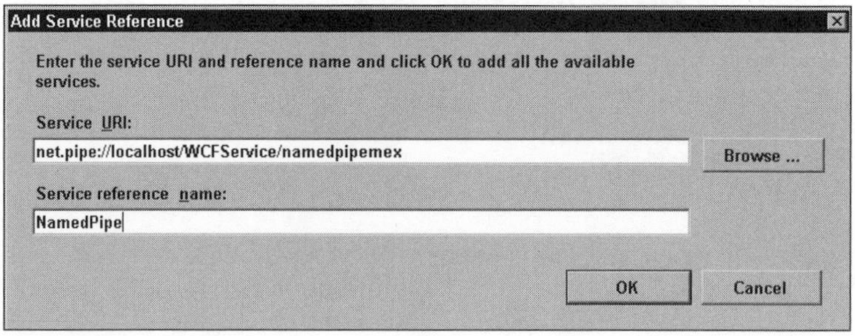

Add Service Reference

Enter the service URI and reference name and click OK to add all the available services.

Service URI:

net.pipe://localhost/WCFService/namedpipemex   Browse ...

Service reference name:

NamedPipe

OK   Cancel

Figure 6-2

The same concept for a service URI applies here as it did when adding the TCP service reference. The URI is a combination of the Named Pipe base address and the endpoint relative address.

The next step is to make some modifications to the form and to modify the client code. Open Form1 in design mode and add two more text boxes, and change the caption of button1 to "Go - Add" and the caption of button2 to "Go - Subtract". Next, modify the client code as follows:

```
using System;
using System.Collections.Generic;
using System.ComponentModel;
using System.Data;
using System.Drawing;
using System.Text;
using System.Windows.Forms;
using System.ServiceModel;

namespace WCFClientApp
{
  public partial class Form1 : Form
  {
    private int _Selection;

    public Form1()
    {
      InitializeComponent();
    }

    private void button1_Click(object sender, EventArgs e)
    {
      switch (_Selection)
      {
        case 0:
          TCP.ServiceClassClient client = new
WCFClientApp.TCP.ServiceClassClient("WSHttpBinding_IServiceClass");

          WCFClientApp.TCP.ExplicitNumbers Val1 = new
WCFClientApp.TCP.ExplicitNumbers();
          Val1.Explicit1 = 2;
          Val1.Explicit2 = 4;

          WCFClientApp.TCP.ExplicitNumbers Val2 = new
WCFClientApp.TCP.ExplicitNumbers();

          Val2.Explicit1 = 6;
          Val2.Explicit2 = 8;

          WCFClientApp.TCP.ExplicitNumbers result = client.Add(Val1, Val2);
          textBox1.Text = result.Explicit1.ToString();
          textBox3.Text = result.Explicit2.ToString();
          break;

        case 1:
          NamedPipe.ServiceClassClient client1 = new
WCFClientApp.NamedPipe.ServiceClassClient("WSHttpBinding_IServiceClass1");

          WCFClientApp.NamedPipe.ExplicitNumbers Val3 = new
          WCFClientApp.NamedPipe.ExplicitNumbers();
          Val3.Explicit1 = 1;
```

```
            Val3.Explicit2 = 3;

            WCFClientApp.NamedPipe.ExplicitNumbers Val4 = new
        WCFClientApp.NamedPipe.ExplicitNumbers();
            Val4.Explicit1 = 5;
            Val4.Explicit2 = 7;

            WCFClientApp.NamedPipe.ExplicitNumbers result1 = client1.Add(Val3, Val4);
            textBox1.Text = result1.Explicit1.ToString();
            textBox3.Text = result1.Explicit2.ToString();
            break;

        case 2:
            break;
        }
    }

    private void button2_Click(object sender, EventArgs e)
    {
      switch (_Selection)
      {
        case 0:
          TCP.ServiceClassClient client = new
WCFClientApp.TCP.ServiceClassClient("WSHttpBinding_IServiceClass");

            WCFClientApp.TCP.ExplicitNumbers Val1 = new
        WCFClientApp.TCP.ExplicitNumbers();
            Val1.Explicit1 = 8;
            Val1.Explicit2 = 6;

            WCFClientApp.TCP.ExplicitNumbers Val2 = new
        WCFClientApp.TCP.ExplicitNumbers();
            Val2.Explicit1 = 4;
            Val2.Explicit2 = 2;

            WCFClientApp.TCP.ExplicitNumbers result = client.Subtract(Val1, Val2);
            textBox2.Text = result.Explicit1.ToString();
            textBox4.Text = result.Explicit2.ToString();
            break;

        case 1:
          NamedPipe.ServiceClassClient client1 = new
WCFClientApp.NamedPipe.ServiceClassClient("WSHttpBinding_IServiceClass1");

            WCFClientApp.NamedPipe.ExplicitNumbers Val3 = new
        WCFClientApp.NamedPipe.ExplicitNumbers();
            Val3.Explicit1 = 7;
            Val3.Explicit2 = 5;

            WCFClientApp.NamedPipe.ExplicitNumbers Val4 = new
        WCFClientApp.NamedPipe.ExplicitNumbers();
            Val4.Explicit1 = 3;
            Val4.Explicit2 = 1;

            WCFClientApp.NamedPipe.ExplicitNumbers result1 = client1.Subtract(Val3, Val4);
```

```
        textBox2.Text = result1.Explicit1.ToString();
        textBox4.Text = result1.Explicit2.ToString();
        break;

     case 2:
       break;

  }
}

private void radioButton1_CheckedChanged(object sender, EventArgs e)
{
  _Selection = 0;
  textBox2.Text = "";
  textBox1.Text = "";
  textBox3.Text = "";
  textBox4.Text = "";
}

private void radioButton2_CheckedChanged(object sender, EventArgs e)
{
  _Selection = 1;
  textBox2.Text = "";
  textBox1.Text = "";
  textBox3.Text = "";
  textBox4.Text = "";
}

private void Form1_Load(object sender, EventArgs e)
{
  radioButton1.Checked = true;
}
}
}
```

Once you have made the changes, run the client application. Select the desired transport and click either the Add or Subtract button. The results will look like those shown in Figure 6-3.

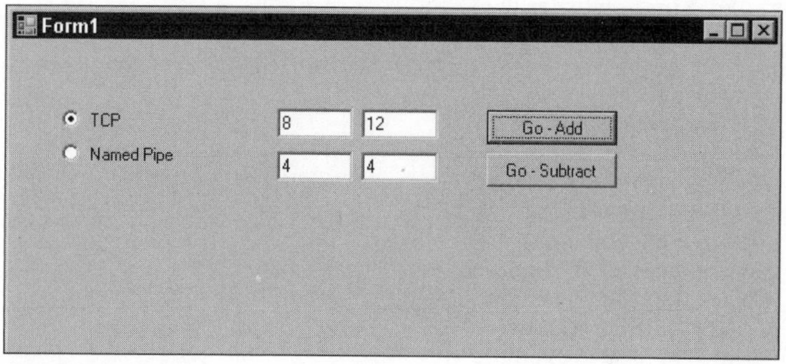

Figure 6-3

In this example, both the client and service use complex numbers. Taking a look at the client code, an instance of the ExplicitNumbers type is created and used to take two numbers and pass them to the service. Those numbers are accepted, calculated, and returned to the client. The data contract is defined on the service and understood by the client when the ExplicitNumbers type is instantiated.

Message Contract

This next example focuses on the use of a message contract. As explained earlier, message contracts exist to provide increased control of the structure of the message and the data in the SOAP message. However, the majority of the time the functionality can be accomplished by using data contracts and defining the message schema. Message contracts provide better control and flexibility, such as letting you map specific types to SOAP messages and adding custom SOAP headers.

This section defines a simple message contract to help illustrate how message contracts are used. A custom user-defined message is defined to pass between the client and the service.

Go back to the WCFService project and modify the service code as follows:

```
using System;
using System.ServiceModel;
using System.Collections.Generic;
using System.Runtime.Serialization;
using System.IO;

namespace WCFService
{
    [ServiceContract]
    public interface IServiceClass
    {
        [OperationContract]
        string InitiateOrder();

        [OperationContract]
        BookOrder PlaceOrder(BookOrder request);

        [OperationContract]
        string FinalizeOrder();
    }

    [MessageContract]
    public class BookOrder
    {

        private string isbn;
        private int quantity;
        private string firstname;
        private string lastname;
        private string address;
        private string ordernumber;

        public BookOrder(BookOrder message)
        {
```

```
            this.isbn = message.isbn;
            this.quantity = message.quantity;
            this.firstname = message.firstname;
            this.lastname = message.lastname;
            this.address = message.address;
            this.ordernumber = message.ordernumber;
        }

        [MessageHeader]
        public string ISBN
        {
            get { return isbn; }
            set { isbn = value; }
        }

        [MessageBodyMember]
        public int Quantity
        {
            get { return quantity; }
            set { quantity = value; }
        }

        [MessageBodyMember]
        public string FirstName
        {
            get { return firstname; }
            set { firstname = value; }
        }

        [MessageBodyMember]
        public string LastName
        {
            get { return lastname; }
            set { lastname = value; }
        }

        [MessageBodyMember]
        public string Address
        {
            get { return address; }
            set { address = value; }
        }

        [MessageBodyMember]
        public string OrderNumber
        {
            get { return ordernumber; }
            set { ordernumber = value; }
        }

    }

public class ServiceClass : IServiceClass
{
```

```
string IServiceClass.InitiateOrder()
{
    return "Initiating Order...";
}

public BookOrder PlaceOrder(BookOrder request)
{
    BookOrder response = new BookOrder(request);
    response.OrderNumber = "12345678";
    return response;
}

string IServiceClass.FinalizeOrder()
{
    return "Order placed successfully.";
}


    }
}
```

Before continuing, take a look at the preceding code. In this example, a custom message that contains the order information for a book is defined and passed between the client and service. The message contains a single message header and a small handful of message body members. Together, these make up the custom message.

The header contains the ISBN number of a book (this one, to be exact), and the body contains information about the person placing the order. The message is sent to, and processed by, the service that contains the message. When the message is processed, an order number is updated in the message and the message is sent back to the client for processing.

The great part is that because this is WCF no changes need to be made in the host application. And even if any changes were needed, you can make them directly in the configuration file, negating the need for a recompilation.

There are still changes that need to be made to the client application. Add a few more message boxes so that you have a total of six. Align them horizontally, and set the enabled property of the bottom text box to False. Next, remove one of the buttons and add two labels below the remaining button, and add six more labels to the left of the text boxes as labels for the text boxes. From the top label down, label them as ISBN, Quantity, First Name, Last Name, Address, and Order Number. Next, change the caption of the button to Place Order. Your form should look something like Figure 6-4. Keep in mind, you're not shooting for an aesthetically pleasing UI, but for functionality.

Lastly, modify the underlying code to look like the following:

```
using System;
using System.Collections.Generic;
using System.ComponentModel;
using System.Data;
using System.Drawing;
using System.Text;
using System.Windows.Forms;
```

```csharp
using System.ServiceModel;

namespace WCFClientApp
{
    public partial class Form1 : Form
    {
        private int _Selection;

        public Form1()
        {
            InitializeComponent();
        }

        private void button1_Click(object sender, EventArgs e)
        {
            int intval;

            switch (_Selection)
            {
                case 0:
                    TCP.ServiceClassClient client = new
WCFClientApp.TCP.ServiceClassClient("WSHttpBinding_IServiceClass");

                    lblResponse1.Text = client.InitiateOrder();

                    WCFClientApp.TCP.BookOrder Val1 = new
WCFClientApp.TCP.BookOrder();
                    Val1.ISBN = textBox1.Text;
                    int.TryParse(textBox2.Text, out intval);
                    Val1.Quantity = intval;
                    Val1.FirstName = textBox3.Text;
                    Val1.LastName = textBox4.Text;
                    Val1.Address = textBox5.Text;

                    WCFClientApp.TCP.BookOrder result = client.PlaceOrder(Val1);
                    textBox2.Text = Val1.OrderNumber;

                    lblResponse2.Text = client.FinalizeOrder();

                    client.Close();

                    break;

                case 1:
                    NamedPipe.ServiceClassClient client1 = new
WCFClientApp.NamedPipe.ServiceClassClient("WSHttpBinding_IServiceClass1");

                    lblResponse1.Text = client1.InitiateOrder();

                    WCFClientApp.NamedPipe.BookOrder Val2 = new
WCFClientApp.NamedPipe.BookOrder();
                    Val2.ISBN = textBox1.Text;
```

```
                int.TryParse(textBox2.Text, out intval);
                Val2.Quantity = intval;
                Val2.FirstName = textBox3.Text;
                Val2.LastName = textBox4.Text;
                Val2.Address = textBox5.Text;

                WCFClientApp.TCP.BookOrder result = client.PlaceOrder(Val2);
                textBox2.Text = Val2.OrderNumber;

                lblResponse2.Text = client1.FinalizeOrder();

                client1.Close();

                break;

          case 2:
                break;
      }
}

private void radioButton1_CheckedChanged(object sender, EventArgs e)
{
    _Selection = 0;
    textBox1.Text = "";
    textBox2.Text = "";
    textBox3.Text = "";
    textBox4.Text = "";
    textBox5.Text = "";
    textBox6.Text = "";
}

private void radioButton2_CheckedChanged(object sender, EventArgs e)
{
    _Selection = 1;
    textBox1.Text = "";
    textBox2.Text = "";
    textBox3.Text = "";
    textBox4.Text = "";
    textBox5.Text = "";
    textBox6.Text = "";
}

private void Form1_Load(object sender, EventArgs e)
{
    radioButton1.Checked = true;
}

    }
}
```

Run the host application followed by the client application. When the form opens, enter the information displayed in Figure 6-4 and click the Place Order button.

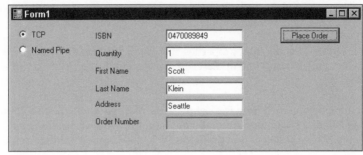

Figure 6-4

You should immediately get back an order number, which will be displayed in the Order Number text box, as shown in Figure 6-5. You should also get back processing information in the labels below the button letting you know that the order is initiating, and a final feedback letting you know the order has been placed.

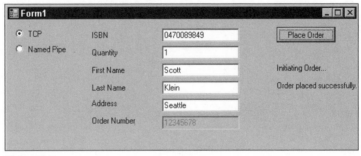

Figure 6-5

When the Place Order button was clicked, the service sent the defined custom message to the client, which then filled out the message header and message body members with information. The message was then sent back when the PlaceOrder method was called, at which point the service processed the message.

Realistically, instead of returning a simple order number, the PlaceOrder method could be expanded to do much more, such as verifying that the book is in stock, looking up title information, and so on. But you get the concept, which is the purpose of this example. A message was defined and passed back and forth between the client and service containing custom-defined information.

Summary

The purpose of this chapter was to dig deep into contracts and to help you understand the different aspects of the functionality they provide. A couple of examples were provided to introduce you to data and message contracts. You have been using service contracts throughout the book so you should have a good understanding of how they work. However, this chapter did spend some time covering the different properties and parameters available to the `[ServiceContract]` attribute.

This chapter also covered the different properties and parameters for the `[DataContract]` and `[MessageContract]` attributes. More of these are explored in later chapters as different communication patterns are discussed.

With the information you learned from the last three chapters (4, 5, and 6), you should have a good understanding of Windows Communication Foundation from the service side (and a little from the client side). Chapter 7 changes focus and discusses WCF and communication from the client side.

7

Clients

Up until now this book has mainly focused WCF service implementations. The last three chapters have discussed the components necessary to build a Windows Communication Foundation service. Chapter 4 discussed addresses, Chapter 5 discussed bindings, and Chapter 6 discussed contracts. Each of these is essential in building a successful service. It is time, however, to change the focus and take a good look at the client, the piece of the equation that utilizes everything you have learned so far.

This chapter covers the following topics:

- ❑ Client architecture
- ❑ Client communication patterns
- ❑ Creating client code
- ❑ Defining client bindings and endpoints

Client Architecture

A Windows Communication Foundation client is an application used to invoke functionality exposed by a service. The client application will communicate with the service via a service endpoint. In order to do that the client needs to know several pieces of information about the service, such as the address at which the endpoint is communicating, the binding the service is using, and the service contract. Each of these elements has been discussed in the previous chapters.

A good look under the hood of a client will reveal some important things about its makeup. One of the things you will find is a channel built on binding settings specified in the configuration file. Just to be clear, these bindings are the same bindings that have been discussed in the past couple of chapters. These bindings allow the client and service to appropriately and effectively communicate.

The second thing you will find is the implementation of the IClientChannel interface. This interface defines the operations that allow developers to control channel functionality, such as closing the client session and disposing of the channel. It exposes the methods and functionality of the SystemServiceModel.ChannelFactory class.

Lastly, you will find a generated service contract, which provides the functionality that turns client method calls into outgoing messages, and turns incoming messages into information that your client application can readily use in the form of return values and output parameters.

Clients communicate with service endpoints through a proxy, as shown in Figure 7-1. A proxy class is what the client manipulates to communicate to a service. This communication takes place via a channel. Once that proxy (and channel) is created, the client can access any exposed methods (service operations) on that endpoint.

Figure 7-1

There are two ways to create client proxies, both of which are discussed in this chapter:

❑ The first method is to create the proxy from generated code, that is, code that is automatically generated from the metadata provided by the service. This is done by using the Service Model Metadata Utility Tool Svcutil.exe. The Svcutil utility creates an instance of the derived class ClientBase that is then accessible to the client.

❑ The second method is by creating the proxy dynamically through code using a ChannelFactory object. This is provided by the System.ServiceModel.ChannelFactory class. This method allows for greater control by the developer, such as creating new client channels from an existing channel factory.

Client Objects

A Windows Communication Foundation client must contain two base object interfaces, the ICommunicationObject interface and the IExtensibleObject interface.

ICommunicationObject

The ICommunicationObject interface is one of the core components that define basic communication object functionality. The responsibility of this object is to define the contract for the basic state for all communication objects in the system; for example, is the communication object opened or closed, or in the process of opening or closing. These objects include channels, listeners, dispatchers, factories, and service hosts.

A state transition is the transition from one state to another; for example, the communication channel transitioning from an "opening" state to an "open" state.

This interface defines a set of methods for initiating state transitions. These methods are:

- **Open:** Causes a communication object to transition from the Created state to the Opened state.
- **Close:** Causes a communication object to transition from its current state to the Closed state.
- **Abort:** Causes a communication object to instantly transition from its current state into the Closed state.

This interface also defines notification events for state transitions. These include:

- **Opening:** This event is fired when the communication object transitions from Created to Opened, such as when the Open or BeginOpen method is invoked.
- **Closing:** This event is fired when the communication object transitions from Opened to Closed, such as when the Close or BeginClose method is invoked.
- **Opened:** This event is fired when the communication object is finished transitioning from Opening to Opened.
- **Closed:** This event is fired when the communication object is finished transitioning from Closing to Closed.
- **Faulted:** This event is fired when the communication object enters the Faulted state.

This interface also includes a set of methods that define asynchronous versions of the Open and Close methods:

- **BeginOpen:** Begins an asynchronous operation to open a communication object.
- **BeginClose:** Begins an asynchronous operation to close a communication object.
- **EndOpen:** Completes an asynchronous operation to open a communication object.
- **EndClose:** Completes an asynchronous operation to close a communication object.

This interface has a single State property, of type CommunicationState, which is used to return the current state of the object.

When an ICommunicationObject is instantiated, its default state is Created. This is not readily intuitive because many assume that it's defaulted to Opened. While in the Created state, the ICommunicationObject can be configured but it cannot send or receive communication. For example, any of the events listed earlier can be registered. Once the object is in the Open state, it can send and receive messages, but it no longer can be configured.

The Open method must be called for the object to enter the Opened state. The object will stay in the Open state until its transition to the Closed state is finished. The Close method allows any unfinished work to be completed before transitioning to the Closed state. The Abort method does not exit gracefully, meaning all unfinished work is ignored. The Abort method can also be used to cancel any and all outstanding operations, and that includes outstanding calls to the Close method. Keep in mind that the Abort method will cause any unfinished work to be cancelled. Use transactions, discussed in Chapter 9, if you want work grouped as a single unit.

IExtensibleObject

The IExtensibleObject interface provides extensible behavior in the client, meaning that it enables the object to be involved in custom behaviors. In WCF, the extensible object pattern is used to add new functionality to existing runtime classes, thereby extending current components, as well as adding new state features to an object.

This interface exposes a single property to provide this functionality. The Extensions property, of type IExtenstionCollection, is used to return a collection of extension objects that can then be used to extend the existing runtime classes.

Client Channels

Windows Communication Foundation clients contain two base channel interfaces, the IClientChannel interface and the IContextChannel interface.

IClientChannel

The IClientChannel interface defines the extended ClientBase channel operations. It contains a number of methods and properties that can be used to define the outbound request channel behavior and the request/reply channel behavior of the client application.

For example, the AllowInitializationUI property can be used to tell WCF to open a channel without an explicit call to open it. There are also a small handful of methods that you can use to return the credential information.

The IClientChannel interface inherits from the IContextChannel interface (discussed next) as well as the ICommunicationObject and IExtensibleObject interfaces discussed earlier. This allows client applications to have access to client-side runtime functionality directly.

IContextChannel

The IContextChannel interface defines the session state of the channel. This information includes the SessionId, Input and Output session, as well as the local and remote endpoints that are currently communicating with the client in the session. This information is provided by the following properties:

- ❏ **InputSession:** Returns the input session for the channel.
- ❏ **OutputSession:** Returns the output session for the channel.
- ❏ **LocalAddress:** Returns the local endpoint for the channel.
- ❏ **RemoteAddress:** Returns the remote address connected with the channel.
- ❏ **SessionId:** Returns the current session identifier.
- ❏ **OperationTimeout:** Returns, or sets, the time in which the operation has to complete. If the operation does not complete in the specified time, an exception is thrown.
- ❏ **AllowOutputBatching:** Tells WCF to store messages before handing them off to the transport.

There are two AllowOutputBatching properties, one that is applied at the channel level and one that is applied at the message level. Setting the AllowOutputBatching at the message level does not override the channel-level AllowOutputBatching property. If the message-level AllowOutputBatching property is set to true, the message will be sent immediately even if the AllowOutputBatching property is set to true at the channel level.

Keep in mind that the AllowOutputBatching property can affect the performance of the system because you are telling WCF to store outgoing messages in a buffer and send them out with other messages as a group. Your message delivery needs will affect how this setting is configured. Setting this property to true means that message throughput and delivery is essential to you, and setting it to false will reduce latency.

Channel Factories

It is important that you understand the client objects and client channel objects because both of these utilize the ChannelFactory object. The ChannelFactory object is responsible for creating and supporting all the runtime client invocations.

As stated earlier, you can either create clients on demand using the ChannelFactory or by using the Service Model Metadata Utility svcutil.exe. The svcutil utility automatically generates the handling of the ChannelFactory, but as stated before, creating the channels on demand provides you more control over the creation and handling of the channels. For example, you can repeatedly create a new channel from an existing factory.

The following code illustrates using the ChannelFactory to create a channel to a service by specifying the service contract name:

```
EndpointAddress ea = new EndpointAddress("tcp.net://localhost:8000/WCFService");
BasicHttpBinding bb = new BasicHttpBinding();
WCFClientApp.TCP.IServiceClass client =
    ChannelFactory<IServiceClass>.CreateChannel(bb, ea);
client.PlaceOrder(Val1);
```

In this example, the address and binding were specified in code and passed as parameters to the CreateChannel method.

The following section details the ChannelFactory class, which is used to create and manage channels that are used by the clients to send messages and communicate with service endpoints.

ChannelFactory Class

The following sections list many of the important constructors, properties, and methods of the ChannelFactory class.

Constructors

The ChannelFactory class has a single constructor called ChannelFactory, and it is used to instantiate a new instance of the ChannelFactory class, as illustrated in the previous example. The following code snippet, taken from the previous example, shows the instantiation of the ChannelFactory class:

```
WCFClientApp.TCP.IServiceClass client =
    ChannelFactory<IServiceClass>.CreateChannel(bb, ea);
```

Properties

The following properties are exposed by the ChannelFactory class:

❑ **Credentials:** Returns the credentials used by the client to communicate with the service endpoint, via the channel created by the factory.

❑ **Endpoint:** Returns the endpoint that the channel created by the factory connect.

❑ **State:** Returns the value of the current communication object state.

The use of credentials requires a reference to the System.ServiceModel.Description namespace, which needs to be added via a `using` statement:

```
using System.ServiceModel.Description;
```

Once you have access to the System.ServiceModel.Description namespace, you can configure client and service credentials as well as provide credentials for authenticating on the proxy side. The following example illustrates how to provide credentials for proxy side authentication when creating a channel:

```
WCFClientApp.TCP.ServiceClassClient("WSHttpBinding_IServiceClass");

ChannelFactory<TCP.IServiceClass> factory = new
    ChannelFactory<TCP.IServiceClass>("WSHttpBinding_IServiceClass");

TCP.IServiceClass channel = factory.CreateChannel();

ClientCredentials cc = new ClientCredentials();
cc.UserName.UserName = "scooter";
cc.UserName.Password = "wcfrocks";
factory.Credentials = cc;
```

The following example illustrates how to use the Endpoint property to return the service endpoint on which the channel was produced:

```
WCFClientApp.TCP.ServiceClassClient("WSHttpBinding_IServiceClass");

ChannelFactory<TCP.IServiceClass> factory = new
    ChannelFactory<TCP.IServiceClass>("WSHttpBinding_IServiceClass");

Console.WriteLine(factory.Endpoint);
```

Methods

The following methods are exposed by the ChannelFactory class. The BeginClose, BeginOpen, EndClose, and EndOpen methods are used in asynchronous communication.

❑ **Abort:** Immediately transitions the communication object from its current state into the *closing* state.

❑ **BeginClose:** Begins an asynchronous operation to close the current communication object.

❑ **BeginOpen:** Begins an asynchronous operation to open a communication object.

❑ **Close:** Transitions the object from its current state into the *closed* state.

❑ **EndClose:** Finishes the asynchronous *close* on the current communication object.

❑ **EndOpen:** Finishes the asynchronous *open* on the current communication object.

❑ **Open:** Transitions the object from the *created* state into the *opened* state.

The following can be used to explicitly open a channel:

```
WCFClientApp.TCP.ServiceClassClient("WSHttpBinding_IServiceClass");

ChannelFactory<TCP.IServiceClass> factory = new
    ChannelFactory<TCP.IServiceClass>("WSHttpBinding_IServiceClass");

TCP.IServiceClass channel = factory.CreateChannel();

factory.Open();

channel.DoSomething();
```

The following can be used to implicitly open a channel:

```
WCFClientApp.TCP.ServiceClassClient("WSHttpBinding_IServiceClass");

ChannelFactory<TCP.IServiceClass> factory = new
    ChannelFactory<TCP.IServiceClass>("WSHttpBinding_IServiceClass");

TCP.IServiceClass channel = factory.CreateChannel();

channel.DoSomething();
```

The difference between the two previous examples is that by explicitly opening the channel you have more control over the creation and management of the channel.

Be sure to close the channel factory when you are done with it:

```
factory.close();
```

CreateChannel Method

The CreateChannel method creates a channel of a specific type to a specified endpoint. Typically in code you will create a channel that is configured with a specific binding and endpoint. In most of the examples you have seen, a channel has been created to an endpoint that has been configured with a specific binding, as shown here:

```
EndpointAddress ea = new EndpointAddress("tcp.net://localhost:8000/WCFService");
BasicHttpBinding bb = new BasicHttpBinding();
ChannelFactory<TCP.IServiceClass> cf = new
    ChannelFactory<IServiceClass>("BasicHttpBinding_IServiceClass");
TCP.IServiceClass ch = cf.CreateChannel(bb, ea);
textbox1.Text=ch.AddNumbers;
```

The CreateChannel method takes a number of overloads that can be used to create the channel as described in the following table.

Overload	Description
CreateChannel()	Creates a channel of an IChannel type.
CreateChannel(EndpointAddress)	Creates a channel used to send messages to the specified endpoint address.
CreateChannel(String)	Creates a channel used to send messages to a service whose endpoint is configured in a specified way.
CreateChannel(Binding, EndpointAddress)	Creates a channel used to send messages to a service endpoint at the specified endpoint and configured with the specified binding.
CreateChannel(EndpointAddress, Uri)	Creates a channel used to send messages to a service endpoint at the specified endpoint through the specified transport address.
CreateChannel(Binding, EndpointAddress, Uri)	Creates a channel used to send messages to a service endpoint at the specified endpoint and configured with the specified binding and transport address.

Asynchronous communication is discussed later on in this chapter.

Client Communication Patterns

Now that you understand how channels are created and function, this section describes the different types of communication that can take place between the client and the service endpoint.

One-Way

One-way communication is just that, it is communication in a single direction. That direction flows from the client to the service. No reply is sent from the service, and the client does not expect a response. In this scenario, the client sends a message and continues execution.

Figure 7-2 illustrates a one-way communication. The client sends a message to the service, and execution takes place on the service. No response is sent back to the client from the service.

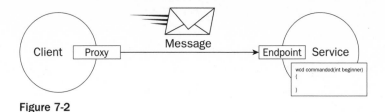

Figure 7-2

Because there is no response from the service in one-way communication, any errors generated by the service during the processing of the message are not communicated back to the client, therefore the client has no idea if the request was successful or not.

For a one-way, single direction communication, the `IsOneWay` parameter on the `[OperationContract]` is set to True. This tells the service that no response is required. The following code example illustrates setting a one-way communication:

```
[ServiceContract]
public interface IServiceClass
{
    [OperationContract(IsOneWay=true)]
    string InitiateOrder();

    [OperationContract]
    BookOrder PlaceOrder(BookOrder request);

    [OperationContract(IsOneWay=true)]
    string FinalizeOrder();
}
```

In this example, the service contains three available operations, two of which are defined as one-way operations. The InitiateOrder and FinalizeOrder operations are defined as one-way operations, whereas the PlaceOrder operation is not. When the client calls the InitiateOrder service operation, it will immediately continue processing without waiting for a response from the service. However, when the client calls the PlaceOrder service operation, it will wait for a response from the service before continuing.

Request-Reply

Request-reply communication means that when the client sends a message to the service, it expects a response from the service. Request-reply communication also means that no further client execution takes place until a response is received from the service.

Figure 7-3 illustrates a request-reply communication. The client sends a message to the service, the service operation takes place, and a responding message is sent back to the client. Further client execution is paused until the responding message is received by the client.

Figure 7-3

In Windows Communication Foundation, there are two ways to specify a request-reply communication. The first method is to set the value of the IsOneWay parameter on the [OperationContract] to False. This tells the service that a response is required.

The default value for the IsOneWay parameter is False, so the second method is to not include the IsOneWay parameter at all and the operation will be a request-reply communication by default.

The following code example, taken from the previous example, illustrates setting a request-reply communication:

```
[ServiceContract]
public interface IServiceClass
{
    [OperationContract(IsOneWay=false)]
    string InitiateOrder();

    [OperationContract]
    BookOrder PlaceOrder(BookOrder request);

    [OperationContract(IsOneWay=true)]
    string FinalizeOrder();
}
```

In this example the service contains three available operations, two of which are defined as request-reply operations. The InitiateOrder and PlaceOrder operations are defined as request-reply operations, whereas the FinalizeOrder operation is a one-way communication. The InitiateOrder is explicitly defined as a request-reply communication by setting the IsOneWay parameter to False, whereas the PlaceOrder method is a request-reply communication by default because no specific communication method is specified, thereby being a request-reply communication by default.

Therefore, the client will wait for a response from both the InitiateOrder and PlaceOrder operations, but not on the FinalizeOrder operation.

Duplex

Duplex communication is the ability of both the client and service to initiate communication, as well as respond to incoming messages; in other words, bi-directional communication, or duplex messaging pattern. With duplex communication, the service can not only respond to incoming messages, but it can also initiate communication with the client by sending request messages seeking a response message from the client.

The client communication with the service does not change, meaning that it still communicates with the service via a proxy. However, the service communicates with the client via a callback, as shown in Figure 7-4.

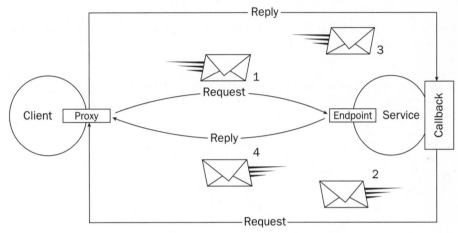

Figure 7-4

Setting up duplex communication requires changes both on the client and the service. The following sections describe the service and client requirements for building duplex communication service and client. A full example is given at the end of the chapter.

Service

In all of the examples so far the WCF service has consisted of a single interface and a class that implements that interface. For duplex communication, the service must contain two interfaces. The purpose of the first, or primary, interface is used for client-to-service communication, meaning that it is used to receive messages from the client, as you have seen in all the examples so far. The second interface, or callback interface, is used for service-to-client communication, to send messages from the service to the client. The trick to remember is that both of these contracts must be designated as one-way contracts because the second interface, or callback, is handling the communication from the service to the client.

The following example illustrates how to define a duplex service contract. The first step is to define the interface that makes up the service side of the duplex contract:

```
[ServiceContract(SessionMode = SessionMode.Required)]
public interface IDuplexService
{
    [OperationContract(IsOneWay = true)]
    void Add(int bignumber);

    [OperationContract(IsOneWay = true)]
    void Subtract(int bignumber);
}
```

The second step is to create the callback interface. This is the interface that will send the results of the preceding operations back to the client:

```
public interface IDuplexServiceCallback
{
  [OperationContract(IsOneWay = true)]
  void Calculate(int bignumber);
}
```

The third step is to apply the callback interface to the service contract, as shown in the following code. This links the two interfaces:

```
[ServiceContract(SessionMode = SessionMode.Required),
    CallbackContract = typeof(IDuplexServiceCallback)]

public interface IDuplexService
{
  [OperationContract(IsOneWay = true)]
  void Add(int bignumber);

  [OperationContract(IsOneWay = true)]
  void Subtract(int bignumber);
}
```

Now the service code looks like the following:

```
[ServiceContract(SessionMode = SessionMode.Required),
    CallbackContract = typeof(IDuplexServiceCallback)]

public interface IDuplexService
{
  [OperationContract(IsOneWay = true)]
  void Add(int bignumber);

  [OperationContract(IsOneWay = true)]
  void Subtract(int bignumber);
}

public interface IDuplexServiceCallback
{
  [OperationContract(IsOneWay = true)]
  void Calculate(int bignumber);
}
```

Lastly, the service class needs to implement the duplex service contract. To do this correctly, a service behavior needs to be added to the class. This is accomplished by adding the [ServiceBehavior] attribute to the service class. Once the behavior attribute has been added, the PerSession value of the InstanceContextMode parameter on that behavior attribute needs to be set. This creates an instance of the service for each outbound duplex session:

```
[ServiceBehavior(InstanceContextMode = InstanceContextMode.PerSession)]
public class DuplexServiceClass : IDuplexService
{
```

```
    int answer = 0;

    IDuplexServiceCallback Callback
    {
      get
      {
        return OperationContext.Current.GetCallbackChannel<IDuplexServiceCallback>();
      }
    }

    public void Add(int bignumber)
    {
      answer += bignumber;
      Callback.Calculate(answer);
    }
}
```

At this point you have the basis for a service that supports duplex communication. The service contains two interfaces, one of which is the callback for sending messages to the client. You also have a service class that implements the duplex service.

The second part of this equation is to modify the client to handle duplex communication.

Client

For duplex communication, the client must also take some responsibility for this type of communication, and therefore must implement the callback contract. It does this by implementing the callback interface of the duplex contract:

```
public class ClientCallback : IDuplexServiceCallback
{
  public void Calculate(answer);
  {
    textbox1.text = answer.ToString();
  }
}
```

The last step for the client is to build a mechanism to handle the message on the callback interface. This is done by creating an instance of the InstanceContext in the client class:

```
InstanceContext ic = new InstanceContext(new ClientCallback());
```

From here, you create the client and make calls to the service operations:

```
DuplexServiceClient client = new DuplexServiceClient(ic);

int val = 100;
client.Add(val);
```

Duplex Client Using the DuplexChannelFactory

The preceding code examples didn't specify how the client proxy was created because there are multiple ways to create the proxy. All of the examples in the book so far have used an added service reference.

However, the same can be accomplished using the svcutil utility, or by using the ChannelFactory as discussed earlier in this chapter.

The DuplexChannelFactory class provides the ability to create and maintain duplex channels, which are used by clients to send and receive messages between endpoints. It is through the duplex channel that clients and services can communicate with each other independently. This is important because both sides can initiate communication with the other party.

Creating a duplex client proxy using the DuplexChannelFactory is quite simple and not that different from the examples given earlier in this chapter using the ChannelFactory. The CreateChannel method of the DuplexChannelFactory class allows you to create a duplex client proxy. This method requires the service contract name as a generic parameter. The following example illustrates how to create a duplex channel that the client and service can use for communication:

```
EndpointAddress ea = new EndpointAddress("tcp.net://localhost:8000/WCFService");
BasicHttpBinding bb = new BasicHttpBinding();

InstanceContext callbackLocation = new InstanceContext(
DuplexChannelFactory(TCP.IServiceClass> dcf = new
  DuplexChannelFactory<WCFClient.TCP.IServiceClass>
  (callbackLocation);

TCP.IServiceClass ch = dcf.CreateChannel(bb, ea);
textbo1.Text =  ch.AddNumbers;

((IServiceClass).client).Close();
((IServiceClass).client).Dispose();
```

As you can see, using the ChannelFactory to create duplex client communication is easy.

Lastly, operations of a service can be called and accessed synchronously or asynchronously. The next section discusses calling a service asynchronously.

Asynchronous

Calling methods asynchronously allows applications to continue processing other work while the called method is still executing.

Like the duplex communication, asynchronous operations require specific changes to the client and to the service. So, like the duplex example, the following sections describe the service and client requirements for building an asynchronous communication service and client.

Service

Asynchronous operations divide the operation into two separate but related operations. The first operation is the *Begin* operation, which the client calls to start operation processing. In a *Begin* operation, two additional parameters need to be passed to the operation and the return value is a System.IAsyncResult. The first parameter(s) in the *Begin* method is the value or values you wish to pass it. The second parameter is a callback object, and the third parameter is the state object. The callback object is provided by the client and runs when the called operation is complete. The state object is the state of the callback function when the operation is finished. For example, you would normally pass the client proxy because this tells the callback function to automatically call the *End* operation and return the result.

The second operation is a matching *End* operation that takes the System.IAsyncResult as a parameter and returns a return value. The End operation does not need an [OperationContract] attribute.

The Begin operation must contain the AsyncPattern property with the value of that property set to True.

The following code illustrates defining an asynchronous communication service operation:

```
[ServiceContract]
public interface IAsyncService
{
   [OperationContract(AsyncPattern = true)]
   IAsyncResult BeginAdd(int val1, int val2, AsyncCallback cb, object astate);

   int EndAdd(IAsyncResult result);
}

Public class AsyncServiceClass : IAsyncService
{
   public IAsyncResult BeginAdd(int val1, int val2, AsyncCallback cb, object astate)
   {
     //do some addition
   }

   Public int EndAdd(IAsyncResult ar)
   {

   }
}
```

The service is now set up to communicate asynchronously, so the next step is to tell the client to communicate the same way.

Client

On the client side of an asynchronous service, the client simply needs to pass the correct parameters and make sure that the returned results are of the IAsyncResult type. To access the asynchronous service operation, the client first calls the Begin operation, which in the following example is the BeginAdd operation. In that call, a callback function is specified through which the results are returned, in this case the callbackAdd function. When the callback function executes, the client calls the End operation to obtain the results, which in the following example is the EndAdd operation:

```
private void button1_Click(object sender, EventArgs e)
{
  WCFClientApp.TCP.IServiceClass client =
    ChannelFactory<IServiceClass>.CreateChannel(bb, ea);

  IAsyncResult ar = client.BeginAdd(2, 2, callbackAdd, client);

  client.Close();
```

```
    }

    Static void callbackAdd((IAsyncResult AR)
    {
      int result ((WCFClientApp.TCP.IServiceClass)ar.AsyncState).EndAdd);
      textbox1.Text = result
    }
```

Asynchronous communication enables applications to be more flexible in their communication by way of maximizing communication throughput and a balanced interactivity.

Creating Client Code

Most, if not all, of the examples so far throughout the book have used an added service reference to consume the service and build the client. However, the Service Model Metadata Utility Tool (svcutil.exe) has been mentioned briefly as a method of generating client code. The syntax and options for this tool were covered in detail in Chapter 3.

This section provides a few examples of using the Service Model Metadata Utility Tool to generate client code.

Generating Client Code

The svcutil utility is a command-line tool that generates client code from service metadata. From this tool, proxy classes, contracts (data, service, and message), and configuration files can be generated to be added to your client application.

The svcutil utility assumes a number of defaults if left blank, such as the language and the output file name. The default language is C# and the output filename that is generated is taken from the service contract namespace.

Even though the two aforementioned values are defaulted, it is good practice to specify those values to make sure you are getting what you are intending. The following example illustrates specifying the language and output file for the examples in Chapter 6:

```
svcutil.exe net.tcp//localhost:8000/WCFService/tcpmex
/o:c:\wcfclientapp\wcfclientapp\client.cs /l:c#
```

The following example shows how to specify the language, the name for the generated code, and the filename for the generated configuration file:

```
svcutil.exe net.tcp//localhost:8000/WCFService/tcpmex
/o:c:\wcfclientapp\wcfclientapp\client.cs
/config:c:\wcfclientapp\wcfclientapp\output.config /l:c#
```

You also have the ability to generate message contract types by using the `/messageContract` switch (or the short form `/mc`). For example, the following generates a message contract type.

```
svcutil.exe net.tcp//localhost:8000/WCFService/tcpmex /o:c:\wcfclientapp\
wcfclientapp\client.cs /messageContract
```

The `/messageContract` switch tells WCF that the message being passed between the service and the client is the parameter. Remember the message example from Chapter 6? The following code is from that example, and in the highlighted line the message is being passed from the client to the service. The `/messageContract` switch generated the client code to be able to tell the system that the message is the parameter.

```
WCFClientApp.TCP.BookOrder Val1 = new WCFClientApp.TCP.BookOrder();
Val1.ISBN = textBox1.Text;
int.TryParse(textBox2.Text, out intval);
Val1.Quantity = intval;
Val1.FirstName = textBox3.Text;
Val1.LastName = textBox4.Text;
Val1.Address = textBox5.Text;

WCFClientApp.TCP.BookOrder result = client.PlaceOrder(Val1);
textBox2.Text = Val1.OrderNumber;
```

The svcutil utility can also export metadata for contracts, services, and data types contained in compiled assemblies. The `/servicename` option allows you to specify the service you would like to export. Chapter 6 also contained a data contract example, and that example could have easily used the `/dataContractOnly` option to export the contract types defined in the data contract. For example, the following command exports the data types from the data contract example in Chapter 6:

```
svcutil.exe net.tcp//localhost:8000/WCFService/tcpmex /dataContractOnly
```

Defining Client Bindings and Endpoints

You saw in the first few chapters that the examples used code to define the bindings, the addresses, and to create the endpoints. The following code was taken from the first example in Chapter 5 where everything was defined in code.

The first two lines define the addresses and transports of the service endpoints. The second line creates a service host for the service passing in the two addresses. The third and fourth lines define the two bindings that the endpoints will use.

The remaining code defines the endpoints that will be exposed on the service, associates the addresses and bindings with those endpoints, and then finally associates those endpoints with the service and the service host and then starts the service host:

```
Uri bpa = new Uri("net.pipe://localhost/NetNamedPipeBinding");
Uri tcpa = new Uri("net.tcp://localhost:8000/TcpBinding");

sh = new ServiceHost(typeof(ServiceClass), bpa, tcpa);

NetNamedPipeBinding pb = new NetNamedPipeBinding();
NetTcpBinding tcpb = new NetTcpBinding();

ServiceMetadataBehavior mBehave = new ServiceMetadataBehavior();
sh.Description.Behaviors.Add(mBehave);
sh.AddServiceEndpoint(typeof(IMetadataExchange),
MetadataExchangeBindings.CreateMexTcpBinding(), "mex");

sh.AddServiceEndpoint(typeof(IMetadataExchange),
MetadataExchangeBindings.CreateMexNamedPipeBinding(), "mex");

sh.AddServiceEndpoint(typeof(IServiceClass), pb, bpa);
sh.AddServiceEndpoint(typeof(IServiceClass), tcpb, tcpa);

sh.Open();
```

Although this works, hopefully you have learned over the past few chapters that this method is not the most efficient method. Suppose you wanted to add a binding or endpoint address? That would require you to modify the code and rebuild the application.

The following is the configuration-based version of the preceding code. The same endpoints, addresses, and bindings are specified. This configuration should look familiar because it is the exact same configuration from the service host project that the past handful of examples from the last three chapters have used:

```xml
<?xml version="1.0" encoding="utf-8" ?>
<configuration>
  <system.serviceModel>
    <services>
      <service name ="WCFService.ServiceClass"
behaviorConfiguration="metadataSupport">
        <host>
          <baseAddresses>
            <add baseAddress="net.pipe://localhost/WCFService"/>
            <add baseAddress="net.tcp://localhost:8000/WCFService"/>
            <add baseAddress="http://localhost:8080/WCFService"/>
          </baseAddresses>
        </host>
        <endpoint address="tcpmex"
                  binding="mexTcpBinding"
                  contract="IMetadataExchange"/>
        <endpoint address="namedpipemex"
                  binding="mexNamedPipeBinding"
                  contract="IMetadataExchange"/>
        <endpoint address="" binding="wsHttpBinding"
contract="WCFService.IServiceClass"/>
      </service>
    </services>
```

```
            <behaviors>
              <serviceBehaviors>
                <behavior name="metadataSupport">
                  <serviceMetadata httpGetEnabled="false" httpGetUrl=""/>
                </behavior>
              </serviceBehaviors>
            </behaviors>
          </system.serviceModel>
        </configuration>
```

The great thing about this is that the only hosting code necessary is the following two lines:

```
sh = new ServiceHost(typeof(WCFService.ServiceClass));
sh.Open();
```

Now suppose you want to add an additional binding or endpoint address? Is a recompile necessary? Not at all. The only thing you need to modify is the configuration file to add the necessary components.

The purpose of this section is to illustrate that defining endpoints (addresses and bindings) can be done a number of ways. There are benefits to both, but the majority of the time you should steer toward using configuration rather than inline code.

Typed versus Untyped Services

Chapter 3 spent a page or two discussing the different types of services. The two major types are typed and untyped services. As explained in Chapter 3, typed services function a lot like a class method, in that they take parameters and return results if needed. Untyped services let the developer have much more control and flexibility by providing the ability to work at the message level. The following two sections take a look at the client side on how to work with the two types of services.

Invoking Operations of a Typed Services

Most of the examples so far in this book have utilized typed services. The client calls the service using a proxy, and the service can return a result if necessary. With typed services the parameters and return values are primitive or complex data types, as shown in the following example:

```
textBox1.Text = client.AddNumbers(5, 5).ToString();
textBox2.Text = client.MultiplyNumbers(5, 5).ToString();

client.DeleteOrder(OrderID);
```

Typed services also support ref and out parameters as well:

```
string ordernumber;
client.PlaceOrder(string title, int quantity, out ordernumber);
```

Typed services can also accept and return complex data structures through the use of data contracts. These data structures can be used as parameters and return values. Data contracts are discussed in Chapter 6.

Invoking Operations of an Untyped Service

Untyped services require a bit more work but also provide much more control and flexibility. At this level, the developer works directly with the message itself. The key to keep in mind here is that requests and responses are in the form of a message, meaning that the client initiates a request (in the form of a created message) and sends that to the service. If a response from the service is required, that response is also in the form of a message.

The following example, taken from the message service example in Chapter 6, illustrates working with a message directly. An instance of the message is created, the header and body elements that are defined on the service side are populated and serialized into the message, and the message is passed to the service:

```
WCFClientApp.TCP.BookOrder Val1 = new WCFClientApp.TCP.BookOrder();

Val1.ISBN = textBox1.Text;
int.TryParse(textBox2.Text, out intval);
Val1.Quantity = intval;
Val1.FirstName = textBox3.Text;
Val1.LastName = textBox4.Text;
Val1.Address = textBox5.Text;

WCFClientApp.TCP.BookOrder result = client.PlaceOrder(Val1);
```

Based on the example in Chapter 6 and the information here in this section you can agree that although working at the message level provides a more granular level of control, it also opens up a wider opportunity for error. An intimate knowledge of the service and what it expects is necessary to ensure a well-functioning client and service. This is certainly not to steer you away from using untyped services and working at the message level, because the experience can be rewarding.

Useful Information

This chapter has covered a lot of information necessary to build and use Windows Communication Foundation clients. This section discusses a few topics that should be considered when building clients, specifically the creation and use of client and channel objects.

Initializing Channels Interactively

A little-known functionality in Windows Communication Foundation is the ability to dynamically define and create a user interface that lets the user select credentials. These credentials are used to create a channel prior to the timeout timers being fired.

This functionality is provided via the IInteractiveChannelInitializer interface and can be used by developers by calling either the System.ServiceModel.ClientBase.DisplayInitializationUI or System.SerivceModel.IClientChannel.DisplayInitializationUI. Either of these need to be called before the channel is opened and the first operation is called.

The explicit approach is to open the channel directly, and the implicit approach is to open it by calling the first operation of the session.

Session and Channel Duration

Windows Communication Foundation contains two groups of channels that are available for creating client channel objects:

- ❑ **Datagram:** A channel in which all messages are unassociated. If an input or output operation message fails, subsequent operations are not affected and can use the same channel.

- ❑ **Sessionful:** Channels in which a session on one side is always correlated and connected with the corresponding session on the other side. Both sides of the session must agree on the connection requirements or else a fault is generated. The majority of the WCF-provided bindings support sessions by default.

Sessions are very useful in WCF. Through sessions the developer can determine whether the message exchange between the client and service is successful. If the Close method is called on an open session channel, and the Close method returns successfully, then the session was successful. It can be considered successful for two reasons:

- ❑ All delivery guarantees specified by the binding were met.

- ❑ The service side did not call the Abort method on the channel before calling Close.

A calling application should open the channel, use the channel, and close the channel, and wrap these steps inside a try block. See the section "Exception Handling" for more information on handling exceptions and the try block.

Blocking Issues

Windows Communication Foundation applications can communicate in one-way or request-reply mode. In a request-reply communication, the client blocks further processing until either a return value is received or an exception is thrown. This is also true when an application calls an operation asynchronously on a WCF client object or channel. The client does not return until either the data is written to the network by the channel layer or an exception occurs.

One-way communication can make clients more responsive, but one-way communication can also block as well. The selected binding and previous messages can also block, having an impact on client processing; for example, in a situation where too many messages are sent to the service that the service has trouble processing them. In this case the client will block until the service can process the messages or until an exception is thrown or the timeout period has been reached.

Another scenario is where the ConcurrencyMode is set to Single but the binding uses sessions. In this scenario, the dispatcher forces ordering on incoming messages preventing further messages from being read off of the wire until the service has had a chance to process previous messages. The client will block in this scenario as well and may return an exception depending on whether the service could process the message before the timeout period was reached on the client.

Inserting a buffer between the client object and the send operation can help alleviate some of these blocking problems. You have two options at your disposal:

- ❑ Asynchronous calls

- ❑ In-memory message queue

Both of these options will help the client object return much more quickly. You have the ability to use one or the other, or both; however, you are still limited by the size of the thread pool and message queue.

One-way communication should be used in the following scenarios:

❑ The client is not affected by the result of the invoked operation.

❑ The NetMsmqBinding or MsmqIntegrationBinding bindings are used.

The type of communication depends on your requirement. If your application needs to keep processing while an operation is completing, you should create an asynchronous method pair on the service contract interface that your WCF client can take advantage of.

Exception Handling

As stated earlier, the opening, use, and closing of a session should be done within a try block, simply for the reason that the conversation can be determined as successful if an exception was not generated. If an exception was caught it is recommended that the session be aborted.

The following example illustrates the try/catch method of opening and closing sessions:

```
private void button1_Click(object sender, EventArgs e)
{
  try
  {

    WCFClientApp.TCP.IServiceClass client =
      ChannelFactory<IServiceClass>.CreateChannel(bb, ea);

      // do some cool stuff

    client.Close();
  }
  Catch (CommunicationException ce)
  {
    // do something with the exception
  }
}
```

This example is simplistic but provides the basis for catching exceptions and determining if the session was successful. Other exceptions can also be tracked such as timeout exceptions and FaultException exceptions.

Windows Communication Foundation also recommends that the using statement not be used solely for the fact that the end of the using statement can cause exceptions that can mask exceptions that you may want to know about. The following URL provides more information on this subject:

```
http://msdn2.microsoft.com/en-us/library/aa355056.aspx
```

Client Programming Example

The final section of this chapter contains two examples. The first example illustrates how to use the ChannelFactory class to create a channel on the client to send messages with the service endpoint. The second example illustrates a duplex service contract, or a message exchange pattern.

ChannelFactory

Open up your WCFService project and modify your service code as follows:

```
using System;
using System.ServiceModel;
using System.Collections.Generic;
using System.Runtime.Serialization;
using System.IO;

namespace WCFService
{
    [ServiceContract]
    public interface IServiceClass
    {
        [OperationContract]
        int AddNumbers(int number1, int number2);

        [OperationContract]
        int SubtractNumbers(int number1, int number2);

        [OperationContract]
        int MultiplyNumbers(int number1, int number2);

        [OperationContract]
        string GetText();

    }

    public class ServiceClass : IServiceClass
    {
        string IServiceClass.GetText()
        {
            StreamReader sw = new StreamReader(@"c:\wrox\WCFServiceTest.txt");
            return sw.ReadLine();
        }

        int IServiceClass.AddNumbers(int firstvalue, int secondvalue)
        {
            return firstvalue + secondvalue;
        }

        int IServiceClass.SubtractNumbers(int firstvalue, int secondvalue)
        {
            return firstvalue - secondvalue;
```

```
            }

            int IServiceClass.MultiplyNumbers(int firstvalue, int secondvalue)
            {
                return firstvalue * secondvalue;
            }


        }
    }
```

You can see that the service code is not that complicated. In fact, it looks very similar to the first example in Chapter 5. This service contract exposes a few mathematical operations plus an operation that reads from a text file. Compile the service to make sure everything is ok. Be sure that the WCFServiceTest .txt file exists in the \Wrox directory and that the text file contains some text. If your text file is not located in the C:\Wrox directory, be sure to modify the path in the StreamReader line of code.

The next step is to modify the client application. Nothing needs to be done to the service host, so the focus now is to modify the client. Open Form1 in design mode and make sure there are four text boxes on the form, with the names textbox1, textbox2, textbox3, and textbox4. Next, place a button to the right of each text box, with the names button1, button2, button3, and button4. Again, you are going for functionality, not form design. Once you are done, your form should look like the picture in Figure 7-5 (which appears later in the chapter).

Next, right-click the form and select View Code, and modify the code behind the form as follows:

```csharp
using System;
using System.Collections.Generic;
using System.ComponentModel;
using System.Data;
using System.Drawing;
using System.Text;
using System.Windows.Forms;
using System.ServiceModel;
using System.ServiceModel.Channels;

namespace WCFClientApp
{

    public partial class Form1 : Form
    {
        private int _Selection;
        private int val1 = 5;
        private int val2 = 5;
        private int result;

        public Form1()
        {
            InitializeComponent();
        }

        private void Form1_Load(object sender, EventArgs e)
        {
```

```
                radioButton1.Checked = true;

        }

        private void button1_Click(object sender, EventArgs e)
        {

            switch (_Selection)
            {
                case 0:
                    //TCP.ServiceClassClient client = new
                    //
WCFClientApp.TCP.ServiceClassClient("WSHttpBinding_IServiceClass");
                    ChannelFactory<TCP.IServiceClass> factory = new
ChannelFactory<TCP.IServiceClass>("WSHttpBinding_IServiceClass");
                    TCP.IServiceClass channel = factory.CreateChannel();

                    result = channel.AddNumbers(val1, val2);
                    textBox1.Text = result.ToString();

                    factory.Close();

                    break;

                case 1:
                    //NamedPipe.ServiceClassClient client1 = new
                    //
WCFClientApp.NamedPipe.ServiceClassClient("WSHttpBinding_IServiceClass1");
                    ChannelFactory<NamedPipe.IServiceClass> factory1 = new
ChannelFactory<NamedPipe.IServiceClass>("WSHttpBinding_IServiceClass1");
                    NamedPipe.IServiceClass channel1 = factory1.CreateChannel();

                    result = channel1.AddNumbers(val1, val2);
                    textBox1.Text = result.ToString();

                    factory1.Close();

                    break;

                case 2:
                    break;
            }
        }

        private void button2_Click(object sender, EventArgs e)
        {
            switch (_Selection)
            {
                case 0:
                    //TCP.ServiceClassClient client = new
                    //
WCFClientApp.TCP.ServiceClassClient("WSHttpBinding_IServiceClass");
                    ChannelFactory<TCP.IServiceClass> factory = new
ChannelFactory<TCP.IServiceClass>("WSHttpBinding_IServiceClass");
```

```
                                  TCP.IServiceClass channel = factory.CreateChannel();

                                  result = channel.SubtractNumbers(val1, val2);
                                  textBox2.Text = result.ToString();

                                  factory.Close();

                                  break;

                          case 1:
                                  //NamedPipe.ServiceClassClient client1 = new
                                  //
WCFClientApp.NamedPipe.ServiceClassClient("WSHttpBinding_IServiceClass1");
                                  ChannelFactory<NamedPipe.IServiceClass> factory1 = new
ChannelFactory<NamedPipe.IServiceClass>("WSHttpBinding_IServiceClass1");
                                  NamedPipe.IServiceClass channel1 = factory1.CreateChannel();

                                  result = channel1.SubtractNumbers(val1, val2);
                                  textBox2.Text = result.ToString();

                                  factory1.Close();

                                  break;

                          case 2:
                                  break;
                      }

              }

          private void button3_Click(object sender, EventArgs e)
          {
              switch (_Selection)
              {
                  case 0:
                          //TCP.ServiceClassClient client = new
                          //
WCFClientApp.TCP.ServiceClassClient("WSHttpBinding_IServiceClass");
                          ChannelFactory<TCP.IServiceClass> factory = new
ChannelFactory<TCP.IServiceClass>("WSHttpBinding_IServiceClass");
                          TCP.IServiceClass channel = factory.CreateChannel();

                          result = channel.MultiplyNumbers(val1, val2);
                          textBox3.Text = result.ToString();

                          factory.Close();

                          break;

                  case 1:
                          //NamedPipe.ServiceClassClient client1 = new
                          //
WCFClientApp.NamedPipe.ServiceClassClient("WSHttpBinding_IServiceClass1");
                          ChannelFactory<NamedPipe.IServiceClass> factory1 = new
ChannelFactory<NamedPipe.IServiceClass>("WSHttpBinding_IServiceClass1");
```

```
                    NamedPipe.IServiceClass channel1 = factory1.CreateChannel();

                    result = channel1.MultiplyNumbers(val1, val2);
                    textBox3.Text = result.ToString();

                    factory1.Close();

                    break;

                case 2:
                    break;
            }

        }

        private void button4_Click(object sender, EventArgs e)
        {
            switch (_Selection)
            {
                case 0:
                    //TCP.ServiceClassClient client = new
                    //
WCFClientApp.TCP.ServiceClassClient("WSHttpBinding_IServiceClass");
                    ChannelFactory<TCP.IServiceClass> factory = new
ChannelFactory<TCP.IServiceClass>("WSHttpBinding_IServiceClass");
                    TCP.IServiceClass channel = factory.CreateChannel();

                    string strresult = channel.GetText();
                    textBox4.Text = strresult;

                    factory.Close();

                    break;

                case 1:
                    //NamedPipe.ServiceClassClient client1 = new
                    //
WCFClientApp.NamedPipe.ServiceClassClient("WSHttpBinding_IServiceClass1");
                    ChannelFactory<NamedPipe.IServiceClass> factory1 = new
ChannelFactory<NamedPipe.IServiceClass>("WSHttpBinding_IServiceClass1");
                    NamedPipe.IServiceClass channel1 = factory1.CreateChannel();

                    string result1 = channel1.GetText();
                    textBox4.Text = result1;

                    factory1.Close();

                    break;

                case 2:
                    break;
            }

        }

        private void radioButton1_CheckedChanged(object sender, EventArgs e)
```

```
        {
            _Selection = 0;
            textBox1.Text = "";
            textBox2.Text = "";
            textBox3.Text = "";
            textBox4.Text = "";
        }

        private void radioButton2_CheckedChanged(object sender, EventArgs e)
        {
            _Selection = 1;
            textBox1.Text = "";
            textBox2.Text = "";
            textBox3.Text = "";
            textBox4.Text = "";
        }


    }
}
```

The first thing you should notice is that an extra "using" statement was added. In order to create and manage channels, you need to import the System.ServiceModel.Channels namespace.

The next thing you should notice is the construction and management of the channel. This is easily accomplished via the following two lines:

```
ChannelFactory<TCP.IServiceClass> factory = new
    ChannelFactory<TCP.IServiceClass>("WSHttpBinding_IServiceClass");

TCP.IServiceClass channel = factory.CreateChannel();
```

The first line initializes a new instance of the ChannelFactory class. This is necessary to create the channel. In the constructor of this class, you pass the name of the endpoint in which this channel will communicate.

The second line creates the channel which is used to communicate with the client, and the third and fourth lines call the exposed method and display the results:

```
result = channel.AddNumbers(val1, val2);
textBox1.Text = result.ToString();
```

This example uses a configuration file to configure the endpoints. The other non-recommended option is to specify everything via code, as follows:

```
BasicHttpBinding bind = new BasicHttpBinding;
EndpointAddress ea = new EndpointAddress("");
ChannelFactory<IServiceClass> factory = new
    ChannelFactory<IServiceClass>(bind);

factory.CreateChannel(ea);
```

As you have gathered by now, the configuration route is the best method in most cases, so that is the route this example follows.

The same method, using the ChannelFactory, is used for the three mathematic expressions and to retrieve the text, and used for both the TCP and Named Pipe binding.

Build the project to make sure no errors are found. If everything looks good, run the host project to instantiate the service, and then run the client app. When the form displays, click the buttons to the right of each text box (see Figure 7-5).

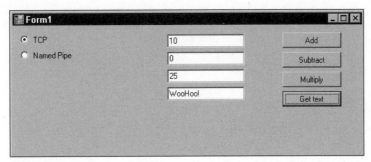

Figure 7-5

The numbers you are adding, subtracting, and multiplying are hard coded, but the intent is to show you how the ChannelFactory class works.

Duplex

This last example illustrates how to define a duplex contract. As you learned earlier, duplex communication allows for both the client and service to initiate communication. When the client establishes a session with the service, the client provides a means in which the service can send messages back to the client. This "service-to-client" communication is provided via a channel that is established by the client.

So, with that, time to get started. Open the service project and modify the service code to look like the following:

```
using System;
using System.ServiceModel;
using System.Collections.Generic;
using System.Runtime.Serialization;
using System.IO;

namespace WCFService
{
    [ServiceContract(SessionMode = SessionMode.Required,
CallbackContract=typeof(IServiceDuplexCallback))]
    public interface IServiceClass
    {
        [OperationContract(IsOneWay=true)]
```

```
            void AddNumber(int number);

            [OperationContract(IsOneWay=true)]
            void SubtractNumber(int number);
    }

    public interface IServiceDuplexCallback
    {
            [OperationContract(IsOneWay = true)]
            void Calculate(int result);
    }

    [ServiceBehavior(InstanceContextMode=InstanceContextMode.PerSession)]
    public class ServiceClass : IServiceClass
    {

        int result = 0;

        public void AddNumber(int number)
        {
            result += number;
            callback.Calculate(result);
        }

        public void SubtractNumber(int number)
        {
            result -= number;
            callback.Calculate(result);
        }

        IServiceDuplexCallback callback
        {
            get { return
OperationContext.Current.GetCallbackChannel<IServiceDuplexCallback>(); }
        }
      }
    }
```

Again, the first thing you should notice is that there are two interfaces defined, a primary interface and a secondary interface. The primary interface is for client-to-service communication. The secondary interface is the callback interface, which provides the service-to-client communication.

The second thing you should notice is the two properties of the [ServiceContract] attribute. The first attribute is the SessionMode attribute. The value of this property is set to Required, meaning that the contract requires a sessionful binding and a context needs to be established to link the messages going between the client and service. The second property is the CallbackContract, which sets the callback in which the service will communicate with the client.

Lastly, the service class implements the primary interface. Nothing new there, but what is new is that the class has been given a service behavior. This is accomplished by tagging it with the [ServiceBehavior] attribute. This needed to be done because the behavior that the class needs to be given is the PerSession instance mode. This is so that the service can maintain the result for each session.

Also defined in the class is a private property that the service will use to send messages back to the client via the previously defined callback interface.

Build the service to make sure everything is ok.

Next, open up the service host application and run it to start the service. Did it work? It shouldn't have. Why didn't it? The answer is because you are trying to start a service that supports duplex service contracts with an endpoint binding that does not support duplex service contracts.

Don't worry, the fix is simple, and this time it requires a change in the configuration file of the host application. Open the configuration file (`app.config`) and modify the line that is highlighted in the following code. Change the binding from `wsHttpBinding` to `wsDualHttpBinding`. This is the appropriate binding that is designed for use with duplex service contracts:

```xml
<?xml version="1.0" encoding="utf-8" ?>
<configuration>
  <system.serviceModel>
    <services>
      <service name ="WCFService.ServiceClass" behaviorConfiguration=
"metadataSupport">
        <host>
          <baseAddresses>
            <add baseAddress="net.pipe://localhost/WCFService"/>
            <add baseAddress="net.tcp://localhost:8000/WCFService"/>
            <add baseAddress="http://localhost:8080/WCFService"/>
          </baseAddresses>
        </host>
        <endpoint address="tcpmex"
                  binding="mexTcpBinding"
                  contract="IMetadataExchange"/>
        <endpoint address="namedpipemex"
                  binding="mexNamedPipeBinding"
                  contract="IMetadataExchange"/>
        <endpoint address="" binding="wsDualHttpBinding"
contract="WCFService.IServiceClass"/>
        <!--<endpoint address="mex" binding="mexHttpBinding" contract=
"IMetadataExchange"/>-->
      </service>
    </services>
    <behaviors>
      <serviceBehaviors>
        <behavior name="metadataSupport">
          <serviceMetadata httpGetEnabled="false" httpGetUrl=""/>
        </behavior>
      </serviceBehaviors>
    </behaviors>
  </system.serviceModel>
</configuration>
```

Next, the client:

```csharp
using System;
using System.Collections.Generic;
using System.ComponentModel;
```

```csharp
using System.Data;
using System.Drawing;
using System.Text;
using System.Windows.Forms;
using System.ServiceModel;
using System.ServiceModel.Channels;

namespace WCFClientApp
{

    public partial class Form1 : Form
    {
        private int _Selection;
        private int val1 = 5;
        private int val2 = 5;

        public Form1()
        {
            InitializeComponent();
        }


        private void Form1_Load(object sender, EventArgs e)
        {
            radioButton1.Checked = true;

        }

        private void button1_Click(object sender, EventArgs e)
        {

            switch (_Selection)
            {
                case 0:
                    //TCP.ServiceClassClient client = new
                    //    WCFClientApp.TCP.ServiceClassClient("WSHttpBinding_
IServiceClass");
                    InstanceContext ic = new InstanceContext(new CallbackHandler());
                    TCP.ServiceClassClient client = new WCFClientApp.TCP
.ServiceClassClient(ic);
                    client.AddNumber(val1);
                    client.AddNumber(val2);
                    //client.Close();

                    break;

                case 1:
                    //NamedPipe.ServiceClassClient client1 = new
                    //
WCFClientApp.NamedPipe.ServiceClassClient("WSHttpBinding_IServiceClass1");
                    InstanceContext ic1 = new InstanceContext(new
CallbackHandler1());
                    NamedPipe.ServiceClassClient client1 = new WCFClientApp
.NamedPipe.ServiceClassClient(ic1);
                    client1.AddNumber(val1);
```

```
                        client1.AddNumber(val2);

                        break;

                    case 2:
                        break;
                }
            }

        private void button2_Click(object sender, EventArgs e)
        {
            switch (_Selection)
            {
                case 0:
                    //TCP.ServiceClassClient client = new
                    //
WCFClientApp.TCP.ServiceClassClient("WSHttpBinding_IServiceClass");
                        InstanceContext ic = new InstanceContext(new
CallbackHandler());
                        TCP.ServiceClassClient client = new WCFClientApp.TCP
.ServiceClassClient(ic);
                        client.SubtractNumber(val1);
                        client.SubtractNumber(val2);
                        //client.Close();

                        break;

                    case 1:
                        //NamedPipe.ServiceClassClient client1 = new
                        //    WCFClientApp
.NamedPipe.ServiceClassClient("WSHttpBinding_IServiceClass1");
                        InstanceContext ic1 = new InstanceContext(new
CallbackHandler1());
                        NamedPipe.ServiceClassClient client1 = new WCFClientApp
.NamedPipe.ServiceClassClient(ic1);
                        client1.SubtractNumber(val1);
                        client1.SubtractNumber(val2);

                        break;

                    case 2:
                        break;
                }

            }

        private void radioButton1_CheckedChanged(object sender, EventArgs e)
        {
            _Selection = 0;
            textBox1.Text = "";
            textBox2.Text = "";
        }

        private void radioButton2_CheckedChanged(object sender, EventArgs e)
        {
```

```
            _Selection = 1;
            textBox1.Text = "";
            textBox2.Text = "";
        }

    }

    public class CallbackHandler : TCP.IServiceClassCallback
    {
        public void Calculate(int result)
        {
            Console.WriteLine(result);
        }
    }

    public class CallbackHandler1 : NamedPipe.IServiceClassCallback
    {
        public void Calculate(int result)
        {
            Console.WriteLine(result);
        }
    }
}
```

What did you notice about this client code that is different from the other examples? If you answered "hey, there's an additional class," you have answered wisely. The client needs to provide a mechanism for receiving the messages that are coming from the service, and the CallbackHandler class accomplishes precisely that task. This class implements the service callback interface of the duplex contract. As such its sole purpose is to receive incoming messages from the service.

Build the project to make sure no errors are found. If everything looks good, run the host project to instantiate the service, and then run the client app. When the form displays, click the buttons to the right of each text box (see Figure 7-6).

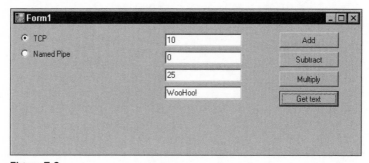

Figure 7-6

Slick, huh? You can see what duplex service contracts can do.

Summary

The purpose of this chapter was to give you a much better look at the client as it pertains to Windows Communication Foundation. The chapter began by providing an overview and discussion of the WCF client architecture, and the different objects and interfaces that make up and define that architecture.

From there the chapter moved on to the different communication patterns and the differences between them. Several examples were given to provide you with some know-how as to their capabilities and general use, as well as when one pattern would be more beneficial than the others.

A detailed discussion regarding the generation of client code using the Service Model Metadata Utility Tool followed. The purpose of this section was to shed some light as to the options you have for generating client code. In addition other options you have available were discussed, such as adding a service reference and when one method might be better than the other, and which one offers functionality that the other does not.

Lastly, this chapter covered the creation and defining of endpoints and their associated components, both in code and configuration. This topic rehashed, albeit ever so lightly, the pros and cons of code versus configuration.

From here the discussion in Chapter 8 moves on to the topic of WCF services as whole units and not just individual concepts.

8

Services

This chapter focuses on those items that are specific to the service side of Windows Communication Foundation. The chapters up until now have been dealing with topics and concepts that apply to the service and the client, and a lot of that still applies to the service itself. Yet, there are some items that are service specific, and this chapter delves into those.

As a quick recap, Chapters 4 through 6 discussed addresses, bindings, and contacts; concepts that apply to both the service and the client. Chapter 7 focused on the client itself and discussed topics that addressed WCF from the perspective of the client such as consuming WCF services, channels, and communication patterns.

This chapter covers the following topics:

- ❏ Overview of WCF service concepts
- ❏ Behaviors
- ❏ Error handling

Overview

When you write a book you spend a lot of time organizing and laying out the topics and content that you are going to write about. A good portion of that time is trying to figure out the best way to organize and lay out the topics that will provide a smooth flow of content and benefit the reader the most. Do you discuss bindings first, or addresses? Maybe discussing contracts first would make more sense. These are the types of questions that keep an author up at night (besides writing).

It is hard to understand, let alone build, Windows Communication Foundation services without first understanding addresses, bindings, and contracts because that is what defines a WCF service. That is why three chapters were dedicated to those specific topics. With that information firmly stored on your cerebral hard drive, this section spends a few pages providing an overview of those topics and discusses some aspects that are particular to WCF services.

Service Types

You have read about the different WCF service types a couple of times so far in this book, but they are worth mentioning briefly again. There are three types of services in WCF, and they are the following:

- ❑ Typed
- ❑ Untyped
- ❑ Typed message

Which service type you use is basically determined by how you want your service to accept and return parameters.

Typed

You learned in previous chapters that a typed service is the least complicated of the three service types and they provide most of the functionality that you will need when developing WCF services. Remember that a typed service is a lot like a class method or function, in that it can accept one or more parameters and can return a result.

Another common term for typed services is *parameter model*, which defines specifically what this type of service does. Typed, or parameter, services are not limited to the types of parameters and results that can be passed to them. Typed services can accept simple types and even complex types. Return values are not limited in any way, because return values can also be simple or complex types. However, keep in mind that when passing or returning complex types, data contracts must be defined for each type being passed and returned.

With typed services Windows Communication Foundation handles all of the messaging. This means that as a developer, you do not have to work directly at the message level.

The following example illustrates a typed service. A service contract is defined with two operations. The first operation accepts no parameters, and the second operation accepts two parameters (in this case, both parameters are of type Int):

```
[ServiceContract]
public interface IServiceClass
{
    [OperationContract]
    string GetText();

    [OperationContract]
    int MultiplyNumbers(int firstvalue, int secondvalue);
}

public class ServiceClass : IServiceClass
{
    string IServiceClass.GetText()
```

```
    {
        StreamReader sw = new StreamReader(@"c:\wrox\WCFServiceTest.txt");
        return sw.ReadLine();
        //return "Hello World";
    }

    int IServiceClass.MultiplyNumbers(int firstvalue, int secondvalue)
    {
        return firstvalue * secondvalue;
    }
}
```

Typed services also support `ref` and `out` parameters, which have the added benefit of letting the service return multiple results. The following example shows the use of an `out` parameter:

```
public void IServiceClass.MultiplyNumbers(int val1, int val2, out int retval)
{
    retval = val1 * val2;
}
```

As a note, it isn't considered good practice to return more than one parameter in object-oriented programming.

You can see that typed services are simple to work with and are very similar to programming methods you already use.

Untyped

Untyped services are a bit more complicated to work with because they necessitate working directly with the message. In this type of service, you define the messages and their contents. Here you are working at the message level, meaning that message objects are passed back and forth between the client and service, and the service may also return a message object if required. Furthermore, they provide the ability to access the message body, as well as serialize and deserialize the message itself.

The following example is taken from the message contract example in Chapter 6. Instead of sending known types as parameters, message objects are passed between the client and the service:

```
[ServiceContract]
public interface IServiceClass
{
    [OperationContract]
    string InitiateOrder();

    [OperationContract]
    BookOrder PlaceOrder(BookOrder request);

    [OperationContract]
    string FinalizeOrder();
}

[MessageContract]
public class BookOrder
```

```
{

    private string isbn;
    private int quantity;
    private string ordernumber;

    public BookOrder(BookOrder message)
    {
        this.isbn = message.isbn;
        this.quantity = message.quantity;
    }

    [MessageHeader]
    public string ISBN
    {
        get { return isbn; }
        set { isbn = value; }
    }

    [MessageBodyMember]
    public int Quantity
    {
        get { return quantity; }
        set { quantity = value; }
    }

    [MessageBodyMember]
    public string OrderNumber
    {
        get { return ordernumber; }
        set { ordernumber = value; }
    }

}

public class ServiceClass : IServiceClass
{
    string IServiceClass.InitiateOrder()
    {
        return "Initiating Order...";
    }

    public BookOrder PlaceOrder(BookOrder request)
    {
        BookOrder response = new BookOrder(request);
        response.OrderNumber = "12345678";
        return response;
    }

    string IServiceClass.FinalizeOrder()
    {
        return "Order placed successfully.";
    }

}
```

Typed Message

A typed message service, also known as the "message contract model," is where you define the messages and their contents. Here, the messages are Message Contract attributes, meaning that message contracts are used to define typed message classes, sending custom messages in and out of service operations.

The following example, taken from Chapter 6, shows a service contract along with a defined typed message that is used as a parameter in a typed service operation:

```
[ServiceContract]
public interface IBookOrder
{
   [OperationContract]
   void PlaceOrder(Contract MyContract);
}

[MessageContract]
public class MyContract
{
   [MessageHeader]
   string Title;
   [MessageBodyMember]
   decimal cost;
```

Before this chapter gets to the really good information, one last quick review of services and endpoints is in order.

Service Contracts

By now you should have a good grasp of service contracts. A service contains one or more operations, all of which are annotated with specific attributes that define them as WCF services and available service methods, or operations. Methods not tagged with the [OperationContract] attribute are normal methods and are not available or accessible to the client, but can be called internally from within the service. This is analogous to making a web service's method consumable by decorating it with the [WebMethod] attribute.

As you are aware, the signature of a contract is critical because it is the mechanism by which the outside world understands the service. The signature of a service is effectively created by defining a method and annotating it with the [OperationContract] attribute. A service contract is created by grouping the operations within a defined interface and annotating the interface with the [OperationContract] attribute.

The following example shows a simple WCF service and exposed service operations:

```
[ServiceContract]
public interface IServiceClass
{
    [OperationContract]
    string GetText();

    [OperationContract]
```

```
    int MultiplyNumbers(int firstvalue, int secondvalue);
}

public class ServiceClass : IServiceClass
{
    string IServiceClass.GetText()
    {
        StreamReader sw = new StreamReader(@"c:\wrox\WCFServiceTest.txt");
        return sw.ReadLine();
        //return "Hello World";
    }

    int IServiceClass.MultiplyNumbers(int firstvalue, int secondvalue)
    {
        return firstvalue * secondvalue;
    }
}
```

Service Endpoints

Clients can only access a service through service endpoints. Endpoints can be defined in code or in a configuration file. A service can have one or more endpoints, and each endpoint must have an address, a binding, and a service contract. Chapters 4, 5, and 6, respectively, discussed each of these in detail.

The following sections provide a review of defining endpoints in code and in a configuration file.

Specifying in Code

The following example illustrates defining an endpoint in code. As stated earlier, an endpoint needs an address, a binding, and a service contract. The first two lines define the addresses through which the service will be accessed.

The next line creates the service host through which the service will be hosted. The addresses are passed as parameters in the service host constructor.

The next two lines define the bindings that the endpoint will use, and the remaining lines call the AddEndpoint method of the ServiceHost class to add the endpoints, passing the service contract, defined bindings, and defined addresses. The service is then opened and available to clients:

```
Uri bpa = new Uri("net.pipe://localhost/NetNamedPipeBinding");
Uri tcpa = new Uri("net.tcp://localhost:8000/TcpBinding");

sh = new ServiceHost(typeof(ServiceClass), bpa, tcpa);

NetNamedPipeBinding pb = new NetNamedPipeBinding();
NetTcpBinding tcpb = new NetTcpBinding();

ServiceMetadataBehavior mBehave = new ServiceMetadataBehavior();
sh.Description.Behaviors.Add(mBehave);
sh.AddServiceEndpoint(typeof(IMetadataExchange),
```

```
MetadataExchangeBindings.CreateMexTcpBinding(), "mex");

sh.AddServiceEndpoint(typeof(IMetadataExchange),
MetadataExchangeBindings.CreateMexNamedPipeBinding(), "mex");

sh.AddServiceEndpoint(typeof(IServiceClass), pb, bpa);
sh.AddServiceEndpoint(typeof(IServiceClass), tcpb, tcpa);

sh.Open();
```

Specifying in Configuration

The same service endpoints can be defined in a configuration file as shown in the following code. It has been stated a number of times that the preferred method of defining an endpoint is through configuration because of the flexibility and ease of deployment:

```xml
<?xml version="1.0" encoding="utf-8" ?>
<configuration>
  <system.serviceModel>
    <services>
      <service name ="WCFService.ServiceClass"
behaviorConfiguration="metadataSupport">
        <host>
          <baseAddresses>
            <add baseAddress="net.pipe://localhost/WCFService"/>
            <add baseAddress="net.tcp://localhost:8000/WCFService"/>
            <add baseAddress="http://localhost:8080/WCFService"/>
          </baseAddresses>
        </host>
        <endpoint address="tcpmex"
                  binding="mexTcpBinding"
                  contract="IMetadataExchange"/>
        <endpoint address="namedpipemex"
                  binding="mexNamedPipeBinding"
                  contract="IMetadataExchange"/>
        <endpoint address="" binding="wsHttpBinding"
contract="WCFService.IServiceClass"/>
      </service>
    </services>
    <behaviors>
      <serviceBehaviors>
        <behavior name="metadataSupport">
          <serviceMetadata httpGetEnabled="false" httpGetUrl=""/>
        </behavior>
      </serviceBehaviors>
    </behaviors>
  </system.serviceModel>
</configuration>
```

When defining an endpoint in configuration, the ServiceHost object automatically scans the configuration file for defined endpoints. Hence, endpoints can be added, modified, or removed non-invasively. This makes adding endpoints and deployment much easier over defining them in code.

Service Behaviors

Up until now the discussion has focused solely on service contracts that define the inputs, outputs, data types, and exposed functionality of a service. Service contracts, when implemented, create a class that when combined with address and binding information makes the service available to clients.

Yet, given all of this information and functionality, the need to control service execution aspects and characteristics of the service is still critical. For example, how do you control threading issues and manage service instances?

The answer is simple: behaviors. Service behaviors are objects that modify and control the runtime characteristics of Windows Communication Foundation services. When a WCF service contract is implemented you then have the ability to shape many of the execution characteristics of the service. These behaviors, or characteristics, are controlled by configuring a runtime property, or through the defining of custom behaviors.

There are two types of behaviors in Windows Communication Foundation: service behaviors and operation behaviors. They are applied just like all the other WCF objects, by adding attributes. The following two sections discuss the [ServiceBehavior] attribute and the [OperationBehavior] attribute.

Unlike the other attributes that you have learned about so far, such as the [ServiceContract] and [OperationContract] attributes, which are defined inside an interface, the [ServiceBehavior] and [OperationBehavior] attributes are applied to the class that implements the interface.

The following code snippet illustrates how the [ServiceBehavior] and [OperationBehavior] attributes are applied:

```
[ServiceContract]
public interface IServiceClass
{
  [OperationContract]
  int AddNumbers(int number1, int number2);

  [OperationContract]
  int SubtractNumbers(int number1, int number2);

}

[ServiceBehavior]
public class ServiceClass : IServiceClass
{
  [OperationBehavior]
  public int AddNumbers(int number1, int numbers2)
  {
    return number1 + number2;
  }
  [OperationBehavior]
  public int SubtractNumbers(int number1, int numbers2)
  {
    return number1 - number2;
  }

}
```

Just like the other attributes, the `[ServiceBehavior]` and `[OperationBehavior]` attributes have a number of available properties that assist in specifying the behaviors of the service. In the preceding example, the attributes would take on the default values of each property because no properties were explicitly specified.

The following two sections discuss the available properties for both the `[ServiceBehavior]` and `[OperationBehavior]` attributes.

ServiceBehavior Attribute

The `[ServiceBehavior]` attribute comes from the System.ServiceModel.ServiceBehaviorAttribute class and specifies the execution behavior of a service contract implementation. The `[ServiceBehavior]` attribute contains the following properties:

❑ AddressFilterMode

❑ AutomaticSessionShutdown

❑ ConcurrencyMode

❑ ConfigurationName

❑ IgnoreExtensionDataObject

❑ IncludeExceptionDetailInFaults

❑ InstanceContextMode

❑ ReleaseServiceInstanceOnTransactionComplete

❑ TransactionAutoCompleteOnSessionClose

❑ TransactionIsolationLevel

❑ TransactionTimeout

❑ UseSynchronizedContext

❑ ValidateMustUnderstand

These properties are discussed in detail in the following sections.

AddressFilterMode

The AddressFilterMode property gets or sets the address filter mode of the service. This mode is used by the service dispatcher to route incoming messages to the appropriate endpoint. The modes used by this property come from the AddressFilterMode enumeration, and the available values are as follows:

❑ **Any:** Applies a filter that matches on any address of an incoming message.

❑ **Exact:** Applies a filter that matches on the address of an incoming message.

❑ **Prefix:** Applies a filter that matches on the longest prefix of the address of an incoming message.

The following example illustrates using the AddressFilterMode property to apply a filter that matches on any address of an incoming message:

```
[ServiceBehavior(AddressFilterMode=AddressFilterMode = AddressFilterMode.Any)]
public class ServiceClass : IServiceClass
{
  . . .
}
```

The default value for this property is *Exact*.

AutomaticSessionShutdown

The AutomaticSessionShutdown property is used to specify whether to close a session automatically when a client closes an output session. If the property value is true, the service automatically closes its session when the client closes its output session. The service does not close the session until it has finished processing all remaining messages. For custom control of the session, set the value of this property to false.

The following example sets the AutomaticSessionShutdown property to a value of *false*. The service will not close any sessions automatically:

```
[ServiceBehavior(AutomaticSessionShutdown=false)]
public class ServiceClass : IServiceClass
{
  . . .
}
```

The default value for this property is *true*.

An output channel is a channel that can send messages, thus an output session is a session established prior to the acceptance of an output channel, which then sends messages that have a session id for that connection/section. Output sessions are typically not important at the application level. They only come into necessity if you are building channels.

ConcurrencyMode

The ConcurrencyMode property specifies the thread support for the service. The modes used by this property come from the ConcurrencyMode enumeration, and the available values are as follows:

❑   **Single:** The service instance is single threaded and does not accept reentrance calls. If a message arrives while another message is currently being processed, the newly arrived message must wait until the current message is finished being processed.

❑   **Multiple:** The service is multi-threaded. In this mode, synchronization and state consistency must be handled manually because no synchronization guarantees are made. This is because threads can change the service object at any given time.

❑   **Reentrant:** The service is single threaded and can accept reentrant calls.

The following example sets the ConcurrencyMode property to a value of *Single*. The service will be single threaded and not accept reentrant calls:

```
[ServiceBehavior(ConcurrencyMode=ConcurrencyMode.Single)]
public class ServiceClass : IServiceClass
{
  . . .
}
```

Using the reentrant mode is useful when one service calls another service, which calls the first service in return. A reentrant service accepts calls when it calls out. Because of possible state inconsistencies, you must be careful to leave your service object state in a consistent state prior to calling out.

Setting this property to a value of Single tells the system to limit all instances of the service to a single thread of execution. The biggest benefit of this is that there are no threading issues that you have to concern yourself with. Setting the property to a value of Multiple informs the system that service objects can be run on multiple threads, which means thread safety is left up to the developer.

The default value for this property is *Single*.

ConfigurationName

The ConfigurationName property specifies or retrieves the value that is used to locate the service element in a configuration file.

The following example sets the ConfigurationName to a value of "service":

```
[ServiceBehavior(ConfigurationName="service")]
public class ServiceClass : IServiceClass
{
    ...
}
```

The default value for this property is the namespace qualified name of the type without the assembly information.

IgnoreExtensionDataObject

The IgnoreExtensionDataObject property specifies whether to send unknown serialization data between the service and client. In typical communication, most types are defined, and the service knows how to handle each member. For example, the BookOrder type may be defined with ISBN and Quantity elements, and the service expects these elements. It is possible, however, to send elements that the service is not aware of, such as a Title element. In these cases, any Windows Communication Foundation type that implements the IExtensibleDataObject interface stores any extra data sent over. In this example, the service would hang on to the Title element for serialization later and be re-emitted.

The following example sets the IgnoreExtensionDataObject to *true*, which tells the service to ignore any extra data (elements) and to not re-emit them:

```
[ServiceBehavior(IgnoreExtensionDataObject=true)]
public class ServiceClass : IServiceClass
{
    ...
}
```

The default value for this property is *false*.

IncludeExceptionDetailInFaults

The IncludeExceptionDetailInFaults property specifies what is to be done with unhandled exceptions. When the value of this property is *false*, unhandled exceptions are converted into a System.ServiceModel.FaultException of type System.ServiceModel.ExceptionDetail.

The root of this goes back to how exceptions are handled in managed applications. Processing errors are represented as Exception objects in managed applications, and in SOAP applications error information is communicated via SOAP fault messages. Windows Communication Foundation utilizes both types of error systems (Exception objects and SOAP fault messages). Therefore, in WCF any managed exception must be converted to a SOAP fault message to be sent over the wire.

This type of information is extremely useful during development to help debug your service, but it is recommended that this property be set to false in production. For more information on this, see the section titled "Handling Exceptions" later in this chapter.

The following example sets the IncludeExceptionDetailInFaults property to a value of *true*. The service will then send information back to the client about any internal service method exceptions:

```
[ServiceBehavior(IncludeExceptionDetailInFaults=true)]
public class ServiceClass : IServiceClass
{
    ...
}
```

The default value for this property is *false*.

InstanceContextMode

The InstanceContextMode property indicates at what point new service objects are created. There is not a direct connection between the service object and the communication channel, therefore the lifetime of the service object is completely independent of the client-service channel. This property specifies the lifetime of the InstanceContext object. The lifetime of the user-defined object is the lifetime of the InstanceContext by default.

Windows Communication Foundation can create a new InstanceContext object for the following situations:

❑ **PerCall:** A new InstanceContext object is created, and recycled, succeeding each call.

❑ **PerSession:** A new InstanceContext object is created per session, and the instance is not sharable between multiple sessions.

❑ **Single:** A single InstanceContext object is created and used for all incoming calls and is not recycled succeeding the calls.

The following example sets the InstanceContextMode property to a value of *PerSession*. The service will create a new object when a new communication session is initiated by the client. All calls from the client to the service will be handled by the same service object:

```
[ServiceBehavior(InstanceContextMode=InstanceContextMode.PerSession)]
public class ServiceClass : IServiceClass
{
    ...
}
```

The default value for this property is *PerSession*.

For more information regarding InstanceContext and its interaction with WCF services, see the section "InstanceContext" later in this chapter.

ReleaseServiceInstanceOnTransactionComplete

The ReleaseServiceInstanceOnTransactionComplete property specifies whether the current service object is recycled when the current transaction is complete.

The following example sets the ReleaseServiceInstanceOnTransactionComplete property to a value of *true*. The service will recycle the service object:

```
[ServiceBehavior(ReleaseServiceInstanceOnTransactionComplete=true)]
public class ServiceClass : IServiceClass
{
    ...
}
```

The default value for this property is *true*.

TransactionAutoCompleteOnSessionClose

The TransactionAutoCompleteOnSessionClose property specifies whether any pending transactions are to be completed when the current session is closed.

The following example sets the TransactionAutoCompleteOnSessionClose property to a value of *true*. All pending transactions will be complete when the current session is closed:

```
[ServiceBehavior(TransactionAutoCompleteOnSessionClose=true)]
public class ServiceClass : IServiceClass
{
    ...
}
```

The default value for this property is *false*.

TransactionIsolationLevel

The TransactionIsolationLevel property specifies the transaction isolation level of the service. The levels used by this property come from the System.Transactions namespace and its IsolationLevel enumeration. To specify one of the following values, you will need to add a reference to the System.Transactions namespace and include a *using* statement to that namespace.

The available values are as follows:

❑ **Chaos:** The pending changes from more highly visible transactions cannot be overwritten.

❑ **ReadCommitted:** Volatile data cannot be read during the transaction, but can be modified.

❑ **ReadUncommitted:** Volatile data can be read and modified during the transaction.

❑ **RepeatableRead:** Volatile data can be read but not modified during the transaction. New data can be added during the transaction.

❑ **Serializable:** Volatile data can be read but not modified during the transaction. No new data can be added during the transaction.

❑ **Snapshot:** Volatile data can be read. Prior to modifying any data, the transaction looks to see if the data has been changed by another transaction. An error is raised if the data has been changed. The process allows the current transaction access to previously committed data.

❑ **Unspecified:** A different isolation level is being used other than the one specified, and the level is undeterminable.

Volatile data is defined as data that will be affected by a transaction. When creating a transaction you can also specify the isolation level to be applied to that transaction. The level of access that other transactions have to volatile data before your transaction completes is called the isolation level. The isolation level you specify on your transaction, when your transaction is created, determines the access to the volatile data of other transactions before your transaction is finished.

You can see by taking a look at the preceding list that ReadUncommitted provides the lowest isolation level. This level allows multiple transactions to read and modify data at the same time, leading to possible data corruption.

The highest level is Serializable. Though this level offers the highest protection, it does require that one transaction complete before another transaction begins.

The isolation level you select can have an impact on performance in your application. There are trade-offs that you will probably need to ask yourself about in order to decide which level to select. Do you want multiple transactions operating simultaneously on a data store, which offers little or no protection against data corruption but is the faster performing? Or, does data integrity mean more to you with each transaction completing prior to other transactions being given the OK to operate on the data? These are the questions you need to ask yourself prior to selecting the appropriate isolation level for your environment.

The following example sets the TransactionIsolationLevel property to a value of *ReadCommitted*. While the current transaction is reading/modifying data, other transactions can read the volatile data but cannot modify it:

```
[ServiceBehavior(TransactionIsolationLevel=System.Transactions.IsolationLevel.ReadC
ommitted)]
public class ServiceClass : IServiceClass
{
   ...
}
```

The default value for this property is *Unspecified*.

TransactionTimeout

The TransactionTimeout property specifies the amount of time, in the form of a TimeSpan object, that a transaction has to complete. Here also there are trade-offs in the amount of time given to a transaction to complete or abort. A higher value might result in fewer timeout exceptions but might not be too pleasing to the user, who might think the system is not responding. On the other hand, a lower timeout value might result in more timeout exceptions but would certainly let the user, as well as the developer, know what is happening.

The following example sets the TransactionTimeout property to a value of *1*. The transaction must complete in one minute or be automatically aborted and rolled back:

❑ **Allowed:** Impersonation is performed if credentials are available and ImpersonateCallerForAllOperations is *true*.

❑ **NotAllowed:** Impersonation is not performed.

❑ **Required:** Impersonation is required.

The following example sets the Impersonation property to a value of *Allowed*. The service will execute using the credentials that are passed from the client, or use its own if none are supplied by the client:

```
[OperationBehavior(Impersonation=ImpersonationOption.Allowed)]
public void AddNumber(int number1, int number2)
{
   result = number1 + number2;
}
```

The default value for this property is *NotAllowed*.

ReleaseInstanceMode

The ReleaseInstanceMode property is used to determine the recycle point of the service object during the course of an operation. This property utilizes the InstanceContextMode property in that the default behavior of this property is to recycle the service object according to the value of InstanceContextMode property.

When dealing with threading, WCF makes no guarantees as to the state of the threads. To be safe, set the InstanceContextMode property to *PerCall*. This will make sure that you get a new object when your service runs.

When using transactions, this property comes in handy to ensure that volatile data is cleaned up before the method call is processed.

The modes used by this property come from the ReleaseInstanceMode enumeration, and the available values are as follows:

❑ **AfterCall:** Recycles the object subsequent to the completion of the operation.

❑ **BeforeAndAfterCall:** Recycles the object prior to calling the operation and subsequent to the completion of the operation.

❑ **BeforeCall:** Recycles the object prior to calling the operation.

❑ **None:** Recycles the object according to the InstanceContextMode.

The following example sets the ReleaseInstanceMode property to a value of *AfterCall*. The service object will be recycled after the successful completion of the operation:

```
[OperationBehavior(ReleaseInstanceMode=ReleaseInstanceMode.AfterCall)]
public void AddNumber(int number1, int number2)
{
   result = number1 + number2;
}
```

The default value for this property is *None*.

TransactionAutoComplete

The TransactionAutoComplete property specifies whether to commit the current transaction automatically. If the value of this property is set to *true* and no unhandled exceptions are found, the current transaction is automatically committed. If exceptions do occur, the transaction is cancelled. If the property is set to a value of *false*, the transaction will need to be completed or cancelled directly via code.

The following example sets the TransactionAutoComplete property to a value of *true*. All transactions will be automatically committed if no exceptions are found:

```
[OperationBehavior(TransactionAutoComplete=true)]
public void AddNumber(int number1, int number2)
{
  result = number1 + number2;
}
```

The default value for this property is *true*, and is defaulted to this value for a reason. As stated, a value of false means that the transaction will need to be completed or aborted manually through code. Letting the system automatically commit the current transaction also lets the system deal with related tasks such as cancelling and rolling back the transaction if an exception occurs. Setting this property to a value of false means that the developer will need to deal with those issues as well as others, such as dealing with exceptions. It is best to let the system handle the transactions unless there are specific reasons you want to manually control the transaction.

TransactionScopeRequired

The TransactionScopeRequired property specifies whether the associated method requires a transaction scope. If a flowed transaction is available, the method will execute within that transaction, otherwise a new transaction is created and used for that method execution. A flowed transaction is a situation in which a transaction id is passed over the wire and used on the receiving side to perform work by enlisting in the corresponding transaction and executing within the scope of that transaction.

The following example sets the TransactionScopeRequired property to a value of *true*. All calls to the service must run on the same thread that is specified by the SynchronizationContext:

```
[OperationBehavior(TransactionScopeRequired=true)]
public void AddNumber(int number1, int number2)
{
  result = number1 + number2;
}
```

The default value for this property is *false*.

Using Configuration to Specify Behaviors

The previous two sections showed how to apply service and operation behaviors via code. It is also possible to specify behaviors via configuration. The following configuration file, taken from one of the examples in Chapter 7, shows how to set service throttling:

```
<?xml version="1.0" encoding="utf-8" ?>
<configuration>
  <system.serviceModel>
```

```
    <services>
        <service name ="WCFService.ServiceClass"
behaviorConfiguration="metadataSupport">
            <host>
              <baseAddresses>
                <add baseAddress="net.pipe://localhost/WCFService"/>
                <add baseAddress="net.tcp://localhost:8000/WCFService"/>
                <add baseAddress="http://localhost:8080/WCFService"/>
              </baseAddresses>
            </host>
            <endpoint address="tcpmex"
                      binding="mexTcpBinding"
                      contract="IMetadataExchange"/>
            <endpoint address="namedpipemex"
                      binding="mexNamedPipeBinding"
                      contract="IMetadataExchange"/>
            <endpoint address="" binding="wsDualHttpBinding"
contract="WCFService.IServiceClass"/>
            <!--<endpoint address="mex" binding="mexHttpBinding"
contract="IMetadataExchange"/>-->
        </service>
    </services>
    <behaviors>
        <serviceBehaviors>
          <behavior name="metadataSupport">
            <serviceDebug includeExceptionDetailInFaults="true"/>
            <serviceMetadata httpGetEnabled="false" httpGetUrl=""/>
            <serviceThrottling maxConcurrentCalls="10" maxConcurrentInstances="5"
maxConcurrentSessions="5"/>
            <serviceSecurityAudit auditLogLocation="Application"
suppressAuditFailure="false"/>
          </behavior>
        </serviceBehaviors>
    </behaviors>
  </system.serviceModel>
</configuration>
```

The <serviceDebug> element contains a number of properties that specify debugging and help information for a Windows Communication Foundation service. In the preceding example, the IncludeExceptionDetailInFaults attribute specifies to include exception information in the detail of the SOAP faults, just like the property defined earlier.

Throttling

Windows Communication Foundation lets you set throttling limits on your service. Throttling is the concept of limiting the amount of work a service can accept. You can see in the previous configuration file that limits can be set on concurrent calls, concurrent instances, and concurrent sessions.

Throttling is controlled by adding the <serviceThrottling> element within the <behavior> element in the service or host application configuration file. You can then specify the attributes of the <serviceThrottling> element to define the throttling behavior of your service.

The maxConcurrentCalls attribute lets you specify the maximum number of concurrent calls for a service. If the maximum number of concurrent calls has been met when a new call is placed, the call is queued and will be processed when the number of concurrent calls is below the specified maximum number. The default is 16 but a value of 0 is equal to Int32.MaxValue.

The maxConcurrentInstances attribute lets you specify the maximum number of concurrent service instances. If a request for a new instance is received and the maximum number has already been reached, the request is queued up and will be completed when the number of instances is below the specified maximum. The default value is Int32.MaxValue.

The maxConcurrentSessions attribute lets you specify the sessions that service can have. More specifically, it specifies the maximum number of connections to a single service. In reality, it will accept more than the specified limit, but the key is that only the channels below the specified limit will be active. The default value for this attribute is 10, but setting this value to 0 is equal to setting it to Int32.MaxValue.

InstanceContext

This chapter has mentioned services and InstanceContext a number of times, so it is only fitting to spend a few paragraphs discussing the differences between the two. It was stated earlier that there is not a direct connection between the service object and the communication channel; therefore the lifetime of the service object is completely independent of the client-service channel.

This is where the InstanceContext comes in. The InstanceContext class is a runtime object whose sole purpose is to bind a channel to an instance of the service object. This is a very useful feature because it allows for the separation of the channel and service. The lifetime of the channel is now disconnected from the lifetime of the service, each being controlled and handled independently.

Why would you want to do this? By managing them separately, you can continue to have open, and maintain, a secure and reliable channel while simultaneously disposing of a service when your transaction or operation is finished. You can keep the channel open and bind it to another instance of a service when you are ready to use it.

By default, when a message is received by the service, a new InstanceContext is created. However, this is controlled by setting the InstanceContextMode property, discussed a few pages ago. This property controls the exact lifetime of the service object. This property gives you the flexibility to maintain state across multiple calls from the same client, multiple calls from multiple clients, or where state does not need to be maintained over calls at all.

Handling Exceptions

As much as developers would like to think that they write error-free code, all applications will have their fair share of errors that will throw exceptions. Windows Communication Foundation services are no "exception" (pun intended). Therefore, it would be wise to build error handling into your WCF service.

It was stated earlier that Windows Communication Foundation utilizes two types of error systems (Exception objects and SOAP fault messages). Processing errors are represented as Exception objects in managed applications, and in SOAP applications error information is communicated via SOAP fault messages. Therefore, in WCF any managed exception must be converted to a SOAP fault message to be sent over the wire back to the client.

Two types of SOAP faults can be sent back to the client:

❑   **Declared:** The operation has a `[FaultContract]` attribute, which specifies a custom SOAP fault type.

❑   **Undeclared:** Faults that are not specified in the operation contract.

It is recommended that service operations declare their faults via the `[FaultContract]` attribute. This formally specifies all SOAP faults that a client should expect to receive throughout the course of normal operation. To maximize the level of security, only the information that a client needs to know regarding the exception should be returned in the SOAP fault.

Declared SOAP faults come in handy for architecting interoperable, distributed applications that are stout enough to support any environment and situation. Yet, there may be times when undeclared SOAP faults may be more useful, such as for debugging purposes where unexpected situations can occur and information can be sent back to the client.

One of the ways you can get internal service operation exception information is by setting the IncludeExceptionDetailInFault property to true. This property is available on the ServiceBehaviorAttribute and ServiceDebugBehavior classes and allows the clients to get sensitive information specific to internal service operations, such as personal identifiable information. This information helps in debugging a service application.

The following code snippet shows how to enable IncludeExceptionDetailInFault using a configuration file:

```
<behaviors>
  <serviceBehaviors>
    <behavior>
      <serviceDebug includeExceptionDetailInFaults="true"/>
    </behavior>
  </serviceBehaviors>
</behaviors>
```

Due to the amount and type of data returned by setting the IncludeExceptionDetailInFault to true, it is recommended that this property be set to true only during development and not be enabled during production.

FaultException

The FaultException class represents a SOAP fault and should be used in a service to create an untyped, or undeclared, fault to return to the client, typically for debugging purposes. From the client side, FaultException objects returned from the service can be caught and inspected to determine whether an unknown or generic fault has occurred.

The FaultException extends the CommunicationException object so it is important to catch FaultExceptions before catching any CommunicationException faults.

Fault exceptions should be thrown when you want the stream to be passed to the constructor, which are then made available to the client and can be called using the FaultException.ToString method.

The following example illustrates how to use a try/catch block to catch and manage exceptions thrown from the service:

```
Try
  // call the operations of the service
  ...
catch (FaultException fe)
{
  // do something with the exception
}
```

There are two reasons why you would want to use the FaultException class:

❑ For debugging purposes when a SOAP fault can be sent to the client from a service

❑ When faults are not part of the service contract and you want to catch SOAP faults on the client

FaultContract Attribute

Although there might be times when the FaultException class will be beneficial, such as in the two scenarios just given, the general recommendation is to use the FaultContract attribute to return strongly typed SOAP faults.

SOAP-based applications such as Windows Communication Foundation communicate error information using SOAP fault messages. Exception information must be converted from exceptions into SOAP faults prior to sending the information to the client.

Use the FaultContract attribute to specify one or more specific exception conditions. These conditions are then added as explicit SOAP fault messages to the WSDL (Web Service Description Language) description, which are returned to the client by the operation. When returning faults, you have two options:

❑ Using the default service exceptions behaviors

❑ Specifying how exceptions are mapped to fault messages

The second option, specifying how exceptions are mapped to fault messages, requires that you decide the conditions under which a client needs to be informed of errors. Once these conditions are identified a custom SOAP fault can be defined with the operation tagged as returning a SOAP fault. For example, the BookOrder operation might return information to customers informing them that the quantity of books they have ordered is not available or that their credit card could not be processed.

The fault message can contain very sensitive information so there are a few recommendations that should be followed. First, only send information in a SOAP fault back to the client that the client needs to know. Second, set the ProtectionLevel property. Failure to follow these recommendations will increase security problems.

This attribute has some of the same properties as the other attributes discussed previously:

❑ **Action:** Defines the action of the fault message.

❑ **DetailType:** Returns the type of the detail object serialized in the message.

❑ **Name:** Defines the name of the fault message.

❑ **Namespace:** Defines the namespace of the fault message.

❑ **HasProtectionLevel:** Specifies the level of protection of the fault message.

As stated earlier, the IncludeExceptionDetailsInFaults property can be used to help in debugging. This can be set through the configuration file, and when set, automatically returns exception information to the client, which appears as FaultException exceptions.

The following example illustrates how to use the FaultContract attribute to return a SOAP fault. The first step is to configure the service appropriately by adding the FaultContract attribute to those operations that you want to return SOAP faults:

```
[ServiceContract]
public interface IWCFService
{
  [OperationContract]
  [FaultContract(typeof(OrderFault),ProtectionLevel=ProtectionLeve.EncryptAndSign)]
  String BookOrder(string ISBN, int Quantity)
}

[DataContract]
public class OrderFault
{
  private string info;

  Public OrderFault(string Message)
  {
    This.info = Message
  }

  [DataMember]
  public string msg
  {
    Get { return this.info; }
    Set { this.info = value; }
  }

  Class WCFService : IWCFService
  {
    Public string BookOrder(string ISBN, int Quantity)
    {
      int BooksOnHand = 10;
      //check book quantity vs. order quantity
      If (Quantity <= BooksOnHand)
        return "Order placed"
      else
        throw new FaultException<OrderFault>(new OrderFault("You ordered too many
books"));
    }
  }
}
```

On the client side the SOAP fault is received and dealt with, as shown here:

```
private void Form1_Load(object sender, EventArgs e)
{
  TCP.ServiceClassClient client = new
    WCFClientApp.TCP.ServiceClassClient("NetTcpBinding_IServiceClass");
  try
  {
    client.BookOrder("123456", 11);
  }
  catch (FaultException<OrderFault> of)
  {
    MessageBox.Show(of.Detail.Message);
  }
  catch (FaultException unknownFault)
  {
    MessageBox.Show(unknownFault.Message);
  }

}
```

Although this code is a very simple code snippet, it provides the necessary information to return a SOAP fault and have it processed appropriately by the client.

Programming Example

This last section walks you through building a service that uses several of the behaviors you learned about earlier in the chapter. Open the WCFService project you have been working with so far and replace the existing code with the following code:

```
using System;
using System.Transactions;
using System.ServiceModel;
using System.Collections.Generic;
using System.Runtime.Serialization;
using System.IO;

namespace WCFService
{
    [ServiceContract(SessionMode = SessionMode.Required)]
    public interface IServiceClass
    {
        [OperationContract]
        string GetText();

        [OperationContract]
        int MultiplyNumbers(int firstvalue, int secondvalue);
    }

    [ServiceBehavior(AutomaticSessionShutdown=true,
        ConcurrencyMode=ConcurrencyMode.Single,
        IncludeExceptionDetailInFaults=false,
```

```
                InstanceContextMode=InstanceContextMode.PerSession,
                UseSynchronizationContext=true)]
        public class ServiceClass : IServiceClass
        {

            [OperationBehavior(AutoDisposeParameters=true,
                TransactionAutoComplete=true,
                TransactionScopeRequired=true)]
            string IServiceClass.GetText()
            {
                StreamReader sw = new StreamReader(@"c:\wrox\WCFServiceTest.txt");
                return sw.ReadLine();
                //return "Hello World";
            }

            [OperationBehavior(AutoDisposeParameters = true,
                TransactionAutoComplete = true,
                TransactionScopeRequired = true)]
            int IServiceClass.MultiplyNumbers(int firstvalue, int secondvalue)
            {
                return firstvalue * secondvalue;
            }


        }
    }
```

Take a quick look at the service code. You should notice that the service interface definition is very similar to other examples. What is different is that this class implements the service interface. The class itself is annotated with the [ServiceBehavior] attribute, and the corresponding methods are annotated with the [OperationBehavior] attribute.

In this example, several properties are applied to the service behavior itself and each operation behavior. For example, the *AutomaticSessionShutown* property is set to *true*, which automatically closes the session when the client closes its output session.

On the operations themselves, the *TransactionAutoComplete* property is set to *true*, which tells the service to automatically commit the transaction.

Compile the service to make sure no errors are found. The next step is to modify the host application. What needs to be modified here is the configuration file, and the only reason this needs to be modified is because the last example dealt with duplex communication. Because this example does not use duplex communication you need to set it back. Simply change the binding property of the highlighted line from *wsDualHttpBinding* to *wsHttpBinding*:

```xml
<?xml version="1.0" encoding="utf-8" ?>
<configuration>
  <system.serviceModel>
    <services>
      <service name ="WCFService.ServiceClass"
behaviorConfiguration="metadataSupport">
        <host>
          <baseAddresses>
            <add baseAddress="net.pipe://localhost/WCFService"/>
            <add baseAddress="net.tcp://localhost:8000/WCFService"/>
```

```
                    <add baseAddress="http://localhost:8080/WCFService"/>
                </baseAddresses>
            </host>
            <endpoint address="tcpmex"
                      binding="mexTcpBinding"
                      contract="IMetadataExchange"/>
            <endpoint address="namedpipemex"
                      binding="mexNamedPipeBinding"
                      contract="IMetadataExchange"/>
            <endpoint address="" binding="wsHttpBinding"
    contract="WCFService.IServiceClass"/>
            <!--<endpoint address="mex" binding="mexHttpBinding"
    contract="IMetadataExchange"/>-->
        </service>
    </services>
    <behaviors>
      <serviceBehaviors>
        <behavior name="metadataSupport">
          <serviceMetadata httpGetEnabled="false" httpGetUrl=""/>
        </behavior>
      </serviceBehaviors>
    </behaviors>
  </system.serviceModel>
</configuration>
```

Compile the host application and press F5 to start the service.

The next step is to modify the client. Because the last example dealt with duplex communication, the client code behind the form and the configuration file contained endpoint definition information dealing with duplex communication. Both need to be modified to operate correctly.

The easiest way to do that is to delete the current service references and re-add them. However, if you feel that the stars are aligned in your favor and want to try to manually modify the configuration file, go right ahead. The rest of you can delete the service references and re-add them. The information to re-add them is the same as past examples, so that won't be covered here. Remember that you will need the host application running to add the service references.

The following client code, however, assumes that you name the service references TCP and NamedPipe and, given the endpoint definitions in the host application configuration file, specify the service URIs as follows:

```
net.pipe://localhost/WCFService/namedpipemex
```

and

```
Net.tcp://localhost:8000/WCFService/tcpmex
```

Once you have your service references added, change the caption of button1 to "Get Text" and change the caption of button2 to "Multiply." Next, modify the code behind the form as follows:

```
using System;
using System.Collections.Generic;
using System.ComponentModel;
```

```csharp
using System.Data;
using System.Drawing;
using System.Text;
using System.Windows.Forms;
using System.ServiceModel;
using System.ServiceModel.Channels;

namespace WCFClientApp
{

    public partial class Form1 : Form
    {
        private int _Selection;
        private int val1 = 5;
        private int val2 = 5;

        public Form1()
        {
            InitializeComponent();
        }


        private void Form1_Load(object sender, EventArgs e)
        {
            radioButton1.Checked = true;

        }

        private void button1_Click(object sender, EventArgs e)
        {

            switch (_Selection)
            {
                case 0:
                    TCP.ServiceClassClient client = new
WCFClientApp.TCP.ServiceClassClient("NetTcpBinding_IServiceClass");
                    textBox1.Text = client.GetText();
                    break;

                case 1:
                    NamedPipe.ServiceClassClient client1 = new
WCFClientApp.NamedPipe.ServiceClassClient("NetNamedPipeBinding_IServiceClass");
                    textBox1.Text = client1.GetText();
                    break;

                case 2:
                    break;
            }
        }

        private void button2_Click(object sender, EventArgs e)
        {
            switch (_Selection)
```

```
                    {
                        case 0:
                            TCP.ServiceClassClient client = new

WCFClientApp.TCP.ServiceClassClient("NetTcpBinding_IServiceClass");
                            textBox2.Text = client.MultiplyNumbers(val1, val2).ToString();
                            break;

                        case 1:
                            NamedPipe.ServiceClassClient client1 = new

WCFClientApp.NamedPipe.ServiceClassClient("NetNamedPipeBinding_IServiceClass");
                            textBox2.Text = client1.MultiplyNumbers(val1, val2).ToString();
                            break;

                        case 2:
                            break;
                    }

                }

                private void radioButton1_CheckedChanged(object sender, EventArgs e)
                {
                    _Selection = 0;
                    textBox1.Text = "";
                    textBox2.Text = "";
                }

                private void radioButton2_CheckedChanged(object sender, EventArgs e)
                {
                    _Selection = 1;
                    textBox1.Text = "";
                    textBox2.Text = "";
                }

            }
        }
```

Compile the client application and press F5 to run the client application. You should be familiar with this form by now, so you can select the transport you want to use and click the appropriate buttons.

Summary

The purpose of this chapter was to provide you with an in-depth look at concepts that are more specific to services. This chapter began by spending a few pages providing an overview of WCF services focusing on how service contracts and their associated endpoints are defined. This information was covered in detail in the past several chapters but provided the basis for the rest of this chapter.

Service behaviors exist so that you can modify the runtime behavior of the service to suit the needs of your application. Therefore it is important that you understand the available options that you can apply to your service in which to control the behavior of your service. Thus, a large portion of this chapter covered the [ServiceBehavior] and [OperationBehavior] attributes and provided an example that illustrates the application of a few of the behavior attributes.

Lastly, and equally important, is the error handling in WCF. Microsoft did not take this subject lightly, and it shows in the functionality it has provided via the *FaultException* class and *FaultContract* attribute. Both of these let you control how errors are handled and managed within the service and communicated back to the client.

With this chapter, you should have garnered a good understanding of Windows Communication Foundation, a foundation in which to start building and expanding what you have learned. It is time to take it to the next level and start discussing topics that will enhance your knowledge, beginning with the discussion of WCF transactions in Chapter 9.

9

Transactions and Reliable Sessions

The first half of this book spent a considerable amount of time looking at the foundation, those pieces and components that make up the basic underlying architecture of Windows Communication Foundation. With all that you have learned so far you should be able to begin building WCF services. You should also be able to build client applications that can access and communicate with those services.

However, the first eight chapters are just the beginning. There is so much more to Windows Communication Foundation, and the rest of this book discusses this functionality.

This chapter discusses two topics or concepts that are fundamental in building successful WCF services:

❑   Windows Communication Foundation transactions

❑   Reliable messaging/sessions

Transactions

Whether you know it or not, you deal with transactions on daily basis. Many times it may not be obvious, but transaction processing occurs nearly everywhere. This section discusses transactions and how they work within the realm of Windows Communication Foundation.

Overview

A transaction is a collection or group of one or more units of operation executed as a whole. Another way to say it is that transactions provide a way to logically group single pieces of work and execute them as a single unit, or *transaction*.

For example, when you place an order online, a transaction occurs. Suppose you order a nice 21-inch wide-screen flat-panel monitor from your favorite online hardware source. Assume you were to pay for this monitor with a credit card. You enter the information required on the screen and click the "Place Order" button. At this point, two operations occur. The first operation takes place when your bank account is debited the amount of the monitor. The second operation occurs when the vendor is credited that amount. Each of those operations is a single unit of work.

Now imagine that one of those operations fails. For example, suppose that the money was removed from your bank account for the purchase of the monitor, but the payment to the vendor failed. First, you wouldn't receive your anxiously awaited monitor, and second, you would lose the amount of money for the cost of the monitor. I don't know about you, but I would be quite unhappy if this happened.

Conversely, a payment could be made to the vendor without debiting your account. In this case, the debit from your account failed but the payment to the vendor succeeded. You would likely receive the purchase item without having paid for it. Although this scenario is preferable to the former one, neither is acceptable in that in either case, someone is not receiving what is rightfully theirs.

The solution to this is to wrap both of these individual operations into a single unit of execution called a transaction. A transaction will make sure that both operations succeed or fail together. If either of the operations fails, the entire unit of work is cancelled and any and all changes are undone. At this point, each account is in the same state it was before you attempted your purchase. This undoing is known as "rolling back" the transaction.

This ensures that you receive your monitor and the vendor receives its money. Both parties are now happy and your confidence in doing business online hasn't wavered.

A pure and successful transaction has four characteristics. You can use the mnemonic aid "ACID" to help you remember each of them:

- ❑ Atomic
- ❑ Consistent
- ❑ Isolated
- ❑ Durable

Atomic

The word "atomic" comes from the Greek word "atamos," meaning "indivisible; cannot be split up." In computing terms, this meaning also applies to transactions. Transactions must be atomic, meaning either all the operations of the transactions succeed or none of them succeed (that is, all successful operations up to the point of failure are rolled back).

In the case of the monitor order, the money is removed from the bank account and deposited into the vendor bank account. If either of those operations fails, each account returns to the state it was in prior to the start of the purchase attempt.

Consistent

Consistent transactions mean that the outcome is exactly what you expected it to be. If you purchase the monitor for $300 and you have $1000 in the bank account, consistent transactions mean that you expect to be charged $300 and have $700 remaining in the bank account when the transaction is committed and complete.

Isolated

Isolated transactions are "private," meaning that no one else knows about the transaction until it is committed.

For example, suppose you have $1000 in a bank account from which to purchase the monitor. You purchase the monitor for $300, and during the purchase of the monitor, while the transaction is taking place, your husband or wife is at the local ATM checking the balance of the account from which the money for the monitor is being withdrawn.

Isolated transactions are invisible to all other transactions, and in this example the husband or wife would see a balance of $1000. In fact, if the husband or wife were to withdraw money from the ATM while the online purchase was taking place, both transactions would be isolated transactions, completely unknown to one another.

Durable

Durable transactions must survive failures. When a transaction is complete, it is "committed," meaning that the changes have taken effect. For a transaction to be durable, it must maintain its committed state if there is a failure.

What is a failure? It could be a power outage, hardware failure, and so on. Regardless of the failure, the transaction must survive it.

Suppose that after the processing of the transaction, someone yanks the power cord out of the server that is processing your order. A durable transaction survives this failure. When the power is restored to the server, the result of the transaction must be in the committed state.

Transaction Attributes in System.ServiceModel

When version 2.0 of the .NET Framework was released, it included a new namespace (System.Transactions) that makes transaction programming easy and efficient. The *System.Transactions* namespace supports transactions initiated by many platforms including SQL Server, MSMQ, ADO.NET, as well as MSDTC (Microsoft Distributed Transaction Coordinator).

Windows Communication Foundation utilizes the many available objects of this namespace to provide all the necessary transaction capabilities you will need when building your WCF services and client applications.

ServiceBehavior Attribute

You learned about the `[ServiceBehavior]` attribute in Chapter 8, but it is being mentioned again here because there are three properties belonging to this attribute that deal with handling and managing transactions. Each is shown in the following list:

❑   **TransactionAutoCompleteOnSessionClose:** Specifies whether pending transactions are completed when the current session closes.

❑   **TransactionIsolationLevel:** Determines the isolation level of the transaction.

❑   **TransactionTimeout:** Specifies the period in which a transaction has to complete.

The first of these is the *TransactionAutoCompleteOnSessionClose* property. It should be used for cases where you want to ensure that transactions are completed when the session is closed. As such, the transaction will either be committed or rolled back when the session is closed, depending on its state.

The one that needs to be highlighted here is the *TransactionIsolationLevel* property. This property determines how the data is handled when other transactions make modifications to the data. It also has an impact on how long your transaction can hold locks on the data, protecting it from other transactions. For a review of the available values for this property, see Chapter 8.

The *TransactionTimeout* property determines how long the transaction can run before it is cancelled. If the transaction has not completed before the timeout value has been reached, the transaction is rolled back. Great care must be taken when choosing a timeout interval. Too high of an interval will cause needless wait times when a failure has occurred. Too small of an interval will cause the transaction to fail before it has had time to complete.

These properties are properties of the `[ServiceBehavior]` attribute, which is applied to the class that implements the service interface. The following code snippet shows the three transaction properties applied to the `[ServiceBehavior]` attribute:

```
[ServiceBehavior(TransactionAutoCompleteOnSessionClose=true,
     TransactionIsolationLevel=IsolationLevel.ReadCommitted,
     TransactionTimeout="00:00:30")]
public class ServiceClass : IServiceClass
{
    [OperationBehavior]
    string IServiceClass.GetText()
    {
        StreamReader sw = new StreamReader(@"c:\wrox\WCFServiceTest.txt");
        return sw.ReadLine();
    }
}
```

In this case, the TransactionAutoCompleteOnSessionClose property is set to true, the TransactionIsolationLevel is set to ReadCommitted, and the TransactionTimeout is set to 30 seconds. The TransactionTimeout property value is of a Timespan object.

Prior to running the example, make sure that the `WCFServiceTest.txt` file exists and contains at least a few words of text. This example has the text file residing in the `Wrox` directory in the root of the C drive. If yours is located somewhere else, make sure the example is pointed to the correct location.

OperationBehavior Attribute

The `[OperationBehavior]` attribute was also covered in Chapter 8 but it bears briefly repeating because it also has a couple of properties related to transactions. The two properties are:

- ❑ **TransactionAutoComplete:** Specifies that transactions will be auto-completed if no exceptions occur.

- ❑ **TransactionScopeRequired:** Specifies whether the associate method requires a transaction.

The characteristics of a successful transaction were discussed earlier in this chapter. Both the *TransactionAutoComplete* property and *TransactionScopeRequired* property help fulfill the *durable* requirement because it will automatically complete a transaction, thus ensuring that the specific operation is successful.

The following example illustrates a service operation that is annotated with the `[OperationBehavior]` attribute, which specifies the two transaction properties:

```
[OperationBehavior(TransactionAutoComplete=true,
TransactionScopeRequired=true)]
string IServiceClass.GetText()
{
    StreamReader sw = new StreamReader(@"c:\wrox\WCFServiceTest.txt");
    return sw.ReadLine();
}
```

In this example, the TransactionAutoComplete property is set to true and the TransactionScopeRequired property is set to true as well.

TransactionFlow Attribute

The `[TransactionFlow]` attribute is used to specify the level at which a service operation can accept a transaction header. This attribute has a single property and is the attribute used to annotate a service operation method. The values for this property come from the TransactionFlowOption enumeration and are shown in the following list:

- ❑ **Allowed:** Transaction may be flowed.

- ❑ **Mandatory:** Transaction must be flowed.

- ❑ **NotAllowed:** Transaction cannot be flowed.

This property and the associated values are used to indicate whether transaction flow is enabled for the associated method.

The following example illustrates a service operation that is annotated with the `[TransactionFlow]` attribute, which specifies the level at which the operation is willing to accept incoming transactions. This example sets the level at *mandatory*, signifying that transactions are required for this operation:

```
[TransactionFlow(TransactionFlowOption.Mandatory)]
int IServiceClass.MultiplyNumbers(int firstvalue, int secondvalue)
{
    return firstvalue * secondvalue;
}
```

The default value for this property is *NotAllowed*.

A flowed transaction is a situation in which a transaction id is passed over the wire and used on the receiving side to perform work, usually enlisting in the corresponding transaction and executing within that scope.

WS-Atomic Transaction

Windows Communication Foundation utilizes the WS-AT (WS-Atomic Transaction) protocol to flow transactions to other applications. The WS-AT protocol is an interoperable protocol that enables distributed transactions to be flowed using web service messages, and incorporates a two-phase commit protocol to facilitate the outcome between distributed applications and transaction managers. The transaction protocol used when flowing a transaction between a client and service is determined by the binding that is exposed on the endpoint.

You do not need to use this protocol if your communication is using strictly Microsoft technology (WCF). Simply enabling the TransactionFlow attribute will get you the desired results. However, this protocol will be necessary if you are flowing transactions to other platforms and third-party technologies.

Specifying Transactions Through Configuration

On the client side, transaction flow is enabled via the binding. The following configuration file was taken from the behavior example in Chapter 8. If you remember in that example, several properties on the [ServiceBehavior] and [OperationBehavior] attributes were set so that they enabled transactions on the service. When the service references were added to the client, the client interrogated the consumed service and set the appropriate binding attributes in the configuration file.

Transaction flow is enabled by setting the value of the *transactionFlow* attribute to true, as shown by the highlighted line in the following code:

```xml
<?xml version="1.0" encoding="utf-8" ?>
<configuration>
  <system.serviceModel>
    <bindings>
      <wsHttpBinding>
        <binding name="WSHttpBinding_IServiceClass"
                 closeTimeout="00:01:00"
                 openTimeout="00:01:00"
                 receiveTimeout="00:10:00"
                 sendTimeout="00:01:00"
                 bypassProxyOnLocal="false"
                 transactionFlow="true"
                 hostNameComparisonMode="StrongWildcard"
                 maxBufferPoolSize="524288"
                 maxReceivedMessageSize="65536"
                 messageEncoding="Text"
                 textEncoding="utf-8"
                 useDefaultWebProxy="true"
                 allowCookies="false">
          <readerQuotas maxDepth="32"
                        maxStringContentLength="8192"
                        maxArrayLength="16384"
                        maxBytesPerRead="4096"
```

```
                            maxNameTableCharCount="16384" />
            <reliableSession ordered="true"
                             inactivityTimeout="00:10:00"
                             enabled="false" />
            <security mode="Message">
              <transport clientCredentialType="Windows"
                         proxyCredentialType="None"
                         realm="" />
              <message clientCredentialType="Windows"
                       egotiateServiceCredential="true"
                       algorithmSuite="Default"
                       establishSecurityContext="true" />
            </security>
          </binding>
        </wsHttpBinding>
      </bindings>
      <client>
        <endpoint address="http://localhost:8080/WCFService"
                  binding="wsHttpBinding"
                  bindingConfiguration="WSHttpBinding_IServiceClass"
                  contract="WCFClientApp.TCP.IServiceClass"
                  name="NetTcpBinding_IServiceClass">
          <identity>
            <userPrincipalName value="Scott@Avalon" />
          </identity>
        </endpoint>
      </client>
    </system.serviceModel>
  </configuration>
```

You should now understand how WCF handles transactions, so this next section and the rest of the chapter discuss reliable sessions.

Reliable Sessions

Whether you are building ASP.NET web services or delving into Windows Communication Foundation services, message delivery is critical. Reliable messaging is defined as a mechanism to successfully deliver messages in between distributed applications irrespective of any failures of the dependent components.

The following link discusses the WS-Reliable Messaging specification and can be useful to understand more about the WS-Reliable Messaging protocol:

```
http://www-128.ibm.com/developerworks/library/specification/ws-rm/
```

The following section discusses reliable messaging and how to enable it.

Overview

Reliable sessions in Windows Communication Foundation provide a reliable transfer of messages from one point to another, from the source to its destination. Reliable messaging should be ensured regardless of message transfer failure or other failures, such as transport or network failure.

WCF inherits its reliable messaging from the implementation of the SOAP reliable messaging protocol, which provides reliable messaging between two endpoints. The reliable delivery of the message is provided regardless of the number of intermediaries the message encounters along the way and irrespective of their SOAP support.

The following sections illustrate enabling reliable sessions through configuration.

Message Exchange

On the service, reliable messaging in enabled by including the `<reliableSession>` element to the appropriate binding and setting the *enabled* attribute to *true*. The following application configuration file shows how to enable reliable sessions on the service:

```xml
<?xml version="1.0" encoding="utf-8" ?>
<configuration>
  <system.serviceModel>
    <services>
      <service name ="WCFService.ServiceClass"
behaviorConfiguration="metadataSupport">
        <host>
          <baseAddresses>
            <add baseAddress="net.pipe://localhost/WCFService"/>
            <add baseAddress="net.tcp://localhost:8000/WCFService"/>
            <add baseAddress="http://localhost:8080/WCFService"/>
          </baseAddresses>
        </host>
        <endpoint address="tcpmex"
                  binding="mexTcpBinding"
                  contract="IMetadataExchange"/>
        <endpoint address="namedpipemex"
                  binding="mexNamedPipeBinding"
                  contract="IMetadataExchange"/>
        <endpoint address="" binding="wsHttpBinding"
bindingConfiguration="Binding1" contract="WCFService.IServiceClass"/>
        <!--<endpoint address="mex" binding="mexHttpBinding"
contract="IMetadataExchange"/>-->
      </service>
    </services>
    <bindings>
      <wsHttpBinding>
        <binding name ="Binding1">
          <reliableSession enabled ="true" ordered ="true"/>
        </binding>
      </wsHttpBinding>
    </bindings>
    <behaviors>
      <serviceBehaviors>
        <behavior name="metadataSupport">
          <serviceMetadata httpGetEnabled="false" httpGetUrl=""/>
        </behavior>
      </serviceBehaviors>
    </behaviors>
  </system.serviceModel>
</configuration>
```

On the client, the *enabled* attribute of the `<reliableSession>` element also needs to be set to a value of *true*, as shown by the following highlighted code:

```xml
<?xml version="1.0" encoding="utf-8" ?>
<configuration>
  <system.serviceModel>
    <bindings>
      <wsHttpBinding>
        <binding name="WSHttpBinding_IServiceClass"
                 closeTimeout="00:01:00"
                 openTimeout="00:01:00"
                 receiveTimeout="00:10:00"
                 sendTimeout="00:01:00"
                 bypassProxyOnLocal="false"
                 transactionFlow="true"
                 hostNameComparisonMode="StrongWildcard"
                 maxBufferPoolSize="524288"
                 maxReceivedMessageSize="65536"
                 messageEncoding="Text"
                 textEncoding="utf-8"
                 useDefaultWebProxy="true"
                 allowCookies="false">
          <readerQuotas maxDepth="32"
                        maxStringContentLength="8192"
                        maxArrayLength="16384"
                        maxBytesPerRead="4096"
                        maxNameTableCharCount="16384" />
          <reliableSession ordered="true"
                           inactivityTimeout="00:10:00"
                           enabled="true" />
          <security mode="Message">
            <transport clientCredentialType="Windows"
                       proxyCredentialType="None"
                       realm="" />
            <message clientCredentialType="Windows"
                     egotiateServiceCredential="true"
                     algorithmSuite="Default"
                     establishSecurityContext="true" />
          </security>
        </binding>
      </wsHttpBinding>
    </bindings>
    <client>
      <endpoint address="http://localhost:8080/WCFService"
                binding="wsHttpBinding"
                bindingConfiguration="WSHttpBinding_IServiceClass"
                contract="WCFClientApp.TCP.IServiceClass"
                name="NetTcpBinding_IServiceClass">
        <identity>
          <userPrincipalName value="Scott@Avalon" />
        </identity>
      </endpoint>
    </client>
  </system.serviceModel>
</configuration>
```

Also, it is recommended that you set the InstanceContextMode to PerSession so that a separate class instance is maintained for each client, as shown here:

```
[ServiceBehavior(InstanceContextMode=InstanceContextMode.PerSession)]
public class ServiceClass : IServiceClass
{
    [OperationBehavior]
    string IServiceClass.GetText()
    {
        StreamReader sw = new StreamReader(@"c:\wrox\WCFServiceTest.txt");
        return sw.ReadLine();
    }
}
```

Refer to Chapter 8 for the discussion on InstanceContext and the InstanceContextMode.

> *Make sure the* WCFServiceText.txt *file exists. You can use the file that is included with the code download or simply create a text file.*

Setting the InstanceContextMode to PerSession specifies that each service object will handle requests from one client channel.

The following built-in bindings support reliable messaging:

❑ NetTCPBinding

❑ wsHttpBinding

❑ NetNamedPipeBinding

❑ wsDualHttpBinding

❑ wsFederationBinding

❑ MsmqIntegrationBinding

Three of these, NetNamedPipeBinding, MsmqIntegrationBinding, and wsDualHttpBinding have reliable messaging enabled by default.

To summarize, reliable messaging should be used in cases where both the client and service may not operate online at the same time because at the transport level, reliable sessions can overcome any failures due to a loss of network connectivity for whatever reason.

Securing Messages

Messages can also be secured within a reliable session using one of the built-in bindings. Securing a session requires that the client and service be configured to exchange messages inside a reliable session and a set of credentials be specified that will be used to authenticate the service.

The first step is to configure the endpoint binding configuration that enables reliable messaging (see the previous section).

The second step is to add a `<security>` element to the appropriate binding. Inside the `<security>` element, the clientCredentialType attribute of the `<message>` element needs to be set.

Credentials are used by WCF to establish identity. Your passport or driver's license both serve as credentials verifying your identity. WCF uses credentials to establish identity and establish capabilities. Credentials come in many forms, such as username/password combinations or certificates.

Setting the clientCredentialType attribute of the `<message>` element depends on the security mode, such as Message or Transport. The following lists the credential types when using Transport security:

- ❑ **None:** Specifies that the client does not need to present any credentials.
- ❑ **Basic:** Basic authentication is required for the client.
- ❑ **Digest:** Digest authentication is required for the client.
- ❑ **Ntlm:** NTLM authentication is required for the client.
- ❑ **Windows:** Specifies Windows authentication.
- ❑ **Certificate:** Client authentication is performed via an X.509 certificate.

The following lists the credential types when using Message security:

- ❑ **None:** Specifies that the client does not need to present any credentials.
- ❑ **Windows:** SOAP messages can be exchanged using Windows credentials.
- ❑ **Username:** The service requires authentication via a username.
- ❑ **Certificate:** Client authentication is performed via an X.509 certificate.
- ❑ **IssuedToken:** Authentication is performed using a custom token type configured according to a security policy. The default token type is SAML.

Although setting the credential type to a value of None might be OK for testing, specifying a value None does not qualify as securing an application. Why try to enforce security without enforcing security? It's like adding a lock to your front door to keep people out but intentionally leaving the door unlocked. Sure, it's there if you wanted to lock the door at some point, but it's not stopping anything.

Windows Communication Foundation does not allow cryptographic operations with a username credential type, such as encrypting data. However, WCF does ensure that the transport is secure when username credentials are used. That is, you cannot use a UserName token to encrypt or sign messages; WCF never derives a security key from the password because this usually results in weak keys. For transport security, the confidentiality and integrity is usually provided by SSL (based on the service's certificate).

The following configuration example illustrates how to secure messages using Windows authentication. A `<security>` element has been added to the appropriate binding, setting the mode attribute to Message and specifying the credential type of the `<message>` element to *Windows*, specifying that Windows credentials will be used to authenticate to the service:

```
<?xml version="1.0" encoding="utf-8" ?>
<configuration>
  <system.serviceModel>
    <services>
```

```
        <service name ="WCFService.ServiceClass"
behaviorConfiguration="metadataSupport">
          <host>
            <baseAddresses>
              <add baseAddress="net.pipe://localhost/WCFService"/>
              <add baseAddress="net.tcp://localhost:8000/WCFService"/>
              <add baseAddress="http://localhost:8080/WCFService"/>
            </baseAddresses>
          </host>
          <endpoint address="tcpmex"
                    binding="mexTcpBinding"
                    contract="IMetadataExchange"/>
          <endpoint address="namedpipemex"
                    binding="mexNamedPipeBinding"
                    contract="IMetadataExchange"/>
          <endpoint address="" binding="wsHttpBinding"
bindingConfiguration="Binding1" contract="WCFService.IServiceClass"/>
          <!--<endpoint address="mex" binding="mexHttpBinding"
contract="IMetadataExchange"/>-->
        </service>
      </services>
      <bindings>
        <wsHttpBinding>
          <binding name ="Binding1">
            <security mode="Message"/>
              <message clientCredentialType="Windows"/>
            </security>
          </binding>
        </wsHttpBinding>
      </bindings>
      <behaviors>
        <serviceBehaviors>
          <behavior name="metadataSupport">
            <serviceMetadata httpGetEnabled="false" httpGetUrl=""/>
          </behavior>
        </serviceBehaviors>
      </behaviors>
    </system.serviceModel>
</configuration>
```

On the client, the equivalent information needs to be set in the configuration file to secure messages. The following highlighted section of code shows the information that needs to be specified to secure messages within a reliable session. Inside the <security> element for the appropriate binding, the clientCredentialType attribute specifies the type of authentication that will be used to authenticate to the service:

```
<?xml version="1.0" encoding="utf-8" ?>
<configuration>
  <system.serviceModel>
    <bindings>
      <wsHttpBinding>
        <binding name="WSHttpBinding_IServiceClass"
                 closeTimeout="00:01:00"
                 openTimeout="00:01:00"
                 receiveTimeout="00:10:00"
```

```
                    sendTimeout="00:01:00"
                    bypassProxyOnLocal="false"
                    transactionFlow="true"
                    hostNameComparisonMode="StrongWildcard"
                    maxBufferPoolSize="524288"
                    maxReceivedMessageSize="65536"
                    messageEncoding="Text"
                    textEncoding="utf-8"
                    useDefaultWebProxy="true"
                    allowCookies="false">
            <readerQuotas maxDepth="32"
                        maxStringContentLength="8192"
                        maxArrayLength="16384"
                        maxBytesPerRead="4096"
                        maxNameTableCharCount="16384" />
            <reliableSession ordered="true"
                        inactivityTimeout="00:10:00"
                        enabled="true" />
            <security mode="Message">
                <transport clientCredentialType="Windows"
                        proxyCredentialType="None"
                        realm="" />
                <message clientCredentialType="Windows"
                        egotiateServiceCredential="true"
                        algorithmSuite="Default"
                        establishSecurityContext="true" />
            </security>
          </binding>
        </wsHttpBinding>
      </bindings>
      <client>
        <endpoint address="http://localhost:8080/WCFService"
                binding="wsHttpBinding"
                bindingConfiguration="WSHttpBinding_IServiceClass"
                contract="WCFClientApp.TCP.IServiceClass"
                name="NetTcpBinding_IServiceClass">
          <identity>
            <userPrincipalName value="Scott@Avalon" />
          </identity>
        </endpoint>
      </client>
    </system.serviceModel>
</configuration>
```

Queues

The concept behind queues is to provide reliable communication between sender and receiver, regardless of the environment and parties involved. Direct transport protocols such as TCP or HTTP offer little or no guarantee for a safe and successful message delivery if either the sender or receiver were to quit communicating. In a direct transport scenario, both the sender and receiver must be running to ensure that the application is working correctly.

Queued transport offers a different story. Queued transport provides isolation between the sender and receiver so that if either the sender or receiver were to stop functioning or the communication between them breaks down, the other party can continue to function and the delivery of the message is still queued and available for delivery.

A good metaphor is the telephone before voice mail. In order for telephone communication to happen, both parties had to be available. This caused many to sit around and wait for important phone calls, effectively consuming a very hefty bit of their resources. Queuing is similar to voice mail, in that callers can leave you a message telling you exactly what they would have said if they got through. You can then act on that information and proceed accordingly.

Windows Communication Foundation provides support for queues by leveraging Microsoft Message Queuing (MSMQ) as a transport. Reliable communication is provided despite the fact that there could be network failures or a breakdown in communication between sender and receiver. The roll of the queue is to catch any messages sent between sender and receiver, and to send them to their destination.

Windows Communication Foundation recommends queues in the following scenarios:

❑ **Disconnected operations:** When either the sending, receiving, or processing parties have the potential of becoming disconnected.

❑ **Loosely coupled applications:** Sending and receiving independence, in that the sending application is not dependent on how fast the receiving application can process incoming messages, or that the sending of a message has no direct connection to the act of receiving and processing a message.

❑ **Load leveling:** When the sender is sending messages faster than the receiver can process them. In this scenario, queues can take much of the load off of the receiver and feed the messages to the receiver.

❑ **Failure isolation:** Either the sender or receiver can fail without affecting the other party. In this scenario, the receiver can fail but the sending application can still send messages successfully. When the receiving application is functioning properly the queue can then start to feed messages.

To fully understand how queues work, a few terms need to be defined. A Queue Manager manages a collection of queues. The Queue Manager has the responsibility for accepting messages that are sent to its queue from other Queue Managers, as well as sending messages to other remote queues. Both the sender and receiver have their own Queue Managers.

In the case of the sender and receiver, the sender has a Transmission Queue, which is managed by its Queue Manager and the receiver has a Target Queue, which is managed by its own Queue Manager.

Basic queue behavior is illustrated in the following steps:

1. The client sends the message to a queue. The address on the message is the address of the Target Queue.
2. The client's Queue Manager sends the message to the outgoing queue.
3. The client's Queue Manager tracks down the Target Queue owned by the Queue Manager of the receiver, and sends the message to the Target Queue.
4. The receiving application requests a message from the Target Queue.
5. The Queue Manager of the Target Queue hands the message to the receiving application.

Through the Queue Manager, multiple instances of the receiving application can read from the same queue. This provides a higher message throughput enabling the farming out of work. Also, either the sending or receiving application can fail without affecting the other party.

Queues can also take advantage of transactional messaging. In this scenario, messages are sent and received from the queue within a transaction. Suppose a message was sent or received in a transaction, and at some point during the processing the transaction was rolled back. The result would be as if the message was never sent to the queue or received from the queue.

> *Latency is the delay, in time, from when the client sends a message and the time the message is received by the service. In high latency there is no way of knowing how long a message takes to reach the Target Queue when the message is sent. Therefore, it is recommended that the sending, receiving, and process-ing of a message not be wrapped in a single transaction, but spread out over several transactions. Including these actions in a single transaction would create a transaction that would not be committed for an undetermined amount of time.*

WCF and Queues

In Windows Communication Foundation, the bindings specify how messages are exchanged. Operationally, this means that the binding includes the details of how the messages are to be exchanged. Queuing in Windows Communication Foundation is no different.

WCF includes two built-in bindings that take advantage of message queuing: NetMsmqBinding and MsmqIntegrationBinding. The NetMsmqBinding is the WCF-provided queued binding that allows end-points to communicate using MSMQ. The binding exposes MSMQ-specific properties to enable MSMQ communication. However, not all MSMQ features and properties are supported. The NetMsmqBinding binding only supports a subset of MSMQ features and properties that most developers would deem ade-quate for their MSMQ needs. Refer to Chapter 5 for more information on the NetMsmqBinding.

The MsmqIntegrationBinding is the other system-provided binding that is used to integrate WCF with an existing MSMQ application written in C, C++, or COM. Most of the properties that apply to the NetMsmqBinding also apply to the MsmqIntegrationBinding except for three differences:

- ❑ The operation contract for MsmqIntegrationBinding only takes a single parameter that is of type MsmqMessage, where the type parameter is the body type.

- ❑ Serializers such as XML are provided to assist in the serialization and deserialization of the mes-sage body.

- ❑ Many of the MSMQ native message properties are exposed for use in the MsmqMessage.

Both the NetMsmqBinding and the MsmqIntegrationBinding have several properties that affect how messages are transferred between queues. These two properties, the ExactlyOnce property and the Durable property, were discussed earlier in Chapter 5 but are repeated here.

The ExactlyOnce property ensures that the message will not be duplicated if it has already been success-fully delivered. This property also ensures that the message will not be lost. To enable this functionality the property must be set to true, but if it is set to false, the system will do its best to transfer the message. The default setting for this property is true.

The dead letter queue, also discussed in Chapter 5, is a queue that stores messages that are unable to be delivered. Although the ExactlyOnce property will do its best to deliver the message, in the case that the message delivery fails, the message and associated reason will be recorded in the dead letter queue. This also happens if the TimeToLive expires before the message can be delivered.

The Durable property ensures that MSMQ stores the message to disk. This has the benefit of having access to the message even though the MSMQ service was stopped and restarted. Very sweet. However, to get this functionality you need to set this property to true. Otherwise the message will be lost if the MSMQ service is ever stopped and restarted. Luckily, this property defaults to a value of true.

Please refer to Chapter 5 to see the other properties for these two bindings.

The following list should be "kept in mind" when using WCF queued bindings:

❑ Service operations must be one-way. By default, the queued binding provided with WCF does not support duplex communication.

❑ Generating a WCF client using metadata exchange requires an additional HTTP endpoint on the service so that queued communication can be configured correctly. By adding the extra endpoint, the service can be queried directly to generate the WCF client and obtain the necessary binding information.

❑ Additional configuration outside of WCF will be necessary, depending on the queued binding.

The following example illustrates queued communication between a WCF client and WCF service using the NetMsmqBinding. To enable queuing, changes need to be made in the service, the service host, and the client.

To enable queuing on the service, a few simple changes need to be made, as shown in the code that follows. The first step is to set the IsOneWay property of the OperationContract attribute to true. The second step is to add an OperationBehavior attribute to the operation, setting the TransactionScopeRequired and TransactionAutoComplete properties to true:

```csharp
using System;
using System.Transactions;
using System.ServiceModel;
using System.Collections.Generic;
using System.Runtime.Serialization;
using System.IO;

namespace Wrox.WCF.Chapter9.WCFService
{
    [ServiceContract]
    public interface IServiceClass
    {
        [OperationContract(IsOneWay=true)]
        int MultiplyNumbers(int firstvalue, int secondvalue);
    }

    public class ServiceClass : IServiceClass
    {

        [OperationBehavior(TransactionScopeRequired=true,
TransactionAutoComplete=true)]
        int IServiceClass.MultiplyNumbers(int firstvalue, int secondvalue)
        {
```

```
                return firstvalue * secondvalue;
        }

    }
}
```

Next, the host application needs a few changes as well.

The first thing to do is to add a reference to the System.Messaging and System.Configuration namespaces, and to reference those in the hosting application as shown here:

```
using System;
using System.Collections.Generic;
using System.ComponentModel;
using System.Data;
using System.Drawing;
using System.Text;
using System.Windows.Forms;
using System.ServiceModel;
using System.ServiceModel.Description;
using WCFService;
using System.Messaging;
using System.Configuration;
```

The next step is to add the following highlighted code in the form's load event. The first line reads the "QueueName" value out of the AppSettings section of the configuration file. This value contains the name of the transactional queue. That value is then passed to the next line of code, which checks to see if the queue exists, and to create it if it does not exist:

```
namespace Wrox.WCF.Chapter9.WCFServiceHost
{
    public partial class Form1 : Form
    {
        ServiceHost sh = null;

        public Form1()
        {
            InitializeComponent();
        }

        private void Form1_Load(object sender, EventArgs e)
        {
            string QueueName = ConfigurationManager.AppSettings["QueueName"];

            if (!MessageQueue.Exists(QueueName))
                MessageQueue.Create(QueueName, true);

            sh = new ServiceHost(typeof(WCFService.ServiceClass));

            sh.Open();

            label1.Text = "Service Running";
        }

        private void Form1_FormClosing(object sender, FormClosingEventArgs e)
```

```
            {
                sh.Close();
            }
        }
    }
```

Next, the configuration file for the host application needs to be modified. To begin, the `<appSettings>` section needs to be added to hold the name/value pair that contains the name of the transactional queue used in the preceding code. The relevant fragment is shown here:

```
    <appSettings>
      <add key="QueueName" value=".\private$\WCFQueuedServiceSample"/>
    </appSettings>
```

The next change is to set the appropriate base address, using the net.msmsq address format:

```
<baseAddresses>
            <add baseAddress="net.msmq://localhost/private/
WCFQueuedServiceSample"/>
            <add baseAddress="http://localhost:8080/WCFService"/>
        </baseAddresses>
```

Lastly, the appropriate address, binding, and contract for the endpoint are set as shown in the third highlighted section. The binding is set to the WCF built-in NetMsmqBinding:

```
<endpoint address="msmqmex"
                  binding="NetMsmqBinding"
                  contract="IMetadataExchange"/>
```

The complete layout for the configuration file is shown next with the relevant portions highlighted:

```
<?xml version="1.0" encoding="utf-8" ?>
<configuration>
  <appSettings>
    <add key="QueueName" value=".\private$\WCFQueuedServiceSample"/>
  </appSettings>
  <system.serviceModel>
    <services>
      <service name ="WCFService.ServiceClass"
behaviorConfiguration="metadataSupport">
        <host>
          <baseAddresses>
            <add baseAddress="net.msmq://localhost/private/
WCFQueuedServiceSample"/>
            <add baseAddress="http://localhost:8080/WCFService"/>
          </baseAddresses>
        </host>
        <endpoint address="msmqmex"
                  binding="NetMsmqBinding"
                  contract="IMetadataExchange"/>
        <endpoint address="" binding="wsHttpBinding" contract="WCFService
.IServiceClass"/>
```

```
        <!--<endpoint address="mex" binding="mexHttpBinding"
contract="IMetadataExchange"/>-->
        </service>
    </services>
    <behaviors>
      <serviceBehaviors>
        <behavior name="metadataSupport">
          <serviceMetadata httpGetEnabled="false" httpGetUrl=""/>
        </behavior>
      </serviceBehaviors>
    </behaviors>
  </system.serviceModel>
</configuration>
```

Finally, the client needs to be modified. A reference to the System.Transactions and System.Messaging namespaces need to be added to the project and aliased in the application. The examples so far have been using a Windows Forms application for the client:

```
using System;
using System.Collections.Generic;
using System.ComponentModel;
using System.Data;
using System.Drawing;
using System.Text;
using System.Windows.Forms;
using System.ServiceModel;
using System.ServiceModel.Channels;
using System.Transactions;
using System.Messaging;
```

Next, a TransactionScope object is created to write to the transaction queue. Within the transaction scope, a queued call to the Complete method is made, committing the transaction:

```
namespace Wrox.WCF.Chapter9.WCFClientApp
{

    public partial class Form1 : Form
    {
        private int val1 = 5;
        private int val2 = 5;

        public Form1()
        {
            InitializeComponent();
        }

        private void Form1_Load(object sender, EventArgs e)
        {

        }

        private void button2_Click(object sender, EventArgs e)
        {
```

```
        TCP.ServiceClassClient client = new
          WCFClientApp.TCP.ServiceClassClient("NetTcpBinding_IServiceClass");

            using (TransactionScope ts = new
TransactionScope(TransactionScopeOption.Required))
            {
                textBox2.Text = client.MultiplyNumbers(val1, val2).ToString();
                ts.Complete();
            }
        }
    }
}
```

The client won't work unless the necessary changes are made to the configuration file. The appropriate address and binding must be specified to be able to communicate with the service, as shown here:

```
<client>
    <endpoint address="net.msmq://localhost/private/WCFQueuedServiceSample"
       binding="NetMsmqBinding"
       contract="IMetadataExchange"/>
</client>
```

Your homework assignment for this chapter is to take the preceding code and finish this example. The preceding code will get you most of the way there.

Queuing Best Practices

This section lists a few "best practices" items to close out this chapter. The topics discussed here are recommended practices for WCF queued communication. A lot of the items were touched upon in this chapter, but most are worth repeating and explaining a bit further.

When your environment requires reliable messaging from end to end, the following practices are recommended:

❑   **Reliable Transfer:** Make sure that the ExactlyOnce and Durable properties are set to true. These properties were discussed earlier in this chapter, but you need to be aware that there is a performance decision that needs to be made. By default, both of these properties are true to ensure a reliable end-to-end queued messaging environment is in place. But having these set to true comes at a performance cost because making the message durable means that the messages are each written to disk. The tradeoff is that if the service restarts, the messages are not lost.

❑   **Transactions:** Using transactions ensures end-to-end reliability by ensuring that the message was received. When used with the ExactlyOnce property, messages are guaranteed to be delivered to the target queue if/when it becomes operational and the messages will not be lost if the application fails.

❑   **Use dead letter queues:** Dead letter queues are a necessity for reliable messaging. Messages can fail delivery for a number of reasons including network failure, authentication failure, or simply that the message could not be delivered in the allotted time. Dead letter queues make sure that you are notified if a message cannot be delivered.

❑ **Use poison-message handling:** Poison-message handling helps recover from messages that fail to be processed. A poisoned message is a message that fails repeated delivery attempts. The ReceiveErrorHandling property of the MsmqBindingBase class determines how a poisoned message is handled. When ReceiveErrorHandling is set to a value of *Drop*, the MsmqBindingBase simply drops the message, resulting in a loss of data. A value of *Move*, available only on Windows Vista, moves the poisoned message to a poisoned message queue. A value of *Reject*, available only on Windows Vista, tells MSMQ to send a message back to the sending queue manager informing it that the message cannot be delivered and that the message is being put in the sending queue manager's dead letter queue. A value of *Fault* sends a fault to the listener causing the ServiceHost to fault.

One of the things that can ensure the demise of a WCF service is its inability to handle and process the messages that are sent to it. High throughput on a service endpoint can be achieved by considering the following recommendations:

❑ **Use throttling:** Throttling the number of messages in the pipeline can significantly help performance. For information on throttling, refer to the section titled "Throttling" in Chapter 8.

❑ **Use transacted batching:** Transacted batching guarantees that multiple messages can be read/processed in a single transaction. This helps optimize transaction commits, which considerably increases performance. There is a cost to batching, however. If a message within a batch fails to be processed successfully (a poisoned message), the entire batch is rolled back. However, transacted batching is still preferred because poisoned messages are uncommon.

❑ **Use concurrency:** There is an upside and downside to using concurrency. The upside is that throughput is increased. The downside is that contentions to shared resources can happen.

Farms of services should also be considered in a large transaction environment.

Summary

The purpose of this chapter was to give you an in-depth look at bindings and their properties and to show you how to use bindings to communicate with service endpoints. This chapter began by defining the concept of a binding and then spent quite a few pages discussing the built-in, preexisting bindings and their attributes. These bindings should be able to cover most application requirements.

The last part of this chapter provided several examples to illustrate how to implement bindings and the options you have available to take advantage of the predefined bindings.

Custom bindings are discussed later in this book.

10

Security

It goes without saying that security should play a large role anytime sensitive data is transmitted from one location to another. In a distributed environment, the importance of sending and securing messages cannot be overstated. Communication between the sender and receiver should be protected against so that only authorized parties can access it and each involved party can be confident of the communication's integrity. On a daily basis, most of us lock a door of some sort or other. Moreover, we live in an increasingly digital time where many assets exist in a digital form. Why should we be any more cavalier about securing them than we are about any other asset? Or take the common "he said, she said" phenomenon, when one party claims another party said something the latter party denies. How much time has been wasted by people trying to figure out who's telling the truth (or if either party is telling the truth)?

As you have surely gathered by now, Windows Communication Foundation allows for the communication of messages over many protocols, and the need for securing this communication is great. The whole mantra of Windows Communication Foundation is the ability to reliably, efficiently, and *securely* communicate SOAP messages over a large number of supported protocols.

This chapter discusses the different security aspects of Windows Communication Foundation and how to take advantage of them. Security is a huge topic, but this chapter focuses on message security from the point of WCF. Therefore, this chapter discusses the following:

❑   WCF security overview

❑   Security behaviors

❑   Clients/services

❑   Best practices

Security Overview

Windows Communication Foundation is a distributed application platform in which SOAP messages are communicated between clients and services. Securing and ensuring the safe delivery of these messages is of the utmost importance to prevent lost or stolen information or system attacks. Building upon the Online Purchase example used in the discussion of transactions, there's actually a little more to safe and secure online commerce than making sure it runs transactionally. For instance, after making the purchase and having your account debited, what would happen if someone changed the transaction amount in between when it was debited from your account and credited to the vendor's account? What if your account was debited for $250.00 yet only $1.00 was credited to the vendor, while the remainder found its way to Joe Hacker's account?

Fortunately, WCF provides a flexible platform for securing messages that takes advantage of a large number of existing standards and technologies.

The wonderful thing about Windows Communication Foundation security is that it uses existing concepts and technologies that you are likely already familiar with in order to secure WCF messaging. WCF builds on these existing security technologies to provide a very robust and versatile secure messaging infrastructure.

On the surface, security as a whole may seem a little complex, yet the great thing about Windows Communication Foundation is that securing messages is not that difficult once you understand some of the concepts and scenarios in which it applies.

Concepts

As stated earlier, WCF utilizes new as well as existing concepts and technologies to implement security, but regardless of what technology is used, the concepts behind them are the same. Therefore, this section discusses some of those concepts to assist you in understanding the foundation of the security mechanisms of WCF.

Some of the basic and fundamental security concepts include the following:

- ❑ Integrity
- ❑ Confidentiality
- ❑ Authentication
- ❑ Authorization

Each of these concepts fundamentally applies to any distributed messaging system in which messages are sent from a source sender to a receiving destination.

Integrity

Integrity means that the message arrives at the receiver in the same form, and with the same contents, as it had when it left the sender. You need to trust that a message has not been altered or tampered with en route between the sender and the receiver. Digitally signing a message can reasonably ensure the integrity of a message remains intact.

Confidentiality

Message confidentiality protects the message so that the planned recipient of the message is the only one who can view the message. This helps ensure that the message is not viewed or interrogated while in transit between sender and receiver. Any parts of a message that are intended for a specific receiver should be read only by that receiver.

Authentication

Authentication is the act of definitively identifying an individual entity, or requesting evidence of identity. Typically, this has been "one-sided," meaning authenticating the sender of the message. However, in a distributed messaging system, authentication must take place on both sides of the transmission, the sender and the receiver. The process of authenticating both the sender and receiver ensures that the message isn't altered while in transit, commonly known as man-in-the-middle attack, proving each party to be who they claim to be.

Authorization

Authorization occurs after authentication, and is the process of specifying the resources, functionality, and features to which the authorized entity has access.

Think of authentication and authorization much like the process of logging into a computer that belongs in a network domain. When you log in, you provide a set of credentials that authenticates you as a valid network user. Authorization then takes place, which indicates the network resources (network shares, drives, printers, and so on) that you have access to.

Authentication and authorization in WCF operate much like the preceding scenario, but on a larger scale. Authentication happens on both the sender and receiver, at which point the authorized entity is given permission to specific resources or functionality.

Windows Communication Foundation also utilizes the following mechanisms in which WCF can be deployed in various infrastructures:

❑ **Windows Identity:** The ability to map a user's Internet identity to his or her Windows identity.

❑ **Public Key Infrastructure:** PKI employs digital certificates and certificate authorities, whose responsibility is to validate and authenticate each entity that is involved in an electronic transaction.

❑ **X.509:** X.509 are certificates that are a main form of credentials within a security application.

❑ **Kerberos:** Kerberos is not so much a technology as it is a specification that defines the creation of security mechanisms for authenticating users on a Windows domain. In a Kerberos environment, a user requests an encrypted "permit" from an authoritative source, which can then be used to be granted access to services or resources on the network.

As a "Did you know?" fact, did you know that the word Kerberos comes from Greek mythology? In Greek mythology, Kerberos was a three-headed monster with a tail of a snake. Kerberos guarded the gate to Hades (Greek underworld). His job was to make sure that the dead did not leave and the living did not enter. According to Greek mythology, Kerberos was overcome several times by different individuals, including Heracles, but never by brute strength. In most cases, he was lulled to sleep. In Heracles' case, he won the beast over by treating it with kindness.

Who would have ever thought that you would learn Greek mythology by reading a .NET book?

Why WCF Security?

Windows Communication Foundation provides a strong security system for distributed applications and it accomplishes this by dividing security into three distinct, functional areas:

❑ Transfer Security

❑ Access Control

❑ Auditing

Transfer Security

Transfer Security is responsible for providing message integrity, confidentiality, and authentication Each of these were defined previously. Windows Communication Foundation builds on this security to include quite a few modes of transfer security. Those modes include the following:

❑ **None:** In this mode, no security is provided at the transport or message level.

❑ **Message:** At this level, SOAP-message security is employed. Messages are secured using WS-Security standards. This level of security ensures message confidentiality, integrity, and authentication for sender and receiver.

❑ **Transport:** Secure transport protocols such as HTTP are used to ensure message confidentiality, integrity, and authentication.

❑ **Mixed:** Both message-level and transport-level security are employed.

❑ **Both:** This level of security is available only in the netMsmqBinding binding. This mode provides protection and authentication on both levels.

Control Access / Authorization

Another name for Access Control is *authorization*, which was defined earlier as the process of specifying the resources, functionality, and features to which the authorized entity has access. Access Control features in Windows Communication Foundation are enabled through several different mechanisms, which range in complexity. The access technologies are the following:

❑ PrinciplePermissionAttribute

❑ ASP.NET Membership Provider

❑ ASP.NET Role Provider

❑ Authorization Manager

❑ Identity Model

PrinciplePermission Attribute

The *PrinciplePermission* attribute is applied to a WCF service method and is used to restrict access to a service method. When applied to a method, it can be used to demand membership to a specific Windows Group or ASP.NET role. It can also be used to deny access to specific resources.

The *PrinciplePermission* attribute has several parameters that can be applied to control method access. The first parameter defines the SecurityAction that will be applied to the method. Those actions are defined as follows:

❑ **Assert:** The calling code can access the identified resource by the current permission object, even if callers higher in the stack have not been granted permission to the resource.

❑ **Demand:** All callers higher in the call stack are required to have been granted the permission specified by the current permission object.

❑ **Deny:** Access to the resource by the current permission object is denied to callers, even if they have been granted permission to access.

❑ **LinkDemand:** The immediate caller is required to have been granted the specified permission.

❑ **PermitOnly:** Only the resources specified by the permission object can be accessed, even if the code has been granted permission to access other resources.

❑ **RequestMinimum:** The request for the minimum permissions required for code to run.

❑ **RequestOptional:** The request for the additional permissions that are optional to run.

❑ **RequestRefuse:** The request for permissions that might be misused will not be granted to the calling code.

It should be noted that the RequestMinimum, RequestOptional, and RequestRefuse actions can only be used within the scope of the assembly.

The rest of the parameters that can be specified are as follows:

❑ **Authenticated:** A Boolean value.

❑ **Role:** The name of the role in which the SecurityAction applies.

❑ **Unrestricted:** A Boolean value.

For example, the following code snippet illustrates how to apply the *PrinciplePermission* attribute. The *SecurityAction* property is set to Demand and the *Role* property has a value of Dev. In this example, the PrinciplePermission attribute is used to "demand" that users of this method belong to the Dev role:

```
[PrinciplePermission(SecurityAction=SecurityAction.Demand, Role="Dev"]
Public int Multiple(Number1 int, Number2 int)
{

}
```

The PrinciplePermission attribute is best used to control access to resources on the machine in which the service is running and the users of the service are part of the same Windows domain the service is running in.

ASP.NET Membership and Role Provider

Both the ASP.NET Membership and ASP.NET Role providers are used to manage site membership and role authorization. The ASP.NET membership provider contains a database in which user credentials can be stored. The purpose of this database is to set up accounts for the site or service. This allows users to establish accounts that are then used to gain access to the site. The ASP.NET Role provider provides the ability to manage site authorization using roles, letting the developer define and create roles for users. This information is also stored in a database. A role is a named set of users grouped together that share the same security privileges.

Windows Communication Foundation can utilize both of these features within a service to provide further access control. Both of these features allow developers to create sites that let users of the site create accounts and be assigned roles.

Although WCF does not directly provide methods to populate the ASP.NET membership database, developers can integrate this functionality into their application by using a binding that supports username/password credentials, such as the WSHttpBinding.

To configure the membership provider, the following things must take place:

❑ Modification of the `Web.config`

❑ Modification of the service configuration file to add the username/password combination and membership provider

First, the `Web.config` must be modified to include the appropriate information. Under the `<system.web>` element, the following needs to be added:

```
<membership defaultProvider="SqlProvider" userIsOnlineTimeWindow="10">
  <providers>
    <clear />
      <add
        name="MembershipProvider"
        type="System.Web.Security.SqlMembershipProvider"
        connectionStringName="conn"
        applicationName="SecuritySampleApp"
        enablePasswordRetrieval="true"
        enablePasswordReset="true"
        requiresQuestionAndAnswer="true"
        requiresUniqueEmail="false"
        passwordFormat="Hashed"
  </providers>
</membership>
```

Next, the service configuration file must be modified to accept the username and password combination. This is done by using the wsHttpBinding binding and setting the security mode to *Message*, as shown here:

```
<bindings>
  <wsHttpBinding>
    <binding name="MembershipBinding">
      <security mode="Message">
        <message clientCredentialType="UserName" />
      </security>
    </binding>
  </wsHttpBinding>
</bindings>
```

While in the service configuration file, the service behavior must be modified to use the membership provider, as follows:

```
<behaviors>
  <serviceBehaviors>
    <behavior name="MembershipProviderBehavior">
      <serviceCredentials>
        <userNameAuthentication
          userNamePasswordValidationMode="MembershipProvider"
          membershipProviderName="SqlMembershipProvider" />
      </serviceCredentials>
    </behavior>
  </serviceBehaviors>
</behaviors>
```

As previously discussed, the Role provider works together with the Membership provider to enable users to create accounts with a site and be assigned to roles therein. Together membership and roles allow users to log in and gain access to whatever features and resources their roles have been given access to.

Windows Communication Foundation can take advantage of these features by enabling and configuring the Role provider, which is a multi-step process:

1. Modify the `Web.config` file under the `<system.web>` element.

2. Add a `<roleManager>` element setting its *enabled* property to *true*, as shown here:

```
<roleManager enabled="true" defaultProvider="SqlRoleProvider">
  <providers>
    <add name="SqlRoleProvider"
      type="System.Web.Security.SqlRoleProvider"
      connectionstring="conn"
      applicationname="SecuritySampleApp"
  </providers>
</roleManager>
```

3. The next step is to tell your WCF service to use the enabled Role Manager by modifying the service configuration file and adding the appropriate behavior, as follows:

```
<behaviors>
  <serviceBehaviors>
    <behavior name="RoleProviderBehavior">
      <serviceAuthorization principleName="UseASPNetRoles"
        roleProviderName="SqlRoleProvider" />
    </behavior>
  </serviceBehaviors>
</behaviors>
```

With the Membership and Role providers working together, developers can now build WCF services that take advantage of this great ASP.NET functionality.

Authorization Manager

The Authorization Manager, combined with the ASP.NET Role provider, enables developers to define and build distinct operations that can be grouped together as tasks. Site administrators can then grant tasks, or individual operations, to roles. The Authorization Manager is available through an MMC (Microsoft Management Console) snap-in, which lets administrators manage the roles, tasks, operations and users visually.

Via Authorization Manager integration, authorization to the service is accomplished through the Authorization Manager. Windows Communication Foundation can take advantage of the Authorization Manager by integrating it into an application by configuring the Authorization Manager ASP.NET Role provider for the ASP.NET application that is hosting the web service.

Because the Authorization Manager is combined with the ASP.NET Role provider, enabling the Authorization Manager is very similar to enabling the Role provider:

1. Modify the `Web.config` file under the `<system.web>` element.

2. Add a `<roleManager>` element setting its *enabled* property to *true*, but this time setting the default provider to *AzManRoleProvider*, as shown here:

```
<roleManager enabled="true" defaultProvider="AzManRoleProvider">
  <providers>
    <add name="AzManRoleProvider"
      type="System.Web.Security.SqlRoleProvider"
      connectionstring="conn"
      applicationname="SecuritySampleApp" >
  </providers>
</roleManager>
```

3. Tell your WCF service to use the enabled Authorization Manager by modifying the service configuration file and adding the appropriate behavior, as follows:

```
<behaviors>
  <serviceBehaviors>
    <behavior name="RoleProviderBehavior">
      <serviceAuthorization principleName="UseASPNetRoles"
        roleProviderName="AzManRoleProvider" />
    </behavior>
  </serviceBehaviors>
</behaviors>
```

You can start to see that each level of Access Control mechanisms provides increased granularity. A key point is that this granularity may not be necessary, in which case it doesn't have to be used. But it is available if the application's security needs require it.

Identity Model

The Identity Model, the most complex of the available Access Control mechanisms, allows you to manage claims and policies to authorize clients through a set of well-defined APIs. This model provides the ability to interrogate each claim within a credential and subsequently compare that claim to the policies set for a service, at which point you can approve or deny access.

Windows Communication Foundation provides two authorization methods. The first is through existing CLR constructs, and the second is through a claim-based model called the Identity Model. A claim is a combination of the following:

❑ **A claim type:** A kind of claim defined by the Identity Model API, which is a member of the ClaimType enumeration. The following table lists the available values of the ClaimType enumeration.

Member	Description
Custom	Specifies Custom types of claims
Group	Specifies Group types of claims
GroupAndCustom	Specifies both Group types and Custom types of claims
None	

❑ **A right:** A capability over a resource.

❑ **A value:** On object over which a right has claimed.

Claims define the capabilities of an entity, which are usually used to define or gain access to resources. Claims can be grouped into *Claim Sets* which, when connected with a specific entity, can be also defined as a *key*. It is the individual claims that define the shape of the key. Claims are the expression of a right to a specific value. Rights define the type of access to a resource, such as "Read," "Modify," or "Delete." A value is the physical object to which the right is applied. For example, a value could be a file, a document, or a database.

WCF utilizes the Identity Model as the foundation for authorization processing by creating claims on incoming messages. The *ServiceAuthorizationBehavior* class is used to allow authorization policies to be included as part of the service. These policies, referred to as *external authorization* policies, allow claim-based processing on local policies or by interacting with remote services.

Auditing

Auditing is the process of logging security events. Security events are written to the Windows Event Log and include events such as logon successes and failures. Tracking events such as these allows system administrators to monitor their systems for possible attacks. From the developer standpoint, these events can help developers debug problems related to security in their application. However, logging to the Windows Event Log can be costly and has a strong propensity to be overused. Unnecessary and/or verbose logging can cause a log to fill up quickly, which itself can cause problems. Many developers have tried to track down problems using event logging, only to later find out that their very logging was the major source of a problem!

In Windows Communication Foundation there are two levels of security audits:

❑ Service authorization, which authorizes the caller

❑ Message level, which checks the validity of the message and authenticates the caller

In both of these cases the audits can be checked for both success and failure.

Credentials

A common theme you should be noticing throughout this discussion is the concept of authentication, which is the process of validating an identity. To authenticate something, credentials must be supplied, which are in turn used to facilitate the authentication. These credentials are used to provide proof of identity of an entity. Credentials are essentially data that verify identity and/or capabilities, and involve presenting two items of information during authentication. The first is the actual presentation of data. The second is the presentation of the proof of possession of the data, meaning that during authentication the credentials must show proof that they contain the necessary data.

An example of this would be a driver's license or some other form of identification that has the possessor's picture, such as a government-issued passport. These documents, or forms of identification, contain data pertaining to the individual's identity and capabilities. The proof of possession is presented in the form of the individual's picture.

The following is a list of transport credential types supported by Windows Communication Foundation:

❑ **None:** The client does not need to specify any credentials. Also known as an Anonymous Client.

❑ **Basic:** Specified Basic authentication. Transmits passwords across the network in a clear text, unencrypted form.

❑ **Digest:** Specifies Digest Authentication. Only works with Windows Active Directory accounts, sending a hash value over the network rather than plain text.

❑ **NTLM:** Windows authentication using SSPI (Security Support Provider Interface) negotiation on a Windows domain.

❑ **Windows:** Specifies Windows authentication using SSPI on a Windows domain. SSPI will either pick Kerberos or NTLM. Kerberos is tried first.

❑ **Certificate:** Client authentication performed using a certificates, usually X.509.

These values can be used in applications that need to utilize transfer security and can be used in either code or configuration binding settings.

The following is a list of message client credential types supported by Windows Communication Foundation:

❑ **None:** The service can interact with anonymous clients.

❑ **Windows:** SOAP messages are exchanged using Windows authentication credentials.

❑ **Username:** The service requires that the client be authenticated with a username.

❑ **Certificate:** The service requires that the client be authenticated using a certificate.

❑ **Windows CardSpace:** The service requires that the client be authenticated using a Windows CardSpace.

These values can be used in applications that need to utilize message security and can be used in either code or configuration binding settings.

Windows Communication Foundation supports two types of credentials, which are applied through behaviors: service credential behaviors and channel credential behaviors, which contain the actual credential data. These credentials are used to meet the security requirements defined through bindings. It is through the use of credential types, defined previously, that the WCF programming model allows credential values and validators to be specified via service and channel behaviors.

In summary, why use WCF security? Because of the following:

❏ Message integrity

❏ Message confidentiality

❏ Service and client authentication

❏ Replay detection

Windows Communication Foundation does not introduce new security mechanisms but instead utilizes infrastructures that are already in existence. WCF integrates extremely well with these technologies and takes advantage of existing security features and practices.

Moreover, WCF supports a large number of credential types and authentication methods while still supporting existing standards and providing the ability to interoperate with existing technologies. This enables the ability to successfully and securely run in a distributed environment and on distributed platforms.

Security Behaviors and Bindings

The following sections discuss built-in runtime security behaviors and the system-provided bindings included with Windows Communication Foundation that include security schemes.

Security Behaviors

Chapter 8 spent quite a bit of time discussing service behaviors and how they can be applied to affect the runtime behavior of both the service and endpoint. This does not change when applied to security. Security behaviors provide control over a wide variety of options such as credentials, auditing, authentication, and authorization.

The `<serviceCredentials>` and `<clientCredentials>` elements are used to set credential values for a service or client and are child elements of the `<serviceBehaviors>` section. The security mechanism being used determines whether credentials need to be set. Just as important, the security mechanism depends on the transport being used.

Just like everything else in WCF, security behaviors can be defined in code or through configuration settings. The following four sections discuss behaviors related to security functions.

Service Credentials

The `<serviceCredentials>` section is used to configure service credentials. It contains four child elements, which are outlined here:

- ❏ **<serviceCertificate>:** This element is used to specify an X.509 certificate that will authenticate the service to the client using Message security mode.

- ❏ **<certificate> of <clientCertificate>:** During duplex communication, use the `<certificate>` element when the service needs the certificate of the client in advance to securely communicate with the client.

- ❏ **<authentication> of <clientCertificate>:** Use the `<authentication>` element to customize how clients will authenticate.

- ❏ **<issuedTokenAuthentication>:** This element is the repository for STS certificates. Tokens are issued in a three-phase scenario. First, a client is handed over to a Secure Token Service (STS) when attempting to authenticate. The STS authenticates the client and issues the client a token, which the client then hands to the service.

The CertificateValidationMode attribute of the `<authentication>` element contains several values that determine the level of client authentication. These include *None, ChainTrust, PeerOrChainTrust, PeerTrust,* or *Custom*. The default is *ChainTrust*, which is the most secure mode.

The general layout of the elements is as follows:

```
<serviceCredentials>
  <clientCertificate>
    <authentication />
    <certificate />
  </clientCertificate>
  <serviceCertificate />
  <issuedTokenAuthentication>
    <knownCertificates>
    </knownCertificates>
  </issuedTokenAuthentication>
</serviceCredentials>
```

The following example illustrates some of the attributes for the given elements:

```
<serviceCredentials>
  <clientCertificate>
    <authentication
      includeWindowsGroups="false"
      certificateValidationMode="PeerTrust"/>
    <certificate x509FindType="FindBySubjectName"/>
  </clientCertificate>
  <serviceCertificate x509FindType="FindByIssuerName"/>
    <issuedTokenAuthentication>
      <knownCertificates>
        <add
          findValue=""
          storeLocation="LocalMachine"
          storeName=""
          x509FindType="FindBySubjectName"/>
      </knownCertificates>
    </issuedTokenAuthentication>
</serviceCredentials>
```

Client Credentials

Client credentials are used to validate and authenticate the client with the service in the cases where authentication on both sides is necessary. Client credentials are configured via the `<endpointBehaviors>` section.

The `<clientCredentials>` element contains the following child elements:

- ❏ **<clientCertificate>:** Specifies the certificate the client uses to authenticate.
- ❏ **<httpDigest>:** Used with Active Directory on Windows and IIS.
- ❏ **<issuedTokens>:** Contains the elements that are used to configure the local token issuer and/or the STS behavior.
- ❏ **<localIssuer> of <issuedTokens>:** The address of the default STS is of a URL format.
- ❏ **<issuerChannelBehaviors> of <issuedTokens>:** This element is used to specify STS behaviors.

The general layout of the elements is as follows:

```
<endpointBehaviors>
  <behavior name="TCPEndPointBehavior">
    <clientCredentials>
      <clientCertificate/>
      <httpDigest/>
      <issuedToken>
        <localIssuer />
        <issuerChannelBehaviors>
          <add />
        </issuerChannelBehaviors>
      </issuedToken>
    </clientCredentials>
  </behavior>
</endpointBehaviors>
```

The following example illustrates some of the attributes for the given elements:

```
<endpointBehaviors>
  <behavior name="TCPEndPointBehavior">
    <clientCredentials>
      <clientCertificate/>
      <httpDigest impersonationLevel="Anonymous"/>
      <issuedToken maxIssuedTokenCachingTime="0">
        <localIssuer address="" />
        <issuerChannelBehaviors>
          <add behaviorConfiguration="ClientBehavior"
            issuerAddress="www.wrox.com"/>
        </issuerChannelBehaviors>
      </issuedToken>
    </clientCredentials>
  </behavior>
</endpointBehaviors>
```

The preceding example illustrates how the `<clientCredentials>` element is used along with its sub-elements, but obviously the sub-elements you will use will depend on your needs and environment.

Service Authorization

The <serviceAuthorization> element is used to configure authorization and role providers. Some of this information was discussed when the [PrinciplePermission] attribute was discussed. This attribute is applied to a service method specifying the user groups that will be authorized against a protected method.

The <serviceAuthorization> element is applied to the Web.config file as follows:

```
<membership defaultProvider="SqlProvider" userIsOnlineTimeWindow="10">
  <providers>
    <clear />
      <add
        name="SqlProvider"
        type="System.Web.Security.SqlMembershipProvider"
        connectionStringName="conn"
        applicationName="SecuritySampleApp"
        enablePasswordRetrieval="true"
        enablePasswordReset="true"
        requiresQuestionAndAnswer="true"
        requiresUniqueEmail="false"
        passwordFormat="Hashed"
  </providers>
</membership>
```

Remember that a corresponding step is to configure the service to use the supplied service authorization:

```
<behaviors>
  <behavior name="ServiceBehavior">
    <serviceAuthorization principlePermissionMode="UseAspNetRoles"
      roleProviderName="SqlProvider" />
  </behavior>
</behaviors>
```

The default value for the [PrinciplePermission] attribute is "UseWindowsGroups."

Service Audit

The <serviceSecurityAudit> element is used to specify where the audit log is to be written to as well as the types of events to write. The following example writes the successful authentication attempts to the application log and logs all successes:

```
<serviceBehaviors>
  <behavior name="ServiceBehavior">
    <serviceSecurityAudit AutditLogLocation="Application"
      suppressAuditFailure="true"
      serviceAuthorizationAuditLevel="Success"
      messageAuthenticationAuditLevel="Success" />
  </behavior>
</serviceBehaviors>
```

This code example specifies settings related to the auditing of a specific behavior. All audit events are written to the Application Event Log, as specified by the AuditLogLocation being set to a value of

"Application". As well, successful service authorization events and successful message authentication events are audited.

Bindings

Windows Communication Foundation comes with a large number of predefined bindings, of which all but one include security enabled by default. This section lists each binding and a quick summary of their corresponding security features.

BasicHttpBinding

This binding is not secure by default. It is specifically designed to interoperate with ASMX web services. If security is enabled the binding will interoperate with existing IIS security mechanisms such as Integrated Windows security, Basic authentication, and Digest.

BasicHttpBinding supports the following:

❑   HTTPS transport security

❑   HTTP Basic authentication

❑   WS-Security

This binding is designed to be used with existing technologies such as ASMX web services and WSE applications.

WSHttpBinding

This binding implements the WS-Security specification by default, and provides interoperability with other services and applications that implement the WS-* specification, such as WS-Reliable Messaging. WSHttpBinding supports the following:

❑   HTTPS transport security

❑   HTTPS transport protection with SOAP message credential security for caller authentication

❑   WS-Security

WSDualHttpBinding

This binding works with duplex service operations and implements the WS-Security specification for message-based transfer security. WSDualHttpBinding provides the following:

❑   WS-Reliable Messaging for reliability

❑   WS-Security for transfer security and authentication

❑   HTTP for message delivery

❑   Text/XML message encoding

Transport security is not available with this binding.

NetTcpBinding

This binding is designed for machine-to-machine communication. By default it provides the following:

- ❑ Transport-layer security
- ❑ Windows security for transport security and authentication
- ❑ TCP for transport
- ❑ Binary message encoding
- ❑ WS-Reliable Messaging

Optionally, the following can be enabled:

- ❑ Message-layer security via WS-Security
- ❑ Transport security with message credential

NetNamedPipeBinding

This binding is designed for process-to-process communication, typically on the same machine. By default it provides the following:

- ❑ Transport security for message transfer and authentication
- ❑ Named Pipes for message delivery
- ❑ Binary message encoding
- ❑ Encryption and message signing

Optionally, the following can be enabled:

- ❑ Authentication using Windows security

MsmqIntegrationBinding

This binding is designed for WCF clients and services that interoperate with non-WCF MSMQ endpoints. By default it provides the following:

- ❑ MSMQ transport security

This binding allows security to be disabled. By default, this binding uses transport security.

NetMsmqBinding

This binding is designed for WCF services that require MSMQ queued message support. By default it provides the following:

- ❑ MSMQ transport security
- ❑ SOAP-based message security

❏ Concurrent transport and message security

❏ Client credential types supported

The Certificate credential type is only supported when the security mode is set to either *Both* or *Message*.

This binding uses transport security by default, and allows security to be disabled.

WSFederationBinding

This binding uses WS-Security by default.

The following table lists the bindings and the associated modes that they support.

Binding	Transport Mode	Message Mode	Transport with MessageCredential
BasicHttpBinding	Yes	Yes	Yes
WSHttpBinding	Yes	Yes	Yes
WSDualHttpBinding	No	Yes	No
NetTcpBinding	Yes	Yes	Yes
NetNamedPipeBinding	Yes	No	No
NetMsmqBinding	Yes	Yes	No
MsmqIntegrationBinding	Yes	No	No
wsFederationBinding	No	Yes	Yes

Securing Clients and Services

Windows Communication Foundation provides three methods for providing security:

❏ Transport

❏ Message

❏ TransportWithMessageCredential

As you have learned by now, transport security is dependent on the binding and subsequent transport used. The bindings in the previous section discussed each binding and their security support level. For example, the BasicHttpBinding binding does not provide security by default. All of the other bindings do support security by default. Transport security does have its advantages. For example, message streaming is possible and transport security performance is excellent.

However, transport security has the following disadvantages:

❑ Hop to hop only; meaning that the security is not applied at the message level. An issue when the path from source to destination contains one or more intermediaries.

❑ Not extensible in that it has a limited set of credentials.

❑ It is transport dependent.

So why would you use message security over transport security? There are several reasons:

❑ End-to-end security

❑ Multiple transport support

❑ Increased flexibility

❑ Increased support for credentials

End-to-end security means that the message is secure from transmission to receipt. Suppose a message is routed through one or more intermediaries between the sender and its ultimate destination. Transport security is point-to-point, meaning that once it hits the first intermediary, the message is not secure anymore because the first intermediary has grabbed the message from the wire and read it. Message security is end-to-end, no matter how many intermediaries the message passes through.

Message security allows messages to be secured over multiple transports. The benefit from this is that you are not relying on the transport for security.

Message security also provides increased flexibility over transport security in that individual parts of the message can be encrypted. Earlier it was mentioned that using this method enables the receiver, whether an intermediary or the final destination, to view the parts of the message that were intended only for them.

Message security is based on the WS-Security specification, which provides a more extensible framework that allows the transmitting of any time of claim within the SOAP message. WCF security allows multiple types of authentication and claims without any modifications.

Message security and transport security differ in a number of ways, but the most apparent difference is that message security includes the credentials and claims directly in the message.

Yet, there are some disadvantages to message security:

❑ Performance

❑ Streaming

❑ XML-level security

Message streaming is not possible with message security, and also requires the implementation of XML-level security mechanisms. Transport security does not require the implementation of XML-level security concepts. These XML-level security concepts, when used, must be understood by the communicating parties, therefore message security is limited by this fact in that it could affect interoperability.

Transport and message security are added by adding the appropriate section in the configuration for the client and service. The following example enables transport security:

```
<bindings>
  <WSHttpBinding>
    <binding name="TransportSecurity">
      <security mode="Transport">
        <transport clientCredentialType="Windows" />
      </security>
    </binding>
  </WSHttpBinding>
</bindings>
```

The following enables message security for WSHttpBinding:

```
<bindings>
  <WSHttpBinding>
    <binding name="MessageTransport">
      <security mode="Message">
        <message clientCredentialType="Windows" />
      </security>
    </binding>
  </WSHttpBinding>
</bindings>
```

However, you could have the best of both worlds by using both transport and message security. The benefit of this is that the transport security provides the integrity and confidentiality, while the message security provides the credential piece. The following uses simple WSHttpBinding with the TransportWithMessageCredential mode:

```
<bindings>
  <WSHttpBinding>
    <binding name="TransportMessage">
      <security mode="TransportWithMessageCredential">
        <message clientCredentialType="UserName" />
      </security>
    </binding>
  </WSHttpBinding>
</bindings>
```

You are not limited to using one or the other either. The following sets *clientCredentialType* for the *message* security to *NTLM* and to *Windows* for the *transport* security:

```
<bindings>
  <NetTcpBinding>
    <binding name="TransportMessage">
      <security mode="TransportWithMessageCredential">
        <message clientCredentialType="NTLM" />
        <transport clientCredentialType="Windows" />
      </security>
    </binding>
  </NetTcpBinding>
</bindings>
```

The piece that provides the transport-level security is determined by the transport when the security mode is set to TransportWithMessageCredential. Therefore, the clientCredentialType property can only be set on a message security object, not a transport security object (it will be ignored on a transport security object).

Best Practices

When creating Windows Communication Foundation applications, the following information should be taken into consideration:

- ❑ **Revert after impersonation:** Be sure to revert to the original identity after impersonating a client.

- ❑ **Careful impersonation:** Impersonate *only* when needed when using the *WindowsIdentity* class. Control the scope of impersonation by using the Impersonate method.

- ❑ **Metadata:** Get your metadata from a trusted source and secure the metadata exchange endpoint with either transport- or message-level security (to prevent tampering with the service metadata).

- ❑ **Local issuer:** When an issuer address and binding are used for a specific binding, the local issuer is not used for any endpoints that use the specified binding. As a result, clients need to make sure that they do not use such a binding if they expect to use the local issuer.

Summary

The topic of security can be very intimidating and somewhat overwhelming. The purpose of this chapter was to provide some insight into the realms of WCF security and show you that it does not need to be as difficult as it would seem.

WCF does not build or introduce new security features to complicate security even further. However, it does a very good job using the technologies and concepts that already exist to build a very robust and flexible security infrastructure.

The beginning of this chapter gave an overview of WCF security to help lay the foundation for the rest of the chapter and to help lay to rest any security fears. From there the chapter discussed specific WCF security features as they apply to bindings and behaviors and how they can be used to control the security behavior of your WCF application.

From there, you read about transport and message security and how they differ and the pros and cons of each, leading to the best practices section that gave a brief list of things to consider when looking at security for your WCF application.

11

Customizing Windows Communication Foundation

Stating that Windows Communication Foundation is extensible would be a gross misrepresentation of its capabilities. It should be fairly obvious by now that the extensible characteristics of WCF are what make it a strong distributed application platform.

The list of features and classes that can be extended is impressive, including topics such as security, the ServiceHost, bindings, the channel layer, and many others. One could probably fill a small book on nothing more than extending WCF. However, I don't have that kind of time. I have a deadline to meet. But you get the drift, so this chapter focuses on three topics that provide the developer some great options for extending WCF.

This chapter discusses the following WCF extensibility topics:

- ❑ ServiceHost/Service Model layer
- ❑ Channel layer
- ❑ Bindings

When talking about extending WCF, there are really only two major layers:

- ❑ The application layer
- ❑ The channel layer

The "glue layer" is the bindings because the application layer doesn't know about the channel implementations. Therefore, bindings are discussed last.

Extending ServiceHost and Service Model Layer

At the root of Windows Communication Foundation is the Service Model layer. Chapter 3 spoke somewhat about the service model, defining what it is and what it is comprised of. However, the WCF Service Model layer has the responsibility of grabbing incoming messages off of the wire (channel), converting them to method invocations, and, if necessary, replying to the caller with the results.

The extensibility of the service model allows the modification of many of its features regarding the client and the dispatcher functionality. The following two sections discuss the extensibility options available to those two WCF features.

Client

In Windows Communication Foundation, a client channel object has the responsibility of converting method calls into outgoing messages and converting incoming messages into results. To accomplish this, WCF contains two classes that are used in the processing of client objects and channels: the *ClientRuntime* class and the *ClientOperation* class. Both are members of the *System.ServiceModel.Dispatcher* namespace.

The *ClientOperation* class translates all outbound objects and converts them into messages. Furthermore, it verifies that the outbound message conforms to the target contract. At that point it hands the message off to the *ClientRuntime* class, which creates and manages all outbound channels.

These two classes are also used as the primary extensions in which to customize WCF client objects and channel processing. In most cases there is more than likely no need to customize the client. WCF comes with a superb service model that should fulfill most needs. Yet, as you have surely learned by now, WCF provides developers the ability and flexibility to have more control of the system if the need requires it. What would be those needs?

❑ **Custom data model:** Rather than use the built-in data or serialization models, you can define your own model.

❑ **Custom logging:** Using the message interceptor interfaces, you can log different messages that flow through the endpoint.

❑ **Custom message validation:** You can view or modify incoming or outgoing messages of a WCF client.

❑ **Custom parameter validation:** You can view or modify single operations of an incoming or outgoing message.

❑ **Custom message transformations:** You can apply specific transformations to a message at runtime.

The following two sections discuss how to use the *ClientRuntime* and *ClientOperation* classes to extend the WCF client.

ClientRuntime Class

The ClientRuntime class provides the insertion point for extending the client functionality of WCF client objects for all messages handled by the client. It is used to modify all runtime behavior for all messages within a contract. This class contains a number of properties that can be used to extend the client and intercept messages and add client behavior:

❑ **CallbackDispatchRuntime:** Returns the dispatch runtime object for service-initiated callback clients.

❑ **ContractClientType:** Returns the type of contract associated with a client.

❑ **ContractName:** Returns the name of the contract associated with the client.

❑ **ContractNamespace:** Returns the namespace of the contract associated with the client.

❑ **OperationSelector:** Accepts a custom operation selector object.

❑ **ChannelInitializers:** Enables the addition of a channel initializer, which can examine and change the client channel.

❑ **Operations:** Returns a collection of the ClientOperation object. These objects allow you to add custom message interceptors providing functionality specific to the message of that operation.

❑ **ManualAddressing:** Enables applications to turn off automatic addressing headers.

❑ **MessageInspectors:** Returns a collection of *IClientMessageInspector* objects. These objects let you add custom message interceptors for all messages moving through a WCF client.

❑ **Via:** Sets the value of the destination of the message at the transport level.

These properties allow developers to add extension objects that provide, for example, the ability to perform custom channel initialization, to process messages in a specific contract, and to add other custom client behaviors.

ClientOperation Class

The ClientOperation class is used to modify client runtime behaviors and is the insertion point at which all custom extensions are made that are targeted to only use a single service operation. The properties of the ClientOperation class, listed here, provide a mechanism by which custom objects can be inserted into the client system:

❑ **Action:** Returns the action of the operation.

❑ **BeginMethod:** Specifies the begin method associated with an asynchronous operation.

❑ **DeserializeReply:** Specifies a value indicating that the *Formatter* property value is used to deserialize the reply message.

❑ **EndMethod:** Specifies the end method associated with an asynchronous operation.

❑ **FaultContractInfos:** Returns a collection of FaultContractInfo objects, which represent the specified SOAP faults for an operation.

❑ **Formatter:** Specifies the formatter that is used to serialize objects into a message and deserialize messages into objects.

❑ **IsInitiating:** A value indicating whether a session can be started by a message to this operation.

❑ **IsOneWay:** A value indicating that the operation is one-way.

❑ **IsTerminating:** A value indicating that the current operation is the last operation in a session.

❑ **Name:** Returns the operation name.

❑ **ParameterInspectors:** Specifies a collection of *IParameterInspector* objects that can interrogate and make changes to inbound and outbound objects on a specific client method.

❑ **Parent:** Returns the ClientRuntime object.

❑ **ReplyAction:** Returns the action of the reply message of the current operation.

❑ **SerializeRequest:** Specifies whether the Formatter object serializes an outbound object, controlling who serializes an outbound message.

❑ **SyncMethod:** Returns the message associated with the current operation.

Custom extension objects can be inserted by using several built-in interfaces. The *IServiceBehavior* interface lets you modify or insert custom extensions across an entire service. The *IOperationBehavior* interface implements methods that can be used to extend the runtime behavior of an operation of a service or client application. The *IContractBehavior* interface contains methods that are used to extend runtime behavior for a contract in a service or client application. Lastly, the *IEndpointBehavior* interface contains methods that are used to extend the runtime behavior of an endpoint contract in a service or client application.

By implementing these interfaces and using the ClientRuntime and ClientOperation classes and their associated properties, you have everything at your disposal to extend the WCF client and insert custom extension objects.

For example, the following class implements the *IServiceBehavior, IEndpointBehavior*, and *IOperationBehavior* classes. Each class behavior implemented requires the *AddBindingParameters, ApplyDispatchBehavior*, and *Validate* methods be used to implement the appropriate behavior:

```
using System;
using System.Collections.Generic;
using System.Text;
using System.ServiceModel;
using System.ServiceModel.Channels;
using System.ServiceModel.Dispatcher;
using System.ServiceModel.Description;
using System.ServiceModel.Configuration;

namespace WCFClientApp
{
    class Class1 : IServiceBehavior, IEndpointBehavior, IOperationBehavior
    {
        #region IServiceBehavior Members
        public void AddBindingParameters(ServiceDescription sd,
            ServiceHostBase shb,
            System.Collections.ObjectModel.Collection<ServiceEndpoint> ep,
            BindingParameterCollection bpc)
        {
            //
        }

        public void ApplyDispatchBehavior(ServiceDescription sd,
            ServiceHostBase shb)
        {
            //
```

```
    }

    public void Validate(ServiceDescription sd, ServiceHostBase shb)
    {
        //
    }

    #endregion

    #region IEndpointBehavior Members

    public void AddBindingParameters(ServiceEndpoint se,
        BindingParameterCollection bpc)
    {
        //
    }

    public void ApplyClientBehavior(ServiceEndpoint se, ClientRuntime cr)
    {
        //
    }

    public void ApplyDispatchBehavior(ServiceEndpoint se,
        EndpointDispatcher ed)
    {
        //
    }

    public void Validate(ServiceEndpoint se)
    {
        //
    }

    #endregion

    #region IOperationBehavior Members

    public void AddBindingParameters(OperationDescription od,
        BindingParameterCollection bpc)
    {
        //
    }

    public void ApplyClientBehavior(OperationDescription od,
        ClientOperation co)
    {
        //
    }

    public void ApplyDispatchBehavior(OperationDescription od,
        DispatchOperation dop)
    {
        //
    }

    public void Validate(OperationDescription od)
```

```
        {
            //
        }

        #endregion

    }
}
```

The Validate method is used in the following situations:

❑ When used with the IServiceBehavior interface, the Validate method is used to verify whether the current service can execute properly within your scenario.

❑ When used with the IEndpointBehavior interface, the Validate method is used to verify that the endpoint is meeting your intended criteria.

❑ When used with the IOperationBehavior interface, the Validate method is used to verify that the operation is meeting your intended criteria.

The AddBindingParameters method is used in the following situations:

❑ When used with the IServiceBehavior interface, this method is used to pass custom data to binding elements that support the contract implementation.

❑ When used with the IEndpointBehavior and IOperationBehavior interfaces, this method is used to pass runtime data to bindings that support custom behaviors.

The ApplyDispatchBehavior method is used in the following situations:

❑ When used with the IServiceBehavior interface, this method provides the ability to alter runtime property values and insert custom extension objects such as error handlers.

❑ When used with the IEndpointBehavior and IOperationBehavior interfaces, this method can be used to implement an extension of the service across an operation.

The ApplyClientBehavior method is used with the IEndpointBehavior and IOperationBehavior interfaces to implement an extension of the client across an operation.

The following example illustrates how to insert an IClientMessageInspector into the client runtime. It is inserted into the client runtime by adding it to the MessageInspectors property of the ClientRuntime class:

```
public void ApplyClientBehavior(ServiceEndpoint se, ClientRuntime cr)
{
    cr.MessageInspectors.Add(new Inspector());
    foreach (ClientOperation co in cr.Operations)
      op.ParameterInspectors.Add(new Inspector());

}
```

Implementing an operation in most scenarios will usually be enough to meet your customization needs. However, endpoint behaviors and contract behaviors are at your disposal. These behaviors achieve the same results by locating the OperationDescription for a specific operation and attaching the behavior.

Dispatcher

The channel layer, part of the service model, has the responsibility of performing the conversion between the programming model and the message exchange. Two components that assist in this conversion are the ChannelDispatcher dispatcher and the EndpointDispatcher dispatcher. These two service components are assigned the tasks of receiving messages, accepting new channels, dispatching and invocating operations, and processing responses.

As messages arrive, the ChannelDispatcher pings each associated EndpointDispatcher object to determine which endpoint can accept and process the message. When the ChannelDispatcher finds an available EndpointDispatcher, the ChannelDispatcher hands the message off to that EndpointDispatcher.

The channel dispatcher is tasked with grabbing messages out of the channel and handing them to the associated endpoint dispatcher. The EndpointDispatcher object processes the messages received from the ChannelDispatcher. The message processing of the EndpointDispatcher object is accomplished by two classes of the EndpointDispatcher object. The DispatchRuntime class routes messages to the appropriate DispatchOperation, which then calls the appropriate method that implements the operation.

Through these two classes, you can customize the processing of the dispatcher. The DispatchRuntime and DispatchOperation classes let you extend the dispatcher at the contract and operation level.

The following lists the benefits and reasons of extending the dispatcher:

- **Custom message logging:** The ability to interrogate and log sets of messages flowing through an endpoint.

- **Custom message validation:** The ability to enforce that a message is valid for a specific schema.

- **Custom data model:** The ability to have a data serialization model other than the WCF-supported models.

- **Custom parameter validation:** The ability to enforce that typed parameters are valid.

- **Custom message transformations:** The ability to apply specific transformations to a message during runtime.

- **Custom operation dispatching:** The ability to implement dispatching on something other than action.

- **Custom authorization behaviors:** The ability to extend the contract or operation runtime pieces to implement custom access control.

- **Object pooling:** The ability to pool instances instead of allocating a new instance for each call.

- **Custom error handling:** The ability to define how local errors are processed and how faults are communicated back to the client.

- **Instance leasing:** The ability to employ a leasing pattern for instance lifetime.

The following two sections discuss how to use the *DispatchRuntime* and *DispatchOperation* classes to extend the WCF client.

DispatchRuntime Class

The *DispatchRuntime* class provides the ability to intercept and extend the dispatcher at the contract scope, meaning all messages for a specific contract. It is used to change the default behavior of a specific endpoint or a service as a whole. The *DispatchRuntime* class contains the following properties to accomplish this:

- ❑ **AutomaticInputSessionShutdown:** The value that determines if the service closes an input session when the client closes an output session.

- ❑ **CallbackClientRuntime:** Returns the *ClientRuntime* object representing the installation point for extensions to outbound calls to a duplex callback endpoint.

- ❑ **ChannelDispatcher:** Returns the *ChannelDispatcher* for the current dispatch runtime object.

- ❑ **ConcurrencyMode:** Specifies whether an instance of a service processes messages concurrently or sequentially.

- ❑ **EndpointDispatcher:** Returns the *EndpointDispatcher* for the current dispatch runtime.

- ❑ **ExternalAuthorizationPolicies:** Specifies the external authorization policies for authorizing users based on a set of claims.

- ❑ **IgnoreTransactionMessageProperty:** Specifies whether to ignore the *TransactionMessageProperty*.

- ❑ **ImpersonateCallerForAllOperations:** Specifies a value that determines if the service will attempt to impersonate using credentials supplied by the incoming message.

- ❑ **InputSessionShutdownHandlers:** Returns a collection of IInputSessionShutdown objects, which are used to determine how input sessions are closed via a custom handler.

- ❑ **InstanceContextInitializers:** Returns a collection of IInstanceContextInitializer objects, which are used to check or change an InstanceContext when first created.

- ❑ **InstanceContextProvider:** Specifies the IInstanceContextProvider used by the *DispatchRuntime*.

- ❑ **InstanceProvider:** Specifies the IInstanceProvider object used to control the lifespan (creation and destruction) of service objects.

- ❑ **MessageAuthenticationAuditLevel:** Specifies a value that determines whether successful message authentication events are written to the event log.

- ❑ **MessageInspectors:** Returns a collection of *IDispatchMessageInspector* objects used to attach a custom message inspector to all incoming and outgoing messages through the endpoint.

- ❑ **Operations:** Returns a collection of *DispatchOperation* objects used to control the execution behavior of a specific operation.

- ❑ **OperationSelector:** Specifies the *IDispatchOperationSelector* object, which controls the selection of a destination *DispatchOperation* for a specific message.

- ❑ **PrinciplePermissionMode:** Specifies a value that determines how the *CurrentPrinciple* property (of the System.Threading namespace) is set.

- ❑ **ReleaseServiceInstanceOnTransactionComplete:** Specifies a value that determines whether the service object recycled after a successfully completed transaction.

- ❑ **RoleProvider:** Specifies the custom *RoleProvider* used by *DispatchRuntime*.

- ❑ **SecurityAuditLogLocation:** Specifies the location of the audit log.

❏ **ServiceAuthorizationAuditLevel:** Specifies a value that controls which service authorization events are audited.

❏ **ServiceAuthorizationManager:** Returns the *ServiceAuthorizationManager*, which provides authorization checking for the *DispatchRuntime*.

❏ **SingletonInstanceContext:** Specifies the singleton *IInstanceContextProvider* used by the *DispatchRuntime*.

❏ **SuppressAuditFailure:** Specifies a value that determines whether to suppress exceptions that occur during logging which are non-critical.

❏ **SynchronizeContext:** Specifies the synchronization context that is used to invoke service operations.

❏ **TransactionAutoCompleteOnSessionClose:** Specifies a value indicating whether to auto-complete the current transaction when the session closes.

❏ **UnhandledDispatchOperation:** Specifies the operation to which unrecognized messages are dispatched.

At first glance, these properties might seem overwhelming. There certainly are quite a few. However, they can be grouped into four dispatcher extensibility areas that are exposed by this class:

❏ **Channel components:** Used to customize how the channel dispatcher accepts and closes channels. Includes *ChannelDispatcher, ChannelInitializer,* and *InputSessionShutdownHandlers* properties.

❏ **Message components:** Used to customize each processed message. Includes *MessageInspectors, OperationSelector, Operations,* and *ErrorHandlers* properties.

❏ **Instance components:** Used to customize the creation, lifetime, and disposal of instances of the service type. Includes *InstanceContextInitializers, InstanceContextLifetimes,* and *InstanceProvider* properties.

❏ **Security components:** Used to control security-related aspects. Includes *SecurityAuditLogLocation, ImpersonateCallerForAllOperations, MessageAuthenticationAuditLevel, PrinciplePermissionMode, ServiceAuthorizationAuditLevel,* and *SuppressAuditFailure* properties.

Once the custom extension objects are assigned to a *DispatchRuntime* property, the installing behavior is then added to the associated collection of behaviors. The custom extension objects can also be inserted into a collection by a service behavior, a contract behavior, or an endpoint behavior. This task can be done either programmatically or through the application configuration file by adding a custom *BehaviorExtensionElement*.

DispatchOperation Class

The DispatchOperation class provides the ability to intercept and extend the dispatcher at the operation scope, meaning all messages in a given operation. This class has the following properties:

❏ **Action:** Returns the action of the operation.

❏ **AutoDisposeParameters:** Specifies whether the parameters are to be disposed of automatically.

❏ **CallContextInitializers:** A collection of ICallContextInitializer objects, which define the methods that enable the initialization and recycling of thread-local storage.

❏ **DeserializeRequest:** Specifies a value indicating the *Formatter* property to be used to deserialize the request message.

- ❑ **FaultContractInfos:** Returns a collection of FaultContractInfo objects, which represent the specified SOAP faults for an operation.

- ❑ **Formatter:** Specifies the formatter that is used to serialize objects into a message and deserialize messages into objects.

- ❑ **Impersonation:** Specifies a value indicating the level of impersonation required by the operation.

- ❑ **Invoker:** Specifies the *IOperationInvoker* object, which initiates the user-defined method.

- ❑ **IsOneWay:** A value indicating that the operation is one-way.

- ❑ **IsTerminating:** A value indicating that the current operation is the last operation in a session.

- ❑ **Name:** Returns the name of the operation.

- ❑ **ParameterInspectors:** Specifies a collection of IParameterInspector objects used to view and change inbound and outbound objects of a particular method.

- ❑ **Parent:** Returns the DispatchRuntime object.

- ❑ **ReleaseInstanceAfterCall:** Specifies a value indicating whether to recycle the service object after a call.

- ❑ **ReleaseInstanceBeforeCall:** Specifies a value indicating whether to recycle the service object before dispatching the call.

- ❑ **ReplyAction:** Returns the action of the reply message of the operation.

- ❑ **SerializeReply:** Specifies a value indicating whether the *Formatter* object should serialize reply messages.

- ❑ **TransactionAutoComplete:** Specifies a value that indicates whether the current transaction auto-completes after the return of a successful operation.

- ❑ **TransactionRequired:** Specifies a value that indicates whether the operation must execute inside a transaction.

Although this class cannot be inherited, it is the place where runtime changes are made and the insertion point for custom extensions scoped to a single service operation.

The following example illustrates how an operation behavior attaches a parameter inspector at runtime. The ApplyDispatchBehavior method takes two parameters. The first parameter is the operation being executed and is for examination use only. The second parameter is the runtime object that exposes customization properties for the operation defined in the first parameter:

```
public void ApplyDispatchBehavior(OperationDescription od,
    DispatchOperation dop)
{
    dop.ParameterInspectors.Add(new Inspector());
}
```

Incoming and outgoing messages can be inspected and modified for a single operation on a single WCF client object or service by implementing the IparameterInspector interface and inserting it into the service or client runtime:

```
public void ApplyDispatchBehavior(ServiceEndpoint se, EndpointDispatcher, ed)
{
  ed.DispatchRuntime.MessageInspector.Add(new Inspector());
  foreach (DispatchOperation dop in ed.DispatchRuntime.Operations)
    dop.ParameterInspectors.Add(new Inspector());
}
```

As well, it can be done via configuration, as shown in the following partial configuration:

```
<client>
  <endpoint behaviorConfiguration="clientInspector" ...>
  </endpoint>
</client>
<behaviors>
  <endpointBehaviors>
    <behavior name = "clientInspector">
      <clientInterceptors />
    </behavior>
  </endpointBehaviors>
</behaviors>
<extensions>
  <behaviorExtensions>
    <add name="clientInterceptors"
      type="Microsoft.WCF.Service, HostApp" />
  </behaviorExtensions>
</extensions>
```

In this configuration, the Microsoft.WCF.InspectorInserter is the behavior extension type and the HostApplication is the name of the assembly the class has been compiled into.

Behaviors

You learned in Chapter 8 about behaviors and the fact that they allow you to modify default behaviors. Windows Communication Foundation also lets you add custom extensions that can inspect and validate service configuration settings or modify runtime behaviors in WCF clients and services.

In WCF, behavior types are added to the service or endpoint description objects prior to those objects being used by WCF. Together, the behavior types and description objects create a runtime that executes a WCF service or client, which when called during runtime, can access runtime properties and methods that modify the runtime behaviors that are constructed via the address, binding, and contract.

WCF contains four kinds of behaviors, each corresponding to a specific scope of access:

❑ **Service:** Primary method of modifying the service runtime as a whole via the IServiceBehavior interface. Service behaviors can be added by:

   ❑   Applying an attribute on the service class.

   ❑   Adding the behavior to the behaviors collection on ServiceDescription programmatically.

   ❑   Adding a custom BehaviorExtension element to the configuration.

❑ **Contract:** Used to extend both the WCF client and service runtime across a contract via the IContractBehavior interface. Contract behaviors are added to a contract via the following:

    ❑ Creating a custom attribute that can be used on the contract interface.

    ❑ Adding the behaviors to the behaviors collection on a ContractDescription.

❑ **Endpoint:** Used to modify the service as a whole or a client runtime for a specific endpoint. Endpoint behaviors are added to a service through the following two ways:

    ❑ Adding the behavior to the Behaviors property.

    ❑ Adding a custom BehaviorExtension element to the configuration.

❑ **Operation:** Used to extend the client and service runtime for each operation. Operation behaviors are added to an operation via the following:

    ❑ Creating a custom attribute on the method that models the operation.

    ❑ Adding the behavior to the behaviors collection on a constructed OperationDescription.

The WCF behavior methods and the client and service runtime classes provide a great way to modify and extend WCF runtime components to extend your applications. For a more in-depth look at behaviors, refer to Chapter 8.

Extending the Channel Layer

Chapter 2 discussed the WCF channel stack and the importance it plays in the communication process. However, it bears reviewing to understand how to build custom channels.

The channel layer of Windows Communication Foundation has the responsibility of exchanging messages between the client and services. It accomplishes this via the Windows Communication Foundation channel stack. This stack is multi-layered. At the top layer sits the application, at the bottom lays the transport channel, and in the middle sits one or more protocol channels.

The transport channel sends a message to, and receives a message from, other parties. It is responsible for adapting the channel stack to the underlying transport and transforming the Message object into the format that is used to communicate with other parties. The protocol channels are responsible for providing the communication functionality and each operates on the messages that are flowing through the stack. Regardless of the channel, messages flow through the stack as Message objects.

The WCF channel stack is a communication stack layered with one or more channels, each with the responsibility of processing messages. At the top of the stack is the application. At the bottom of the stack is the transport channel, responsible for adapting the channel stack to the underlying transport and sending and receiving messages. In between the application and transport are the protocol channels. These protocol channels provide the communication functionality including reliable delivery.

Messages flow through the stack as Message objects, with the protocol channels operating on the messages as they flow through the stack.

Channel stacks are created using a factory pattern. Bindings are used to create the channel stack on both the sending side and receiving side. The binding on the sending side is used to build a ChannelFactory. On the receiving side the binding is used to create an IChannelListener to listen for incoming messages.

The channel factory builds a channel stack, which the application can then use to send messages. The IChannelListener takes incoming messages and hands them to the listening application by creating channel stacks.

It is through this channel object model where the interfaces exist that are necessary in creating and implementing channel factories, channel listeners, and channels. Channel factories provide the ability to create channels used in sending messages (and closing any channels they created when the channel factory is closed). Channel listeners listen for incoming messages. The channel listener takes incoming messages and hands them to the layer above via the channels created by the channel listener.

The following sections discuss several areas that can be used to extend the channel.

Client Channel

Creating a Windows Communication Foundation client application that uses channel-level programming requires the following steps:

- ❏ Create a binding
- ❏ Create/build a channel factory
- ❏ Create a channel
- ❏ Send request
- ❏ Read reply
- ❏ Close channel objects

These steps provide the ability to create an application that sends messages and processes reply messages. The following code illustrates the steps that enable a client to send a message and read a reply message:

```
CustomBinding cb = new CustomBinding ();
cb.Elements.Add(new TcpTransportBindingElement());

IChannelFactory<IRequestChannel> cf =
  cb.BuildChannelFactory<IRequestChannel>(new BindingParameterCollection());

cf.Open();

IRequestChannel chnl = cf.CreateChannel(new
  EndpointAddress("net.tcp//localhost:8000/CoolApp"));

Message reqmess =
  Message.CreateMessage(MessageVersion.Soap12WSAddressing10,
  "http://wrox.com/requestaction", "Message body data");

Message repmess = chnl.Request(reqmess);

textbox1.text = "Sending message...";
```

```
string MessageData = repmess.GetBody<string>();
textbox2.text = MessageData;

reqmess.Close();
repmess.Close();
chnl.Close();
cf.Close();
```

In this code, a binding is created, which is then used to create a channel factory. Once the channel factory is opened, a channel is created with a specific endpoint address. This channel is then used to send a message via the CreateMessage method, and to read the reply message.

Service Channel

Creating a Windows Communication Foundation service application that uses channel-level programming is very similar to that of building a client channel. The following steps are required:

❑   Create binding

❑   Build channel listener

❑   Open channel listener

❑   Read request and send reply

❑   Close channel objects

The following code illustrates the steps that enable a service to receive and process messages:

```
CustomBinding cb = new CustomBinding();
cb.Elements.Add(new TcpTransportBindingElement());

IChannelListener<IReplyChannel> lis =
                cb.BuildChannelListener<IReplyChannel>(new
  Uri("net.tcp//localhost:8000/CoolApp"),
  new BindingParameterCollection());

lis.Open();

IReplyChannel repchnl = lis.AcceptChannel();

repchnl.Open();

RequestContext rc = repchnl.ReceiveRequest();

Message reqmes = rc.RequestMessage;

Message repmes = Message.CreateMessage(MessageVersion.Soap12WSAddressing10,
  "",
```

```
    "");

rc.Reply(repmes);

reqmes.Close();

rc.Close();

repchnl.Close();

lis.Close();
```

In this code, a binding is created, which is then used to create a channel listener. Once the channel listener is opened, requests are then read and a reply is sent, followed by the closing of the channel objects.

Channel Development

Several important steps are necessary to develop a protocol or transport channel in which to extend your WCF application layer. The following lists the steps necessary to create a user-defined channel:

❑   Select the appropriate MEP (Message Exchange Pattern)

❑   Create the channel factory and listener

❑   Add a binding element

❑   Handle exceptions

The following sections discuss these steps in more detail.

Choosing Message Exchange Pattern

Developing a custom transport requires several steps, the first of which is deciding the appropriate MEP (Message Exchange Pattern) for your application. There are three MEPs from which to choose:

❑   **Datagram:** The client sends a message and does not expect a response. Typically called a "fire and forget" exchange. Even though the send operation may complete on the client, it does not ensure that the endpoint has received the message.

❑   **Request-Response:** The client sends a message and a response is received.

❑   **Duplex:** Allows a client to send an arbitrary number of messages and be received by the service in any order.

Each of these MEPs support sessions, so in reality you can say that there are six MEPs. Each session correlates messages on a channel. For example, a request-reply pattern that does not support sessions is a standalone session in which the client sends a message and the service sends a reply message, such that the request and reply are correlated. Equally, a request-reply pattern that supports sessions implies that all request and reply messages on a channel are correlated with each other.

To fully understand sessions, a couple of terms need to be defined. "Connection-oriented" is a way of sending data in which both the sender and receiver use a predefined protocol to establish an end-to-end connection prior to any data being sent. The contrast is "connection-less," which means that data can be sent from sender to receiver without prior arrangement. That is, the sender can send data to the receiver without first making sure the receiver is ready and available to receive the data.

In Windows Communication Foundation, sessionful protocols are similar to connection-oriented network protocols, and sessionless WCF protocols are similar to connection-less protocols. Each new session established by the client with a corresponding service corresponds to a new sessionful session on each side.

For example, a client creates a new sessionful channel and sends a message. The channel listener on the service receives the message and determines that it pertains to a new session and therefore creates a new sessionful channel. The sessionful channel is then handed off to the application through which the message is received by the application, as well as all other messages sent in the same session and sessionful channel. This process is repeated when the same client or another client creates a new sessionful channel and sends a message.

The concept here is that there is no correlation between channels and sessions without sessions.

Channel Factory and Channel Listener

There are three categories of channel objects:

❑ **Channels:** The interface between the application and channel stack.

❑ **Channel listeners:** Create the channels on the receiving side.

❑ **Channel factories**: Create channels on the sender side to start the communication.

Listeners create channels and receive messages from the layer below and hand the messages to the layer above via the channel created by the channel listener. When the listener receives a message from the layer below, it places the message in a queue (think of it like an in-memory queue or temporary holding location). The channel itself then grabs the messages from the "queue" and passes them to the layer above when a message is asked for.

Channel factories also create channels and are used to send messages. Like channel listeners, channels take the message from the layer above, process them, and hand them off to the layer below. Channel factories have the additional task of closing any channels they create.

Add Binding Element

Bindings and binding elements are where the WCF application model is associated with channel factories and channel listeners. Bindings provide the ability to use custom channels without the need to write code at the channel level. BindingElement lets developers connect a WCF application to a channel. The benefit of this is that you don't have to know the type information for your channel.

A custom BindingElement can be implemented by including a class that inherits from BindingElement. This allows you to create a channel with any binding using the BindingElement and configure the binding to use it.

The BindingElement you create is responsible for creating the associated ChannelFactory and ChannelListener by overriding the CanBuildChannelFactory and CanBuildChannelListener implementations (which indicate that the binding element can build a channel factory and channel listener, respectively, for the specific type of channel).

Alternatively, you can use the BuildChannelFactory and BuildChannelListener to build channels of a specific type from the binding context and a channel listener to accept channels of a specific type.

For example, the following code uses the BuildChannelFactory of type IRequestChannel with a TcpTransportBindingElement:

```
CustomBinding cb = new CustomBinding();
TcpTransportBindingElement el = new TcpTransportBindingElement();
BindingParameterCollection bpc = new BindingParameterCollection();
BindingContext bc = new BindingContext(cb, bpc);

IChannelFactory<IRequestChannel> factory =
  el.BuildChannelFactory<IRequestChannel>(bc);

factory.Open();
EndpointAddress ea = new
  EndpointAddress("net.tcp://localhost:8000/CoolChannelApp");

IRequestChannel reqchan = factory.CreateChannel(ea);
reqchan.Open();
Message request =
  Message.CreateMessage(MessageVersion.Default, "this stuff rocks!");

Message response = reqchan.Request(request);
textBox1.Text = response.Headers.Action.ToString;
reqchan.Close();
factory.Close();
```

Likewise, the following code uses the BuildChannelListener of type IReplyChannel for accepting channels. The return value is the IChannelListener of type IChannel from the context:

```
CustomBinding cb = new CustomBinding();
TcpTransportBindingElement el = new TcpTransportBindingElement();
BindingParameterCollection bpc = new BindingParameterCollection();
Uri ba = new Uri("net.tcp://localhost:8000/CoolChannelApp");
String relativeAddress = "net.tcp://localhost:8000/CoolChannelApp/WCFService";
BindingContext bc = new BindingContext(cb, bpc, ba, relativeAddress,
  ListenUriMode.Explicit);

IChannelListenr<IReplyChannel> listen =
  el.BuildChannelListener<IReplyChannel>(bc);

listen.Open();
IReplyChannel repchan = listen.AcceptChannel();
repchan.Open();
RequestContext rc = repchan.ReceiveRequest();
Message message = rc.RequestMessage;

if (message.Headers.Action == "this stuff rocks!")
{
  Message replymessage = Message.CreateMessage(MessageVersion.Default, "I KNOW!");
```

```
      rc.Reply(replymessage);
}

message.Close();
repchan.Close();
listen.Close();
```

The benefit of adding new binding elements is that it allows you to substitute or enhance the system-provided bindings when the system-provided bindings may not provide the functionality requirements of your service.

Creating a new protocol binding element begins by extending the BindingElement class. At the very least, the BindingElement.Clone method must be implemented. The Clone method, when overridden, returns a copy of the binding element object. Also, be sure to implement the Channels.IChannel .GetProperty generic method, which will return the ChannelProtectionRequirement class for the binding element.

New transport binding elements can also be created, which are used to extend the TransportBindingElement interface. Here also the Clone method must be implemented.

Extending Bindings

Bindings are a collection of binding elements that are examined at runtime at the point that the client or service endpoint is being constructed. As explained earlier, bindings are the "glue layer" between the application and the channel layer. In other words, both the binding and the binding elements are the connection between the application programming model and the channel model.

Bindings specify the transport, protocol, and encoding required to connect to an endpoint. Custom bindings and extensions allow the developer to implement additional functionality that might be required to support additional features within an application.

The following sections discuss custom bindings.

Building Custom Bindings

Windows Communication Foundation includes the CustomBinding class, which provides the ability to construct a custom binding when the built-in bindings do not meet your binding needs. Custom bindings are constructed from the built-in binding elements, or can include existing custom binding elements.

Custom bindings are built through the use of the CustomBinding class, which comes from a collection of binding elements. These elements, some of which are required and others of which are optional, are expected to be in a certain order:

- ❑ The optional TransactionFlowBindingElement is first, which allows the flow of transactions.

- ❑ The optional ReliableSessionBindingElement follows, which provides a reliable session functionality.

- ❑ The SecurityBindingElement is next, which enables security features such as authentication and confidentiality.

Although the first three elements are optional, the next two elements are required. The first required element is the message encoding binding element, which can be one of the following:

- ❑ TextMessageEncodingBindingElement
- ❑ BinaryMessageEncodingBindingElement
- ❑ MtomMessageEncodingBindingElement

Of course, you can also use your own message encoder as well.

The next required element is the transport element, which can be one of the following WCF-provided values:

- ❑ BasicHttpBindingElement
- ❑ NetNamedPipesBindingElement
- ❑ NetTcpBindingElement
- ❑ NetMsmqBindingElement
- ❑ WSHttpBindingElement
- ❑ WsDualHttpBindingElement
- ❑ WsFederationBindingElement

You are also free to use your own transport here as well.

As you have learned previously, only the transport and encoding layers are required, and the transaction, reliability, and security layers are not required. Therefore, if your application does not require transaction, reliability, or security functionality, those binding elements do not need to be included.

The following code illustrates the order of these bindings within a configuration file:

```
<bindings>
  <customBinding>
    <binding name="CustomBind">
      <transactionFlow/>
      <reliableSession/>
      <security/>
      <textMessageEncoding/>
      <tcpTransport/>
    </binding>
  </customBinding>
</bindings>
```

Modifying a WCF Built-in Binding

You have learned by now that Windows Communication Foundation provides many built-in bindings. Bindings, in WCF, are constructed of binding elements, with each binding element being derived from the BindingElement class. These built-in bindings let you configure some aspects (properties) of the binding, but they do not give you full access to the properties of the binding elements.

WCF-provided bindings have the responsibility of creating and configuring their own binding elements, but when creating a custom binding, the developer has the responsibility. Therefore, creating a custom binding requires several steps.

The previous section discussed the required and optional binding elements necessary to create a custom binding. The following example uses code to create a custom binding.

The first step is to create an instance of the system-provided binding:

```
NetTcpBinding binding = new NetTcpBinding();
```

With an instance of the binding created, you can optionally set properties on the binding, such as setting its security mode:

```
binding.Security.Message.ClientCredentialType = TcpClientCredentialType.Windows;
binding.Security.Mode = SecurityMode.Message;
```

The next step is to create a custom binding from the binding instance you created:

```
CustomBinding cb = new CustomBinding(binding);
```

Next, create a BindingElementCollection from one of the custom binding's properties:

```
BindingElementCollection bec = cb.CreateBindingElements();
```

Lastly, loop through the binding collection looking for the transport binding element for the custom binding you just added. When you find it, you have access to its properties.

```
foreach (BindingElement be in bec)
{
  if (be is TcpTransportBindingElement)
  {
    TcpTransportBindingElement tcpbe = (TcpTransportBindingElement)be;
    // set properties
  }
}
```

In this example, the NetTcpBinding was used but you can do the same with all the other WCF-provided bindings to customize them.

User-Defined Bindings

This last section discusses how to create a user-defined binding. A user-defined binding is a binding that is not provided by Windows Communication Foundation, and WCF provides three ways to create a user-defined binding:

❑　Create a custom binding based on the CustomBinding class. This option was discussed earlier.

❑　Create a class that derives from a built-in binding. This option was discussed earlier.

❑　Create a new binding type. This provides complete control over the binding implementation as a whole.

Binding elements, discussed previously, denote a processing step when a message is sent or received. The three types of binding elements supplied by WCF are the following:

❑ **Protocol:** Denote steps that work with messages on a higher level. Any channel that is created by these bindings can add, delete, or modify the message content.

❑ **Transport:** Signify the communication of encoded messages on a transport protocol.

❑ **Encoding:** Signify transformations between a messages and encodings to be sent.

The order of binding elements is critical when creating new bindings. The order of the binding elements was discussed earlier; however, it is repeated here:

❑ First is the TransactionFlow binding element.

❑ The ReliableSession binding element follows.

❑ Next is the Security binding element.

❑ The Encoding binding element is next.

❑ Lastly, the Transport binding element is used.

Remember that the first three binding elements are optional, but the Encoding and Transport binding elements are required.

Creating your own binding elements enables you to customize many aspects of the binding elements, including the way the stack of bindings is created. You can also include the components that are included in the binding element.

A user-defined binding must at least implement the CreateBindingElements method and the Scheme property. The Scheme property sets the URI scheme specifying the transport used by the channel and listener factories built by the bindings. For example, NetTcpBinding will return "net.tcp".

The CreateBindingElement returns a new BindingElementCollection, as shown in the example in the previous section. This ordered collection holds the binding elements for the binding, with the Protocol binding element first, the Encoding binding element second, and the Transport binding element last.

Summary

This chapter focused on the customization of Windows Communication Foundation, focusing on three specific areas. The first part of the chapter discussed how to extend the ServiceHost using the ClientRuntime and ClientOperation classes, which provide the insertion point for extending the client functionality of WCF client objects for all messages handled by the client, and modify client runtime behaviors, respectively. This was followed up by discussing the DispatchRuntime and DispatchOperation classes, which provide the ability to intercept and extend the dispatcher at the contract scope class, and provide the ability to intercept and extend the dispatcher at the operation scope, respectively.

The second major section of this chapter discussed the channel layer and the available ways to extend the channel layer. The client channel section outlined the steps necessary to create an application that sends messages and processes reply messages. The service channel section outlined and discussed the steps that enable a service to receive and process messages.

This chapter covered the topic of channel development, discussing the steps that are necessary to develop a protocol or transport channel in which to extend your WCF application layer.

An important aspect of extending the channel layer is channel factories and channel listeners. Channel factories are responsible for creating channels, which are used for sending messages. This section discussed the aspects of creating and utilizing channel factories and channel listeners to extend your application.

Lastly, the topic of extending bindings was discussed. Bindings are the "glue layer" between the application and the channel layer. This section discussed how to build and utilize custom bindings in the case where WCF-provided bindings do not meet the requirements of your service.

Next, in Chapter 12, the topic of interoperability and integration is discussed.

12

Interoperability and Integration

A recurring theme that has been evident in nearly every chapter so far is the ability of Windows Communication Foundation to "play nice" with other technologies. WCF provides many benefits, and one of them is the ability to communicate with other platforms and technologies.

Interoperation and integration are the abilities to communicate with other platforms (like Linux) and to interact with other technologies (like Java). This chapter discusses the interoperability and integration features in Windows Communication Foundation.

It can't be stated enough the importance of interoperability and integration in Windows Communication Foundation. Although WCF is a near replacement for a lot of the technology you use today, such as web services, Web Service Enhancements, and Remoting, it would not be a very good idea for Microsoft to ask you to toss out much of your existing functionality that you worked so hard on, only to replace it with the "new and improved."

This is why there is such an emphasis on the integration and interoperability of Windows Communication Foundation. WCF allows you to enhance and build upon existing applications and technology without giving up on your existing technologies.

This chapter covers the following topics:

- ❑ WS-* interoperability
- ❑ Integration with legacy systems

Interoperability

Interoperability is the ability to communicate with other platforms through standard protocols (such as SOAP). One of the major benefits of SOAP is that it is platform independent.

Web Service Protocol Support

Windows Communication Foundation includes web service protocols that contain extensibility points and options that the developer can use to interoperate with web services.

WCF is designed and built to interoperate with web services that support the Web Services Specification, known as the WS-* specifications. As such, WCF comes with three system-provided bindings that facilitate interoperability. These bindings are shown in the following list:

❑ **BasicHttpBinding:** WCF services can use this binding to configure and expose endpoints. These endpoints in turn can communicate with *.asmx-based web services as well as clients and services that comply with the WS-I Basic Profile 1.1.

❑ **WsHttpBinding:** Supports distributed transactions as well as secure and reliable sessions.

❑ **WsDualHttpBinding:** Support for duplex communication and communication via SOAP intermediaries.

A brief synopsis of each of these bindings follows:

❑ **BasicHttpBinding:** Using the HTTP transport, suitable for communicating with WS-Basic Profile web services.

❑ **WSHttpBinding:** Similar to the BasicHttpBinding, this binding offers a secure and interoperable communication using the HTTP transport. Though it offers message security like its BasicHttpBinding sibling, WSHttpBinding also offers transaction and reliable messaging support as well as WS-Addressing. However, this binding does not support duplex service contracts.

❑ **WsDualHttpBinding:** A mere copy of the WSHttpBinding except for the fact that the WSDualHttpBinding supports duplex communication and communication via SOAP intermediaries. (Although a complete discussion of intermediaries is a discussion unto itself, an intermediary can be defined as an entity that brokers additional functionality in between a client and a service.) This binding lets both services and clients send and receive messages. This binding requires that the client have a public URI, providing a callback endpoint for the service.

Through these system-provided bindings developers can leverage the protocols supported by WCF. Table 12-1 lists the protocols supported by both the BasicHttpBinding and WsHttpBinding.

Table 12-1

Category	Protocol	Information
Transport	HTTP 1.1	Uses the HTTP and HTTPS transports.
Messaging	MTOM	Not used by default.

Category	Protocol	Information
Metadata	WSDL 1.1	WCF uses WSDL to describe services.
Metadata	WS Policy	WS-Policy and domain-specific used together to describe service requirements and capabilities.
Metadata	WS Policy Attachment	Implements WS-Policy attachments to attach policy expressions at different scopes in WSDL.
Metadata	WS Metadata Exchange	WS-MetadataExchange implemented to return XML Schema, WSDL, and WS-Policy.

To enable the MTOM protocol, set the messageEncoding attribute to *Mtom* as shown here:

```
<wsHttpBinding>
  <binding messageEncoding="Mtom">
</wsHttpBinding>
```

Table 12-2 lists the protocols supported by the BasicHttpBinding.

Table 12-2

Category	Protocol	Information
Messaging	SOAP 1.1	Implements the SOAP 1.1 message protocol.
Security	WSS SOAP Message Security 1.0	For username/password and X.509-based security.
Security	WSS SOAP Message Security Username Token Profile 1.0	
Security	WSS SOAP Message Security X.509 Token Profile 1.0	

Table 12-3 lists the protocols supported by both the WsHttpBinding and WsDualHttpBinding.

Table 12-3

Category	Protocol	Information
Messaging	SOAP 1.2	
Messaging	WS-Addressing 2005/08	Implements the WS-Address recommendation allowing for asynchronous messaging, message correlation, and transport-neutral addressing.

Table continued on following page

Category	Protocol	Information
Security	WSS SOAP Messaging Security 1.0*	Used when the securityMode attribute is set to "WSSecurityOverHttp".
Security	WSS SOAP Message Security Username Token Profile 1.1	Used when the wsSecurity authenticationMode attribute is set to "username".
Security	WSS SOAP Message Security X509 Token Profile 1.1	Enables message protection when the wsSecurity authenticationMode attribute is set to "Username", "None", or "Certificate".
Security	WSS SOAP Message Security Kerberos Token Profile 1.1	Enables authentication and message protection when the wsSecurity authenticationMode attribute is set to "Windows".
Security	WS Secure Conversation	Provides secure session.
Security	WS Trust	
Reliable Messaging	WS-Reliable Messaging	Used when the binding is configured to use reliableSessions.
Transactions	WS Atomic Transactions	Enables the communication between transaction managers.
Transactions	WS Coordination	Enables the flow of transaction context. The flow-Transaction attribute must be set to "Allowed" or "Required".

MTOM stands for Message Transmission Optimization Mechanism and enables a client and web service to efficiently send large amounts of data across the wire, taking advantage of the WS-* specifications. In WCF, the MTOM standard lets you take large data elements that are contained within a message and externalize them, meaning that the data is carried alongside the message as pure binary data minus any encoding.

It is through the WS-* specifications that interoperability is provided in Windows Communication Foundation. The built-in bindings discussed previously are provided to simplify service configuration for interoperability. From a "best practices" perspective, these bindings should be used for all interoperability needs in your application.

WSE (Web Service Enhancements)

WCF services are compatible with WSE 3.0. This interoperability is available to .NET clients when a WCF service is configured to use the WS-Addressing specification of August 2004.

The following two sections describe how to enable a WCF service and client to interoperate with WSE 3.0. The first section discusses how to enable a WCF service to interoperate with a WSE client. The second section discusses how to enable a WCF client to interoperate with a WSE web service.

WCF Service

Enabling a WCF service to interoperate with a WSE 3.0 client is a two-step process:

1. Define a custom binding for the WCF service.

2. Instruct the service to use the custom binding.

On the surface, it really is that simple. Underneath, however, there is a bit more to it but even the behind-the-scenes processing is fairly simple.

In the configuration file for the service, a `<customBinding>` element must be added to the `<bindings>` section. A name for the custom binding must be added to identify it. Once this is done the authentication mode and WS-Security specification version must then be specified, accomplished by adding a `<Security>` element to the `<binding>` element and adding the AuthenticationMode attribute and specifying one of the values in the following list. The WS-Security specification version must be compatible with WSE 3.0.

When interoperating with WSE the authentication mode must be set to one of the following values:

❑ **AnonymousForCertificate:** Specifies that the initiator is anonymous, and that the responder is authenticated.

❑ **Kerberos:** Specifies that the initiator and responder are authenticated using the Kerberos protocol.

❑ **MutualCertificate:** Specifies that the initiator and responder are authenticated with X.509 version 3 certificates.

❑ **UserNameOverTransport:** Specifies that the initiator is authenticated using a username token, and that the responder is authenticated by SSL over HTTPS.

❑ **UserNameForCertificate:** Specifies that the initiator is authenticated using a username token, and the responder's certificate is available to the initiator out-of-band.

Also, to interoperate with WSE 3.0 the value of the *messageSecurityVersion* attribute of the `<security>` element must be set to *WSSecurity11WSTrustFebruary2005WSSecurityConversationFebruary2005 WSSecurityPolicy11BasicSecurityProfile10*. Yeah, that's a long one to type but that is what it needs to be set to. To make things even more involved, this value is case sensitive and spaces are taken as literal (which means any inappropriate ones will cause this to fail). Regardless of the length, what it does do is get the message security version. This specific security version requires the Basic Security Profile, which is based on WS-Security 1.1, WS-TrustFebruary2005, WS-SecurityConversation2005, and WS-SecurityPolicy1.1 security specifications.

For example, the following configuration sets the authentication mode to Kerberos and the messageSecurityVersion to interoperate with WSE 3.0:

```
<bindings>
  <customBinding>
    <binding name ="CustBind">
      <security authenticationMode="Kerberos"
messageSecurityVersion="WSSecurity11WSTtrustFebruary2005WSSecureConversationFebruary
2005WSSecurityPolicy11BasicSecurityProfile10">
      </security>
    </binding>
  </customBinding>
</bindings>
```

Lastly, don't forget to modify the services section to reference the custom binding:

```
<services>
  <service behaviorConfiguration = "ServBehav" Name="MyWCFService">
    <endpoint binding="endpointbinding" address="" bindingConfiguration="CustBind"
      Contract="WCFService">
    </endpoint>
  </service>
</services>
```

This section discussed WCF service interoperability with WSE 3.0 web services. The next section discusses WCF client interoperability with WSE 3.0 web services.

WCF Client

Configuring a WCF client to work with a WSE 3.0 web service takes a little more work but is certainly doable. The first step is to create a class that represents the binding that will communicate with the WSE web service. That class needs to derive from the System.ServiceModel.Channels.Binding class:

```
public class wseHttpBinding : Binding
{
  //
}
```

The next step is to define properties on that class that mandate specific functionality. The following properties can be set on the class:

❑   **RequireDerivedKeys:** Specifies whether derived keys are required.

❑   **EstablishSecurityContext:** Specifies whether secure sessions are used.

❑   **MessageProtectionOrder:** Specifies whether signature confirmations are required.

❑   **SecurityAssertion:** Specifies message protection settings.

The following references are needed to support WSE 3.0 functionality:

```
using System.Security.Cryptography.X509Certificates;
using System.ServiceModel.Security;
```

For example, the following code snippet defines the four properties just described:

```
private wseSecurityAssertion assert;
private bool DerKeyReq;
private bool estSecCntxt;
private bool SigConfReq;
private MessageProtectionOrder messProtOrd;

public Wrox.WCF.Chapter12.WseSecurityAssertion sa
{
  get { return assert; }
  set { assert = value; }
}

public bool RequireDerivedKeyes
```

```
{
  get { return DerKeyReq; }
  set { DerKeyReq = value; }
}

public bool EstablishSecurityContext
{
  get { return estSecCntxt; }
  set { estSecCntxt = value; }
}

public bool RequireSignatureConfirmation
{
  get { return SigConfReq; }
  set { SigConfReq = value; }
}

public MessageProtectionOrder MessageProtectionOrder
{
  get { return messProtOrd; }
  set { messProtOrd = value; }
}
```

The next step is to override the CreateBindingsElements method. The purpose of overriding this method is to set specific binding properties:

```
public override BindingElementCollection CreateBindingElements()
{
  BindingElementCollection bec = new BindingElementCollection();
  SecurityBindingElement sbe;
  BindingElement be;

  Switch (assertion)
  {
    case WseSecurityAssertion.UsernameOverTransport:
      be = new HttpsTransportBindingElement();
      sbe = (TransportSecurityBindingElement)
        SecurityBindingElement.CreateUserNameOverTransportBindingElement();
      break;

    case WseSecurityAssertion.MutualCertificate10:
      be = new HttpTransportBindingElement();
      sbe = SecurityBindingElement.CreateMutualCertificateBindingElement(
MessageSecurityVersion.WSSecurity10WSTrustFebruary2005WSSecureConvesationFebruary20
05WSSecurityPolicy11BasicSecurityProfile10);
      break;

    case WseSecurityAssertion.UsernameForCertificate:
      be = new HttpTransportBindingElement();
      sbe = (SymmectricSecurityBindingElement)SecurityBindingElement.
        CreateUserNameForCertificateBindingElement();
      break;

    case WseSecurityAssertion.AnonymousForCertificate:
      be = new HttpTransportBindingElement();
      sbe = (SymmectricSecurityBindingElement)SecurityBindingElement.
```

```
            CreateAnonymousForCertificateBindingElement();
        break;

    case WseSecurityAssertion.MutualCertificate11:
        be = new HttpTransportBindingElement();
        sbe = SecurityBindingElement.CreateMutualCertificateBindingElement(

MessageSecurityVersion.WSSecurity11WSTrustFebruary2005WSSecurityConversations2005WS
SecurityPolicy11);
        break;

    case WseSecurityAssertion.Kerberos:
        be = new HttpsTransportBindingElement();
        sbe = (SymmectricSecurityBindingElement)SecurityBindingElement.
          CreateKerberosBindingElement();
        break;

    default;

    }

    bec.Add(sbe);

    //Add message encoder
    TextMessageEncoding

    bec.Add(be);

    return bec;

}
```

Lastly, in the client, code needs to be added to set the binding properties:

```
EndpointAddress ea = new EndpointAddress(new
  Uri ("http://localhost/WSETest/WSEService.asmx"),
  EndpointIdentity.CreateDnsIdentity("WSEServer"));

WseHttpBinding bi = new WseHttpBinding();

WSSecurityAnonymousServiceSoapClient cli = new
  WSSecurityAnonymousServiceSoapClient(bi, ea);

cli.ClientCredentials.ServiceCertificate.SetDefaultCredentials(
  StoreLocation.LocalMachine, StoreName.My,
  X509FindType.FindBySubjectDistinguishedName, "CN=WSEServer");
```

You can also set properties on the binding as well, such as the properties discussed earlier:

```
bi. SecurityAssertion = WseSecurityAssertion.Kerberos
bi.RequiredDerivedKeys = True
```

Getting a WCF client to communicate with a WSE 3.0 service requires only a few steps, as detailed in this section. WCF provides clients the ability to be wire-level compatible with WSE 3.0 web services quite easily. As long as you follow the August 2004 WS-Addressing specification version, this code should function properly.

ASP.NET Web Services

Windows Communication Foundation and ASP.NET web services can interoperate quite easily. Interoperability can be achieved by making sure that both the ASP.NET web service and the WCF service adhere to the WS-I Basic Profile 1.1 specification. As long as the ASP.NET web service adheres to the WS-I Basic Profile 1.1 specification, the WCF clients can interoperate by using the WCF-provided *BasicHttpBinding* binding.

The following link provides an in-depth look at the BasicProfile specification:

```
http://www.ws-i.org/Profiles/BasicProfile-1.1-2004-08-24.html
```

The preferred method of interoperating these two technologies is by using current ASP.NET 2.0 functionality. A custom interface should be created and the [WebService] and [WebMethod] attributes should be applied to it.

You may have picked up on the fact that I mentioned adding these attributes to an interface, rather than a class. Why? The answer is that interfaces define contracts and in this case, that's precisely what we're trying to do, define a contract for operations. Take a look at the following example:

```
[WebService]
public interface ITest
{
  [WebMethod]
  string TestMethod(string val);
}

public class TestService : ITest
{
  public string TestMethod(string val);
  {
    //
  }
}
```

This example creates an interface named ITest and applies the [WebService] attribute to it. Therein, it creates a method named TestMethod and applies the [WebMethod] attribute to this. With the only distinction being that this is an interface as opposed to a class, this should look identical to the traditional way you create and expose web services.

WCF/ASP.NET Compatible Endpoints

Endpoints can be added that are compatible with ASP.NET web service clients as well, and they can be defined and configured via code or via a configuration file.

Endpoint via Code

To add a WCF endpoint via code requires the following:

❑　Create a new BasicHttpBinding

❑　Add a new endpoint to the service host

❑　Enable an HTTP/GET metadata endpoint

The following code illustrates these steps:

```
using System;
using System.Collections.Generic;
using System.Text;
using System.ServiceModel;
using System.ServiceModel.Description;

[WebService]
public interface ITest
{
  [WebMethod]
  string TestMethod(string val);
}

public class TestService : ITest
{
  public string TestMethod(string val);
  {
    //
  }
}

class CoolProgram
{
  static void Main(string[] args)
  {
    string ba = "http://localhost:8000/wcfhost/";
    ServiceHost sh = new ServiceHost(typeof(TestService), new Uri(ba));

    BasicHttpBinding bhb = new BasicHttpBinding();

    Sh.AddServiceEndpoint(typeof(ITest), bhb, "TestMethEP");

    sh.Open();
    // do something
    sh.Close();
  }
}
```

An optional step would be to enable transport security for the defined endpoint. This can be done by setting the security mode for the binding to *Transport*.

Endpoint via Configuration

Conversely, a WCF endpoint that is ASP.NET compatible can be defined through a configuration file. The steps for this are no different than those for the preceding example. This means that a new BasicHttpBinding binding must be defined, an endpoint must be defined that uses the new binding, and HTTP/GET must be enabled as shown in the following configuration code:

```
<system.ServiceModel>
  <services>
    <service name="TestService" behaviorConfiguration="GetHttpMD">
      <endpoint address="TestMethEP" contract="ITest" binding="basicHttpBinding" />
    </service>
  </services>
  <behaviors>
    <serviceBehaviors>
      <behavior name="GetHttpMD">
        <serviceMetadata httpGetEnabled="true" />
      </behavior>
    </serviceBehaviors>
  </behaviors>
</system.ServiceModel>
```

In this configuration, a service metadata behavior is used to enable metadata support for HTTP GET.

Windows Communication Foundation offers many interoperability features, as you have learned in this section. The following section discusses the integration features of WCF.

Integration

Integration is the ability to interact with other technologies. Most companies will have already devoted a lot of time to the development of these technologies and won't want to simply toss them aside. Instead they would like to extend the functionality of their existing code. The following two sections discuss the integration of COM+ and MSMQ with WCF to extend existing logic.

COM+

Integrating Windows Communication Foundation with existing COM+ components lets you extend your existing applications as opposed to having to rewrite their logic. WCF makes this extensibility quite easy. Basically, it requires only a few steps to expose a COM+ interface as a web service and no changes need to be made to the original component.

You can accomplish this in four steps.

The first step is to determine if the COM+ component interface can be exposed as a web service. The following types of interfaces are supported:

❑   Interfaces that pass object references as parameters

❑   Interfaces that pass types that are not compatible with the .NET Framework COM interop

- ❑ COM+ infrastructure interfaces
- ❑ Component interfaces that are marked as private to the application
- ❑ System application interfaces
- ❑ Interfaces for applications that have application pooling enabled when hosted by COM+
- ❑ Enterprise Services component interfaces that have not been added to the GAC (Global Assembly Cache)

The next step is to select the appropriate hosting mode. COM+ has the ability to expose web services in one of the following hosting modes:

- ❑ COM+-hosted
- ❑ Web-hosted
- ❑ Web-hosted in-process

Afterwards the COM+ Service Model Configuration Tool should be used to add a web service for the interface. See the following section entitled "COM+ Service Model Configuration Tool" for information regarding this tool.

Lastly, optional service settings can be added and configured via the configuration file.

As COM+ component interfaces are exposed as web services, the contract and specifications are automatically determined by an application initialization mapping. This mapping basically states that there is a single service for each exposed COM class. Additionally, the service contract is derived from the definition of the chosen component's interface, and the operations of the selected contract are derived from the methods of the component's interface definition.

This mapping also specifies that the operations in the contract are derived from the methods on the component's interface definition, and that the parameters for the exposed web service methods are derived from the COM interoperability type.

From a security perspective, defining security for exposed services is accomplished just like it is in other WCF services, through configuration settings for the WCF channel.

COM+ Service Model Configuration Tool

The COM+ Service Model Configuration Tool is a command-line tool that lets you configure a COM+ interface to be exposed as a web service. As a command-line tool it has no user interface, but a number of available command-line switches can be used. This tool is located in the following directory:

```
C:\WINDOWS\Microsoft.NET\Framework\v3.0\Windows Communication Foundation
```

Table 12-4 lists the modes in which the COM+ Service Model Configuration Tool can be used.

Table 12-4

Option	Short Form	Description
install	/i	Installs a configuration for a COM+ interface for Service Model integration.
uninstall	/u	Uninstalls a configuration for a COM+ interface from Service Model integration.
list	/l	Lists the information about COM+ applications and components that have interfaces that are configured for Service Model integration.

Table 12-5 lists the flags available for use with the COM+ Service Model Configuration Tool.

Table 12-5

Option	Short Form	Description
/application:	/a	Specifies the COM+ application to configure.
/contract:	/c	Specifies the COM+ component and interface that will be configured as the contract for the service.
/hosting:	/h	Specifies whether to use the COM+ hosting mode or the web hosting mode. Values are *complus* or *was*.
/website:	/w	Specifies the web site for hosting when web hosting is used.
/webDirectory:	/d	Specifies the virtual directory for hosting when web hosting is used.
/mex	/x	Adds a MEX service endpoint to the default service configuration. This is to support clients that want to obtain a contract definition from the service.
/id	/k	Displays the application, component, and interface information as IDs.
/nologo	/n	Prohibits the COM+ Service Model Configuration Tool from showing the logo.
/verbose	/v	Outputs warnings or informational text as well as encountered errors.
/help	/?	Displays the usage information.
/partial		Creates a service configuration when the specified interface includes one or more method signatures that can be exposed.

The following command line adds an interface to a COM+ component that will be exposed as a web service. For example, if you had an existing COM+ BookOrder component that you wanted to expose as a web service, you would execute the following:

```
ComSvcConfig.exe /install /application:BookOrder /contract:BookOrders.IBookOrder,
IOrder /hosting:was /verbose
```

In this example, a BookOrders COM+ application exists, and the IOrder interface of the BookOrders .IBookOrder component is added to the list of available interfaces that will be exposed as web services. The service will use the web hosting mode, and the /verbose option is added, indicating that warnings will be displayed in addition to the any errors generated.

The following command line removes the IBookOrder interface from the BookOrder.IBookOrder component:

```
ComSvcConfig.exe /uninstall /application:BookOrder /contract:BookOrders.IBookOrder,
IOrder
```

MSMQ

If you are using MSMQ (Microsoft Message Queuing) to ensure a reliable transfer of messages, Windows Communication Foundation allows for the integration of your existing message queuing applications with WCF applications. Integration is accomplished by using the Message Queuing Integration Binding, which converts MSMQ messages to and from WCF messages. The benefit of this is that you can use a WCF client to call into an MSMQ receiver application. In fact, the reverse is true as well, in that your existing MSMQ sending applications can call into WCF services.

This section discusses how to use the MsmqIntegrationBinding binding to integrate MSMQ and WCF.

WCF Service and MSMQ Client

Creating a WCF service that can receive messages from an MSMQ client requires the following steps:

❑ Define a WCF service interface

❑ Implement the interface and apply the necessary attributes

❑ Specify the MsmqIntegrationBinding in the configuration file

Following these steps, a WCF service interface must first be defined for receiving queued messages from an MSMQ sending application:

```
[ServiceContract]
public interface IBookOrder
{
    [OperationContract(IsOneWay=true, Action="*"]
    void ProcessBookOrder(QueueMessage<BookOrder> msg);
}
```

Next, the implementation of the interface must be applied along with the appropriate behavior attributes:

```
public class BookOrderProcess : IBookOrder
{
  [OperationContract(TransactionScopeRequired=true, TransactionAutoComplete=true)]
  public void ProcessBookOrder(QueueMessage<BookOrder> msg)
  {
    // process the book order
  }
}
```

Lastly, the MsmqIntegrationBinding must be specified in the configuration file:

```
<bindings>
  <msmqIntegrationBinding>
    <binding name="BookOrderProcessBind">
      <security mode="Transport">
    </binding>
  </msmqIntegrationBinding>
</bindings>
```

Obviously you will need a host for this service and instantiate the ServiceHost, which uses the configured binding. This can be accomplished as follows:

```
Uri ba = new Uri(ConfigurationManager.AppSettings("QueueAddress");
ServiceHost sh = new ServiceHost(typeof(IBookOrder), ba));
sh.Open();
```

Equally you will need to specify the following in the configuration file:

```
</configuration>
  <appSettings>
    <add key="QueueAddress" value=".\private$\BookOrders" />
  </appSettings>

  <system.ServiceModel>
    <services>
      <service name="BookOrderProcess">
        <endpoint address = "msmq.formatname:DIRECT=OS:.\private$\BookOrders"
          binding = "msmqIntegrationBinding"
          bindingConfiguration="BookOrderProcessBind"
          contract = "WCFService" >
        </endpoint>
      </services>
    </services>
  </system.ServiceModel>
</configuration>
```

Following these steps will allow you to use the Message Queuing integration binding to convert Message Queuing messages to and from WCF messages.

Summary

Integration and interoperability play a large role in Windows Communication Foundation for several reasons, and hopefully you can see why after going through this chapter. Primarily, it allows you to use existing applications and architecture without the need of rewriting existing applications.

This chapter was broken out into two main sections, integration and interoperability. The chapter began by discussing interoperability and how easily WCF interoperates with web services by implementing a large number of web services protocols. It then discussed how easy and flexible it is to interoperate with WSE 3.0 and ASP.NET web services using existing technologies.

The chapter then followed that up by discussing integration and specifically discussed integrating with COM+ applications and MSMQ applications. WCF provides a very slick command-line tool that lets you configure a COM+ interface to be exposed as a web service.

The next section of the book focuses on the management side of Windows Communication Foundation and discusses topics such as hosting and deployment as well as WCF Management tools.

Part III
Deploying Windows Communication Foundation

13

Deploying Windows Communication Foundation

The last 11 chapters have all focused on designing and building Windows Communication Foundation services as well as the clients that access these services. Now that you have those services built and tested, the next logical step is to deploy and install them to their appropriate production environment.

This chapter discusses some topics that will assist in installing and deploying your new services as well as some ideas about upgrading and troubleshooting existing services.

Thus, this chapter covers the following:

❑   Installing Windows Communication Foundation services

❑   Upgrading existing services

❑   Troubleshooting WCF service installations

Installing WCF Services

Prior to installing your new WCF service, a few things need to be done in order to successfully install and deploy it, including making sure you are installing it on an operating system that supports WCF as well as installing the required software components. This section discusses the requirements for successfully installing a WCF service.

Support Operating Systems

Windows Communication Foundation is supported on the following operating systems:

❑ Windows XP with Service Pack 2

❑ Windows Server 2003 with Service Pack 1

❑ Windows Vista

Windows Communication Foundation is installed with Windows Vista by default.

Required Software

To successfully run a WCF service requires the installation of the following components:

❑ .NET Framework 3.0

❑ IIS (Internet Information Services)

❑ MSMQ (Microsoft Message Queuing)

Depending on how you plan on hosting your WCF service, IIS will only be required if you plan on hosting your service in IIS. MSMQ is only required if you plan on utilizing the MSMQ transport for message communication.

.NET Framework

The .NET Framework 3.0 will ship as part of Windows Vista, but is available as a separate download for Windows XP and Windows Server 2003. Version 3.0 can be downloaded from the following location:

```
http://www.microsoft.com/downloads/details.aspx?FamilyId=10CC340B-
F857-4A14-83F5-25634C3BF043&displaylang=en
```

This will need to be installed on any machine in which you plan on running a Windows Communication Foundation service.

Internet Information Services

If you plan on hosting a WCF service in IIS, you will need to install IIS or ensure that IIS is installed on the computer that will be hosting the WCF service. To install IIS, open the Control Panel and select Add/Remove Windows Components.

In the Windows Components Wizard shown in Figure 13-1, select the Internet Information Services (IIS) option from the list of components and click Next. Depending on how the operating system was installed, you may be required to have the operating system CD/DVD handy.

In order to successfully host and run a WCF service in IIS, ASP.NET must also be installed. ASP.NET is installed by default as part of the .NET Framework 3.0. Note that if the .NET Framework is not installed on the box that will be hosting the WCF service, ASP.NET will be installed when you install the .NET Framework 3.0.

However, it is critical that you install IIS prior to installing the .NET Framework because the .NET Framework requires certain IIS components to be in place.

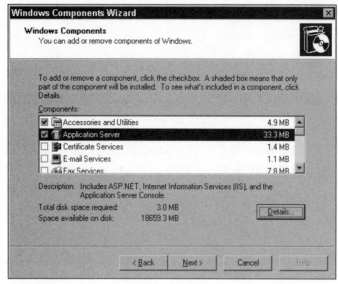

Figure 13-1

Once IIS is installed and configured, open Windows Explorer and navigate to the root of your system drive. You should see a folder called `intepub`. Open that folder and you should see a folder called `wwwroot`. To test that IIS is operational, open Microsoft Notepad and type in the following:

```html
<html>
   <body>
     <H1>
       Ready for Windows Communication Foundation!
     </H1>
   </body>
</html>
```

Save this file as `WCFTest.htm` in the `\inetpub\wwwroot` folder, as shown in Figure 13-2.

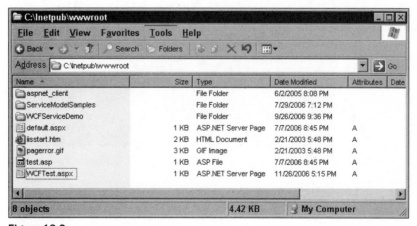

Figure 13-2

Next, open Internet Explorer or your favorite browser and type in the following address:

```
http://localhost/WCFTest.aspx
```

The browser should then display what's shown in Figure 13-3.

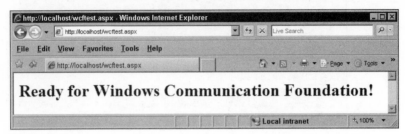

Figure 13-3

You are now ready to install your WCF service. This is discussed later in the chapter.

Microsoft Message Queuing

If you plan on utilizing the MSMQ transport for message communication, you will need to install the necessary MSMQ components. To install MSMQ, open the Control Panel and select Add/Remove Windows Components.

In the Windows Components Wizard shown in Figure 13-4, select the Message Queuing option from the list of components and click Next. Depending on how the operating system was installed, you may be required to have the operating system CD/DVD available.

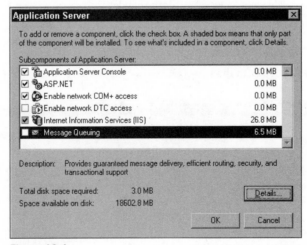

Figure 13-4

With the Message Queuing option selected, click the Details button to select the specific MSMQ options for your MSMQ installation. Clicking the Details button will open the Message Queuing detail form shown in Figure 13-5.

At the minimum, you want to select the *Common* option, which provides the basic functionality for local messaging services. If you are using MSMQ with Active Directory Authentication, you will want to select the Active Directory Integration option. This option provides MSMQ integration with Active Directory if the computer is part of a Windows domain.

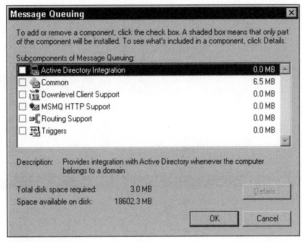

Figure 13-5

Installing the WCF Service

Once you have everything installed, the next step is to install your new WCF service. This section discusses the steps necessary to install your service.

IIS

To install your WCF service in IIS, you will first need to create a virtual directory and then copy the WCF service components into the new directory. For instructions on how to create a virtual directory, refer to the example in Chapter 3.

Once the virtual directory is created and ready, there are two ways to install the WCF service. You can deploy the service in source form or in binary form. In binary form you simply place the compiled binary assemblies within a \bin folder underneath the virtual directory. The Web.config file and the .svc file need to be placed underneath the virtual directory.

To deploy the service using the source form you place the source code (.vb or .cs file), the Web.config file, and the .svc file underneath the virtual directory. The .svc file then needs to reference the source code as follows:

```
<%@service name = "<file>"%>
```

Figures 13-6 and 13-7 show the structure of the virtual directory using binary deployment.

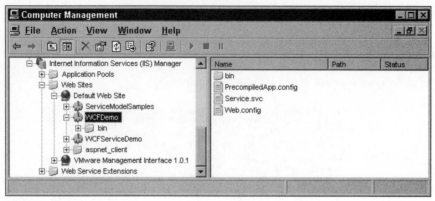

Figure 13-6

Figure 13-7 shows the contents of the bin directory.

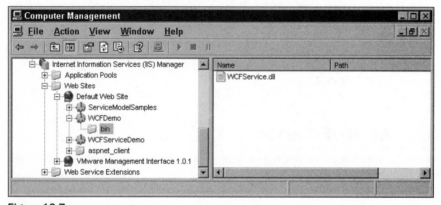

Figure 13-7

The service can now be consumed and utilized by a client.

Though the preceding scenario walked you through installing the service manually, you can also use installers to accomplish this task as well. Several installers are available that will automate the install process, such as Wise and InstallShield.

All the examples in this chapter walk you through installing the service and related components manually so that you will understand the steps and requirements necessary to successfully install and deploy a WCF service. Once you understand these steps, you can add these steps into your favorite installer program.

Windows Service

Chapter 15, "Hosting Windows Communication Foundation Services," discusses the different ways in which a Windows Communication Foundation service can be hosted. Therefore this section does not discuss how to build a Windows service in which to host the WCF service. It does, however, discuss how to deploy the WCF service via a Windows service.

Once the Windows service has been built and compiled, it can be installed and registered as a Windows service by using the InstallUtil utility, which is installed as part of the .NET Framework. The InstallUtil utility is a command utility that installs and registers the service as a Windows service.

The syntax for installing the service is as follows:

```
C:\Windows\Microsoft.NET\Framework\v2.0.50727\InstallUtil
C:\Windows\System32\WCFServhost.exe
```

This utility is also installed with the Windows SDK and is installed in the following location:

```
Program Files\Microsoft SDKs\Windows\v6.0\Bin
```

The new Windows service can then be started by using the net start and net stop commands. The following starts the newly installed Windows service:

```
net start WCFServhost
```

The following stops the Windows service:

```
net stop WCFServhost
```

The Windows service can be uninstalled and unregistered by running the InstallUtil command utility with the /u parameter, as shown here:

```
C:\Windows\Microsoft.NET\Framework\v2.0.50727 /u
C:\Windows\System32\WCFServhost.exe
```

WCF Service Configurations

By now you should have a good grasp on how services and their related endpoints are defined in configuration files. Once WCF services are installed and running, making changes is simple, letting you add new endpoints or configure existing endpoints.

There are a number of things to keep in mind when deploying and configuring your WCF service. The first thing to consider is the environment in which your service will be hosted. Windows Communication Foundation services are specifically designed to optimally operate in any Windows process which supports managed code. Regardless of the hosting environment, however, the deployment strategy will differ in different degrees. As stated earlier, Chapter 15 discusses the different ways in which a Windows Communication Foundation service can be hosted.

The second aspect to consider is the security of your service. Any time you have a program that is based on the exchange of SOAP messages, the security of those messages is critical. Every party that is communicating must be able to identity one another and limit what the other parties can do. When deploying your WCF service, make sure you consider the security aspects as they apply to your environment. Security was discussed in Chapter 10.

Regardless of the deployment strategy, your goals for deploying and configuring your WCF service should be flexible enough as to not interrupt the production solution and application in your environment.

Upgrading Services

One of the great things about Windows Communication Foundation is the way that services can be upgraded. This is one of the requirements and principles of SOA as discussed in Chapter 1, in that a service should not disrupt the functionality and functions of the rest of the solution.

Now, this can certainly be true a majority of the time. However, a lot of it depends on how your WCF service is deployed. If you are familiar with ASP.NET web services, you know that deploying a new version of the web service is as simple as copying a new assembly into the \bin directory (and Web.config if necessary), which is often referred to as XCopy deployment.

Luckily WCF services hosted in IIS operate the same way. Upgrading a WCF service hosting in IIS is as simple as copying the new assembly or source code (along with the Web.config and .svc file if necessary) into the appropriate locations in the virtual directory, and IIS/ASP.NET will utilize the new service automatically.

WCF services hosted in a Windows service is another matter, however. WCF services hosted in IIS or WAS (Windows Process Activation Service) watch the file, and when the service changes they gracefully restart the working process. They even go so far as allowing requests to the old library continue to their natural end.

Windows Services and other hosts will require that you restart the hosting environment. For example, if you are hosting your WCF service in a Windows service, you will need to restart the Windows service manually in order for the changes to be available.

Troubleshooting WCF Installations

So now your service is installed, configured, and running. Now you can breathe a sigh of relief because you are done and nothing else can go wrong. Uh huh, and it's not hot in the Sahara. Whether you want to believe it or not, you are going to need to be prepared to run into some sort of problems and know where to do your sleuthing. The trick, Sherlock, is knowing where to begin your investigation.

Client/Service Communication

If the client cannot communicate with the service, you can't automatically assume that the problem is with the client. Your best bet is to start looking at the service first. Your first test is to use the ServiceModel Metadata Utility Tool (svcutil.exe) utility and try to access it with this utility. For example, you could execute a statement like the following:

```
svcutil.exe net.tcp//localhost:8000/WCFService/tcpmex /o:c:\wcfclientapp\
wcfclientapp\client.cs /config:c:\wcfclientapp\wcfclientapp\output.config /l:c#
```

If you are hosting the service in IIS you can try to access the service from the local machine and again from another computer. For example, open a browser and type in the following:

```
http://localhost/WCFService/Service.svc
```

If either of these scenarios is successful, then you can start looking at the client.

The first thing you should check is the configuration settings. You should know by now that a client and service need to agree on the ABCs of services. A client and service need to agree on their addresses, bindings, and contract definitions (service, data, and message). Your service and client could be error free, but if the ABCs don't match up, they won't communicate.

If a review of the configuration files doesn't visually turn up any discrepancies, you can use the svcutil utility to generate client code and configuration. With the generated files you can compare your original client code and configuration file with the generated files and look for any discrepancies. You can also use the generated code and try and access the service.

Unexpected Service Behavior

You may also run into the scenario where your client and service are communicating but the service isn't behaving as you expected. This is typically because of unhandled exceptions in the service. You learned in Chapter 8 that the way to catch these is by utilizing the IncludeExceptionDetailInFaults property of the [ServiceBehavior] attribute, which will return all unhandled exceptions to the client:

```
[ServiceBehavior(IncludeExceptionDetailInFaults=true)]
public class ServiceClass : IServiceClass
{
    ...
}
```

The key to this property is that you typically do not want to keep it on in your production system. Once you have used it to find the problem in your service, turn it off.

You also have two more resources at your disposal to help debug unexpected service behavior. The first of these choices is to enable tracing. Tracing allows you to view the events that lead up to the error that can help pinpoint the problem. The trace output can be viewed in the SvcTraceViewer tool and provide a great in-depth look at the events that transpired up to the error and shed some great insight. Tracing is covered in detail in Chapter 14.

The other resource at your fingertips is message logging. Message logging provides the ability to store messages (sent and received) that can then be viewed and inspected later. Why is this important? Because message logging provides the unique ability to look inside the message that encountered the problem, its contents might divulge incorrect or invalid message content or structure. Message logging is also covered in Chapter 14 in more detail.

Exceptions

When I started writing this chapter, I thought it would be a really nice "bonus" to include a section that listed the top five or so errors that developers commonly get when they first start working with Windows Communication Foundation.

After some digging around and discussing this with my contacts at Microsoft, I decided to supply something better that I cannot take credit for. Instead of discussing a "Top 5," a link is included that is a WCF troubleshooting guide put together by the Ralph Squillace at Microsoft. After reading this article, it is much better than any "Top 5" I could put together. The following link describes some of the common issues in WCF and what you can do to solve them:

```
http://msdn2.microsoft.com/en-us/library/aa702636.aspx
```

Summary

Deploying and troubleshooting a WCF service can be a smooth process if done correctly. This chapter focused on these specific topics to help you understand the process of deploying a WCF service and pointed out some things that you should watch out for so that your deployment is a success. One of the many great characteristics of Windows Communication Foundation is its ability to configure and upgrade a WCF service without disrupting the flow of a system. The purpose of this chapter was to help you get a grasp of the deployment and upgrading of a WCF service and the requirements necessary to do so.

If you know where to look, troubleshooting a WCF service can also be a fairly smooth process. This chapter spent a few pages discussing the process of how to troubleshoot a WCF service to help your deployment go smoothly.

Then next chapter covers how to manage and administer your WCF services.

14

Managing Windows Communication Foundation

So far you have built and deployed your WCF service, but what now? It doesn't end here because WCF provides a number of tools and functionalities to assist you in rolling out and deploying your WCF service. You know as well as I do that dealing with distributed applications can be a challenge because work is being processed on multiple computers and possibly at more than one location. It may not even stop there because communication may be taking place across organizations as well.

Chapter 13 briefly mentioned a couple of tools that can assist you in troubleshooting and debugging your WCF service: tracing and message logging. This chapter discusses those two tools in detail as well as some others that make managing, configuring, and troubleshooting your WCF service much easier.

The tools provided by WCF integrate extremely well with some of the Microsoft Windows management tools, providing exceptional debugging and troubleshooting capabilities.

This chapter discusses the following topics:

- ❑ Tracing/Service Trace Viewer
- ❑ Message logging
- ❑ The Service Configuration Editor
- ❑ Windows performance counters

Tracing

Chapter 13 briefly mentioned that WCF provides support for tracing. Tracing allows you to capture and view all types of events. Through these captured events you can possibly pinpoint a problem that led up to an error. This section discusses tracing in WCF and the tools at your disposal to turn on tracing and view/dissect the results.

End-to-End Tracing

When a program executes, tracing tracks and records the events that occur in the program. Tracing can be configured to track all events or only events you specify. In a distributed application, tracing can be applied from end to end, thus called *end-to-end tracing*.

Tracing is built upon the System.Diagnostics namespace of the .NET Framework. Two classes comprise most of the functionality provided in this namespace: the Debug class and the Trace class. Together, they allow you to debug your application and trace code execution.

Tracing is turned off by default and must be enabled if you want to start tracing. To enable tracing, you must do two things:

1. First, a trace listener must be created and defined.

2. Second, the trace level must be set to anything other than *off*. Even if you define a listener but do not set the trace level, tracing is still disabled so you must configure both.

Tracing can be enabled via the configuration file or through code. The more appropriate place is via configuration so that you can turn it on and off when you are done debugging. Leaving tracing enabled when you don't need it is a drain on resources and can itself cause problems, so be forewarned, only enable tracing when you need to!

You can enable tracing by adding a `<system.diagnostics>` section in your configuration file. This section needs to be outside of the `<system.servicemodel>` section of the configuration. Each `<system.diagnostics>` section includes a `<source>` section and `<listener>` section, which set the level of information logging and define the listener type, respectively.

Table 14-1 lists the logging information level as defined by the *switchValue* attribute of the `<source>` element.

Table 14-1 Logging Information Level

Level	Tracked Events	User Target
None	None	None
Critical	Out of Memory exception, Stack overflow exception, Application start errors, System hangs, Poison messages	Administrators, Developers

Level	Tracked Events	User Target
Error	All exceptions are logged	Administrators, Developers
Warning	Exceeded timeout, rejected credentials, throttling exceeded, receiving queue nearing capacity	Administrators, Developers
Information	Channels and endpoints created, message enters/leaves transport, configuration read, general helpful information	Administrators, Developers
Verbose	Debugging or application optimization	Administrators, Developers
ActivityTracing	Tracing for transfers, activity boundaries, start/stop	Administrators, Developers
All	All listed events	Administrators, Developers

❑ The *Error* type traces unexpected processing events where the application was still running but was not able to perform the required task.

❑ The *Warning* type traces events where a problem has occurred or may occur although the application is still operating correctly. However, the application may not continue to function as expected.

❑ The *Information* type traces all successful milestones of the execution of the application.

❑ The *Verbose* type traces all low-level events.

❑ The *ActivityTracing* type traces all flow events, including tracing for activity boundaries and endpoint transfers.

The Information, Verbose, and ActivityTracing levels create a lot of traces, which could have a negative impact on the performance of your service.

During application execution, trace data is given to the defined listeners to process, which is provided by WCF.

Trace sources are defined for each assembly in Windows Communication Foundation. Trace sources in WCF are defined as follows:

❑ **System.ServiceModel:** Logs all aspects of WCF processing such as message processing and reading a configuration file.

❑ **System.ServiceModel.MessageLogging:** Logs all messages that are flowed through the system.

❑ **System.ServiceModel.Activation:** Logs the activity of creating and managing service hosts.

❑ **System.IO.Log:** Logs the .NET Framework interface.

❑ **System.Runtime.Serialization:** Logs when objects are read or written.

All traces that are generated with the specific assembly are consumed that are defined for that source.

The following example shows how to enable tracing within a configuration file.

```
<?xml version="1.0" encoding="utf-8" ?>
<configuration>
  <system.serviceModel>
    ...
  </system.serviceModel>

  <system.diagnostics>
    <sources>
      <source name="System.ServiceModel" switchValue="All">
        <listeners>
          <add type="System.Diagnostics.XmlWriterTraceListener"
               name="tracelistener"
               initializeData="c:\logs\traces.svclog" />
        </listeners>
      </source>
    </sources>
  </system.diagnostics>
</configuration>
```

As I found out the hard way, source names are case sensitive. In the preceding example, it is System.ServiceModel, not system.ServiceModel. A mistyped source name will result in events not being logged.

There is, however, an easier way to figure this information so there are no typos and mistakes. The "easier way" is to use the Service Configuration Editor, which is discussed later in this chapter. The Service Configuration Editor tool has a nice user interface that lets you enable all tracing options.

During tracing, WCF captures the events of the service and client such as message processing or the reading and writing of objects. Events are grouped into activities, with an ActivityID assigned to each activity. When a new event is fired, a new activity is created. An example of an event would be sending a message.

Once tracing is enabled and traces have been collected, the next step is to analyze the trace logs. The trace logs can be viewed in the Service Trace Viewer discussed in the following section.

Service Trace Viewer

After tracing has been enabled and you've started collecting information, what do you do with that information? How do you interpret the output and what is the best way to view it? The answer is the Service Trace Viewer tool that is included with Windows Communication Foundation.

Chapter 13 introduced this tool, and its sole purpose is to let you view and help analyze traces. Figure 14-1 shows an example of the Trace Viewer with a trace log loaded.

Traces can be viewed four different ways. The left pane of the viewer shows four tabs that let you pick the way you want to view the traces. The four views are the following:

❑ Activity

❑ Project

❑ Message

❑ Graph

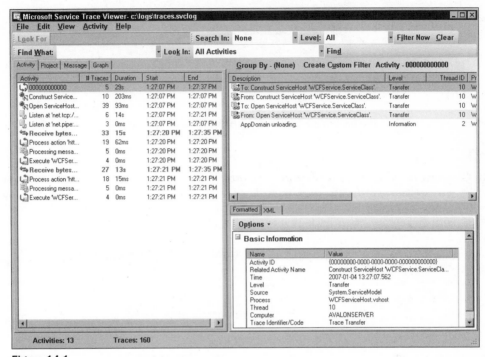

Figure 14-1

Activity

The Activity view lets you see the events of the trace group grouped by activities. The list of activities in the left lists each of the activities and the number of traces for each. By selecting an activity in the left pane, the traces and detailed trace information are displayed in the right pane. Activities are color-coded based on the information they contain. An activity that contains exception information has a red background, and a trace that contains warning information has a yellow background.

Project

The Project tab lets you manage the trace files for the current project. A project lets you organize your traces and view multiple trace files. Projects are managed via the File menu where you can open, save, and close projects. Via the Project tab you can add trace files to the project.

Projects are created by opening a trace file and selecting Save Project from the File menu. Project files are stored with the .stvproj extension. Trace projects can then be opened by selecting Open Project from the File menu, which then loads all traces associated to that project.

Once a project is loaded, selecting the Project tab will show all trace logs associated with that project, as shown in Figure 14-2.

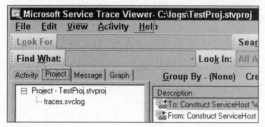

Figure 14-2

Selecting a trace log in the Project tab will show all events associated with that trace in the Activity tab.

Graph

The Graph tab lets you view trace data in chart form for a selected activity. This view lets you see the step-by-step execution of events. The Graph view also shows the interrelationships between multiple trace files as data moves between each trace file. To view an activity in Graph view, select an activity on the Activity tab and then select the Graph tab. Figure 14-3 shows the Graph view of a specific activity.

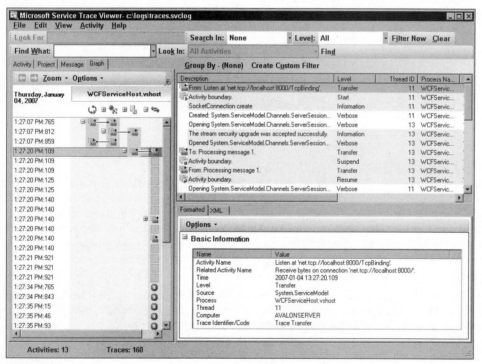

Figure 14-3

It is also possible to view multiple activities at once by using the Ctrl or Shift key and selecting the desired activities.

When you select multiple activities and then click the Graph tab, the applicable traces show in the Graph view with each column representing an activity and each block in the column representing a trace in the activity.

The two panes on the right side of the viewer contain the individual traces for the selected activity and the detail information for each trace. The upper-right pane lists the individual traces for the selected activity. Each line in the trace pane lists the description, level, trace time, and other vital information pertaining to each trace.

The lower-right pane displays the detail information for each trace. When a trace is selected in the upper-right pane, the detailed information for that trace is displayed in the lower-right section. You have three options when viewing detailed trace information. The Formatted view displays the trace information in a clean, organized format that lists the known XML elements in a table/tree view for easy reading.

The XML view displays the selected trace information in XML format.

The Message view displays the message part of the XML of the selected trace information. This information is not viewable when you select a non-message trace.

Filtering Traces

Traces can be filtered using multiple methods including the following:

❑ The Filter toolbar

❑ Built-in filter options

❑ Custom filters

Filter Toolbar

The first method is by using the Filter toolbar, shown in Figure 14-4. If this toolbar is not displayed, you can activate it by selecting the Filter Tool Bar option from the View menu.

Look For Message	Search In: Event ID	Level: Critical	Filter Now Clear

Figure 14-4

The Filter toolbar provides the ability to filter by very granular and specific criteria. The Look For section lets you define the subject to search for when filtering the trace.

The Search In field lets you define the type of filter to apply. The trace file contains certain information that assists you in debugging and following the events that took place during application execution. Each item contains an Event ID as well as the Start Time and Stop Time of the event. Each of these items, as well as others, can be used to filter the trace file output. The following list shows the types of filters you can filter by:

❑ Event ID

❑ Source Name

❑ Process Name

- ❏ Trace Identifier
- ❏ Description
- ❏ Start Time
- ❏ Stop Time
- ❏ Time Range
- ❏ Endpoint Address
- ❏ Application Data
- ❏ Trace Raw Data

The Level option lets you set the minimum trace level to filter by. The following list shows the levels at which you can filter the traces:

- ❏ **All:** Traces at all levels are displayed.
- ❏ **Critical:** Only traces at the Critical level are displayed.
- ❏ **Error And Up:** Only traces at the Error and Critical levels are displayed.
- ❏ **Warning And Up:** Only traces at the Warning, Error, and Critical levels are displayed.
- ❏ **Information And Up:** Only traces at the Information, Warning, Error, and Critical levels are displayed.

Information contained in the Search In and Look For areas is contained in the Level search.

Built-in Filter Options

The Trace Viewer can be configured to display or hide specific traces from the filter results. These options can be set by selecting Filter Options from the View menu, which displays the form shown in Figure 14-5.

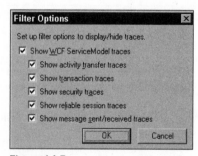

Figure 14-5

By default, the Trace Viewer shows all traces in the results, but using this option you can configure the viewer to remove specific traces from the results of the filter.

Custom Filters

You can also filter the traces by creating custom filters. Custom filters can be created by either using the Template wizard or by creating a filter manually.

Creating a Custom Filter via the Template Wizard

A custom filter can be created by selecting an existing trace in the trace pane in the top-right area of the viewer and clicking the Create Custom Filter button. This button is located at the top of the trace description pane.

Figure 14-6 shows the dialog that opens when you click the Create Custom Filter button. On this form, enter the name for the filter and an optional description.

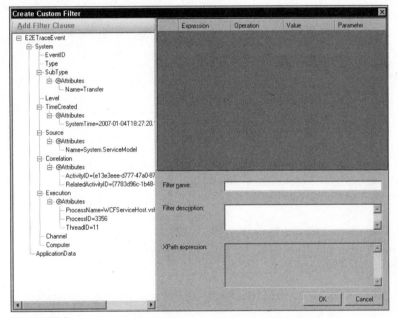

Figure 14-6

On the left side of this dialog is a tree view, which displays the trace record structure selected from the description pane on the main Trace Viewer form. In the tree view, double-click the element you would like to create a filter condition for. Double-clicking a tree view item creates a filter expression in the top-right pane, as shown in Figure 14-7.

In the filter expression section you can freely change the Operation, Value, and Parameter fields to the values that you would like to filter by. As you change the values, you will notice the XPath section in the bottom-right corner of the dialog change.

You can add multiple filter expressions simply by double-clicking the desired node in the tree view. You can also have more than one filter expression for the same node as well.

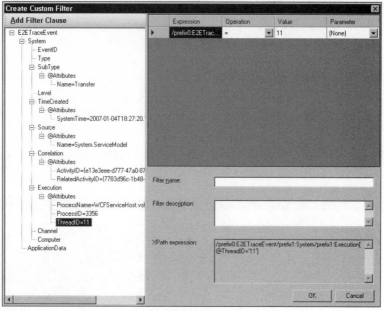

Figure 14-7

When you have completed this form, click OK. The information will then be passed to the Custom Filter dialog, pictured in Figure 14-8. On the Custom Filter dialog, simply click the OK button. The custom filter you just created is now available for use.

Creating a Custom Wizard Manually

A custom filter can be created by selecting the Custom Filters option from the View menu. The dialog shown in Figure 14-8 will appear.

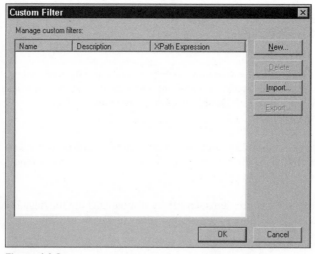

Figure 14-8

In the Custom Filter dialog, click the New button. The New Custom Filter dialog, shown in Figure 14-9, will display. At the minimum, the Filter Name and XPath expression must be specified. Using XPath to create a custom filter allows you to query the trace log for specific, detailed information and narrow down the results returned.

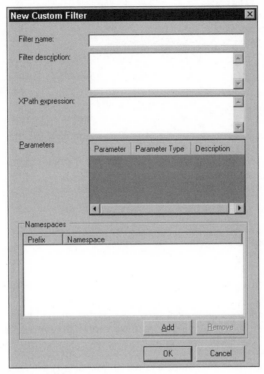

Figure 14-9

Once this form has been filled out, click OK on the New Custom Filter form, and then click OK on the Custom Filter form. Your new custom filter name will now show up in the Search In combo box on the Filter toolbar.

Message Logging

Message logging provides the ability to store messages (sent and received), which can then be viewed and inspected later. Why is this important? Because this provides the unique ability to look inside the message at its contents, which might divulge incorrect or invalid message content or structure.

Messages are not logged by default in Windows Communication Foundation, and therefore to enable message logging a trace must first be added to the System.ServiceModel.MessageLogging trace source. Next, the `<messagelogging>` element must be added underneath the `<system.serviceModel>` element.

The following example illustrates how to enable message logging using the steps just discussed:

```xml
<?xml version="1.0" encoding="utf-8" ?>
<configuration>
  <system.serviceModel>
    <!--endpoint info -- >
    <diagnostics>
      <messageLogging
        logEntireMessage="true"
        logMalformedMessage="false"
        logMessagesAtServiceLevel="true"
        logMessagesAtTransportLevel="false"/>
    </diagnostics>
  </system.serviceModel>

  <system.diagnostics>
    <sources>
      <source name="system.ServiceModel.MessageLogging" switchValue="Verbose">
        <listeners>
          <add type="System.Diagnostics.XmlWriteTraceListener"
               name="message"
               initializeData="c:\log\messages.svc" />
          </add>
        </listeners>
      </source>
    </sources>
  </system.diagnostics>
</configuration>
```

Three logging levels for logging messages can be used to trace the messages, and they are the following:

❑ **Malformed:** Malformed messages are messages that are rejected by WCF at any given point of the message processing. They are logged without any changes, meaning that any discrepancies in the message are logged "as-is." This is enabled by setting the logMalformedMessages attribute to true.

❑ **Service:** Messages that are entering or leaving user code are logged. This includes all infrastructure messages such as transactional, peer channel, and security messages. Reliable Messages are not logged. If a filter has been applied, only those messages that match the filter are logged. This is enabled by setting the logMessagesAtServiceLevel to true.

❑ **Transport:** Messages ready for encoding and decoding are logged. Infrastructure messages are logged such as transactional and security messages. Reliable Messages are also logged at this level. This is enabled by setting the logMessagesAtTransportLevel to true. If a filter has been applied, only those messages that match the filter are logged.

Logging happens immediately for incoming messages:

❑ After the message is formed

❑ When malformed messages are found

❑ At the service level before the message gets to user code

Logging happens immediately for outgoing messages:

❑ After the message leaves user code

❑ Before the message is sent

You can also specify whether the entire message (head and body) is logged or just the header. This is specified by including the logEntireMessage attribute to the `<messageLogging>` element. Setting this option affects the transport and service logging levels, in that the service level logs messages before all encryption and signing of messages, and the transport level logs messages after encryption and signing prior to sending the messages.

The maximum number of logged messages can be set by including the maxMessagesToLog attribute to the `<messageLogging>` element. All messages count toward this number, and when this number is reached, no more messages are logged. The default is 10,000 messages.

To further control the messages that are logged you have the ability to define and apply a filter to the logging. The filter is defined and applied at both the service and transport level, and only those messages that match the filter criteria are logged.

To apply a filter, a `<filters>` element must be underneath the `<messageLogging>` element. The filter must include full XPath syntax. If the syntax is not correct a configuration exception will occur.

The following example illustrates how to configure a filter to return only those messages logged at the service level:

```
<diagnostics>
  <messageLogging
    logMalformedMessage="false"
    logMessagesAtServiceLevel="true"
    logMessagesAtTransportLevel="false"/>
    <filters>
      <add>
      </add>
    </filters>
</diagnostics>
```

The XmlWriterTraceListener outputs its results in the form of an invalid XML file, meaning that it is an XML fragment. This is by design but this means that to view and analyze this file you need to use the Service Trace Viewer, which was discussed earlier in this chapter. This tool provides the ability to view the message log files. When the file is loaded into the viewer, the information can be viewed by selecting the Message tab in the left pane of the viewer.

Windows Communication Foundation provides several predefined listeners for the System.Diangostics namespace. The XmlWriterTraceListener is the standard .NET Framework listener that is used in the first example shown earlier. The other trace listeners are the following:

❑ **DelimtedListTraceListener:** Writes the output to a text writer such as a stream writer or a stream such as a file stream.

❑ **EventLogTraceListener:** Writes the trace output to the event log via System.Diagnostics.Eventlog.

❑ **TextWriteTraceListener:** Directs the output to System.IO.TextWriter or System.IO.Stream such as System.IO.Filestream.

Once you have captured the message logs, you can easily view these logs as well through the Service Trace Viewer. This provides a nice view into the message's content at the point the message was logged.

The next section discusses the Service Configuration Editor, a tool provided by WCF to manage your configuration settings.

Service Configuration Editor

The Service Configuration Editor is a tool provided by Windows Communication Foundation that provides the ability to view and modify configuration file settings. Figure 14-10 shows the Configuration Editor with a configuration file loaded.

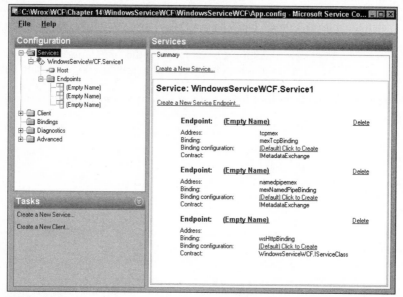

Figure 14-10

The Configuration Editor lets you open four types of files. Figure 14-11 shows the four types of files you can browse to and open. Each option lets you browse, open, and manage WCF configuration files, service, and assembly files.

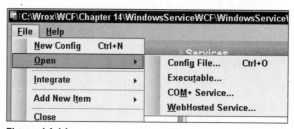

Figure 14-11

The Configuration Editor is divided into three sections. Each section provides specific tasks and information to configure the configuration file. The three sections are the following:

❑   Configuration

❑   Tasks

❑   Detail

Each section is discussed next.

Configuration

The Configuration pane contains a tree view that displays the configuration elements of the configuration file. The tree view contains five nodes that can be expanded and used to configure the configuration file. Those sections are discussed here.

Services

The Services node displays all of the services defined within the configuration file. Each defined service, a sub-element of the `<services>` node, corresponds to a sub-node in the tree underneath the Services node.

By selecting a service node, the detailed information for that service is displayed on a Summary Page in the detail pane on the right side of the form. Expanding the selected service node, the corresponding endpoints for that service are displayed. To configure an endpoint, select the desired endpoint on the left pane, and endpoint detail information will display in the Detail pane in the property grid. New endpoints can be created by right-clicking the Endpoints node and selecting New Service Endpoint from the context menu. Endpoints can also be deleted by right-clicking the desired endpoint and selecting Delete Endpoint from the context menu.

To edit the service configuration, select the desired service in the tree and the corresponding detail service information will display in the Detail pane providing the ability to edit service settings in the property grid. New services can be defined by right-clicking the Services node in the tree view and selecting New Service from the context menu.

One or more base addresses can be configured by selecting the Host node underneath the corresponding service node. The Base Address configuration information will display in the Detail pane. To add a base address, click the New button in the Base Addresses section and enter the base URI address in the dialog box and then click OK.

Client

The Client node displays all defined client endpoints in the configuration file. Like the endpoints in the Services section, new client endpoints can be added and existing endpoints can be deleted or reconfigured. Selecting an endpoint in the tree displays the configuration information in the Detail pane.

Bindings

The Bindings node displays all bindings defined in the configuration file that are used to configure bindings on endpoints. New bindings can be added by right-clicking the Bindings node and selecting New Binding Configuration from the context menu. Figure 14-12 shows the Create New Binding dialog that displays when you add a new binding.

Select the desired binding from the dialog box and click OK. The binding is then displayed underneath the Bindings node in the tree view, and the grid in the Detail pane lets you configure the binding information.

Figure 14-12

Diagnostics

The Diagnostics node displays the configured diagnostics settings that are currently defined in the configuration file. This node lets you do the following:

- ❑ Configure performance counters (turn on or off)
- ❑ Enable or disable Windows Management Instrumentation
- ❑ Configure tracing in WCF (turn on or off)
- ❑ Enable or disable WCF message logging
- ❑ Configure listeners
- ❑ Configure sources

This information comes from, and is stored in, the `<system.diagnostics>` section in the configuration file.

New listeners can be added by right-clicking the Listeners node and selecting New Listener from the context menu. New sources can be added by right-clicking the Sources node and selecting New Source from the context menu.

Advanced

The Advanced node displays the advanced configuration settings that are currently defined in the configuration file. This node lets you configure the following:

- ❑ Endpoint behaviors
- ❑ Service behaviors

❑   Extensions

❑   Host environment

Endpoint Behavior

Endpoint behaviors can be added by right-clicking the Endpoint Behaviors node and selecting New Endpoint Behavior Configuration. Behaviors are a collection of elements that form what is called a *stack*, with each element on the stack containing its own configuration. The element extension of a behavior determines the position of the behavior on the stack.

Through the Configuration Editor, behavior extensions can be added and have their extension position changed. Those elements at the top of the stack are applied first, with the rest of the elements applied in the order specified.

Once an endpoint behavior has been added, behavior elements can be added by clicking the Add button in the Detail section in the Behavior element extension position section. Clicking the Add button displays the form shown in Figure 14-13. This form lets you pick the behavior element extension.

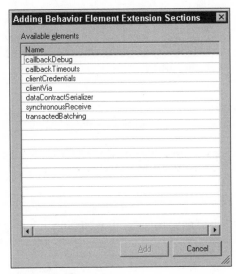

Figure 14-13

Once the behavior extension element has been selected, click OK on the form. To change the position of the element, use the Up and Down buttons to change the selection.

To configure or edit the behavior element position, select the behavior extension element and click the Edit button or double-click the behavior extension element in the grid.

Service Behavior

Service behaviors can be added by right-clicking the Service Behaviors node and selecting New Service Behavior Configuration. The same instructions for adding and configuring behavior element extensions apply here as they do for configuring endpoint element extensions.

Once a service behavior has been added, behavior elements can be added by clicking the Add button in the Detail section in the Behavior element extension position section. Clicking the Add button displays the form shown in Figure 14-14. This form lets you pick the behavior element extension.

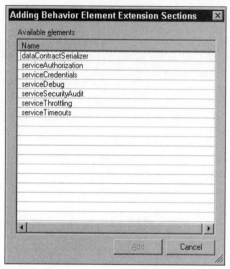

Figure 14-14

Once the behavior extension element has been selected, click OK on the form. To change the position of the element, use the Up and Down buttons to change the selection.

To configure or edit the behavior element position, select the behavior extension element and click the Edit button or double-click the behavior extension element in the grid.

Extensions

The Extensions node lets you add new extensions for bindings, binding elements, and behaviors. Extensions are added in name/type pairs with the name defining the name of the extension in the configuration file and the type defining the extension. The three types of extensions are defined as follows:

❑ **Binding:** Define a full binding type.

❑ **Binding Element:** Define an element of a binding.

❑ **Behavior:** Define an element of a behavior.

Figures 14-13 and 14-14 show the behavior extensions that are available to configure with the associated object (Service or Endpoint).

New extensions can be added by selecting one of the built-in extensions of the Extension nodes and then selecting the New button in the Detail pane. The Extension Configuration Element Editor dialog, shown in Figure 14-15, is displayed to allow you to add a new extension.

Enter a configuration name, then click the ellipsis button to select the extension type in which to add to the configuration.

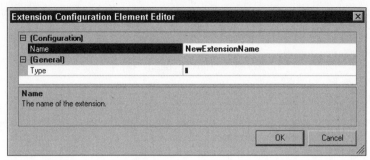

Figure 14-15

Click OK to add the extension element, which will now be displayed in the list of available extensions.

Tasks

The Tasks pane provides links that facilitate adding items based on the node selected in the Configuration section. When a link is selected in the Tasks pane, a wizard is launched that walks you through adding and configuring the appropriate item based on the node you have selected in the Configuration section.

For example, if you have selected the Services Endpoints node in the Configuration pane, a link is displayed in the Tasks pane labeled Create a New Service Endpoint. Clicking this link will start a wizard to walk you through adding and configuring a service endpoint.

Detail

The Detail pane displays the summary and configuration information based on the item selected in the tree node in the Configuration pane. Detailed settings of the configuration are displayed in this section, providing the ability to make modifications to the configuration and viewing summary information if no configuration settings are available.

Performance Counters

Whether you enable performance counters manually in the configuration file or through the Configuration Editor tool, performance counters can be enabled to help manage and troubleshoot performance issues and potential problems.

Windows Communication Foundation can track three types of performance counters. The following type values are valid:

❑ **Off:** Performance counters are disabled.

❑ **All:** All category counters are enabled. Available categories are ServiceModelService, ServiceModelEndpoint, ServiceModelOperation.

❑ **ServiceOnly:** Only the ServiceModelService counter is enabled.

The following example illustrates how to enable performance counters in the configuration file:

```
<configuration>
    <system.serviceModel>
        <diagnostics performanceCountersEnabled="ServiceOnly" />
    </system.serviceModel>
</configuration>
```

The output results of the performance counters can be viewed by using the Performance Monitor application (perfmon.exe) that comes with Windows.

There are three types of performance counters:

❑ **Service:** This counter instance can be retrieved through WMI *Service* instance's CounterInstanceName property. This counter is used to troubleshoot the service performance as a whole.

❑ **Endpoint:** This counter instance can be retrieved through WMI *Endpoint* instance's CounterInstanceName property. This counter lets you view data that details how the endpoint is accepting messages.

❑ **Operation:** This counter instance can be retrieved through WMI *Endpoint* instance's GetOperationCounterInstanceName property. This counter lets you know how the operation performance is and lets you track how the call is being used.

In Performance Monitor, the Service counter is found under the ServiceModelService 3.0.0.0 object, the Endpoint counter is found under the ServiceModelEndpoint 3.0.0.0 object, and the Operation counter is found under the ServiceModelOperation object.

It is through these performance counters that WCF lets you track and gauge your application's performance.

Summary

The intent of this chapter was to provide you with an in-depth look at the available management and configuration tools in Windows Communication Foundation to help you successfully deploy, configure, and manage your WCF service implementations. By default, all the management features are turned off, but through configuration file settings they can be enabled.

This chapter discussed tracing, message logging, and the available tools to view the results of the traces and message output logs.

The remaining part of the chapter discussed the Service Trace Viewer tool, which provides a graphical user interface for viewing the traces and message logs, as well as the Service Configuration Editor, which also provides a graphical user interface that provides the ability to edit configuration files.

From here, Chapter 15 discusses expanding WCF and discusses interoperability and integration.

15

Hosting Windows Communication Foundation Services

Windows Communication Foundation services can be hosted in many different ways. Up until this chapter, all the examples have either hosted the service in IIS or a Windows forms application. But that is just the "tip of the iceberg" because WCF services can also be hosted in a traditional Windows service and a Windows Process Activation Service. For those familiar with .NET Remoting technologies, using Windows services and IIS (itself a Windows service) for a host should appear familiar.

Hosting a WCF service refers to the environment that the service exists and operates in. There are two primary hosting modalities:

❑ Self-hosting, which means that you will build the host environment yourself

❑ Hosted, which means that you will use a built-in hosting environment such as IIS

This chapter discusses the many different hosting scenarios in which to host a WCF service. In particular, this chapter covers the following hosting topics:

❑ Hosting versus self-hosting

❑ Available hosting options

Windows Communication Foundation services are designed to run in any process that supports managed code, including NT services, traditional EXEs, as well as the aforementioned Windows Process Activation Service (WAS). The great thing about this is that the code for your service will look the same regardless of the hosting environment because of the unified programming model that WCF provides for building service-oriented applications.

Hosting versus Self-Hosting

Self-hosting means that developers will need to write their own code, which will in turn be used to host the WCF service. Because IIS is already a service, it effectively obviates the need for this approach, hence allowing one to claim it is not considered self-hosting.

Hosting

In a hosted environment, the developer does not need to create the host application because IIS hosts the WCF service. IIS is aware that the service is a WCF service and works in tandem with ASP.NET to provide the optimal environment. It also helps to control the lifetime properties of the service. IIS manages and controls the lifetime of the service as well as handles the creation and disposal (release of memory, release of system resources) of the service when necessary.

Though the developer does not need to create the host application, in a hosted environment the developer does need to create the directory structure and virtual directory in which to host the service. If you create the service manually you will also need to create the .svc file as well (see Appendix A to read how to use the built-in templates).

A hosted service gets the added benefit of having IIS monitor the health and stability of the service, performing automatic process recycling of the service when it deems necessary.

Self-Hosting

Self-hosting a WCF service means that the developer must create the environment that the service exists in. This hosting application is responsible for the creation (instantiating) and lifetime control of the service. In a self-hosting environment, the host application is responsible for all control aspects of the service, such as the defining of endpoints and the creation of the ServiceHost.

The host application controls the creation and disposal of the service through an instance of the *ServiceHost* class, using the *Open* method of the class to start receiving messages. The *Close* method of the *ServiceHost* class stops the service and disposes of it, thereby preventing clients from further accessing it.

Examples of self-hosted services would include one hosted in a managed application (such as a Windows forms application or console application), or one hosted as a Windows service or a DLL library.

Quick Comparison

The following is a quick comparison of the two hosting types:

❑ In a hosted environment, the activation of the service is automatic; not so for self-hosted.

❑ In a hosted environment, the health of the service is automatically monitored; not so for self-hosted.

❑ In a hosted environment, the service is compiled on demand; not so for self-hosted.

Deciding between a hosted environment and a self-hosted environment depends on the requirements of your application. Self-hosted "managed" applications are easier to deploy and much more flexible, and if hosted in a Windows service offer a secure environment as well as letting the operating system control the service process lifetime. Yet self-hosted applications many times do not lend themselves to being an enterprise solution for services.

Alternatively, hosted services such as IIS offer process recycling and message-based activation, but offer HTTP protocol communication only. Hosted applications also benefit from process health monitoring.

WAS (Windows Process Activation Service) and IIS 7.0 provide additional protocol support, and even WAS does not require IIS.

Hosting Options

This section discusses the available hosting options for hosting a Windows Communication Foundation. The following hosting options are discussed:

- ❏ IIS
- ❏ Managed code
- ❏ Windows service
- ❏ WAS

All of the examples in this book so far have hosted the service in either IIS or self-hosted the service in a Windows forms application. Therefore, the IIS and managed code sections do not go into as much detail as the Windows service and WAS sections.

Hosting in IIS

The very first example this book provided in Chapter 3 was an example of a WCF service hosted in IIS. That example walked you through how to create and build a WCF service manually, even as far as creating and configuring the virtual directory that the WCF service will use in IIS.

This section does not redo that example; rather, it discusses the benefits and requirements of hosting a WCF service in IIS. Feel free to go back and re-read the example in Chapter 3 or to skip ahead to Appendix A, which walks you through using the templates and add-ins to Visual Studio to build and deploy a WCF service in IIS.

Windows Communication Foundation services can be hosted in a few specific versions of IIS. Those versions are the following:

- ❏ IIS 5.1 on Windows XP w/ Service Pack 2
- ❏ IIS 6.0 on Windows Server 2003
- ❏ IIS 7.0 on Windows Vista
- ❏ IIS 7.0 on Windows Server (codename "Longhorn," the next version of Windows Server)

It is vital to note that there are some significant differences between each of these versions. For example, IIS versions 5.1 and 6.0 are limited to HTTP communication only, whereas IIS 7.0 also includes the WAS to allow WCF services to communicate and operate using any WCF-supported network protocol (net.tcp, net.pipe, and net.msmq).

Benefits

There are several reasons why hosting a WCF service in IIS is more beneficial than the other hosting methods. As mentioned earlier in the chapter, hosting a WCF service in IIS provides automatic processing activation, meaning that you as a developer are not responsible for the launching of the service. This is handled by IIS, such that when a message is received for a service, the service is automatically launched if it is not already running.

IIS also provides built-in health monitors that the WCF service can take advantage of. If IIS determines that a specific process of the service is not healthy, that is, a process is not responding or is taking longer than deemed necessary, IIS will automatically recycle the process.

The hosting model for hosting a WCF service in IIS is extremely similar to the hosting model used by ASP.NET and ASMX web services. Because of this similarity, WCF web services hosted in IIS are deployed and managed in the same manner as the ASP.NET application or ASMX web service hosted in IIS. This has the added benefit of allowing WCF services to utilize the ASP.NET shared hosting model. The ASP.NET shared hosting model allows multiple WCF applications to reside in a common worker process for better scalability, meaning that calls within the same process are more efficient than calls that cross processes. This also has an effect on the ability for a web site to span multiple servers as well as a web site to be more resilient against other web sites on the same server.

WCF services hosted in IIS can also take advantage of ASP.NET's compilation model. The ASP.NET compilation model greatly simplifies both the development and deployment process of applications and services hosted in IIS.

These benefits need to be focused on a little more. What benefits can be found by hosting your WCF in IIS? It is time to drill down.

In IIS 5.0 and 6.0 you get the following:

❑ **Idle shutdown:** This helps conserve system resources. When you need to conserve system resources, you can configure IIS to terminate unused worker processes, letting the process gracefully close after a specific period of time. This feature lets you manage resources when the work load is heavy or when processing space is empty.

❑ **Process recycling:** IIS can be configured to periodically restart worker processes. The benefit of this is that you can recycle faulty web applications, ensuring that applications remain healthy and that any system resources are recovered. Worker process recycling comes in handy when you have the following:

    ❑ The web server is hosting an application that has intermittent or undetermined problems that can't seem to be isolated or corrected.

    ❑ An application is leaking memory due to performance monitoring (Task Manager is not the place to monitor memory issues).

    ❑ A scheduled IISReset execution command has been implemented.

❑ **Process health monitoring:** The WWW service (World Wide Web Publishing Service) monitors the health of worker processes by occasionally pinging them to see if they are responding. If the WWW service determines that a worker process is unresponsive, the worker process will be terminated and a replacement worker process will take its place. Likewise, the WWW service maintains an open communication channel with each worker process. Through this open communication channel, a drop in the application communication channel (or slow responding communication channel) can be detected. This indicates to the WWW service that a worker process has failed and another worker process is started.

❑ **Message-based activation:** Services hosted in ASP.NET can be automatically activated upon the arrival of a message. The added benefit of this is that long-running services have the ability to store instance data to disk. The services can be reactivated with their state data restored when a message arrives after a lengthy period.

These features are only available when IIS is running a worker process in isolation mode.

These features can be configured through IIS application pools. An application pool is a configuration that links one or more applications with a set of one or more worker processes. To configure the options just listed, open IIS and expand the Application Pools node as shown in Figure 15-1.

Figure 15-1

Right-click the desired application pool and select Properties from the context menu. This displays the properties dialog for the selected application pool, like the one shown in Figure 15-2.

Through the tabs of this dialog you can configure process recycling, idle timeouts, and other features discussed previously.

All of the features just discussed are all great benefits, but take a look at the big limitation. IIS 5.0 and 6.0 only support the HTTP protocol. So you need to ask yourself, how important is this to you?

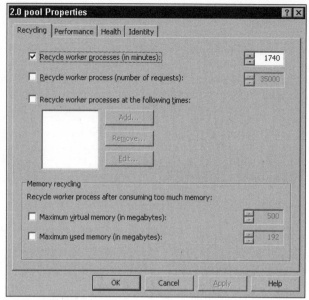

Figure 15-2

A common scenario for running your WCF service in IIS 5.0/6.0 would include wanting to run your WCF service side-by-side with ASP.NET content within an intranet.

What about WAS? With WAS you get all the benefits of IIS plus the following:

❑ **Additional protocols of TCP, Named Pipes, and MSMQ:** Windows Communication Foundation uses the Listener Adapter Interface to communicate activation requests over non-HTTP protocols such as TCP.

❑ **IIS is not required:** WAS is the new process activation service that takes all of the IIS features and enables them to work with non-HTTP protocols.

WAS is discussed in more detail later in this chapter.

You can't forget about Windows Vista and the next version of Windows Server, codenamed "Longhorn." Both of those come with IIS 7.0, which supports all of the WAS benefits plus integration with ASP.NET and IIS content: The best of both worlds.

Although an argument could be made for both hosted and self-hosted services, the choice will boil down to the version of Windows and the transports your service needs to send messages. Hosted services have many benefits as you can surmise from the information in this section, but hosted also has its limitations even as self-hosted has its benefits.

Service Deployment

As you saw in Chapter 3, successfully deploying a WCF service in IIS requires a few steps to get your service up and running. However, that example assumed that you had IIS and WCF already installed and operating correctly, so this section discusses a few items to make sure that when you are ready to develop and deploy your WCF service, your environment is ready.

Though it may appear obvious, you need to have IIS and WCF installed. By default, IIS is not installed with Windows XP and Windows 2003. If you have accepted the default settings when installing either of these operating systems, you will need to go back and add IIS. You can do this through the *Add/Remove Programs* icon found in the Windows Control Panel by selecting *Add/Remove Windows Components*.

The next step is to install Windows Communication Foundation (which is installed as part of the .NET Framework 3.0). You will need to take additional steps, however, if you installed IIS after WCF. If WCF has been installed after IIS, you are good to go because the .NET Framework 3.0 installation process will automatically register all the necessary WCF components with IIS.

If, however, the opposite is true, meaning that IIS was installed *after* WCF, an extra step or two is necessary to register WCF with IIS. This can be accomplished on Windows XP and Windows Server 2003 by running the following command at a command prompt:

```
ServiceModelReg.exe /i <- NEED TO CHECK /x!!!
```

The ServiceModel Registration tool is a command-line tool that is used to manage the registration of ServiceModel on a given (local) machine. You can find this tool in the following location:

```
Windows\Microsoft.NET\Framework\3.0\Windows Communication Foundation
```

For Windows Vista, WCF can be registered with IIS by going into the Windows Control Panel and clicking the Add/Remove Programs icon and selecting Add/Remove Windows Components. From there, run the Windows Component wizard and install the Windows Communication Foundation HTTP Activation Component.

With both IIS and WCF installed, the next step is to create a new IIS application. It is important to note that when you are hosting your WCF service in IIS, the service must reside inside of an IIS application. The example in Chapter 3 walks you through, step-by-step, how to create and deploy a new IIS application and WCF service.

WCF/ASP.NET Side-by-Side

However, it is also possible to host a WCF service inside an existing ASP.NET 2.0 application such as an .ASMX web service. Because ASP.NET provides similar infrastructure for both WCF and ASP.NET including dynamic compilation and AppDomain management, a WCF service can be co-located within a single Application Domain alongside an existing ASP.NET 2.0 application such as an ASPX page or an ASMX web service.

This cohabitating functionality is allowable because even though they share the same AppDomain, the ASP.NET HTTP runtime manages the ASP.NET execution requests without stepping on the requests bound for the WCF service. The WCF service model is responsible for intercepting messages addressed to the WCF service, which then appropriately routes them. The two different frameworks allow the two applications to share the same AppDomain, allowing them to share events and static variables.

The design and intent of a WCF service is to operate and behave completely independent of the hosting environment and associated transport, allowing it to have a consistent behavior. This is because WCF was designed to have a consistent behavior regardless of the hosting environment, whereas the ASP.NET runtime was purposely designed to tightly couple the IIS and ASP.NET hosting environment to take advantage of HTTP communication.

A WCF service that shares the same AppDomain as an ASP.NET application cannot take advantage of some of the features implemented by the HTTP runtime that the ASP.NET application can use. For example:

❑   In its default configuration, WCF will always execute as the IIS process identity. This is true even though ASP.NET is configured to enable impersonation via the configuration option `<identity impersonate = "true" />`.

❑   The WCF security model ignores any URL-based authorization rules that are found in the `<authorization>` element of the System.Web configuration file, if the service is in the same AppDomain secured by the ASP.NET URL authorization rules.

❑   The *Current* property of HttpContext, which gets the HttpContext object for the current HTTP request, will always return NULL when accessed from within a WCF service.

❑   When deciding if a service request should be authorized, the WCF security model does not allow for the ACL (Access Control List) to be applied to the .svc file of the service.

WCF/ASP.NET Compatibility Mode

By default, WCF services are designed to have a consistent behavior regardless of the environment in which they are hosted. This is no different if the service is hosted in IIS, as discussed in the previous section. However, as you have surely found out by now, WCF is extremely flexible and, therefore, when hosting a WCF service in IIS, will allow you to operate your WCF service in "ASP.NET compatibility mode." This means that the WCF service can take full advantage of the ASP.NET HTTP request lifecycle, using the HTTP pipeline. This lets the WCF service behave identically to an ASP.NET web service.

Through the ASP.NET compatibility mode, all of the behaviors previously listed (HttpContext, impersonation, and so on) are now accessible to the WCF service.

The WCF ASP.NET compatibility mode can be enabled by adding the following to the `Web.config` file:

```
<system.serviceModel>
    <serviceHostingEnvironment aspNetCompatibilityEnabled="true" />
</system.serviceModel>
```

Best Practices

Though hosting a WCF service in IIS might seem fairly simplistic, there are a few things to consider that will ensure a successful deployment:

❑   **Avoid absolute URIs:** This has been reiterated a number of times throughout this book. Use *relative* URI addresses, not *absolute* URI addresses when configuring endpoints. Why? Because you have the guarantee that the message-based activation will occur due to the fact that endpoint address will be contained in the set of URI addresses pertaining to the host application.

❑   **Use DLLs:** Implement the service as a DLL (deployed to the \bin directory of the web application). One of the main benefits is that you can reuse the service even outside of the IIS environment.

❑ **Avoid service hosts:** Creating service hosts in a WCF service hosted in IIS is not recommended because they are not known to the host environment and cannot participate in any lifecycle decisions made by IIS.

❑ **Middle-tier scenario:** If you have a service that calls out to other services, instantiate the WCF service proxy once and reuse it across all incoming messages. WCF service proxies are thread safe (no need to synchronize access to a proxy across multiple threads). Remember, though, that instantiating service proxies is expensive.

❑ **State management:** It is recommended that WCF services hosted in IIS should store state information to an external source or process, because IIS recycles the host process, causing any state information stored in memory to be lost.

❑ **Multi-named scenarios:** WCF fully supports services deployed in an IIS web farm but require that special configuration of the IIS web site. The Default Identity of the IIS web site that is hosting the WCF service must use explicit hostnames (*:80:www.wrox.com, for example).

The next section discusses hosting a WCF service in managed code.

Hosting in Managed Code

WCF services can be hosted in any type of managed code application, such as a console application or Windows forms application. All of the examples since Chapter 3 have utilized a Windows forms application to host a WCF service.

Hosting a WCF service in a managed application is known as "self-hosting," which is defined as providing an application domain in which to host your service. A managed application, whether it is a console application or rich client application, contains the appropriate .NET Framework components and assemblies used by the CLR (Common Runtime Language) to successfully host a WCF service.

Of the two options (self-hosting versus hosting in IIS), self-hosting provides the most flexibility for several reasons:

First, the self-hosted service model requires the least amount of infrastructure to deploy. The service code is embedded inside the managed code application and instantiated with only a few lines of code.

Second, your choice of "self-hosted" environments in which to host your service is only limited by those development languages that support the CLR.

As you have seen in most of the examples in this book, creating an instance of the ServiceHost is quite simple, as shown in the following example:

```
private void Form1_Load(object sender, EventArgs e)
{

    sh = new ServiceHost(typeof(WCFService.ServiceClass));
    sh.Open();
}
```

This example, taken from the second example in Chapter 5, shows that it only takes two lines of code to create the ServiceHost and open the service, exposing it to clients. Remember that all of the endpoint definitions (addresses and bindings) were done via configuration.

However, the following code was taken from the first example, illustrating that all of the endpoint definitions are done via code, yet it only takes the same two lines of code to create the ServiceHost and open it:

```
private void Form1_Load(object sender, EventArgs e)
{

    Uri tcpa = new Uri("net.tcp://localhost:8000/TcpBinding");

    sh = new ServiceHost(typeof(ServiceClass), tcpa);

    NetTcpBinding tcpb = new NetTcpBinding();

    ServiceMetadataBehavior mBehave = new ServiceMetadataBehavior();
    sh.Description.Behaviors.Add(mBehave);

    sh.AddServiceEndpoint(typeof(IMetadataExchange),
    MetadataExchangeBindings.CreateMexTcpBinding(), "mex");

    sh.AddServiceEndpoint(typeof(IServiceClass), tcpb, tcpa);

    sh.Open();

}
```

Whether you use a rich client application or a console application is up to you. However, each has respective benefits. For example, a console application provides a quick environment in which to develop, test, and debug your service and host while providing very little in terms of user interface functionality.

Once the service is ready for production, a rich client application, such as a Windows forms application or a WPF (Windows Presentation Foundation) application, can then be used to introduce your application into production. This environment has the added benefit of being able to communicate with external sources, such as in a peer-to-peer environment.

Hosting in a Windows Service

Windows services are a great way to host a WCF service depending on your hosting requirements. Formally known as Windows NT services, Windows services provide a very beneficial hosting environment given the following scenarios:

❑ No user interaction is necessary. If the WCF service is long-running and requires no direct user interaction (has no user interface), hosting the WCF service inside a Windows service should be highly considered.

❑ Explicit activation is required. If your WCF service needs to start and stop automatically rather than wait for incoming messages to dynamically start, your WCF service should be hosted inside a Windows service.

❑ Service requires transports other than HTTP. Windows service applications have access to multiple transports supported by Windows Communication Foundation such as net.tcp and net.pipe.

❑ Long-running processes are required. That is, the process that hosts your service needs to continue running once the process has started. A Windows service provides this functionality, because once a service is started, it is not shut down unless it is manually stopped.

There are important differences between hosting a WCF service in a Windows service and hosting it in IIS.

The IIS hosting environment can only communicate over the HTTP protocol. A Windows service does not have this restriction.

Also, hosting a WCF service in IIS has the ability to be started and stopped dynamically, offering the ability to take advantage of the system resources. However, explicit control over the lifetime of the service is lost in this scenario, and hosting the service in a Windows service should be considered if the need to explicitly control the lifetime of the service is necessary.

Hosting a WCF service inside a Windows service is not much different than hosting the service in any other managed code application. However, certain steps need to be taken that are specific to the Windows service:

❑   The Windows service must inherit from ServiceBase.

❑   Override the OnStart method to open one or more instances of ServiceHost. This provides the ability to host multiple WCF services that can be started and stopped as a group instead of individually.

❑   Override the OnStop method to call OnClosed to safely shut down any WCF services that were started in the OnStart method.

❑   Proper error handling. Use the ServiceController class to gracefully shut down the Windows service if an error occurs.

The example at the end of this chapter creates a Windows service in which to host the WCF service. However, this section outlines the required steps.

Hosting in WAS

WAS is a service that manages the activation and lifetime of a specified worker process. These worker processes contain applications that host WCF services. The focus of the WAS process model is to allow both HTTP and non-HTTP protocols to be used in a hosting environment by removing the dependency on HTTP.

The goal for WAS is to provide a mechanism in which hosted applications can be more flexible, easily manageable, and on top of all that, use resources much more efficiently. In doing so, WAS provides the following:

❑   A more effective way to centrally configure and manage applications.

❑   A more efficient recycling of applications and worker processes to better sustain the health of running applications.

❑   A slimmed-down IIS. The key here is to provide applications the ability to harness the IIS process model without a full installation of IIS.

❑   The dynamic starting and stopping of applications and worker processes for both HTTP and non-HTTP protocols in response to incoming messages.

To accomplish these items, WAS contains several key architectural components:

- ❑ **WAS:** Windows service that controls the creation and lifetime of worker processes.
- ❑ **The Application Manager:** Controls the creation and lifetime of application domains that host applications within the worker process.
- ❑ **Listener adapters:** A Windows service whose responsibility is to take incoming messages that arrive on a given network protocol and communicate with WAS to appropriately route the message to the correct worker process.
- ❑ **Protocol handlers:** Responsible for overseeing the communication between the worker process and each listener adapter. This component runs in the worker process.

Windows Communication Foundation contains the following listener adapters:

- ❑ **W3SVC:** Utilizes the HTTP protocol; this adapter is a common component providing HTTP activation for both IIS 7.0 and WCF.
- ❑ **NetTcpActivator:** Utilizes the net.tcp protocol.
- ❑ **NetPipeActivator:** Utilizes the net.pipe protocol.
- ❑ **NetMsmqActivator:** Utilizes the net.msmq protocol and is used with WCF-based MSMQ applications.

To host WCF services within WAS in Windows Vista requires a few steps. The first step is to install the WCF activation components. You do this as follows:

1. In the Control Panel, select Programs, then Programs and Features.
2. From the Tasks menu, click "Turn Windows Features on or off."
3. Expand the Microsoft .NET 3.0 node. You may need to scroll down to find this node.
4. Select the WCF Non-Http Activation Components.

Figure 15-3 shows the Windows Features dialog with the Windows Communication Non-Http Activation feature selected.

Once this feature is selected, click the OK button.

The next step is to create a WAS site. Make sure you create this site with network protocols you want to use. This can be accomplished by using the appcmd.exe, which is an administrative-level utility installed with IIS 7.0. For example, to support net.tcp activation a net.tcp port must first be bound to the default web site. Open a command prompt and execute the following:

```
%windir%\system32\inetsrv\appcmd.exe set site "Default Web Site" -+ bindings
.[protocol='net.tcp', bindingInformation='8080:*']
```

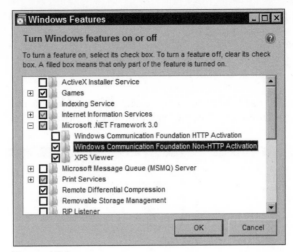

Figure 15-3

Take a look at this command. What this command is doing is adding a net.tcp binding to the default web site that is listening on port 8080 using any hostname. This can also be done with other protocols as well, such as net.pipe.

Using non-Http bindings with WAS requires that the site binding must be added to the WAS configuration. The WAS configuration store is the `applicationHost.config` file, which is located in the following directory:

```
%windir%\system32\inetsrv\config
```

This file is an XML file and can be edited with a number of different editors.

The final step is to create an application in which to host your WCF service. This step is very similar to that of hosting in IIS, but with a few differences:

❑   Define and create a service contract

❑   Implement the service contract

❑   Create a `Web.config` file for the service that uses the configured binding

❑   Create a `Service.svc` file

❑   Drop the `Service.svc` file in the virtual directory

So what are the differences? Remember that the binding is configured on the web site itself, so the address and binding information do not need to be specified in the service implementation. Nor do you need to write code to get that information from the configuration file.

The following section walks you through a hosting example that illustrates many of the topics discussed in this chapter.

Hosting Example

This example illustrates using a Windows service in which to host a WCF service. As mentioned earlier in this chapter, hosting a WCF service inside a Windows service has several benefits and should be used if the condition or environment calls for it.

For this example, you will need to create a new service project. Open Visual Studio 2005, and from the File menu, select New, then Project. This will open the screen shown in Figure 15-4.

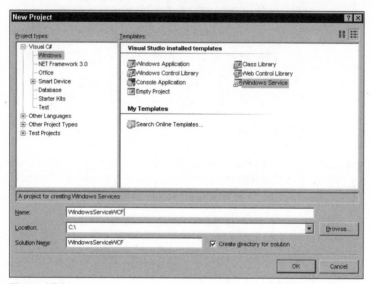

Figure 15-4

Under the *Project Types* section, expand the *Visual C#* node and select the *Windows* project type. In the Templates section, select the Windows Service template. For the project name, enter `WindowsServiceWCF` and set the *Location* to the root of C:\ and make sure the *Create Directory for Solution* checkbox is checked. Click the OK button.

When the project is finished creating, a few things need to be done to get it ready to start adding code. Obviously the System.ServiceModel namespace needs to be added, but there are a few other things to do as well.

First things first, however, so expand the Solution node if it isn't already expanded and right-click the References node. Select *Add Reference* from the context menu to open the Add Reference dialog.

When the dialog opens up, select the Recent tab and you should have listed the System.ServiceModel component. Click OK. You still need to add a few more references, so open the Add References dialog again and this time select the .NET tab, and using the Ctrl key, select the following components:

❑ System.Configuration

❑ System.Configuration.Install

❑ System.Runtime.Serialization

Figure 15-5 shows the two `System.Configuration` components to be added, and the `System.Runtime.Serialization` component is a little farther down in the window.

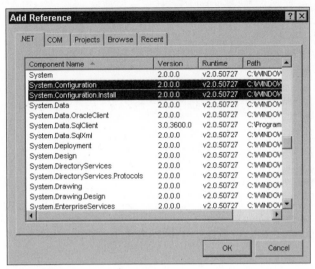

Figure 15-5

With these components highlighted, click the OK button. Almost done. If you look in the Solution Explorer window underneath the project, you will notice that there is a file called `Program.cs`. You don't need that file so go ahead and delete it (right-click the file and select Delete from the context menu).

An application configuration file needs to be added to this project, so right-click the project and select Add ⇨ New Item from the context menu. When the Add New Item dialog appears, select Application Configuration File from the list of templates and click OK (make sure the name of the file is `App.Config`).

Ok, you are done with the changes. Your Solution Explorer should look like Figure 15-6. You are now ready to start adding code.

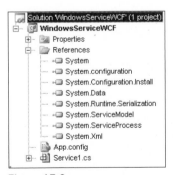

Figure 15-6

Right-click the `Service1.cs` file and select View Code from the context menu. When the code window displays, replace the existing code with the following code:

```csharp
using System;
using System.Configuration;
using System.Configuration.Install;
using System.ComponentModel;
using System.ServiceModel;
using System.ServiceProcess;
using System.IO;

namespace WindowsServiceWCF
{
    [ServiceContract]
    public interface IServiceClass
    {
        [OperationContract]
        string GetText();

        [OperationContract]
        int MultiplyNumbers(int firstvalue, int secondvalue);
    }

    [RunInstaller(true)]
    public class ProjectInstaller : Installer
    {
        private ServiceProcessInstaller process;
        private ServiceInstaller service;

        public ProjectInstaller()
        {
            process = new ServiceProcessInstaller();
            process.Account = ServiceAccount.LocalSystem;
            service = new ServiceInstaller();
            service.ServiceName = "WindowsServiceHostWCF";
            service.StartType = ServiceStartMode.Automatic;
            Installers.Add(process);
            Installers.Add(service);
        }
    }

    public partial class Service1 : ServiceBase, IServiceClass
    {
        public ServiceHost sh = null;

        public static void Main()
        {
            ServiceBase.Run(new Service1());
        }

        public Service1()
        {
            //InitializeComponent();
```

```
            ServiceName = "WindowsServiceHostWCF";
    }

    protected override void OnStart(string[] args)
    {
        if (sh != null)
        {
            sh.Close();
        }

        sh = new ServiceHost(typeof(Service1));

        sh.Open();
    }

    protected override void OnStop()
    {
        if (sh != null)
        {
            sh.Close();
            sh = null;
        }

    }

    string IServiceClass.GetText()
    {
        StreamReader sw = new StreamReader(@"c:\wrox\WCFServiceTest.txt");
        return sw.ReadLine();
        //return "Hello World";
    }

    int IServiceClass.MultiplyNumbers(int firstvalue, int secondvalue)
    {
        return firstvalue * secondvalue;
    }

    }
}
```

The next step is to add the necessary endpoint definition information to the configuration file. However, before you do that, take a look at the preceding code. First, you'll notice that the actual WCF service code is embedded inside of the Windows service itself. Second, the code includes some additional pieces that you have not seen in previous WCF services. The service includes the normal implementation of the service contract, but also includes a Windows Service class and an installer class.

The service implementation of Service1 is the WCF service, but to be classified as a Windows service it needs to inherit from ServiceBase and implement the OnStart and OnStop methods. Lastly, the ProjectInstaller class inherits from Installer, which lets the program be installed as a Windows service.

Ok, now it is time to add the configuration information. Open the app.config file and replace the existing text with the following:

```
<configuration>
  <system.serviceModel>
    <services>
      <service name ="WindowsServiceWCF.Service1"
behaviorConfiguration="metadataSupport">
        <host>
          <baseAddresses>
            <add baseAddress="net.pipe://localhost/WindowsServiceWCF"/>
            <add baseAddress="net.tcp://localhost:8000/WindowsServiceWCF"/>
            <add baseAddress="http://localhost:8080/WindowsServiceWCF"/>
          </baseAddresses>
        </host>
        <endpoint address="tcpmex"
                  binding="mexTcpBinding"
                  contract="IMetadataExchange"/>
        <endpoint address="namedpipemex"
                  binding="mexNamedPipeBinding"
                  contract="IMetadataExchange"/>
        <endpoint address="" binding="wsHttpBinding"
contract="WindowsServiceWCF.IServiceClass"/>
        <!--<endpoint address="mex" binding="mexHttpBinding"
contract="IMetadataExchange"/>-->
      </service>
    </services>
    <behaviors>
      <serviceBehaviors>
        <behavior name="metadataSupport">
          <serviceMetadata httpGetEnabled="false" httpGetUrl=""/>
        </behavior>
      </serviceBehaviors>
    </behaviors>
  </system.serviceModel>
</configuration>
```

This configuration information should look very familiar. This is because this is the same service configuration most of the previous examples have used. The only difference is that this time the service is being hosted inside of the Windows service instead of the normal Windows forms host application the previous examples have used.

Build the project to make sure there are no errors. If there are no errors, set the build mode to Release and build the project again.

The next step is to register the Windows service. From the Start menu, select Run. When the Run dialog opens, type in the following:

```
C:\WINDOWS\Microsoft.NET\Framework\v2.0.50727\installutil.exe
C:\WindowsServiceWCF\WindowsServiceWCF\bin\Release\WindowsServiceWCF.exe
```

The InstallUtil utility is .NET installer tool that allows you to install and uninstall server resources. This tool can be found in the directory listed in the preceding code.

You can also unregister the service by applying the /u switch to the InstallUtil utility as shown in the example:

```
C:\WINDOWS\Microsoft.NET\Framework\v2.0.50727\installutil.exe /u
C:\WindowsServiceWCF\WindowsServiceWCF\bin\Release\WindowsServiceWCF.exe
```

Click OK on the Run dialog. A command window will appear providing output information as to the progress of the service registration and will quickly disappear once the service registration is complete.

Once the service is registered, you will be able to see it in the list of Windows Services in the Computer Management console.

1. Right-click My Computer and select Manage from the context menu. This will bring up the Computer Management console, shown in Figure 15-7.

2. Expand the Services and Applications node.

3. Select the Services node.

4. Scroll down the list of services until you see the service you just registered, which should look like Figure 15-7.

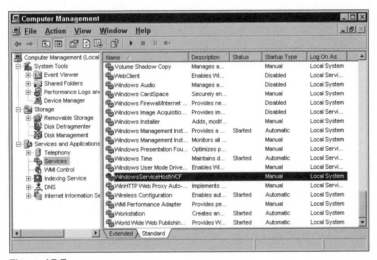

Figure 15-7

To start the service, click the Start button on the toolbar.

The service side is now done. Now it is time to modify the client:

1. Open the WCFClientApp project and open Form1 in design mode.

2. If it does not already have them, place two buttons and two text boxes on the form. The form should still have the familiar TCP and Named Pipe radio buttons.

3. Change the caption of button 1 to Get Text.

4. Change the caption of button 2 to Multiply.

It should look like Figure 15-8.

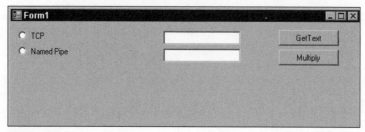

Figure 15-8

Just for safety's sake, go ahead and delete the existing WCF service references and add them back so that the proper references are set. Right-click the Service References node and select Add Service Reference. Re-add the TCP and NamedPipe references again, using the following URI/Reference Name pairs:

❑ TCP

    ❑ URI: net.tcp://localhost:8000/WindowsServiceWCF/tcpmex

    ❑ Reference Name: TCP

❑ Named Pipe

    ❑ URI: net.pipe://localhost/WindowsServiceWCF/namedpipemex

    ❑ Reference Name: NamedPipe

Next, change the code behind the form to the following:

```
using System;
using System.Collections.Generic;
using System.ComponentModel;
using System.Data;
using System.Drawing;
using System.Text;
using System.Windows.Forms;
using System.ServiceModel;
using System.ServiceModel.Channels;

namespace WCFClientApp
{

    public partial class Form1 : Form
    {
        private int _Selection;
        private int val1 = 5;
        private int val2 = 5;

        public Form1()
        {
            InitializeComponent();
```

```
        }

        private void Form1_Load(object sender, EventArgs e)
        {
            radioButton1.Checked = true;

        }

        private void button1_Click(object sender, EventArgs e)
        {

            switch (_Selection)
            {
                case 0:
                    TCP.ServiceClassClient client = new

WCFClientApp.TCP.ServiceClassClient("WSHttpBinding_IServiceClass");
                    textBox1.Text = client.GetText();
                    break;

                case 1:
                    NamedPipe.ServiceClassClient client1 = new

WCFClientApp.NamedPipe.ServiceClassClient("WSHttpBinding_IServiceClass1");
                    textBox1.Text = client1.GetText();
                    break;

                case 2:
                    break;
            }
        }

        private void button2_Click(object sender, EventArgs e)
        {
            switch (_Selection)
            {
                case 0:
                    TCP.ServiceClassClient client = new

WCFClientApp.TCP.ServiceClassClient("WSHttpBinding_IServiceClass");
                    textBox2.Text = client.MultiplyNumbers(val1, val2).ToString();
                    break;

                case 1:
                    NamedPipe.ServiceClassClient client1 = new

WCFClientApp.NamedPipe.ServiceClassClient("WSHttpBinding_IServiceClass1");
                    textBox2.Text = client1.MultiplyNumbers(val1, val2).ToString();
                    break;

                case 2:
                    break;
```

```
        }

    }

    private void radioButton1_CheckedChanged(object sender, EventArgs e)
    {
        _Selection = 0;
        textBox1.Text = "";
        textBox2.Text = "";
    }

    private void radioButton2_CheckedChanged(object sender, EventArgs e)
    {
        _Selection = 1;
        textBox1.Text = "";
        textBox2.Text = "";
    }

    }
}
```

Make sure the WindowsServiceHostWCF Windows service is running and fire up the client. As you select the protocol and click each button, you will get the text back from the text file, and the results form the multiplication method.

Your homework assignment for this chapter is to do the following: The WCF service code was embedded inside the Windows service. In this scenario, you had two projects, the Windows service project and the client project. Modify the Windows service so that instead of embedding the WCF service code inside the Windows service, it references the WCF service used in previous examples. Meaning, the Windows service is much like the Windows forms host application used in previous examples in that it hosts the WCFService service.

Summary

This chapter discussed the different hosting environments in which a Windows Communication Foundation service can be hosted. This intent was to help you recognize and determine the right hosting environment for your WCF service, and to do that this chapter began with a discussion about self-hosting and hosting, what each term means, and their differences.

Hosting refers to hosting a service in IIS, letting IIS manage and control the lifetime of the service, and has the benefit of the developers not needing to write any hosting code.

Self-hosting, on the other hand, gives developers more control and flexibility over the lifetime of the service, but requires them to implement the hosting code for the service.

From there, the different types of self-hosting options were discussed, such as in a Windows service or a Windows forms application.

Lastly, an example was provided, illustrating how to host a WCF service inside a Windows service.

WCF Template Extensions in Visual Studio

In November of 2006, Microsoft released the November 2006 CTP of the Visual Studio 2005 extensions for the .NET Framework 3.0. Those extensions provided support for building .NET Framework 3.0 Windows Communication Foundation and Windows Presentation Foundation applications using the released version of Visual Studio 2005. At the time of this writing, the November release of the VS extensions was the latest.

It was stated at the very beginning of this book that most, if not all, of the examples would be done manually, even though there were Visual Studio extensions and template add-ins available to assist the developer in developing WCF services and applications. The reason given at that time was that doing it manually was to provide a foundation from which to build upon regarding the architecture of WCF.

Taken from Chapter 3, examples were built manually because "...building the service manually will provide a better understanding of the components and procedures necessary to build a WCF service. When using the built-in templates, all the necessary components and references are added to the project for you and it is easy to miss something important that the template added for you."

However, as promised throughout the book, this appendix is here to provide you with some insight to the current set of Windows Communication Foundation extensions and add-ins for Visual Studio 2005. Let me reiterate again that the current set of extensions, as of this writing, is the November 2006 CTP release. Microsoft has made it clear that these tools are a preview of what is targeted to be in the next release of Visual Studio, code-named Orcas.

Because they are CTP, they are not supported by Microsoft but you are "encouraged" to use them with your .NET Framework 3.0 installation.

You can currently get the .NET Framework 3.0 and the Visual Studio 2005 extensions from the following Microsoft site:

```
http://msdn.microsoft.com/windowsvista/downloads/products/default.aspx
```

Toward the middle of the page (directly below the pretty graphic), you will see download links for both the .NET Framework 3.0 and the Visual Studio 2005 Extensions. Make sure you grab the WCF/WPF extensions. There are two download links, one for the WF extensions and one for the WCF/WPF extensions. The setup file for the extensions is currently named `vsextwfx.msi`.

Once you have downloaded the appropriate extensions, install them by running the .msi file. This setup is fairly straightforward so no time will be spent in this appendix walking you through the install.

When the install is complete, you are ready to go. Open Visual Studio and on the Start Page select Create Project, or from the File menu select New ⇨ Project. This will open the New Project dialog. In the *Project Types* section, expand the Visual C# node. Underneath the Visual C# node you will see a new project type called .NET Framework 3.0, shown in Figure A-1.

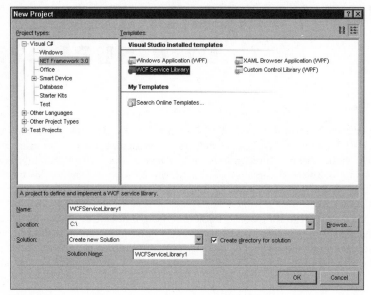

Figure A-1

Selecting the .NET Framework 3.0 project type will display all the available templates in the Templates section of the dialog box. As of the November CTP release, there are four available templates: three for Windows Presentation Foundation and one for Windows Communication Foundation.

Select the WCF Service Library template and make sure the *Create Directory for Solution* checkbox is checked. The default name it gives to the Solution and Project is WCFServiceLibrary1, so feel free to accept the default name.

Click the OK button, and your new WCF application will be created. Once it completes creating the project, expand the Project node as well as the References node, as shown in Figure A-2. You will see that it has somewhat created the beginnings of a WCF service.

You'll notice that it includes the appropriate references, but you may look at this figure and ask yourself, after everything you have learned in the book, shouldn't it have added more? What about a `.svc` file, or a `Web.config` or `app.config` file, at the very least?

Figure A-2

Well, the answer is, "it depends." For now, you get a "generic" project, and at the time of this writing the jury is still out on the decision to include specific templates. So for now, this is what you get. And it becomes more evident once you take a look at the generated service code.

Double-click the `Class1.cs` file and take a few minutes to look at the generated code, which is also shown here:

```
using System;
using System.Collections.Generic;
using System.Text;
using System.ServiceModel;
using System.Runtime.Serialization;

/*

 * HOW TO HOST THE WCF SERVICE IN THIS LIBRARY IN ANOTHER PROJECT
    You will need to do the following things:
    1)    Add a Host project to your solution
        a.    Right click on your solution
        b.    Select Add
        c.    Select New Project
        d.    Choose an appropriate Host project type (e.g. Console Application)
    2)    Add a new source file to your Host project
        a.    Right click on your Host project
        b.    Select Add
        c.    Select New Item
        d.    Select "Code File"
    3)    Paste the contents of the "MyServiceHost" class below into the new Code
File
    4)    Add an "Application Configuration File" to your Host project
        a.    Right click on your Host project
        b.    Select Add
        c.    Select New Item
        d.    Select "Application Configuration File"
    5)    Paste the contents of the App.Config below that defines your service
endpoints into the new Config File
    6)    Add the code that will host, start and stop the service
        a.    Call MyServiceHost.StartService() to start the service and
MyServiceHost.EndService() to end the service
    7)    Add a Reference to System.ServiceModel.dll
        a.    Right click on your Host Project
        b.    Select "Add Reference"
        c.    Select "System.ServiceModel.dll"
```

```
8)    Add a Reference from your Host project to your Service Library project
      a.    Right click on your Host Project
      b.    Select "Add Reference"
      c.    Select the "Projects" tab
9)    Set the Host project as the "StartUp" project for the solution
      a.    Right click on your Host Project
      b.    Select "Set as StartUp Project"


################ START MyServiceHost.cs ################

using System;
using System.ServiceModel;

// A WCF service consists of a contract (defined below),
// a class which implements that interface, and configuration
// entries that specify behaviors and endpoints associated with
// that implementation (see <system.serviceModel> in your application
// configuration file).

internal class MyServiceHost
{
    internal static ServiceHost myServiceHost = null;

    internal static void StartService()
    {
        //Consider putting the baseAddress in the configuration system
        //and getting it here with AppSettings
        Uri baseAddress = new Uri("http://localhost:8080/service1");

        //Instantiate new ServiceHost
        myServiceHost = new
ServiceHost(typeof(WindowsWCFApplication1.service1), baseAddress);

        //Open myServiceHost
        myServiceHost.Open();
    }

    internal static void StopService()
    {
        //Call StopService from your shutdown logic (i.e. dispose method)
        if (myServiceHost.State != CommunicationState.Closed)
            myServiceHost.Close();
    }
}

################ END MyServiceHost.cs ################
################ START App.config or Web.config ################

<system.serviceModel>
<services>
    <service name="WindowsWCFApplication1.service1">
      <endpoint contract="WindowsWCFApplication1.IService1"
binding="wsHttpBinding"/>
    </service>
  </services>
```

```
        </system.serviceModel>

        ################ END App.config or Web.config ################

*/
namespace WCFServiceLibrary1
{
    // You have created a class library to define and implement your WCF service.
    // You will need to add a reference to this library from another project and
add
    // the code to that project to host the service as described below.  Another
way
    // to create and host a WCF service is by using the Add New Item, WCF Service
    // template within an existing project such as a Console Application or a
Windows
    // Application.

    [ServiceContract()]
    public interface IService1
    {
        [OperationContract]
        string MyOperation1(string myValue);
        [OperationContract]
        string MyOperation2(DataContract1 dataContractValue);
    }

    public class service1 : IService1
    {
        public string MyOperation1(string myValue)
        {
            return "Hello: " + myValue;
        }
        public string MyOperation2(DataContract1 dataContractValue)
        {
            return "Hello: " + dataContractValue.FirstName;
        }
    }

    [DataContract]
    public class DataContract1
    {
        string firstName;
        string lastName;

        [DataMember]
        public string FirstName
        {
            get { return firstName; }
            set { firstName = value; }
        }
        [DataMember]
        public string LastName
        {
            get { return lastName; }
            set { lastName = value; }
```

```
            }
        }

    }
```

That was nearly three full pages of code, with one of those pages being a set of step-by-step instructions on what to do next. You will see that it includes everything you need to get you started building a service as well as instructions, and code snippets, to host your application in a Windows service, IIS, or a managed code application.

The great thing about this is that it gives you a great starting point, because the template does not know what type of service you are going to build nor does it know the type of environment you are going to host the service in. Therefore, it provides you with enough information to get started. What is even better is that it breaks everything out into sections, making it easy to read.

Need to know where to begin with your configuration file? No problem, it includes a great piece of code for the beginnings of an `app.config` or `Web.config` configuration file. Are you hosting your WCF service inside of a Windows service? No sweat, because it has a section with some code and instructions for that as well.

The thing to watch out for is that the nine steps at the top of the code should not be "followed step by step from 1 to 9." For example, you do not need to do Steps 2 and 3 if you are hosting your service in IIS. As the comment on the top states, these instructions are there to provide you with the necessary steps on how to host your service (the one created above in the preceding code) in another project. Not all steps apply to all projects so keep that in mind as you build the service.

Your homework for this appendix is to take the preceding template, create a service for it, and host it in IIS. Refer to the example in Chapter 3 if you need some help.

Summary

Although the final release date for the next release of Visual Studio is still in question, Microsoft has recently released the .NET Framework 3.0 and the associated VS template extensions. The template extensions are still in beta and won't be officially released until they are officially released with Orcas.

Thus, it remains to be seen what the final Visual Studio WCF extensions will look like, but this appendix is meant to provide you with a look at the current template plug-in. You might initially think that it is a bit weak, but if you consider the information it provides, it is anything but weak because it gives you a great foundation for building a WCF service and host regardless of the environment you will be hosting the service in.

The intent was to provide you with enough information to get started and to get your cerebral WCF motor going.

Will Microsoft add more templates for the final release? I would honestly think that by the time you are done with this book you would actually be faster doing it manually than through a template. However, the current template is here if you want to use it to jump-start your project.

B

Case Study

I always find it hard to include a case study in a book because in theory, a case study is supposed to provide a real-world example of the technology being discussed in the book. However the term real-world covers a lot of area, so answering the question "What should the case study be about?" can get pretty involved. Because WCF is primarily used for enterprise application development, walking through a typical e-commerce scenario seemed like the obvious choice. However, e-commerce case studies have been done over and over again and I wanted to do something that offered some new perspectives. In talking with some of my co-workers, I gathered some ideas and a couple of them stood out.

With all of the ideas being tossed back and forth, I remembered a case study that had been discussed in one of the early Indigo books. (Indigo, if you weren't aware of it, was the codename Microsoft gave the Windows Communication Foundation prior to deciding on a final name for it.) It wasn't quite real-world in the sense it was something a developer might typically encounter, but it certainly was very real in the sense that it used many of the WCF features that would be used in many typical applications.

After some thought, it came down to two case studies to pick from. The first option was a case study that employed a time-card management system used to track the time a given employee worked. The second was the earlier Indigo case study. I kept asking myself, "Which one of these would provide a better illustration for my readers?" After some thought, I decided to use both. This appendix discusses only one of them, but the download code for this book includes the source code for both projects.

The example discussed in this appendix is an elevator control system. This case study was originally done by David Pallmann in the Microsoft Press book *Programming Indigo*. The main reason for redoing this case study was because at the time the case study was originally done, Windows Communication Foundation was still going through some major architectural changes and as such the case study examples would not work with the final release of the .NET 3.0 Framework and the release of the Windows Communication Foundation.

Before I get started, I want to thank David Pallmann for allowing me to redo this case study. When I was first getting into WCF, his book provided a great foundation on which to build, and I cannot thank him enough for letting me redo this great case study example.

OK, time to begin.

Case Study: Elevator Control System

This case study takes a look at an elevator control system, an application that controls multiple elevators in a building. A real-world system like this would take into consideration many factors, for example the maximum weight each elevator could safely bear and other similar safety requirements. This example, however, is not that complicated. It is fairly simple, and it demonstrates a wide array of the WCF functionality.

If you take a look at the functions of a single elevator, they are relatively simple. Elevators go up and down, stopping at any given floor, and pick people up or drop them off along the way. More specifically, elevators perform the following tasks:

- ❏ Move up and stop at floors with "going-up" requests until all such requests have been completed.

- ❏ Move down, stopping on floors with "going-down" requests until all such requests are completed.

- ❏ Repeat.

If you have ever been waiting for an elevator to go down to the main floor, only to hear it moving up past your floor without stopping, now you know why. It hasn't finished its "going-up" requests, but will surely pick you up on its way down because you are part of its "going-down" requests.

This case study uses the example of a building with a bank of elevators, as shown in Figure B-1. In the following scenario, the movement of the elevators works best when the movement of the elevator cars is coordinated. The coordination of elevator cars allows for the most efficient use of each car.

What is needed is a solution in which the position and direction of the cars are monitored and dispatched to efficiently coordinate the cars.

Think for a minute about the type of requests a car elevator receives—not the "go up" or "go down" requests, but "type" of requests. There are two:

- ❏ **Hall call:** Occurs when someone in the hallway presses the up or down elevator button.

- ❏ **Destination call:** Occurs when someone standing inside the elevator presses a floor button on the button control panel.

Obviously, destination calls will be serviced by the elevator in which you are standing. Hall calls, however, can be serviced by any elevator. The elevator control system needs to decide which elevator will service the hall call.

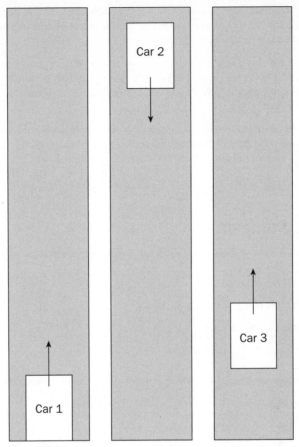

Figure B-1

The elevator control system could micromanage all elevator actions, meaning that the control system could control every aspect of each elevator including hall and destination calls, but that is not what you want. Each elevator should operate autonomously with the control system only being used to determine which elevator should be dispatched to a hall call.

The benefit of this is that even if the elevator control system were to fail, each elevator could continue to provide destination call functionality. Therefore, each elevator and the control system can be considered as self-contained components, and each component as an SOA boundary, perfect for designing an SOA solution.

The problems that the elevator control system needs to solve are the following:

❑   The number of elevator cars. There are x cars.

❑   Each elevator car can be taken out of service and placed in service at any given time.

❑   When an elevator car is in service, that car needs to be able to communicate with the control system. Likewise, the control system needs to be aware of the direction of travel and position of each elevator car.

❑ When a car is not servicing requests, it remains stationary, sitting dormant at the floor where it performed its last service. When a car is servicing requests, it will respond to hall and destination calls autonomously, servicing requests as long as there are requests to be serviced.

❑ Each elevator car maintains its own list of requests, meaning that Car 1 has no idea of the requests Car 2 is servicing. Each car becomes aware of destination requests when someone inside the elevator presses a floor button. Likewise, the car becomes aware of hall requests from the control system.

❑ For each hall call, the control system needs to efficiently determine which of the cars currently in service should be assigned to the call. In this case, "efficiently" will be defined as using the car closest to the floor and available for the direction of the call.

With the problems defined, the next step is to start outlining the solution.

Designing the Solution

The goal is to design a service-oriented solution by performing the following tasks:

❑ Identifying service boundaries

❑ Defining the roles of the service and clients

❑ Selecting a messaging pattern

❑ Designing the contracts and bindings

Each task maps back to a specific area of WCF functionality. Each is discussed in detail in the following sections.

Service Boundaries

As stated earlier, each elevator and control system needs to operate autonomously, each object (elevator car, control system, and so on) being a self-contained unit. This helps determine the service boundaries quite easily such that there is one control system and multiple elevators, as shown in Figure B-2.

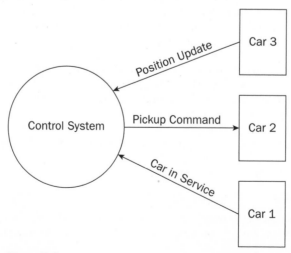

Figure B-2

As you can see from the diagram, the control system itself will be implemented as the service. Each elevator in turn becomes a stateful client of the service.

From what you learned in this book, a two-way messaging pattern is needed because both the client and the service need to communicate with the other party. Each elevator car (the client) needs to inform the control system (the service) of its position and direction of travel, and the control system needs to tell the elevators about hall call requests.

Looking at this you can tell that there is no one-way, synchronous communication about this scenario. This is duplex, asynchronous communication, letting the service and client freely communicate with the other party as events take place.

Service Contract

From what you learned in the previous chapters about duplex messaging patterns, it should be clear that in order to accomplish asynchronous communication, two service contracts are needed. The first interface is for the control system. The second interface is the client callback to the elevator cars. Therefore, the control system (service) will provide the following operations:

❑   **CarInService:** The elevator car informing the control system that it is now in service.

❑   **CarNotInService:** The elevator car informing the control system that it is no longer in service.

❑   **CarUpdate:** The elevator car informing the control system of its new location and direction of travel.

Equally, the elevator car (client) will contain a single operation:

❑   **Pickup:** The control system informing an elevator car of a pickup request (hall call).

As such, the contract contains the following service operation definitions:

```
[ServiceContract(SessionMode=SessionMode.Required,
    CallbackContract=typeof(IElevatorCar))]
public interface IControl
{
  [OperationContract(IsInitiating=true, IsTerminating=false)]
  int CarInService();
  [OperationContract(IsInitiating=false, IsTerminating=true)]
  void CarNotInService();
  [OperationContract]
  void CarUpdate(int floor, bool goingup, bool goingdown);
}

Public interface IElevatorCar
{
  [OperationContract]
  Void Pickup(bool[] upRequests, bool[] downRequests);
}
```

Before moving on, take a look at the preceding service contract. Using the properties of the `OperationContract` attribute, you can see that the operations must be called in a specific order. This is determined by the `IsInitiating` and `IsTerminating` properties. Based on the way they are specified here, the `CarInService` operation must be called first, followed by one or more calls to the `CarUpdate` operation, and finally the `CarNotInService` operation.

It may be instructional to modify this code temporarily and call the methods out of order. If the client calls a non-initiating operation before it calls an initiating one, an `InvalidOperationException` will be thrown. Conversely, if the service is called with a non-initiating operation, a `FaultException` is thrown (An `ActionNotSupported` SOAP Fault is actually raised on the service, but it is raised on the client as a SOAP Fault.)

Looking at the operation contract properties, you can see that a call to the `CarInService` operation begins a new session for the car that is being called into service. This is accomplished by setting the `IsInitiating` property to a value of true, which creates a new instance and starts a new session. As you will see later, the control system will assign a car number to the elevator, which is the operation's return value.

The `CarUpdate` operation is a normal operation (compared to the other two) in that there are no properties set on this operation. This operation simply tells the control system of the car's current location and direction of travel (up or down). Calling this operation prior to calling the `CarInService` operation will result in an error being generated.

The `CarNotInService` operation ends the session for the car that is being removed from service. This is specified by setting the `IsTerminating` property to a value of true. When this operation has completed, the session and instance will be closed.

Finally, you can see the client callback service contract in the preceding code. This enables the control system to respond to a hall call request. The control system will decide which car is better able to service the hall call request and call the car's `Pickup` service operation. The `Pickup` operation contains two parameters, both being arrays of type bool that contain new going-up and going-down requests for that specific car.

With the service ironed out, the next step is to determine the appropriate binding and behaviors for the control system.

Bindings and Behaviors

To determine the appropriate behavior for the control system, the requirements for this application need to be defined. Based on what you know about the application, you can safely assume the following:

- ❑ The need for cross-machine communication
- ❑ Reliable sessions
- ❑ Duplex messaging pattern
- ❑ Exactly-once and in-order delivery assurances

Cross-machine communication is needed because more than likely the client and service won't be running on the same machine in this scenario. Reliable Messaging is needed because the last thing you want is for a passenger to make a hall call request and have it not show up at the control system. The need for duplex communication has already been established, but you also need an in-order/exactly-once delivery assurance. This means that if a passenger makes a hall call, the same elevator won't be sent there twice, and that the requests will be processed in the order they are received.

So which WCF-provided binding provides this functionality? The correct choice is to use the NetTCPBinding. Why? Because the client and service won't be running on the same computer, and more than likely won't be communicating over the Internet, TCP is a protocol of choice. The NetTCPBinding also offers duplex communication and delivery assurance. As a refresher, the MSDN description of the NetTCPBinding is provided here:

"Specifies a secure, reliable, optimized binding suitable for cross-machine communication. By default, it generates a runtime communication stack with WS-ReliableMessaging for reliability, Windows Security for message security and authentication, TCP for message delivery, and binary message encoding."

The service needs to also specify the appropriate instancing and concurrency behaviors, and these behaviors can be applied by specifying the respective properties of the ServiceBehavior attribute:

```
[ServiceBehavior(InstanceContextMode=InstanceContextMode.PerSession,
        ConcurrencyMode=ConcurrencyMode.Multiple)]
class Control : IControl
{
  //
}
```

The properties specified on the ServiceBehavior instruct the service that instancing is per session (InstanceContextMode) and that the service should support multiple threads (ConcurrencyMode.Multiple).

Program Design

With the "under the cover" stuff out of the way, the focus now needs to be turned to the UI (user interface) and the design of the application. This includes not only the UI, but also how the solution will be designed.

To make it easy, the elevator control system will have two programs: the elevator program and the control system program. Each program will be a separate EXE, elevator.exe and control.exe. Only one instance of control.exe, the control system program, will be needed, but multiple instances of the elevator program, elevator.exe, will be created — one for each elevator.

This simulation will have a 10-story building with a bank of three elevators (refer to Figure B-1), the number of floors and maximum number of elevators being defined and set by constants.

Elevator (Client)

The Elevator program will represent a single elevator car, handling destination calls on its own, responding to a button push when a passenger inside the car presses a floor button. The elevator.exe program will contain the following:

❑ **FormElevator.cs:** The main form for the Elevator program. It is the startup form and also creates an instance of the Elevator class.

❑ **ElevatorCar.cs:** The class that implements the elevator car, tracking request lists and kicking off a worker thread that moves the elevator car based on the request.

Figure B-3 shows the user interface of the Elevator program. The Start button puts the elevator in service and the Stop button takes the elevator out of service. The other buttons are the floor buttons, which are used to make destination requests.

Figure B-3

Control (Service)

The control system is the brains behind the elevator system. The control system program, `control.exe`, is the elevator dispatch system for the elevator system. Like the Elevator program, the Control program will contain a form and class. Specifically, it will contain the following:

❑   **FormControl.cs:** The startup form for the control system program. This form creates an instance of the Control class.

❑   **Control.cs:** This class implements the control system, tracking the incoming call requests and running worker threads that move the elevator based on the request.

The purpose of the control form is twofold as shown in the following:

❑   It simulates the building's up and down buttons.

❑   It displays the location and direction of each elevator that is currently in service.

When a user presses the up or down button, the form makes a call to one of the methods of the Control class and registers the hall call. At that point the hall call is assigned to one of the elevators that is in service. The Control class also implements the IControl service contract.

Each elevator car acts as a client to the control system (service), declaring to the control service when it goes in or out of service. The client also sends updates back to the control system as well as retrieving new hall calls.

Figure B-4 shows the user interface for the Control program. The Start and Stop buttons at the top of the form start and stop the service, and the rest of the form shows the status of the elevator control system, including the location and direction of each car. Each car is represented graphically on the form along with individual up and down hall call buttons for each floor.

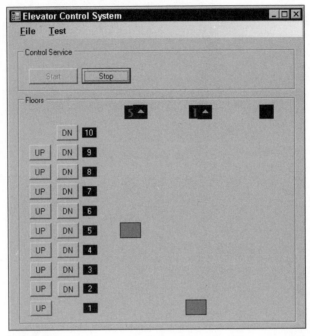

Figure B-4

Building the Solution

This case study uses two Visual Studio projects, each with a form and class.

Project	File	Class	Assembly
Elevator	ElevatorCar.cs	ElevatorCar	Elevator.exe
Elevator	FormElevator.cs	FormElevator	Elevator.exe
Control	Control.cs	Control	Control.exe
Control	FormControl.cs	FormControl	Control.exe

Begin by building the Control project.

Control.cs

Create a new Visual Studio project, naming the project Control. When the project has been created, right-click Form1 in Solution Explorer and select Rename, and rename Form1 to FormControl.

Next, right-click the Elevator project, and from the context menu, select Add ⇨ Class. When the Add New Item dialog appears, the Class template will automatically be selected with a default name of Class1.cs. Simply rename Class1.cs to Control.cs and click the Add button.

Lastly, be sure to add a reference to the System.ServiceModel namespace. This can be accomplished by right-clicking the References node in Solution Explorer and selecting Add Reference from the context menu. The System.ServiceModel namespace should be listed on the Recent tab of the Add Reference dialog box. If for some reason it is not, select the Browse tab and browse to the following location:

```
\Windows\Microsoft .NET\Framework\v 3.0\Windows Communication Foundation
```

With the project ready, it is time to start adding code. The first thing to add is the code in Control.cs. This class is called by FormControl. Enter the following code in the Control.cs class:

```
using System;
using System.ServiceModel;
using System.Threading;
using System.Collections.Generic;
using System.Text;
using Control;

namespace Control
{
    [ServiceContract(SessionMode=SessionMode.Required,
CallbackContract=typeof(IElevatorCar))]
    public interface IControl
    {
        [OperationContract(IsInitiating=true, IsTerminating=false)]
        int CarInService();
        [OperationContract(IsInitiating=false, IsTerminating=true)]
        void CarNotInService();
        [OperationContract]
        void CarUpdate(int floor, bool goingup, bool goingdown);
    }

    public interface IElevatorCar
    {
        [OperationContract]
        void Pickup(bool[] upRequest, bool[] downRequests);
    }

    [ServiceBehavior(InstanceContextMode = InstanceContextMode.PerSession,
        ConcurrencyMode = ConcurrencyMode.Multiple)]
    class Control : IControl
    {
        public const int MaxCars = 3;
        public const int NumberOfFloors = 10;

        int CarNo;

        public static bool UpdateDisplay = false;
        static int NoCars = 0;

        public static int[] CarLocation = new int[MaxCars+1];
```

```
        public static bool[] CarGoingUp = new bool[MaxCars + 1];
        public static bool[] CarPickingUp = new bool[MaxCars + 1];

        public static bool[,] HallCallUp = new bool[MaxCars + 1, NumberOfFloors +
1];
        public static bool[,] HallCallDown = new bool[MaxCars + 1, NumberOfFloors +
1];

        static IElevatorCar[] Callback = new IElevatorCar[MaxCars + 1];

        public int CarInService()
        {
            int car = 0;

            for (int c = 1; c <= NoCars; c++)
            {
                if (CarLocation[c] == 0)
                {
                    car = c;
                    break;
                }
            }

            if (car == 0)
            {
                car = ++NoCars;
            }

            this.CarNo = car;
            Callback[CarNo] = OperationContext.Current
.GetCallbackChannel<IElevatorCar>();
            //lblMessageDisplay.Text = "Car " + CarNo + " in service";
            CarLocation[car] = 1;
            return car;
        }

        public void CarNotInService()
        {
            //lblMessageDisplay.Text = "Car " + CarNo + " out of service";
            CarLocation[CarNo] = 0;
        }

        public void CarUpdate(int floor, bool goingup, bool pickingup)
        {
            CarLocation[CarNo] = floor;
            CarGoingUp[CarNo] = goingup;
            CarPickingUp[CarNo] = pickingup;

            for (int f = 1; f <= NumberOfFloors; f++)
            {
                if (pickingup && goingup && floor == f)
                {
                    for (int car = 1; car <= MaxCars; car++)
                    {
                        HallCallUp[car, f] = false;
```

```
                }
            }
            else if (pickingup && !goingup && floor == f)
            {
                for (int car = 1; car <= MaxCars; car++)
                {
                    HallCallDown[car, f] = false;
                }
            }
        }
    }
    UpdateDisplay = true;
}

public static void HallCall(int floor, bool goingup)
{
    int car = SelectCar(floor, goingup);
    if (car != 0)
    {
        if (goingup)
        {
            HallCallUp[car, floor] = true;
        }
        else
        {
            HallCallDown[car, floor] = true;
        }
    }

    bool[] upRequests = new bool[NumberOfFloors + 1];
    bool[] downRequests = new bool[NumberOfFloors + 1];

    for (int f = 1; floor <= NumberOfFloors; floor++)
    {
        upRequests[f] = HallCallUp[car, f];
        HallCallUp[car, f] = false;
        downRequests[f] = HallCallDown[car, f];
        HallCallDown[car, f] = false;
    }
    Callback[car].Pickup(upRequests, downRequests);
}

static int SelectCar(int floor, bool goingup)
{
    int bestDistance = 10;
    int bestCar = 0;
    int distance = 0;

    for (int car = 1; car <= MaxCars; car++)
    {
        int location = CarLocation[car];
        if (location != 0 && CarGoingUp[car] == goingup)
        {
            if (location < floor)
            {
```

```
                    distance = floor - location;
        }
        else
        {
            distance = location - floor;
        }
        if (distance < bestDistance)
        {
            bestDistance = distance;
            bestCar = car;
        }
    }
}

if (bestCar == 0)
{
    for (int car = 1; car <= MaxCars; car++)
    {
        int location = CarLocation[car];
        if (location != 0)
        {
            if (location < floor)
            {
                distance = floor - location;
            }
            else
            {
                distance = location - floor;
            }
            if (distance < bestDistance)
            {
                bestDistance = distance;
                bestCar = car;
            }
        }
    }
}

//console.writeline
return bestCar;
    }

  }
}
```

The Control.cs class defines the IControl interface and the Control class that implements the IControl interface. This purpose of this class is to track the status of the elevator system, such as location and Elevator car travel direction of those cars currently in service. These values are held in static variables and Boolean arrays, some of which are public so that the control system form can display this information.

This class is called by the FormControl form, which specifies the Control class as the implementation class. A new instance of this class is called every time the service's CarInService operation is called.

There are three service operations defined on this interface:

- ❑ CarInService
- ❑ CarNotInService
- ❑ CarUpdate

There is also an additional method on this class, called HallCall, which is used to register the hall call request when a button is pressed on FormControl.

FormControl.cs

This form is a bit more complicated as far as the UI is concerned. However, it isn't as complicated as it seems. Take a look at Figure B-4, and use it as a guide.

Basically, you need a Start and Stop button. Each of these, respectively, will start and stop an instance of the Control class. You will need to place nine *Up* buttons and nine *Down* buttons on the form with no special properties set.

You will need to place three label controls on the form, each of which will visually represent the elevators. Set the following properties:

- ❑ **Name:** labelCar1, labelCar2, and labelCar3, respectively
- ❑ **BackColor:** Gray
- ❑ **BorderStyle:** FixedSingle
- ❑ **Visible:** False

Three more label controls are needed to represent the current floor for each elevator. Each of the label controls should have its properties set as indicated here:

- ❑ **Name:** labelCar1Floor, labelCar2Floor, labelCar3Floor respectively.
- ❑ **AutoSize:** True
- ❑ **BackColor:** Black
- ❑ **ForeColor:** Red
- ❑ **Text:** "X" (without the quotes)

Finally, three more label controls will be needed to represent the floor direction indicators. Each of the label controls should have its properties set as indicated here:

- ❑ **Name:** labelCar1Direction, labelCar2Direction, and labelCar3Direction, respectively
- ❑ **BackColor:** Black
- ❑ **Font:** Webdings
- ❑ **ForeColor:** LawnGreen

The Text property of the direction label controls will be set via code, so there is no need to specify anything for this property in the designer.

Once the preceding steps have been performed, replace the existing code behind the forms with the following:

```
using System;
using System.ServiceModel;
using System.Collections.Generic;
using System.ComponentModel;
using System.Data;
using System.Drawing;
using System.Text;
using System.Windows.Forms;

namespace Control
{
    public partial class FormControl : Form
    {

        ServiceHost controlservice = null;
        bool initialized = false;
        System.Random random = new System.Random();
        bool TestRandom = false;

        public FormControl()
        {
            InitializeComponent();
        }

        private void FormControl_Load(object sender, EventArgs e)
        {

        }

        private void exitToolStripMenuItem_Click(object sender, EventArgs e)
        {
            Environment.Exit(0);
        }

        private void cmdStart_Click(object sender, EventArgs e)
        {
            Cursor = Cursors.WaitCursor;
            Application.DoEvents();

            cmdStart.Enabled = false;
            cmdStop.Enabled = true;

            Uri uri = new Uri("net.tcp://localhost:8000/ElevatorControl/");
            NetTcpBinding binding = new NetTcpBinding();
            binding.Security.Mode = SecurityMode.None;

            controlservice = new ServiceHost(typeof(Control), uri);

            ServiceMetadataBehavior mBehave = new ServiceMetadataBehavior();
```

```
        controlservice.Description.Behaviors.Add(mBehave);

        controlservice.AddServiceEndpoint(typeof(IMetadataExchange),
            MetadataExchangeBindings.CreateMexTcpBinding(), "mex");

        controlservice.AddServiceEndpoint(typeof(IControl), binding, uri);

        controlservice.Open();

        Cursor = Cursors.Default;
    }

    private void cmdStop_Click(object sender, EventArgs e)
    {
        Cursor = Cursors.WaitCursor;
        Application.DoEvents();
        //controlservice.Close();
        //controlservice = null;
        cmdStart.Enabled = true;
        cmdStop.Enabled = false;
        Cursor = Cursors.Default;

    }

    private void buttonUp1_Click(object sender, EventArgs e)
    {
        buttonUp1.BackColor = Color.Gold;
        Control.HallCall(1, true);
    }

    private void buttonUp2_Click(object sender, EventArgs e)
    {
        buttonUp2.BackColor = Color.Gold;
        Control.HallCall(2, true);
    }

    private void buttonUp3_Click(object sender, EventArgs e)
    {
        buttonUp3.BackColor = Color.Gold;
        Control.HallCall(3, true);
    }

    private void buttonUp4_Click(object sender, EventArgs e)
    {
        buttonUp4.BackColor = Color.Gold;
        Control.HallCall(4, true);
    }

    private void buttonUp5_Click(object sender, EventArgs e)
    {
        buttonUp5.BackColor = Color.Gold;
        Control.HallCall(5, true);
    }

    private void buttonUp6_Click(object sender, EventArgs e)
```

```
{
    buttonUp6.BackColor = Color.Gold;
    Control.HallCall(6, true);
}

private void buttonUp7_Click(object sender, EventArgs e)
{
    buttonUp7.BackColor = Color.Gold;
    Control.HallCall(7, true);
}

private void buttonUp8_Click(object sender, EventArgs e)
{
    buttonUp8.BackColor = Color.Gold;
    Control.HallCall(8, true);
}

private void buttonUp9_Click(object sender, EventArgs e)
{
    buttonUp9.BackColor = Color.Gold;
    Control.HallCall(9, true);
}

private void buttonDown2_Click(object sender, EventArgs e)
{
    buttonDown2.BackColor = Color.Gold;
    Control.HallCall(2, false);
}

private void buttonDown3_Click(object sender, EventArgs e)
{
    buttonDown3.BackColor = Color.Gold;
    Control.HallCall(3, false);
}

private void buttonDown4_Click(object sender, EventArgs e)
{
    buttonDown4.BackColor = Color.Gold;
    Control.HallCall(4, false);
}

private void buttonDown5_Click(object sender, EventArgs e)
{
    buttonDown5.BackColor = Color.Gold;
    Control.HallCall(5, false);
}

private void buttonDown6_Click(object sender, EventArgs e)
{
    buttonDown6.BackColor = Color.Gold;
    Control.HallCall(6, false);
}

private void buttonDown7_Click(object sender, EventArgs e)
{
```

```
        buttonDown7.BackColor = Color.Gold;
        Control.HallCall(7, false);
    }

    private void buttonDown8_Click(object sender, EventArgs e)
    {
        buttonDown8.BackColor = Color.Gold;
        Control.HallCall(8, false);
    }

    private void buttonDown9_Click(object sender, EventArgs e)
    {
        buttonDown9.BackColor = Color.Gold;
        Control.HallCall(9, false);
    }

    private void buttonDown10_Click(object sender, EventArgs e)
    {
        buttonDown10.BackColor = Color.Gold;
        Control.HallCall(10, false);
    }

    private void FormControl_Activated(object sender, EventArgs e)
    {
        if (initialized) return;
        initialized = true;
        while (true)
        {
            Application.DoEvents();
            if (controlservice != null)
            {
                Control.UpdateDisplay = false;
                UpdateDisplay();
                if (TestRandom)
                    RandomHallCall();
                System.Threading.Thread.Sleep(500);
            }
        }
    }

    void UpdateDisplay()
    {
        for (int car = 1; car <= Control.MaxCars; car++)
        {
            Color color;
            string direction = "";
            string location = "";
            int position = 324;
            bool visible;
            Color carColor = Color.DarkGray;

            if (Control.CarLocation[car] == 0)
            {
                location = "X";
                direction = "";
```

```
        color = Color.Red;
        visible = false;
    }
    else
    {
        position = 364 - (Control.CarLocation[car] * 40);
        location = Control.CarLocation[car].ToString();
        color = Color.LawnGreen;
        visible = true;
        if (Control.CarPickingUp[car])
        {
            carColor = Color.White;
        }
        if (Control.CarGoingUp[car])
        {
            direction = "5";
        }
        else
        {
            direction = "6";
        }
    }

    switch (car)
    {
        case 1:
            labelCar1Floor.Text = location;
            labelCar1Direction.Text = direction;
            labelCar1Floor.ForeColor = color;
            LabelCar1.Visible = visible;
            LabelCar1.BackColor = carColor;
            if (position != 0)
                MoveCar(ref LabelCar1, position);
            break;

        case 2:
            labelCar2Floor.Text = location;
            labelCar2Direction.Text = direction;
            labelCar2Floor.ForeColor = color;
            LabelCar2.Visible = visible;
            LabelCar2.BackColor = carColor;
            if (position != 0)
                MoveCar(ref LabelCar2, position);
            break;

        case 3:
            labelCar3Floor.Text = location;
            labelCar3Direction.Text = direction;
            labelCar3Floor.ForeColor = color;
            LabelCar3.Visible = visible;
            LabelCar3.BackColor = carColor;
            if (position != 0)
                MoveCar(ref LabelCar3, position);
            break;
    }
```

```
            }

        for (int floor = 1; floor <= Control.NumberOfFloors; floor++)
        {
            int upCount = 0;
            int downCount = 0;

            for (int car = 1; car <= Control.MaxCars; car++)
            {
                if (Control.CarLocation[car] == floor &&
Control.CarGoingUp[car])
                    upCount++;
                if (Control.CarLocation[car] == floor &&
!Control.CarGoingUp[car])
                    downCount++;
            }

            if (upCount > 0)
            {
                switch (floor)
                {
                    case 1:
                        buttonUp1.BackColor = SystemColors.Control;
                        break;

                    case 2:
                        buttonUp2.BackColor = SystemColors.Control;
                        break;

                    case 3:
                        buttonUp3.BackColor = SystemColors.Control;
                        break;

                    case 4:
                        buttonUp4.BackColor = SystemColors.Control;
                        break;

                    case 5:
                        buttonUp5.BackColor = SystemColors.Control;
                        break;

                    case 6:
                        buttonUp6.BackColor = SystemColors.Control;
                        break;

                    case 7:
                        buttonUp7.BackColor = SystemColors.Control;
                        break;

                    case 8:
                        buttonUp8.BackColor = SystemColors.Control;
                        break;

                    case 9:
                        buttonUp9.BackColor = SystemColors.Control;
```

```
                                        break;
                             }
                   }

                   if (downCount > 0)
                   {
                        switch (floor)
                        {
                             case 2:
                                  buttonDown2.BackColor = SystemColors.Control;
                                  break;

                             case 3:
                                  buttonDown3.BackColor = SystemColors.Control;
                                  break;

                             case 4:
                                  buttonDown4.BackColor = SystemColors.Control;
                                  break;

                             case 5:
                                  buttonDown5.BackColor = SystemColors.Control;
                                  break;

                             case 6:
                                  buttonDown6.BackColor = SystemColors.Control;
                                  break;

                             case 7:
                                  buttonDown7.BackColor = SystemColors.Control;
                                  break;

                             case 8:
                                  buttonDown8.BackColor = SystemColors.Control;
                                  break;

                             case 9:
                                  buttonDown9.BackColor = SystemColors.Control;
                                  break;

                             case 10:
                                  buttonDown10.BackColor = SystemColors.Control;
                                  break;

                        }
                   }
              }
         }

         void MoveCar(ref Label labelCar, int position)
         {
              int StartY = 0, finalY = 0;
              if (labelCar.Location.Y == position) return;
              StartY = labelCar.Top;
              finalY = position;
```

```
            if (StartY < finalY)
            {
                for (int y = StartY; y <= finalY; y += 10)
                {
                    labelCar.Top = y;
                    Application.DoEvents();
                }
            }
            else
            {
                for (int y = StartY; y >= finalY; y -= 10)
                {
                    labelCar.Top = y;
                    Application.DoEvents();
                }
            }
        }

        private void randomToolStripMenuItem_Click(object sender, EventArgs e)
        {
            TestRandom = !TestRandom;
        }

        void RandomHallCall()
        {
            int floor, direction;
            bool goingup;
            floor = random.Next(Control.NumberOfFloors) + 1;
            direction = random.Next(2);
            goingup = (direction == 0) ? true : false;
            if ((goingup && floor == Control.NumberOfFloors || goingup && floor ==
1))
                goingup = !goingup;

            switch (direction)
            {
                case 0:
                    switch (floor)
                    {
                        case 1:
                            buttonUp1.BackColor = Color.Gold;
                            break;

                        case 2:
                            buttonUp2.BackColor = Color.Gold;
                            break;

                        case 3:
                            buttonUp3.BackColor = Color.Gold;
                            break;

                        case 4:
                            buttonUp4.BackColor = Color.Gold;
```

```
                break;

            case 5:
                buttonUp5.BackColor = Color.Gold;
                break;

            case 6:
                buttonUp6.BackColor = Color.Gold;
                break;

            case 7:
                buttonUp7.BackColor = Color.Gold;
                break;

            case 8:
                buttonUp8.BackColor = Color.Gold;
                break;

            case 9:
                buttonUp9.BackColor = Color.Gold;
                break;
        }
        break;
    case 1:
        switch (floor)
        {
            case 2:
                buttonDown2.BackColor = Color.Gold;
                break;

            case 3:
                buttonDown3.BackColor = Color.Gold;
                break;

            case 4:
                buttonDown4.BackColor = Color.Gold;
                break;

            case 5:
                buttonDown5.BackColor = Color.Gold;
                break;

            case 6:
                buttonDown6.BackColor = Color.Gold;
                break;

            case 7:
                buttonDown7.BackColor = Color.Gold;
                break;

            case 8:
                buttonDown8.BackColor = Color.Gold;
                break;

            case 9:
```

```
                        buttonDown9.BackColor = Color.Gold;
                        break;

                    case 10:
                        buttonDown10.BackColor = Color.Gold;
                        break;
                }
                break;
        }
        Control.HallCall(floor, goingup);
    }
  }
}
```

This form has an `Activated` event that runs a continuous loop updating the display if needed before going back to sleep.

Set the solution configuration to Release, and from the Build menu, select Build Solution to ensure that project builds successfully. With the Control piece built, it is time to focus on the elevators.

ElevatorCar.cs

Create a new project named **Elevator**. When the project has been created, right-click Form1 in Solution Explorer and rename Form1 to FormElevator by right-clicking the form and choosing the Rename menu item.

Next, right-click the Elevator project and select Add, then select Class from the context menu. When the Add New Item dialog box appears, the Class template will automatically be selected with a default name of Class1.cs. Simply rename Class1.cs to ElevatorCar.cs and click the Add button.

Next, be sure to add a reference to the System.ServiceModel namespace. Lastly, a few references need to be added. Browse to the \Bin\Release directory of the Control project and double-click on the Control.exe to start the Control program, then click the Start button.

With the Control program running, go back to the Elevator project and right mouse click on the References node and select Add Reference. When the Add Reference dialog appears, select the Browse tab and browse to the \Bin\Release directory of the Control project and double click on the Control.exe file. You should now have a reference to the Control project in your list of refernces.

The next reference is a Service Reference. Open your control project and open the code behind the Control form. In the cmdStart method, highlight and the complete uri, which should be the following:

```
Net.tcp://localhost:8000/ElevatorControl/
```

Go back to the Elevator project and right mouse click on the References node again, but this time select Add Service Reference. When the Add Service Reference dialog appears, paste the URI you copied above into the Service URI field. Next, supply the name ControlService for the Service Reference Name, then click OK.

You'll notice that an app.config was added to the project. As you should know by now, this contains the endpoint configuration information that will be utilized by the client, the elevator. All of the examples in the book used three projects, with one of those projects being the service "host". Unlike those examples, this example will utilize the client as both the host and the client, thus the service reference was added to the client (elevator) project and the app.config subsequently added to this, the client project, as well.

All the services and references have been added, so it is now time to add code.

The first thing to add is the code in ElevatorCar.cs. This class is called by FormElevator. Enter the following code in the ElevatorCar.cs class:

```
using System;
using System.ServiceModel;
using System.Threading;
using System.ServiceModel.Channels;
using System.Collections.Generic;
using System.Text;
using Elevator;

namespace Elevator
{
    [ServiceContract(SessionMode=SessionMode.Required,
CallbackContract=typeof(IElevatorCar))]
    public interface IControl
    {
        [OperationContract(IsInitiating=true, IsTerminating=false)]
        int CarInService();
        [OperationContract(IsInitiating = false, IsTerminating = true)]
        void CarNotInService();
        [OperationContract]
        void CarUpdate(int floor, bool goingup, bool pickingup);
    }

    public interface IElevatorCar
    {
        [OperationContract]
        void Pickup(bool[] upRequests, bool[] downRequests);
    }

    class ElevatorCar : IElevatorCar
    {
        public bool UpdateDisplay = false;
        public static ManualResetEvent workerThreadRunning = new
ManualResetEvent(false);

        ServiceHost sh = null;
        ControlService.ControlClient client = null;

        const int TimeToMoveOneFloor = 500;
        const int TimeToStopAtFloor = 2000;

        public const int NumberOfFloors = 10;

        int ElevatorID = 1;

        bool InService = false;
```

```
    bool Idle = true;
    public bool GoingUp = true;
    public bool PickingUp = false;
    public int CurrentFloor = 1;
    Thread elevatorThread = null;
    int RequestCount = 0;
    int UpRequestCount = 0;
    int DownRequestCount = 0;
    public bool[] UpRequests = new bool[NumberOfFloors + 1];
    public bool[] DownRequests = new bool[NumberOfFloors + 1];

    public ElevatorCar()
    {
        UpdateDisplay = true;
    }

    public int Run()
    {
        sh = new ServiceHost(typeof(Control.FormControl));
        sh.Open();


        InstanceContext site = new InstanceContext(sh);
        client = new Elevator.ControlService.ControlClient(site,
"NetTcpBinding_IControl");

        ElevatorID = controlsystem.CarInService();
        InService = true;
        elevatorThread = new Thread(new ThreadStart(ElevatorRoutine));
        elevatorThread.Start();
        return ElevatorID;
    }

    public void Stop()
    {
        InService = false;
        workerThreadRunning.WaitOne();
    }

    public void Pickup(bool[] upRequests, bool[] downRequests)
    {
        for (int i = 1; i <= 10; i++)
        {
            if (upRequests[i] && !UpRequests[i])
            {
                upRequests[i] = true;
                UpRequestCount++;
                RequestCount++;
            }

            if (downRequests[i] && !downRequests[i])
            {
                downRequests[i] = true;
                DownRequestCount++;
                RequestCount++;
```

```
            }
        }
    }

    public bool IsGoingTo(int floor)
    {
        return (UpRequests[floor] || DownRequests[floor]);
    }

    public void GoToFloor(int floor)
    {
        if (floor == CurrentFloor)
            return;

        bool UpRequest = true;

        if (floor == 1)
            UpRequest = true;
        else if (floor == NumberOfFloors)
            UpRequest = false;
        else if (floor < CurrentFloor)
            UpRequest = false;

        if (!UpRequest)
        {
            if (DownRequests[floor]) return;
            DownRequests[floor] = true;
            DownRequestCount++;
            RequestCount++;
            UpdateDisplay = true;
        }
        else
        {
            if (UpRequests[floor]) return;
            UpRequests[floor] = true;
            UpRequestCount++;
            RequestCount++;
            UpdateDisplay = true;
        }
    }

    void ReportPosition()
    {
        if (controlsystem == null) return;
        controlsystem.CarUpdate(CurrentFloor, GoingUp, PickingUp);
    }

    void ElevatorRoutine()
    {
        try
        {
            workerThreadRunning.Set();
            while (InService)
            {
                ReportPosition();
```

```
                if (Idle)
                {
                    if (RequestCount > 0)
                    {
                        Idle = false;
                        SetDirection();
                    }
                    else
                    {
                        System.Threading.Thread.Sleep(100);
                    }
                }
                else
                {
                    if (MoreAhead() == 0)
                    {
                        ChangeDirection();
                        StopIfNeeded();
                        Idle = true;
                    }
                    else
                    {
                        if (GoingUp && MoreAhead() > 0)
                            MoveUp();
                        else if (!GoingUp && MoreAhead() > 0)
                            MoveDown();
                        StopIfNeeded();
                    }
                }
            }
            controlsystem.CarNotInService();
        }
        finally
        {
            workerThreadRunning.Reset();
        }
    }

    void MoveUp()
    {
        System.Threading.Thread.Sleep(TimeToMoveOneFloor);
        CurrentFloor++;
        UpdateDisplay = true;
        if (CurrentFloor == NumberOfFloors)
            GoingUp = false;
    }

    void MoveDown()
    {
        System.Threading.Thread.Sleep(TimeToMoveOneFloor);
        CurrentFloor--;
        UpdateDisplay = true;
        if (CurrentFloor == 1)
            GoingUp = true;
```

```
}

void ChangeDirection()
{
    GoingUp = !GoingUp;
    ChangeDirectionIfNeeded();
}

void ChangeDirectionIfNeeded()
{
    if (CurrentFloor == 1)
        GoingUp = true;
    if (CurrentFloor == NumberOfFloors)
        GoingUp = false;
}

void StopIfNeeded()
{
    if (GoingUp || CurrentFloor == 1 || CurrentFloor == NumberOfFloors)
    {
        if (UpRequests[CurrentFloor])
        {
            PickingUp = true;
            ReportPosition();
            UpRequests[CurrentFloor] = false;
            UpRequestCount--;
            RequestCount--;
            if (RequestCount == 0)
                Idle = true;
            OpenDoors();
            WaitAtFloor();
            CloseDoors();
            PickingUp = false;
            UpdateDisplay = true;
        }
    }

    if (!GoingUp || CurrentFloor == NumberOfFloors || CurrentFloor == 1)
    {
        if (DownRequests[CurrentFloor])
        {
            PickingUp = true;
            ReportPosition();
            DownRequests[CurrentFloor] = false;
            DownRequestCount--;
            RequestCount--;
            if (RequestCount == 0)
                Idle = true;
            OpenDoors();
            WaitAtFloor();
            CloseDoors();
            PickingUp = false;
            UpdateDisplay = true;
        }
```

```
        }
    }

    void SetDirection()
    {
        int RequestsAbove = 0;
        int RequestsBelow = 0;
        for (int floor = CurrentFloor + 1; floor <= NumberOfFloors; floor++)
        {
            if (UpRequests[floor] || DownRequests[floor])
            {
                RequestsAbove++;
            }
        }

        for (int floor = CurrentFloor - 1; floor >= 1; floor--)
        {
            if (UpRequests[floor] || DownRequests[floor])
            {
                RequestsBelow++;
            }
        }

        if (RequestsAbove > RequestsBelow)
        {
            GoingUp = true;
            Idle = false;
            PickingUp = false;
        }
        else if (RequestsBelow > 0)
        {
            GoingUp = false;
            Idle = false;
            PickingUp = false;
        }
        else
        {
            Idle = true;
        }
    }

    int MoreAhead()
    {
        if (GoingUp)
        {
            return MoreAheadGoingUp();
        }
        else
        {
            return MoreAheadGoingDown();
        }
    }

    int MoreAheadGoingUp()
```

```
        {
            int count = 0;
            for (int floor = CurrentFloor + 1; floor <= NumberOfFloors; floor++)
            {
                if (UpRequests[floor] || DownRequests[floor])
                {
                    count++;
                }
            }
            return count;
        }

        int MoreAheadGoingDown()
        {
            int count = 0;
            for (int floor = CurrentFloor - 1; floor >= 1; floor--)
            {
                if (UpRequests[floor] || DownRequests[floor])
                {
                    count++;
                }
            }
            return count;
        }

        void OpenDoors()
        {
        }

        void CloseDoors()
        {
        }

        void WaitAtFloor()
        {
            System.Threading.Thread.Sleep(TimeToStopAtFloor);
        }
    }
}
```

When the Start button is pressed on the Elevator form, the Run method is called in this Elevator class. The Run method in turn starts up the elevator, initiating a worker thread and establishing a channel to the control service. Through this channel, the elevator car tells the control service that this elevator car is now in service.

The Stop button stops the elevator, telling the control service that this elevator car is now out of service. It then closes the channel and terminates the worker thread.

This class specifies elevator car status information, such as its requests, direction of movement, and current location. Much of this information is scoped with the public modifier. Consequently, FormElevator has access to these properties and it can display that information accordingly.

You should have also seen two Boolean arrays, `UpRequests` and `DownRequests`. These two arrays hold the requests for the corresponding elevator. As the elevator moves to a new floor (up or down), it checks the corresponding array to see if it needs to stop.

Equally, when an action is taken on the class that would require a form display refresh, the Boolean variable `UpdateDisplay` is set to a value of true. When the form refresh is finished, the variable is set to false.

The other methods and subroutines help determine the direction of the elevator. They will also determine whether or not the elevator needs to stop and if the elevator has changed direction.

FormElevator.cs

The last piece for the Elevator project is to work on the form. Using the elevator form shown earlier in Figure B-3 as a basis, change the following properties.

The elevator buttons 1 through 10 should have the following properties specified:

- **BackColor:** Black
- **FlatStyle:** Flat
- **ForeColor:** White
- **UseVisualStyleBackColor:** False
- **Font Size:** 15.75

The current floor display is also a button with the same properties as the floor buttons, with the following difference:

- **ForeColor:** LawnGreen

The direction arrows are labels with the following properties:

- **BackColor:** Black
- **Font:** Webdings
- **FontSize:** 12
- **ForeColor:** LawnGreen
- **TextAlign:** Bottom Left

To get the up arrow and down arrow to display correctly, you need to set the Text property of the Up label to **5** and the Text property of the Down arrow to **6**.

The Service group box next to the buttons should contain two separate label controls. The left label should have the following properties specified:

- **Name:** Label1
- **Text:** Car No.

The right label should have the following properties specified:

- ❏ **Name:** labelCarNo
- ❏ **Text:** "--" (without the quotes)

Once the preceding steps have been performed, replace the existing code behind the form with the following:

```csharp
using System;
using System.Collections.Generic;
using System.ComponentModel;
using System.Data;
using System.Drawing;
using System.Text;
using System.Windows.Forms;

namespace Elevator
{
    public partial class FormElevator : Form
    {
        ElevatorCar elevator = null;
        bool initialized = false;

        public FormElevator()
        {
            InitializeComponent();
        }

        private void FormElevator_Load(object sender, EventArgs e)
        {

        }

        private void FormElevator_Activated(object sender, EventArgs e)
        {
            if (initialized) return;
            initialized = true;
            Application.DoEvents();
            while (true)
            {
                Application.DoEvents();
                if (elevator != null && elevator.UpdateDisplay)
                {
                    UpdateDisplay();
                    elevator.UpdateDisplay = false;
                }
                System.Threading.Thread.Sleep(100);
            }
        }

        private void cmdStart_Click(object sender, EventArgs e)
        {
            Cursor = Cursors.WaitCursor;
```

```
        Application.DoEvents();

        elevator = new ElevatorCar();
        int CarNo = elevator.Run();
        lblCarNo.Text = CarNo.ToString();
        Text = "Elevator No. " + CarNo.ToString();

        cmdStart.Enabled = false;
        cmdStop.Enabled = true;
        Cursor = Cursors.Default;
    }

    void UpdateDisplay()
    {
        buttonCurrentFloor.Text = elevator.CurrentFloor.ToString();
        if (elevator.GoingUp)
        {
            lblGoingUp.ForeColor = Color.LawnGreen;
            lblGoingDown.ForeColor = Color.Black;
        }
        else
        {
            lblGoingDown.ForeColor = Color.LawnGreen;
            lblGoingUp.ForeColor = Color.Black;
        }

        for (int floor = 1; floor <= ElevatorCar.NumberOfFloors; floor++)
        {
            Color buttonForeColor = Color.White;
            Color buttonBorderColor = Color.White;
            if (elevator.IsGoingTo(floor))
            {
                buttonForeColor = Color.Gold;
                buttonBorderColor = Color.Gold;
            }

            switch (floor)
            {
                case 1:
                    button1.ForeColor = buttonForeColor;
                    button1.FlatAppearance.BorderColor = buttonBorderColor;
                    break;

                case 2:
                    button2.ForeColor = buttonForeColor;
                    button2.FlatAppearance.BorderColor = buttonBorderColor;
                    break;

                case 3:
                    button3.ForeColor = buttonForeColor;
                    button3.FlatAppearance.BorderColor = buttonBorderColor;
                    break;

                case 4:
                    button4.ForeColor = buttonForeColor;
```

```
                    button4.FlatAppearance.BorderColor = buttonBorderColor;
                    break;

                case 5:
                    button5.ForeColor = buttonForeColor;
                    button5.FlatAppearance.BorderColor = buttonBorderColor;
                    break;

                case 6:
                    button6.ForeColor = buttonForeColor;
                    button6.FlatAppearance.BorderColor = buttonBorderColor;
                    break;

                case 7:
                    button7.ForeColor = buttonForeColor;
                    button7.FlatAppearance.BorderColor = buttonBorderColor;
                    break;

                case 8:
                    button8.ForeColor = buttonForeColor;
                    button8.FlatAppearance.BorderColor = buttonBorderColor;
                    break;

                case 9:
                    button9.ForeColor = buttonForeColor;
                    button9.FlatAppearance.BorderColor = buttonBorderColor;
                    break;

                case 10:
                    button1.ForeColor = buttonForeColor;
                    button1.FlatAppearance.BorderColor = buttonBorderColor;
                    break;

            }
        }
    }

    private void exitToolStripMenuItem_Click(object sender, EventArgs e)
    {
        Environment.Exit(0);
    }

    private void button1_Click(object sender, EventArgs e)
    {
        elevator.GoToFloor(1);
    }

    private void button2_Click(object sender, EventArgs e)
    {
        elevator.GoToFloor(2);
    }

    private void button3_Click(object sender, EventArgs e)
    {
        elevator.GoToFloor(3);
```

```
        }

        private void button4_Click(object sender, EventArgs e)
        {
            elevator.GoToFloor(4);
        }

        private void button5_Click(object sender, EventArgs e)
        {
            elevator.GoToFloor(5);
        }

        private void button6_Click(object sender, EventArgs e)
        {
            elevator.GoToFloor(6);
        }

        private void button7_Click(object sender, EventArgs e)
        {
            elevator.GoToFloor(7);
        }

        private void button8_Click(object sender, EventArgs e)
        {
            elevator.GoToFloor(8);
        }

        private void button9_Click(object sender, EventArgs e)
        {
            elevator.GoToFloor(9);
        }

        private void button10_Click(object sender, EventArgs e)
        {
            elevator.GoToFloor(10);
        }

        private void cmdStop_Click(object sender, EventArgs e)
        {
            Cursor = Cursors.WaitCursor;
            cmdStop.Enabled = false;
            Application.DoEvents();

            elevator.Stop();

            cmdStart.Enabled = true;
            Cursor = Cursors.Default;
        }
    }
}
```

The FormElevator creates an instance of the ElevatorCar class and calls its Run and Stop methods (via the Start and Stop buttons, respectively) and receives feedback from the ElevatorCar class to display elevator car status on its form.

An important thing to note is the `Activated` event on the form. This routine runs a continuous loop updating the display if needed before going back to sleep.

With both projects in place, compile them both and ensure that no coding errors exist. If everything compiles successfully, you can move on.

Time to Test

Put your hypothetical friend inside the first elevator and do the following to test:

- ❑ Launch the `control.exe` program.
- ❑ When the Control program is running, click the Start button.
- ❑ With the Control program running, launch one to three instances of the `elevator.exe` program.
- ❑ While each instance of the Elevator program is running, click Start on each Elevator Car form, which puts the car into service.

When you click Start on each Elevator Car form, you should see the corresponding car become available on the Control form. If you click the Stop button on any Elevator Car form, you will see that car become unavailable on the Control form.

How it Works

To understand how the elevator control system works, a look at the flow of communication is needed (this is assuming that both the Elevator and Control programs are currently running):

1. When the Start button is pressed on the Elevator Car form, an instance of the ElevatorCar class is created followed by a call to the Run method. The Run method first creates a channel to the control service. It then generates a worker thread from which the `CarInService` operation is called (sending a message to the Control service).

2. The Control service receives the message and creates a new instance of the Control class. As discussed earlier in this chapter, the `CarInService` operation has the `IsInitiating` property set to a value of true. This means that the `CarInService` method must be the first one called when the service is first instantiated. The `CarInService` operation assigns a car number and returns that number to the elevator client.

3. The worker thread of the elevator car runs in a continuous loop. Within this loop, the elevator moves up, moves down, and sits idle. Each one of these actions takes one second. Other actions such as opening and closing doors and waiting on each floor take three seconds. Regardless of the action taken or the time it takes to complete, the `CarUpdate` operation is called. This notifies the control system of which action was taken, such as moving up two floors.

4. Upon executing the `CarUpdate` method of the service, the `CarUpdate` method internally updates its tracking information about the specific elevator car.

When a hall call is issued by the pressing of the up or down button on the control system form, the `HallCall` method is called on the Control class. The purpose of this method is to determine which elevator can most efficiently handle the request. When a determination is made, the request is stored in memory and the value is communicated back to the appropriate car by calling the `Pickup` operation. This operation is executed via the Callback contract.

Each elevator car holds a list of pending requests. When a floor button is pressed inside the elevator (one of the floor buttons on the Elevator Car form), the elevator adds a destination call to its pending request list. It is the responsibility of each elevator to address each request from its own corresponding request list. Thus, the control system does not need to be notified of internal requests, except for sending back direction of travel and location information.

To take an elevator car out of service, simply press the Stop button on the desired Elevator Car form. This calls the `CarNotInService` operation, which stops all communication between that specific elevator and the control system, and also sends a message to the control system. At this point the elevator's worker thread is aborted because it is no longer needed.

The message sent by the client to the control system tells the control system that an elevator is being taken out of service. Thus, the `CarNotInService` operation is called, which terminates the car's instance. This is because the `IsTerminating` property on the `CarNotInService` operation is set to true.

Summary

This appendix used a simple elevator control system to illustrate two-way communication between a client and service, both hosted within a Windows forms application. The elevator control system used a main control system application as the service and one or more elevator cars as the client.

Index

Index

K

Kerberos, 255, 262
[KnownType] **attribute, 144–145**

L

Lightweight Transaction Manager (LM), 45
LinkDemand property, [PrinciplePermission]
    attribute, 257
listenBackLog attribute, NetTcpBinding binding, 98
listeners, 288, 335, 354
listenIPAddress attribute, NetPeerTcpBinding
    binding, 106
LM (Lightweight Transaction Manager), 45
load leveling, queues for, 244
local issuer, security considerations for, 272
LocalAddress property, IContextChannel interface,
    168
<localIssuer> **element, 265**
logging messages. *See also* tracing
    configuring, 335, 338
    custom, 274, 279
    definition of, 333
    enabling, 333–334
    listeners for, 335
    logging levels for, 334
    troubleshooting using, 321
    viewing message logs, 335
logging security events (auditing), 261, 266–267
Logical Datacenter Designer, features for SOA, 8–9
loosely coupled applications, queues for, 244

M

managed code, hosting services in, 351–352
ManualAddressing property, ClientRuntime class,
    275
maxBufferPoolSize attribute
    BasicHttpBinding binding, 90
    NetMsmqBinding binding, 103
    NetNamedPipeBinding binding, 101
    NetPeerTcpBinding binding, 106

    NetTcpBinding binding, 98
    WSDualHttpBinding binding, 94
    WSFederationHttpBinding binding, 96
    WSHttpBinding binding, 92
maxBufferSize attribute
    BasicHttpBinding binding, 90
    NetNamedPipeBinding binding, 101
    NetTcpBinding binding, 98
maxConnections attribute
    NetNamedPipeBinding binding, 101
    NetTcpBinding binding, 99, 100
maxImmediateRetries attribute
    MsmqIntegrationBinding binding, 107
    NetMsmqBinding binding, 103
maxReceivedMessageSize attribute
    BasicHttpBinding binding, 90
    MsmqIntegrationBinding binding, 108
    NetMsmqBinding binding, 103
    NetNamedPipeBinding binding, 101
    NetPeerTcpBinding binding, 106
    NetTcpBinding binding, 99
    WSDualHttpBinding binding, 94
    WSFederationHttpBinding binding, 96
    WSHttpBinding binding, 92
maxRetryCycles attribute
    MsmqIntegrationBinding binding, 108
    NetMsmqBinding binding, 103
Membership provider, ASP.NET, 257–259
MEP (Message Exchange Pattern), 287–288
Message class, 44
message contract model (typed message service),
    134–135, 205
message contracts
    definition of, 11, 35, 145
    [MessageBodyMember] attribute, 149–150
    [MessageContract] attribute, 145–147
    [MessageHeader] attribute, 147–149
    [MessageProperty] attribute, 150–151
    programming, 158–163
    typed message services using, 134–135
<message> **element, 241**
Message Exchange Pattern (MEP), 287–288
message level auditing, 261

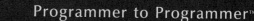